SOUTH CAROLINA AND THE NEW DEAL

SOUTH CAROLINA
AND THE NEW DEAL

JACK IRBY HAYES, JR.

UNIVERSITY OF SOUTH CAROLINA PRESS

UNIVERSITY OF SOUTH CAROLINA *BICENTENNIAL*

© 2001 University of South Carolina

Published in Columbia, South Carolina, by the
University of South Carolina Press

Manufactured in the United States of America

05 04 03 02 01 5 4 3 2 1

Library of Congress Cataloging-in-Publication Data

Hayes, J. I.
  South Carolina and the New Deal / Jack Irby Hayes, Jr.
    p. cm.
  Includes bibliographical references and index.
  ISBN 1-57003-399-4 (alk. paper)
  1. South Carolina—Politics and government—1865–1950. 2. South
Carolina—Economic conditions—20th century. 3. South Carolina—Social
conditions—20th century. 4. New Deal, 1933–1939—South Carolina. I. Title.
F274 .H39 2001
975.7′04—dc21   2001000940

CONTENTS

ILLUSTRATIONS

PREFACE

Since 1933 few states have changed as dramatically as South Carolina. More so than any other state, South Carolina in 1933 was Dixie, the land of cotton. One in every seven acres of farmland, one in every eleven acres of all land, was planted in cotton. The typical industrial worker eked out a livelihood in a cotton mill and spent his leisure time in a cotton mill village where he pastured a cow and cultivated a garden as though he still lived on a farm. The state's agrarian lifestyle and mentality bred self-sufficiency. When coupled with established patterns such as racism, it also bred deference: most blacks deferred to whites, wives to husbands, children to parents, employees to employers, and tenants to landowners. In short, everyone knew "his place." Per-capita income was lowest in the nation; illiteracy, highest. One-party Democratic politics prevailed, and rural dominated urban by a ratio of three to one. Private recreational facilities were scarce; those sponsored by the state, practically nonexistent. Citizens seldom felt the reach of the federal government. Transportation facilities were so inadequate that the average citizen seldom ventured beyond his community and almost never outside his state unless migrating permanently.

Two generations later, South Carolina was America. Its economy balanced agriculture, industry, transportation, and services; international and national corporations; and numerous cash crops. An industrial mentality encouraged specialization instead of self-sufficiency. When coupled with recent racial and gender revolutions, it fostered equality and independence. Advances in education, technical training, and educational television produced an educated citizenry with heightened cultural awareness. Improvements in transportation created a well-traveled citizenry. Urban dominated rural by a ratio of greater than two to one, and each day citizens felt the touch of the federal government. Two-party competitive, Republican-leaning politics had replaced one-party Democratic control. An extensive system of state parks, public beaches, lakes, museums, historic houses, and an award-winning zoo provided plentiful opportunities for recreation.

Because World War II and events in its wake, rather than the New Deal, account for most of these changes, the New Deal was the last decade of an old era and not the first decade of a new one. Nevertheless, the New Deal stimulated innovation that, over time, might have transformed the Palmetto State without the intervention of World War II. And in some areas, New Deal programs were vital indeed.

A few New Deal contributions and changes wrought by them were substantial, others less so, and still others remain ambiguous even today. Among the most important of the substantial ones were the restoration of faith in capitalism, democracy, and progress; prevention of starvation; and salvation from bankruptcy and forfeiture of property of the state's farm owners, mill owners, bankers, and home owners. A continuation of the Hoover doldrums certainly would have imperiled these four groups. Also important were stimulation of the state's economy with an infusion of $533 million in federal funds; physical alteration of the landscape through erosion control, reforestation, and hydroelectric projects; creation of a system of state parks; enactment of the present system of alcoholic beverage control; amelioration of harsh farming conditions by means of rural electrification; and federal regulation of the economy.

Less pervasive were other economic, political, and social initiatives. The New Deal was unable to restore agricultural and industrial prosperity; World War II did that. The effect on African Americans was ambiguous because, although the New Deal helped raise black consciousness, it also displaced black farm tenants and industrial workers. The New Deal bestowed political stardom upon James F. Byrnes, Olin D. Johnston, and Burnet R. Maybank, but it failed to empower any segment of formerly disfranchised citizens. Moreover, the same leaders were in control in 1940 as in 1930. Gov. Olin D. Johnston proposed a "Little New Deal" in areas of social security, education, labor relations, governmental reorganization, and penal reform. However, after the legislature marked up and amended his bills, most of what remained was rather conservative in both tone and scope.

Other areas of daily life were scarcely touched by the New Deal. The predominance of legislative government was not affected. Neither were state fiscal policy and long-range planning. In addition, the New Deal made hardly a dent in prevailing snobbery, racism, sexism, and rugged individualism.

This study is an attempt to delineate the depth and extent of New Deal influence in South Carolina. In the process it portrays how and how well New Deal programs were administered by local bureaucrats and how they were perceived by the average citizen. Chapter 1 assesses the state's political geography, culminating in the presidential election of 1932. Chapter 2 explains the extent to which the six congressmen and two senators in Washington both supported and obstructed the New Deal. Chapters 2 and 9 suggest that the standard description of a First New Deal in 1933 and a Second New Deal in 1935 did not work in South Carolina. Its citizens saw the watershed in 1937, not 1935. Frequent allusions to a more-than-apparent reality emphasize the fact that race was the most important factor in congressional voting, public opinion, and popular motivation. Whites applauded when Franklin D. Roosevelt adhered to prevailing notions of separate but equal in Civilian Conservation Corps (CCC) camps, local Agricultural Adjustment Administration (AAA) committees, Public Works Administration (PWA) housing projects, and Works Progress Administration (WPA) educational programs.[1] They deserted Roosevelt in droves when he disregarded white notions of black inferiority by giving some consideration to antilynching legislation and supporting African American membership in the Democratic Party.

Chapters 3 and 4 deal with relief programs. Inexplicably, African Americans were often over-represented on relief rolls in relation to population percentages. This over-representation is surprising when one considers the prevalent and blatant racial discrimination in all walks of life. The most reasonable explanation is that whites wanted to stanch the sizeable black out-migration that had existed since World War I and threatened to deprive the state of cheap labor. Another unexpected discovery is the generally incompetent administration of relief, owing possibly to the presence of a cavalier mentality and the absence of an entrepreneurial outlook, coupled with the lack of an experienced, trained bureaucracy at the local level. Chapter 5 covers the PWA that forever changed the face of South Carolina with public buildings, public housing, and large hydroelectric projects.

Chapters 6 through 8 consider the cotton economy. The focus in chapters 6 and 7 is on business and labor with particular emphasis on textiles. In assessing the failure of unionization, chapter 7 accepts conclusions by contemporary labor historians and adds as one cause the inability of mill workers to build a coalition of powerful constituencies in favor of unionism. Failing that, the mill workers shifted their focus to state politics and elected a sympathetic governor and like-minded legislators. Chapter 8 covers agriculture, acknowledging that although New

Deal programs did not bring prosperity, they at least reduced the drudg-
ery of life on the farm, improved the quality of farmland, and kept the
farmer in operation long enough for him to thrive during and after World
War II.

Chapter 9 concentrates on politics and public attitude. Although
conservative, South Carolinians were prepared to accept activist government. The agrarian revolt of the 1880s and 1890s under Gov. and later
U.S. senator Benjamin R. ("Pitchfork Ben") Tillman made Carolinians
receptive to innovation and change. In the 1910s the Progressive Movement under Gov. Richard I. Manning taught them to view government
less as "a threat to individual liberty" and more as "a means for solving
the ills of the body politic."[2] Baptist revivals of the early nineteenth century inspired Carolinians to join mass crusades to cleanse society of evils,
which by 1933 certainly included unsound banking, corrupt securities
markets, and inequitable tax structures. The shock of economic depression and absence of solutions from the private sector led Carolinians to
view the federal government as mankind's last, best hope. To no one's
surprise, then, Carolinians initially embraced the New Deal; indeed, they
nearly deified its architect, Franklin D. Roosevelt.

However, the Second New Deal in 1937–1939 brought antilynching
bills, permanent wages and hours policy, Congress of Industrial Organizations (CIO) biracial unionism, sit-down strikes, executive meddling in
the selection of a new Senate majority leader, and continued high unemployment and massive relief spending without agricultural and business
recovery. White opinion leaders simply grew weary of continuing economic uncertainty, threats to rights of property and supplies of cheap
labor, executive aggrandizement, and tampering with the racial status
quo. No doubt, the average white citizen, despite his admiration and love
for FDR, eventually would have followed the dictates of such leaders,
had not World War II intervened to refocus his attention.

Chapter 10 considers the impact of the New Deal on African Amer-
icans. Hundreds of thousands of African Americans benefited from the
Works Progress Administration, Public Works Administration, National
Youth Administration, Civilian Conservation Corps, Federal Emergency
Relief Administration, and Civil Works Administration. As a result
Franklin D. Roosevelt took his place beside Abraham Lincoln and John
Brown in the black pantheon. The professed New Deal concern for the
forgotten American encouraged black Carolinians to become assertive.
Gains in civil rights in the 1940s and 1950s had their genesis in the New

Deal. On the other hand, programs of at least two New Deal agencies—the Agricultural Adjustment Administration and the National Recovery Administration—were counterproductive. Nor did the New Deal alter pernicious social and economic norms in race relations. In short, the impact of the New Deal on African Americans was mixed.

Chapter 11 summarizes chapters 1 through 10 in assessing the impact of the New Deal. It suggests the New Deal was basically conservative. The New Deal relied upon local and state boards, councils, committees, and administrations, which were always subject to local pressure, to implement and in some cases develop policies and guidelines. Despite occasional charges to the contrary, the New Deal was not "straight-jacket methods emanating from Washington." Neither did it ever seriously challenge the racial modus operandi, class structure, gender relations, or centers of political, social, and economic power. For example, mill owners controlled National Recovery Administration policies and circumvented the National Labor Relations Act; the county-seat elite controlled local administration of relief; large farmers dominated the local machinery of the Agricultural Adjustment Administration and associated agencies; and politicians treated both New Deal appointments and funds dispensed as a respective patronage bonanza and giant pork barrel hitherto unknown in American history. In summary, the conservative nature of the New Deal guaranteed its acceptance in conservative South Carolina.

In preparing this work, I received help and encouragement from a number of scholars and institutions. Dr. Daniel W. Hollis directed the first version as a dissertation at the University of South Carolina in 1972. He graciously critiqued and edited my chapters while sharing his rich insights on life and politics in the Palmetto State. More recently, Pres. Frank R. Campbell of Averett College made provisions for financial aid for research trips to several archives. The South Caroliniana Library of the University of South Carolina awarded me the Lewis P. Jones Summer Research Fellowship in 1998, which enabled me to further my research. Administrative support and the use of university facilities were afforded through a faculty research fellowship from the Institute of Southern Studies at the University of South Carolina. I also owe debts of gratitude to the professional staffs of the National Archives, South Carolina Department of Archives and History in Columbia, South Carolina Historical Society in Charleston, and the libraries of Averett College, Duke University, and Clemson University. My greatest debt is to the

South Caroliniana Library. Director Allen Stokes and his staff provided invaluable suggestions and guidance. Several historians were kind enough to read and critique all or portions of the manuscript. These historians include Marvin Cann, William B. Crawley, Walter Edgar, Gilbert C. Fite, Kari Frederickson, Ronald Heinemann, Paul Lofton, Alexander Moore, John Hammond Moore, I. A. Newby, James T. Patterson, Miles S. Richards, Bryant Simon, and Tom Terrill. Gloria Robertson of Averett College patiently processed the manuscript through numerous revisions. Finally, my wife, Bernadine, encouraged me in every phase of the project. She holds the debt I can never repay.

A SOUTH CAROLINA PRIMER | 1

Understanding the voters of South Carolina in 1932 is nearly as simple as *ABCD*. The *A* stands for *a*ncestors, who were worshiped with regularity by the state's 1.7 million citizens. Joining the *A* are four *B*s: *b*lacks, *b*ooze, *B*lease, and *B*aptists. The *C*s include *c*ontrasts, *C*onfederacy, *c*onservatism, and *c*otton, and the two *D*s are *D*epression and *D*emocracy. These eleven factors determined the way in which Carolinians of both races understood the past, interpreted the present, and clarified the future. As building blocks of the state's political culture, these factors fostered a sense of civic duty, legitimated public officeholders, established the extent of political tolerance, and gave definition to terms such as *equality, democracy,* and *liberty.* They also set the precedent for how Carolinians assessed human predicaments, selected heroes, defined the role of government, viewed relations both human and holy, and grouped people into social classes. Finally, in 1932 these factors determined how Carolinians would respond to national political movements such as the New Deal.

South Carolinians liked to joke that they and African natives had one trait in common: both groups worshiped *a*ncestors. Most Carolinians could recite from memory the names of families in their pedigree; many knew by heart a complete genealogy for two centuries or more. Most could also recount an ancestor's role in the founding of the colony, Indian wars, American Revolution, Nullification Controversy, Mexican War, or Secession Crisis. Whites had a special reverence for kinsmen in gray who fought under Robert E. Lee at Gettysburg or wore the red shirt and rode with Wade Hampton in 1876 to "redeem" the Palmetto State from Republican "misrule." Numbering in the hundreds, cousins met often at family reunions, family picnics, and Sunday visits to strengthen the bonds of kinship by reveling in past family glories.[1] Justly proud of their forebears' role in building state and nation, Carolinians were considered "among the rare folk in the South who have no secret envy of Virginians."[2]

*B*lacks, or the issue of race, was perhaps the most important of all the factors. Nearly all whites accepted and acted upon the notion of innate black inferiority. The fact that African Americans made up more than 50 percent of the population from 1820 to almost 1930 accounts in large measure for the development of a siege mentality in the white community, a fierce determination to keep blacks "in their place," and a preoccupation with what political scientist V. O. Key, Jr., has called "the politics of color." Moreover, what South Carolinians thought they knew about their history since 1865 was replete with African American rogues and rascals, lending justification to the hideous stereotypes. In the minds of most whites, their state had endured the harshest Reconstruction of all the former Confederate states—a reconstruction synonymous with black rule, rampant with political corruption, wasteful government, and sordid, incompetent leadership. In the ensuing decades whites resorted to violence, supplemented by legal segregation and disfranchisement, to remove blacks from the political process and deny them the social mobility customarily accorded to whites. It was taken for granted by whites that an African American in politics was either a scoundrel or a tool for scheming whites. As late as 1936 an article in *Time* noted that "trafficking with Negroes for political purposes" continued to be the "supreme sin" among whites in South Carolina.[3]

The moral issue of whiskey, or *booze*, was only slightly less important than race. The Palmetto State entered the twentieth century with a statewide system of liquor dispensaries that sold whiskey purchased and bottled under state auspices. It was generally believed that bootleggers, or "blind tigers," who defied the beverage-control law, sold as much as dispensaries. In 1907 righteous indignation and the increasing power of the "drys," who included a majority of the state's Baptists and Methodists, forced the legislature to allow counties the local option of keeping dispensaries or embracing prohibition. Six counties retained dispensaries until 1915 when a statewide referendum ushered in prohibition. Convinced of the evils of alcohol, Carolinians clung to prohibition throughout the 1920s, and United States senator James F. Byrnes later recalled that any politician who advocated repeal immediately incurred the wrath of his wife and his preacher.[4]

Of equal importance was the *Blease* factor. A perennial candidate for public office for nearly five decades until his death in 1942, Coleman L. ("Coley") Blease voiced the grievances and prejudices of poor white farmers and cotton mill operatives, the state's most numerous industrial workers. Twice governor (1911–1915) and once United States senator (1925–1931), Blease was a demagogue whose attacks on the privileged classes—represented by professional educators, clergymen, newspaper publishers, corporate executives, and urban politicians—fostered class antagonism and earned for Blease the sobriquet "the poor man's friend." To such mongering Blease added a large measure of race baiting. Frequently referring to African Americans as "baboons" and "apes," he praised lynchers and once threatened to "wipe the inferior race from the face of the earth."[5] Reportedly, when mill hands arrived at the polls on election day and discovered that Blease was running for public office, they would leave the polls and return an hour later with a carload of family members to "do right by Coley."[6]

Coley's legions, like most Carolinians, were deeply religious, with Baptists comprising 52 percent of the state's church membership. Actually, the influence of Baptists was greater than this figure indicates because thousands of children attended weekly Baptist services with their parents before being baptized into church membership in early adolescence. The churches they joined practiced congregational polity and Arminian theology. Baptists, distrustful of ecclesiastical hierarchy, insisted upon local control of each congregation by majority rule of its membership. Rejecting infant baptism, they practiced baptism by immersion of believers who professed their faith in, and committed their lives to, Jesus Christ. More comfortable with free will than predestination, they believed that salvation was available to anyone who sought a personal relationship with the Savior. Their worship services were short on liturgy and ceremony and long on emotional uplift and guidance for living. Baptist clergymen inveighed against the evils of vice, including dancing; exhorted followers to undertake righteous crusades to purify America; promised that God prescribed a familial and societal hierarchy of father and male at the apex under Jesus; and warned that license and immorality were affronts to God.[7]

This stronghold of Baptists was also a land of contrasts, the first of four Cs, that occasionally blossomed into conflict. Besides the obvious ones of black versus white and prohibitionists versus repealers, the most noticeable conflicts were Charleston versus the rest of the state, lowcountry versus upcountry, rural versus urban, and townspeople versus mill villagers. Charleston, with more than 62,000 inhabitants, was easily the largest city in South Carolina. The self-proclaimed capital of the Old South, this port city remained the social arbiter of South Carolina, a cosmopolitan city of careful breeding and impeccable taste, replete with elegant mansions, stately churches, yacht club regattas, society balls, colleges, museums, and a medical school. Thriving port facilities, navy yard, and factories making fertilizer, cigars, rubber products, paint, asbestos, and cotton bagging made Charleston somewhat more prosperous than the rest of the state.[8]

Unfortunately, this grand dame had an ego and an attitude. Only a Charlestonian would define the fashionable Battery as the place where the Ashley and Cooper Rivers join to form the Atlantic Ocean, or refuse an offer of a free copy of the *New York Times* because he was not acquainted with anyone in New York City. This city of high life also had a jaded side: open saloons even during prohibition, gambling dens, and brothels that offended the moral sensibilities of Baptists and Methodists in the countryside. More than a century earlier, Methodist bishop Francis Asbury called Charleston "the seat of Satan, dissipation and folly."[9] Even the more tolerant John C. Calhoun chastised Charleston for its "intemperance and debaucheries."[10] He could easily have been referring to the city's political culture. Voting irregularities were rampant, and the city's Democratic machine customarily reported its ballot totals in gubernatorial elections after other localities in order to furnish just enough votes for the candidate it was favoring. In short, Charleston was the city the rest of South Carolina loved to hate, and Charleston acknowledged this hatred with disdain and condescension. So pronounced was this conflict that no Charlestonian had been able to win the governorship for nearly a hundred years.[11]

No less pronounced was the contrast and conflict between lowcountry and upcountry that dated to colonial times. The lowcountry was the eastern 60 percent of the state stretching from the Atlantic coast to a point just east of Columbia in the Midlands. The upcountry was the western one-third of the state beginning west of the Midlands and stretching to the Georgia–North Carolina border in the northwest. Lowcountry was plantation agriculture; upcountry was textile mills. Lowcountry was majority black; upcountry, majority white. To the extent that South Carolina was European, lowcountry was more heavily English; upcountry, more heavily Scotch-Irish and German. Whether true or not, residents in the two areas imagined themselves unique in personality. According to myth, lowcountry folk were to the manner born. They disdained the pursuit of wealth, appreciated leisure, and displayed "courtesy, ease and graceful hospitality."[12] Upcountrymen were described as energetic, materialistic, enterprising, thrifty, industrious, and pioneering. Since 1808 when the state constitution was amended to give the lowcountry control of the state senate and the upcountry control of the state house of representatives, an uneasy truce had prevailed between the two sections. Yet the truce broke down from time to time over matters such as the issuance of bonds to finance public highways.[13] Lowcountry favored bonds; upcountry opposed them.

Rural versus urban was more contrast than conflict because urban businessmen depended upon the countryside for patronage, while rural folk viewed the city as a necessary safety valve in times of rural unemployment. Too, rural folk outnumbered city dwellers by nearly four to one. Moreover, Charleston, Columbia, and to a lesser extent Greenville and Spartanburg were the only cities of any consequence. Still, the contrasts were noticeable. City life seemed fast paced; country life, slower and more deliberate. Urban centers boasted modern conveniences and attractions such as indoor plumbing, electric lights, paved streets, radios, movie theaters, and sophisticated shops. Rural areas had to make do with privies, carbide or kerosene lamps, dirt roads, horse and buggy, hayrides, Sears catalogs, and country stores.[14]

More confrontational were relations between residents of towns and those of mill villages along the periphery of towns. In the 1910s bankers, editors, merchants, and professionals in towns were frequently Progressives who viewed child labor, periodic epidemics, and widespread ignorance in mill villages as societal problems to be solved through government action. In particular, townspeople supported child-labor bills, compulsory health examination and vaccination of school children, and mandatory school attendance. Individualistic, egalitarian, and family-oriented mill workers, on the other hand, resented government intrusion into such "family matters." They found a spokesman in Gov. "Coley" Blease (1911–1915), who championed individualism, opposed compulsory schooling, and promised to pardon "any mill operative who killed a physician for giving his daughter a physical examination without parental consent."[15] Gov. Richard I. Manning (1915–1919) represented townspeople when he pushed through a compulsory education act and child-labor law.[16]

Although mill villagers and townspeople were divided over the proper limits of government intrusion, they united with all white Carolinians in reverence for the Lost Cause, which they called variously the Confederate War or the War between the States, but never the Civil War. In fact, this second *C*, which began at Fort Sumter in Charleston Harbor, was the defining moment in South Carolina history. The abolition of slavery, which destroyed millions of dollars in property, and Gen. William T. Sherman's destructive march through the Carolinas in February–March of 1865 reduced the Palmetto State from one of the wealthiest to one of the poorest states in the Union. Carolina landowners, having converted their national dollars into Confederate currency, were unable in 1865 to pay agricultural workers and had to resort to sharecropping as a permanent substitute for wage labor. The deaths during the war of one-fourth of the state's Confederate soldiers, the maiming of many others, and thefts of personal property and other atrocities committed by Sherman's soldiers left long-lasting bitterness and hatred for the North among the whites of South Carolina. Not until World War I did many Carolinians come to think of themselves as Americans. As late as the Great Depression they still saw themselves as South Carolinians primarily, Southerners secondly, and Americans only thirdly.[17]

Reminders of the Confederate War were everywhere. The annual Confederate Memorial Day celebration, monthly meetings of the United Daughters of the Confederacy, and frequent reunions of Confederate veterans kept the memory alive. So, too, did statues erected in town squares at county seats "sacred to the memory of Confederate dead." The statehouse itself was a constant reminder. Bronze stars in the exterior walls denoted strikes by shells from Sherman's artillery. A few feet away, a statue of George Washington, allegedly defaced by Union soldiers in February 1865, was left marred as a monument to Yankee barbarism. Nearby was a monument to the Confederate dead and an equestrian statue of Confederate general Wade Hampton. Inside, the Confederate flag flew above the desk of the House Speaker.[18]

This rich heritage made white South Carolinians conservative, the third C. Because of reverence for ancestors, they gloried in traditions, liberties, institutions, and lessons that evolved over two and one-half centuries. As farmers, they enjoyed the unhurried pace and deliberate lifestyle of an agricultural society; they respected rights of private property; and they possessed a strong sense of family and community. Many were Baptists because they appreciated local government and were instinctively distrustful of governments that sat miles removed from their constituents. Because of their Protestantism, they accepted man's fallibility and imperfectability, relied for guidance on revelation rather than reason, believed that God prescribed the familial, social, and moral order, and were certain that society and liberty were impossible to maintain without piety and religious faith. As racists, white Carolinians displayed feudal and organic notions of a social order in which everyone knew his place, his privileges, and his responsibilities. Acknowledged by scholars as late as 1941 to be "scornful of innovations" and "not willing to adapt unless thoroughly convinced that it is a good thing," Carolinians deplored social change that was not gradual, natural, unforced, and grounded in practical considerations derived from convention, custom, and tradition.[19] Most Carolinians were taught that social and political duties went hand in hand with liberty and rights. According to the historian Walter Edgar, the most important of these duties was assuring "the good order and the harmony of the whole community," an idea that would have delighted the father of nineteenth-century conservative political thought, Edmund Burke.[20]

The last of four Cs is for cotton, which was king in South Carolina. Slightly more than half of all workers were engaged in agriculture, mostly in the production of cotton. During World War I farmers prospered for the first time after decades of poverty because the federal government imposed no price ceiling on the state's chief money crop. Convinced that cotton won the war and agricultural prosperity would be everlasting, both small- and large-scale farmers borrowed money to buy additional land and equipment. The resulting overproduction and overextension triggered a collapse in 1920 from which South Carolina agriculture did not recover. The price of cotton plunged 56 percent from nearly 38 cents per pound in 1919 to below 17 cents in 1920. Aggravating the problem of price decline was the appearance during the war of the boll weevil and its wholesale devastation of the cotton crop in the early 1920s. Because of this wicked pest, cotton farmers in Williamsburg County, for example, saw their yield decline nearly 93 percent from 37,000 bales in 1920 to 2,700 bales in 1921. Even after chemical insecticides were developed to slow the boll weevil, farmers routinely lost 25 to 35 percent of their crop to weather, insects, and disease. Accordingly, the average value of land in South Carolina dropped 34 percent from over $65 an acre in 1920 to $43 an acre by 1925. During the 1920s farmers abandoned 30,000 of the state's 188,000 farms. The statewide agricultural depression also spelled the doom of bankers and merchants who made loans to finance agricultural expansion. Forty-nine percent of the state's banks closed during the decade.[21]

Of the remaining half of the state's workforce, about one-fourth earned their livelihood from manufacturing, mainly in cotton textiles. Approximately 71 percent of the value of the state's manufactured products sprang from cotton textiles, a single-industry dominance unique to South Carolina. About 80 percent of the industrial workforce labored in 230 cotton mills, and 78 percent of all manufacturing wages went to them. Other industries appeared insignificant in comparison. Fertilizer, the second most valuable industry, had an annual product of only $6.9 million, about one-twenty-fourth that of cotton textiles. The lumber and timber industry, which claimed the second largest labor force, employed only 3,394 workers, or about one-twenty-fourth the number employed by cotton textiles.[22]

In the mid-1920s the cotton textile industry joined cotton farming in economic *d*epression, the first of the two *D*s. The culprits were domestic overproduction and competition from synthetic fibers and overseas manufacturers. Profits evaporated quickly. By early 1929 textile securities were selling for half their 1923 price. Mill owners responded by hiring part-time instead of full-time workers, reducing the workweek, and increasing the machine load per worker. These actions staved off bankruptcy but created a large body of embittered, overworked, malnourished, and underpaid workers.[23]

The Great *D*epression arrived with a jolt in the autumn of 1929. Not far behind was the specter of starvation for hundreds of thousands of farmers and workers. Between 1929 and 1931 the cash value of the state's farm commodities dropped more than 50 percent from $149.7 million to $71.2 million, while the cost the farmer had to pay for goods dropped in percentage by only one-half as much. Cotton, selling for nearly seventeen cents a pound in 1929, brought less than six cents a pound in 1931. In 1932 rural poverty was so severe that taxes were delinquent on 45 percent of the farms in South Carolina. That same year Wyndham Manning of Sumter County reported that more than 1,400 county families were unemployed, hungry, and "practically naked." The deaths by starvation of two Pineville residents prompted a neighbor to observe that "hundreds of Negroes" in that community were "literally starving to death."[24] In September 1932, even after the Red Cross began donating such staples as flour and cloth to the poor in Beaufort, two residents died of starvation.[25]

Continuing bank failures aggravated rural poverty. In October 1931 the Bank of Western Carolina, with headquarters in Aiken and nine branches in rural counties, failed. Then on December 31, Peoples' State Bank closed its doors. With forty-four branches, it was the largest branch bank in the state. This calamity prompted a minor run on other banks the day after New Year's. Five hundred thousand dollars had to be flown by airplane from Charlotte to Columbia to keep the South Carolina National Bank solvent. Gov. Ibra C. Blackwood (1931–1934) pleaded publicly that all "patriotic" South Carolinians leave their deposits alone. Yet, so angry were rural South Carolinians at continuing bank failures that a grand jury in Berkeley County refused to indict two depositors who robbed the closed Moncks Corner branch of Peoples' State Bank of $2,000, a sum they claimed was less than their deposits.[26]

From 1929 to 1932 depression in the cotton textile industry went from bad to worse. The number of days operated declined more than 14 percent from 277 in 1929 to 237 in 1930. Average annual wages dipped 31 percent from $719 in 1929 to $495 in 1932. The number of workers dropped nearly 9 percent from 72,223 in 1929 to 66,032 in 1931. Small wonder that by 1933 the securities of many mills were not even being quoted. Small wonder, also, that the per-capita income of South Carolinians fell 42 percent from $261 in 1929 to $151 in 1932.[27]

Economic depression in the larger cities of South Carolina was just as serious. By May 1932 unemployment in Columbia was twelve times greater than in 1929. Charleston's rate of unemployment increased from 4 percent in 1930 to more than 20 percent by January 1932. Later in January, diminished tax collections forced the port city to pay employees in scrip. That summer, city trucks carried the unemployed to private farms surrounding the city to harvest vegetables donated by the owners. Parent-teacher associations throughout the state funded a school lunch program, while the Red Cross distributed flour milled from wheat donated by the Federal Farm Board.[28]

South Carolinians coped as best they could. First they tried retrenchment. Many families reduced their daily meals from three to two. Breakfast often contained no more than cornbread and syrup. Frequently the evening meal was a glass of buttermilk and a sweet potato roasted in the fireplace. Other families endured the monotony of beans, greens, and cornbread six days a week. Slightly more prosperous families occasionally added grits and molasses and substituted black-eyed peas for beans, biscuits for cornbread. Privation was so widespread, according to Elizabeth M. Hayes of Dillon County, even "nice families" lacked meat for seasoning collard greens. In such an environment, frills like candy were out of the question. In fact, a block of ice purchased on Saturday for iced tea on Sunday was one farm family's only indulgence. "A little sugar" purchased occasionally was another's. Carl Gibbs of Spartanburg County recalls, "You could just look at people and tell they needed food."[29]

Penniless as most people were, they still shared with less fortunate neighbors. Eunice H. Whitaker of Lancaster County remembers the young son of a neighborhood sharecropper coming to their back door at dinnertime to plead, "My Daddy said would you please give us some hot biscuits." Her mother was happy to send the lad home with half of the biscuits prepared for her own family's dinner. Julia Woodson of Liberty remembers that her father, who himself was searching for work, brought home for dinner one evening a young couple and baby who were hitchhiking back to Georgia after an unsuccessful attempt to find work "up north." Mill workers frequently gathered to share a plug of tobacco when one of them was lucky enough to "scrounge" a nickel for purchasing a twist.[30]

Clothing for most people was as basic as their menu. Few children owned more than one pair of shoes. In warm weather they went barefooted. Allison P. Simons of Saluda County recalls that her father, a farmer and sawmill operator, used an awl and anvil to repair his six children's shoes because he had no money to replace them. Cotton mill operatives frequently worked barefooted in warm weather and used pocketknives to remove the splinters of the oily wooden floor from their feet. "Store-bought" clothes were a novelty in most families. Wives and mothers fashioned underwear for the entire family from flour sacks. "Hoover dresses" were often made from feed sacks; hats and caps, from scraps of print cloth; and bed linens, from bolts of muslin. Most families darned socks and patched holes and tears in clothes. Overalls were commonplace in church because many families lacked "church clothes." Paul Wilkerson of Gaffney remembers that he wore and laundered one pair of overalls until they were bleached white.[31]

Other efforts to economize included giving up entertainment that cost money. Few people in the countryside had the ten-cent price of admission to movie theaters. Instead, they joined their neighbors in church activities, hayrides, and field sports, all of which were free. Most rural communities and all mill villages had men's baseball teams that practiced during the week and played games on Saturday. Men in rural communities hunted with rifles; boys, with slingshots. In warm weather children swam in nearby rivers. Both sexes and all ages fished and played checkers. Pitching horseshoes gained popularity. The most popular pastime was visiting, which reinforced both kinship and community bonds. Carl Gibbs of Spartanburg County recalls that a short walk to the grocer on Saturday to purchase sugar might take as long as three hours because of the tendency to visit from front porch to front porch. Nor were extended stays of several days uncommon. Wilburn Hembree of Spartanburg County remembers that children and adults in both host and visiting families would simply "throw down quilts on the floor" at bedtime when extra beds were not available. Factory-made cigarettes gave way to "roll-your-owns." Five cents purchased a cloth pouch of tobacco and enough rolling papers to last several days. According to Paul Wilkerson of Gaffney, the tobacco tasted so vile and smelled so rank that smokers claimed the contents "were a mixture of alfalfa and horse manure . . . without much alfalfa."[32]

Another way of coping was to strive for self-sufficiency. Farm families—and slightly more than half of all South Carolinians were farmers—were able to produce much of what they consumed. Farmers typically cut wood for fuel, grew corn for meal and occasionally wheat for flour, and raised a vegetable garden for canning and preserving. Sweet potatoes from a summer garden could feed a family year-round. They were stored in a sweet potato "bank"—some called it a "hill"—which was a hole dug in the earth, lined with sawdust, surrounded by cornstalks, and covered with pinestraw and dirt. Many families kept chickens that furnished eggs for cooking and meat for Sunday dinner. Many raised hogs whose meat was smoked in the fall at "hog killin' time" and stored year-round in a smokehouse. The more prosperous who had pork to spare ate meat at meals; the less prosperous used the meat to season vegetables. A few farm families kept a cow to milk for cooking, drinking, butter, and cheese. Customarily, in days before refrigeration, a farmer butchering a calf on Saturday would immediately sell the meat throughout the neighborhood for veal steaks on Sunday. The raw steaks were preserved over Saturday night by wrapping them in cloth and lowering them in a well bucket to the cool area just above the water. Many families also grew sorghum to make syrup for the "3-M" diet of meat, meal, and molasses. Families also improvised. An automobile without gasoline became a "Hoover cart" when its body was removed from the chassis, a wooden box with seats added, and a mule hitched to the front for motive power. Self-sufficiency in food, clothing, fuel, and shelter at least brought peace of mind.[33]

Coping also meant reducing expectations and limiting horizons. Economic depression, Carl Gibbs recalls, "taught you not to wish for what you couldn't have." Lacking electricity, most South Carolinians had never yearned for washing machines, ranges, and refrigerators. Many rural people never expected to own an automobile. Clothing had always been basic, and short trips to visit, worship, and shop were the norm. In the 1920s and early 1930s many South Carolinians learned to be satisfied with good health, sound roof, sturdy mule, agreeable weather, square meal, congenial neighbors, solid wash tub, flavorful "smoke," and tasty "chew." Yearning for the unattainable simply meant hoping to have enough money for taxes, mortgage, doctor bills, school supplies, gasoline, movies, vacation, Coca Cola, church tithes, and three meals a day.[34]

Economic depression not only forced entire families into the job market, but it also compelled breadwinners to take on additional responsibilities. Older sons in farm families often took textile jobs and sent money home. Older daughters and unmarried aunts did the same from jobs as clerks in department stores. L. T. Fulmer of Aiken County recalls that his father, a farmer, worked in winter at a local sawmill in order to buy shoes for his family. Five members of the Hembree household in Spartanburg worked at Clifton Manufacturing Company during periods when the mill operated only a few days each month. Lads as young as ten years picked cotton to purchase their first pair of long pants.[35]

Present-day octogenarians from self-sufficient farm families in the 1920s and 1930s recollect, "We were poor then but we never missed a meal," or "We didn't know we were poor because everyone was in the same boat." Unfortunately, this selective recall overlooks the desperate plight of poor sharecroppers, blacks, urban poor, and victims of circumstance. In one area of Pickens County in the west, fully one-fourth of white tenants concentrated so heavily on cotton that they grew no garden, owned no cow for milk or butter, and raised no hogs for meat. Their meager diet was so deficient in niacin that pellagra was pandemic. Sharecroppers in other areas, particularly along the coast, exhibited a high incidence of hookworm, malaria, and malnutrition. A balanced diet was practically unknown there; as one woman put it, "We eat whatever we can scrape up."[36] Small wonder that children in these families missed an average of one-third of each school year.[37]

Blacks and the urban poor suffered as badly. Unemployed whites took over traditional labor-intensive "Negro jobs," leaving blacks to shift for themselves. The luckier ones accepted train tickets from relatives in New York, Baltimore, or Philadelphia and settled permanently "up north." The urban poor had neither plots for gardens nor railroad tickets and had to rely on private charity. In 1931 private charities in Columbia served more than 700,000 free meals to the city's poor. In fact, L. T.

Fulmer, born into a self-sufficient farm family in Aiken County, recalls feeling both guilt and compassion in 1933 when he encountered a Columbia lad at the Civilian Conservation Corps induction center who spoke of frequently missing meals. The next day at Fort Benning, Georgia, several urban youths in Fulmer's company fainted from a combination of factors including hunger.[38]

Adverse circumstances attacked people of all classes. Allison P. ("Polly") Simons of Saluda County, the oldest of six children, lost her father in 1935 when she was seventeen years old. In order to feed the seven survivors and keep their small farm, her mother secured employment in the local school lunch program and used the proceeds from her husband's life insurance to send Polly to business college in Columbia. Polly's younger brothers tended the family garden and worked as day laborers on nearby cotton farms. Later, Polly landed a temporary job in Columbia and sent home a portion of her paycheck each week. The family of Julia Woodson of Liberty in Pickens County was prosperous enough to send two daughters to Queens College in Charlotte before the local bank closed and wiped out the family's savings. Not long afterward the faltering cotton economy drove into bankruptcy the cotton gin manufacturer that employed her father. For several months he was unemployed and forced to support his wife and daughters with the proceeds of a cashed-in life insurance policy. Day after day he searched in vain for work; night after night he paced the floor of his bedroom in desperation. On one occasion, when the family's coal supply was nearly exhausted, an anonymous donor paid to refill the bin. Paul Wilkerson of Gaffney, who was raised by his grandparents, lost his grandfather when the lad was eight years old, forcing the grandmother to become a seamstress after the local bank went bankrupt with their savings and insurance. An aunt who lived in the household secured a job at the local Belk department store to supplement the grandmother's meager income. Eunice H. Whitaker of Lancaster lost her husband shortly after the birth of her child and had to return to her parents' farming household of six children and a paternal grandmother. For people such as the Simons, Woodson, Wilkerson, and Whitaker families, life was indeed hard.[39]

Until the 1950s most Southern voters were *D*emocrats (the second *D*), and none more so than South Carolinians. In the minds of white Southerners, the Democratic Party was the agency of secession and Redemption; the Republican Party, the perpetrator of Reconstruction and black equality. In the period following the Civil War and Reconstruction,

Democrats in the North and the South reached an easy accord: white Southerners would be given a free hand in racial matters in return for their Democratic solidarity. Embrace of Democracy from 1877 to 1932 was easier for white South Carolinians than for other Southerners. After flirting briefly with Federalism in the 1790s, they voted either Democratic-Republican, Democratic, Independent Democratic, or Southern Democratic in every election for president, United States senator, and governor from 1801 to 1860. An occasional Whig won election to the U.S. House of Representatives, but the majority of congressmen were either straight Democrat or some variety of Democrat in states' rights or free-trade clothing. In ten of the thirteen presidential elections following Reconstruction (1880–1928), South Carolina voted more heavily Democratic by percentage than any other state; in the other three, the state cast the second largest percentage of Democratic votes. In short, South Carolina was the most Democratic state in the nation. The Democratic primary in the summer, rather than the general election in November, determined officeholding. And since Democratic senators and congressmen, once elected, seldom left office except by death, South Carolina Democrats acquired seniority and power in Washington out of proportion to the size of the state.[40]

In 1932 every Democrat in South Carolina from the politically powerful to the average voter looked forward to the presidential election. King Cotton was ailing, the Hoover administration was failing, and their party stood an excellent chance of electing only its third president since the Civil War. To earn South Carolina's electoral vote, he need only be Democratic. But to be popular, he would need Southern connections and respectable Protestant ancestry, appreciation of the plight of agriculture and blue-collar labor, respect for individualism and the rights of private property, common-sense solutions to economic depression that drew from the past and involved local control and implementation, acknowledgment of South Carolina's importance in party and institutional councils, sensitivity to the state's racial modus vivendi, and an agenda that minimized contrasts and divisiveness while accentuating harmony and cohesion among whites.

Such a man was already in the offing. On November 12, 1928, former congressman James F. Byrnes, a Spartanburg lawyer who in 1930 would defeat the incumbent Blease for a seat in the United States Senate, congratulated Franklin D. Roosevelt on his election as governor of New York. Byrnes added, "I am now only anxious to have the opportunity to urge your nomination for the presidency."[41] Of like mind was Claud N. Sapp of Columbia, state Democratic Party chairman and former state legislator, who began organizing Roosevelt Southern Clubs in December 1930 and became FDR's state campaign director in March 1932. Two months later, with help from Governor Blackwood and powerful leaders such as state Sen. Richard M. Jefferies of Colleton, the political duo of Sapp and Byrnes was able to elect a delegation pledged to Roosevelt for the National Democratic Convention in Chicago. There, the Carolinians stood firm for FDR, who won the nomination on the fourth ballot. He and running mate John Nance Garner of Texas would oppose the forlorn Hoover-Curtis ticket nominated by the Republicans earlier in June.[42] James A. Farley of New York would manage FDR's campaign.

Since nomination as a Democrat was tantamount to election in South Carolina, the campaign progressed uneventfully through the late summer and early fall. Following conferences with Farley in July and August, Sapp decided that the state party organization would double as the campaign organization. Tactically, the party would emphasize economic issues and avoid the dangerous question of prohibition. Returning from a conference with Farley in August, Sapp remarked with confidence, "I don't see how they can beat us."[43]

Whatever aid in swaying voters the Roosevelt campaign required, South Carolina newspapers were quick to supply. The *Spartanburg Herald* dubbed the whispering campaign regarding Roosevelt's health not only "Blows below the Belt" but also ridiculous because the governorship of New York was only slightly less exacting than the presidency. The *Charleston News and Courier* added that those who whispered Roosevelt was "wanting in strength of character" and too "easygoing" did not realize Roosevelt was simply a gentleman and hence soft spoken and well mannered.[44] The *Barnwell People-Sentinel* suggested that G.O.P. stood for "Great on Promising." The *Camden Wateree Messenger* supposed that Hoover prosperity might be just around the corner, "but from where we are standing it is as dark as the inside of a bull frog's belly and sounds just as doleful." The *Lexington Dispatch News* added that "about the only thing to do is to abolish corners. Then prosperity will have to show itself."[45]

While the press was busy fencing with Republicans, Senator Byrnes was helping with the national campaign. In September he began frequent trips to Roosevelt's "Brains Trust" headquarters in New York where he wrote speeches, offered tactical advice, assessed political situations, predicted congressional attitudes, and accompanied Roosevelt on the nominee's second campaign trip between October 18 and 26. On October 24 the campaign came to Atlanta where Byrnes, Sapp, Blackwood, United States senator Ellison D. ("Cotton Ed") Smith, and eleven other prominent politicians from South Carolina joined Roosevelt and his party for lunch. At a rally that evening in Atlanta's City Auditorium, the principal speakers included Byrnes, Smith, and Blackwood.[46]

Roosevelt's campaign in South Carolina concluded with local rallies organized by county party chairmen. One held in Camden in late October was typical. To music provided by high school bands, the day-long affair featured a parade of 4,000 school children, Boy Scouts, state and local policemen, American Legionnaires with Legion auxiliaries, Confederate and Spanish-American War veterans, National Guard, and Red Shirts—a hoary group of Democrats who had "redeemed" South Carolina from Republican rule in 1876. Following a picnic luncheon, orators Sapp, Blackwood, and former governor John G. Richards addressed the crowd at the courthouse.[47]

Election day, November 8, was a day of jubilation in the Palmetto State, which gave Roosevelt 98 percent of its popular vote, a higher percentage than any other state. In Lancaster County, Roosevelt received 3,103 votes to Hoover's 5; in 23 of the state's 46 counties, Hoover received fewer than 20 votes; and in only 9 counties did he receive more than 50.[48]

Since few had doubted Roosevelt's victory in South Carolina and the nation, there were no immediate efforts to analyze its full implications. The source of this triumph may now be seen as intertwined strands of the state's political past and powerful portents of its future. Central to Roosevelt's success before the Chicago Convention was support he received from influential individuals such as Sapp, Byrnes, and Blackwood. Their reasons for supporting him were not entirely political. Without doubt, they were attracted by his gentlemanly style; moreover, politicians such as Byrnes admired his progressive principles. Not only could Roosevelt claim an ancestry as respectable as any in South Carolina, but he also possessed Southern connections by owning property at Warm Springs, Georgia. But, while Roosevelt the well-born gentleman, transplanted Southerner, and progressive were appealing images, Roosevelt's greatest asset was of a more practical nature: he was a proven winner who could be counted on to dispense patronage to loyal Democrats.

Roosevelt's victory in November was no more surprising than his preconvention success because from 1876 to 1948 a combination of factors made it impossible for any Republican to carry the state. First there was the popular and persistent myth of a harsh, racial-torn, and corrupt Reconstruction that most white voters still equated with the Republican Party.[49] The second and most decisive factor was the "politics of color." To vote Democratic declared a preference for the racial status quo; to vote Republican implied tampering with the delicate social and political order to achieve unworthy ends.[50] The third consideration was the Depression. The prevailing view was that whatever Roosevelt might do as president could not be worse than what Hoover had already done.[51]

No less important was the identification of Roosevelt with Woodrow Wilson, the most beloved president in South Carolina since Thomas Jefferson. In February the *Columbia State* devoted an editorial to comparing Roosevelt and Wilson; in July it noted that Roosevelt's speech accepting the nomination contained "much of the spiritual teachings of Woodrow Wilson"; and in November the *Spartanburg Herald* drew parallels between FDR's entering the White House to fight the Depression and Wilson's entering the Great War to fight Germany.[52] Moreover, South Carolinians associated 1932 with 1876, envisioning a Democratic victory over Hoover as the twentieth-century equivalent of Redemption following Reconstruction. In October, for example, the Roosevelt rally in Camden featured Red Shirt marchers and Red Shirt orators who compared the spirits of 1876 and 1932.[53]

On the day following FDR's election, optimism reigned supreme. Perhaps reflecting the Depression's preparation of people to explore less conservative avenues, the *Spartanburg Herald* suggested that the United States had "turned to the party with the more liberal [Wilsonian] tendency and the more progressive tradition." The *Barnwell People-Sentinel* carried a one-sentence editorial: "Phew! Wasn't that Hoover depression awful?"[54] Yet somehow, only retired admiral Samuel McGowan of Charleston, a subordinate of Roosevelt in the Navy Department during the Wilson administration, really understood what Roosevelt would mean to the nation. Pointing to Roosevelt's precedent-breaking airplane flight to Chicago to accept the nomination, McGowan presciently predicted: "Anybody who thinks he is through springing surprises is mistaken."[55]

THE CONGRESSIONAL DELEGATION AND THE NEW DEAL

1933–1939

Franklin D. Roosevelt's first two administrations produced legislative proposals that were unrivaled in extent or impact since George Washington's first term. Such initiatives from the chief executive would have come to naught, of course, had it not been for favorable action by a complaisant Congress. Its members from South Carolina were in the vanguard of New Dealers during the first administration, less so during the second. In fact, no individual member of Congress was more significant in first erecting and then obstructing the New Deal than Sen. James F. Byrnes, who emerged as the most influential senator from South Carolina—and quite possibly from the entire South—since John C. Calhoun a century earlier.[1] In his role as one of the architects of the New Deal, Byrnes authored, helped craft, or served as administration spokesman for eight major bills. In addition, he served as party whip in the Senate for many others.[2]

Fifty-four years old at the outset of Roosevelt's presidency, Byrnes had only two years of seniority in the Senate. Still, he was already one of its most popular members. Characterized by various colleagues as dapper, gregarious, genial, humorous, and charming, he was also cautious and artful, preferring backstage negotiation to debate on the Senate floor. Byrnes entered national politics in 1910 when he was elected to the House of Representatives for the first of seven consecutive terms. He warmly supported Pres. Woodrow Wilson's Progressive agenda, the New Freedom. After narrowly losing to Blease in the 1924 Senate race, Byrnes bided his time in the Spartanburg law office of Cecil Wyche and former congressman Sam J. Nichols before successfully defeating Blease for reelection in 1930. In the Senate, Byrnes sat on the Appropriations Committee and Banking and Currency Committee.[3]

Byrnes, born in Charleston and having practiced law in Aiken and Spartanburg, was a hybrid of lowcountry and upcountry, a blend that was politically useful in sectional South Carolina. Intellectually, he was a fusion of pragmatism, fiscal conservatism, and Wilsonian Progressivism. In South Carolina politics he was a new breed, leaving the issues of race and booze to his opponents while concentrating instead on social and economic issues. In March 1933 Byrnes was deemed by many political observers to be Roosevelt's "legislative liaison man" and "fair-haired boy," owing to Byrnes's intimate involvement with the Roosevelt campaign. There was even speculation that Roosevelt wanted Byrnes to be Senate majority leader.[4]

Although no senator surpassed Byrnes in constructing the New Deal, few outdid South Carolina's other senator, Cotton Ed Smith, in obstructing it. A farmer by occupation, the sixty-nine-year-old Smith was the senior Democratic member of the Senate and chairman of the Senate Agriculture Committee. He was bulky and ponderous for his medium height, with a baggy, bulldoglike face and several chins—an appearance made even more menacing by a crusty disposition. Smith enjoyed debate, spewed profanity, and used tobacco in all forms. For twenty-five years he had proudly worn the sobriquet Cotton Ed for his unrelenting efforts on behalf of the cotton farmer.[5]

Though colorful, grumpy, and demagogic, Smith boasted a respectable Senate record. He voted the Progressive line under Presidents Taft and Wilson and opposed the return to conservatism under Harding and Coolidge. Ideologically, Smith was a blend of the agrarianism of William Jennings Bryan, Progressivism of Woodrow Wilson, and traditional Southern Democracy. Embracing the motto "Cotton is king, and white is supreme," he opposed protective tariffs, supported currency inflation, advocated white supremacy, adored states' rights, hated Wall Street, and endorsed every program calculated to aid agriculture.[6]

All six South Carolinians in the House of Representatives were men of prominence, stature, and accomplishment who could have been elected to Congress in any era. Most were seasoned lawmakers. Three were or would become committee chairmen during the New Deal. Hampton Pitts Fulmer of Orangeburg in the Second Congressional District was a farmer, rural banker, former state legislator, and second in command of the House Agriculture Committee, whose chairman he became in 1939. Fifty-seven years old in 1933 and a congressman since 1921, he had supported the concept of compulsory crop control for years. The other nationally minded representative was John J. McSwain from Greenville in the Fourth Congressional District containing the four farming and textile counties of Greenville, Spartanburg, Union, and Laurens. Fifty-seven years old in 1933 and a lawyer by profession, McSwain was a former captain in the American Expeditionary Force in France in

World War I and was one of the founders of the South Carolina Department of the American Legion. He had Populist-Progressive antecedents, publicly refusing as a lawyer ever to represent what he termed "unrestricted corporate wealth."[7] He put together an effective political machine of like-minded lawyers, lodge brothers, and cousins in the numerous families of Scotch-Irish descent in the South Carolina piedmont. In Congress since 1921, McSwain chaired the House Military Affairs Committee. Aviation was his hobby, and he was a close friend of the combat-aviator pioneer, Gen. William (Billy) Mitchell. Unfortunately, heart trouble would plague McSwain from 1931 until his death from a heart attack on August 6, 1936.[8]

Completing the delegation were Thomas S. McMillan of Charleston County, Allard Gasque of Florence, James P. Richards of Lancaster, and John C. Taylor of Anderson. The forty-five-year-old McMillan represented the First Congressional District. A lawyer by profession, and a member of the aristocratic and conservative Thomas P. Stoney faction in Charleston, he boasted a distinguished, if brief, career in the lower house of the South Carolina legislature, where he served as speaker for two years before his election to Congress in 1925.[9] Former school superintendent Allard Gasque represented the Sixth Congressional District in the northeastern corner of the state. He had been active in Palmetto politics since at least 1912, serving as a member of the Democratic State Executive Committee (1912–1920) and as chairman of the Florence County Democratic Committee (1919–1923). His ten years of congressional service earned for him the chairmanship of the House Pensions Committee.[10]

The Palmetto delegation contained two freshmen. Forty-three-year-old John C. Taylor of Anderson in the Third District could legitimately be described as self-made, having obtained his college education while working part time in a cotton mill. A farmer, lawyer, and former clerk of the court for Anderson County, he was also part owner of the powerful *Anderson Independent* and *Anderson Daily Mail*. Also new to congressional service, former probate judge James P. Richards of Lancaster in the Fifth District was the youngest of the representatives at thirty-eight. Before service as a lieutenant in World War I, he earned statewide recognition as a baseball and football player at the University of South Carolina.[11]

Voters in the Palmetto State returned these six men to Congress year after year from 1932 to 1936 when McSwain died and was replaced by

G. Heyward Mahon, Jr., of Greenville. Mahon was forty-six years old in 1936, a Baptist, a wealthy and prominent businessman, and son of a politically prominent former Greenville mayor. A major in World War I, he earned both a silver star for battlefield gallantry and a purple heart for wounds that included severe facial disfiguration. He became sufficiently active in the American Legion in the 1920s to serve as a state commander. His innate congeniality and his support of, and from, Senator Byrnes marked him early for a political career, and only his appreciation for the incumbent's popularity deterred him from running for Congress during the early 1930s.[12]

The year 1938 brought three changes within the Palmetto congressional delegation. Mahon lost his bid for renomination to Joseph R. Bryson, a Greenville lawyer, an infantry lieutenant in World War I, and a former state legislator. Taylor also lost his bid for renomination. His successor was former congressman Butler B. Hare, a Saluda native, lawyer, farmer, and former college professor who had served four terms in the U.S. House of Representatives from 1925 to 1933, when he retired because of congressional redistricting. The third change occurred when Allard Gasque died unexpectedly on June 17, 1938, just hours after Congress adjourned. His wife, Elizabeth, served out his unexpired term before being replaced in January 1939 by John L. McMillan of Florence. "Johnny Mac," as he was called, was a lawyer and former secretary to Allard Gasque.[13]

On March 4, 1933, Roosevelt took office and quickly called Congress into special session to deal with the economic crisis. His intention, applauded by the South Carolina congressional delegation, was to use the federal government as an instrument of economic recovery and a means of restoring economic opportunity. States' rights and laissez faire, the Carolinians agreed, practically ruined the Palmetto State in the 1920s. They were convinced that Congress and president should enact legislation to promote recovery in agriculture and business, relief for the unemployed, and reform in such areas as banking, labor-management relations, and investments.

No state delegation was more instrumental in shaping legislation for agricultural recovery than South Carolina's. On March 16, 1933, Roosevelt sent Congress his farm message, embodying what would become the Agricultural Adjustment Act (AAA) of 1933. For years bumper harvests glutted markets and depressed agricultural prices. The president's measure was designed to combat the problem of overproduction through acreage reduction. An additional feature was a processing tax on processors of agricultural commodities (for example, on cotton textile mills) to be used to give farmers parity—that is, the difference between their purchasing power in 1933 and their purchasing power in the period just preceding World War I when agricultural prices were the highest in peacetime history.[14]

The House took speedy action on the president's agricultural initiative, owing both to his request that sponsors allow no unsanctioned amendments and to efforts of House manager Hampton Fulmer, a long-time advocate of acreage-reduction schemes. Fulmer exhorted his colleagues to "get behind the President's farm-relief program to the last ditch." In words that must have made John C. Calhoun roll over in his grave, Fulmer lambasted critics who clothed themselves in the garb of states' rights to complain of Roosevelt's receiving dictatorial power. In fact, he professed regret that the bill stopped short of giving the president "absolute power and control" over production, marketing, and pricing.[15] On March 22 the lower house passed the bill, with every Palmetto representative voting yea.

If Roosevelt believed Senate passage would be as simple, he reckoned without the obstinate chairman of the Senate Agriculture Committee. To the redoubtable Cotton Ed, talk of parity, domestic allotments, and processing taxes was bunkum. A product of the agrarian revolt of the 1890s, Smith advocated currency inflation, mortgage relief, and agricultural loans. Fearful a processing tax would depress cotton prices, he was willing to accept crop reduction only if achieved by having the farmer lease a portion of his land to the government in exchange for cotton held by the Federal Farm Board. Nowhere in the proposed legislation could Smith find his views embodied. In fact, and perhaps most importantly, the agriculture economists who framed the measure had not even consulted him.[16] Even worse, from Smith's perspective, they were men who "flirt[ed] with agriculture as a sideline" and "could not tell a cotton stalk from a jimson weed."[17]

Smith's resistance proved formidable, and the president was forced to invite the Senate Agriculture Committee to the White House for a conference with him, Secretary of Agriculture Henry A. Wallace, and Senate Majority Leader Joseph Robinson. Amid pleas for party solidarity, the meeting produced a compromise whereby the administration's bill would incorporate Smith's plan for exchanging cotton bales for crop reduction agreements, and Smith, in turn, would agree not to oppose the administration's bill.[18] The farm bill then glided through the Senate with Byrnes voting yea and Smith, profoundly disgusted, not voting.[19] Nevertheless, Smith subordinated his feelings to party loyalty and took to the hustings in South Carolina to encourage compliance with the AAA.[20]

Nine months later, on January 23, 1934, Senator Smith delivered a radio address titled "The Cotton Reducing Plan of the AAA," which was designed to persuade all cotton growers to sign new acreage reduction contracts. Smith called the acreage reduction program for cotton a "marvelous success."[21] Yet he knew better, and so did Alabama's senator John Bankhead. Many cotton farmers refused to reduce acreage but benefited from the rise in price caused by those who did. Reminiscent of Populism, Smith's solution was to discard the AAA in favor of a system of federal agricultural banks and warehouses that would lend money to farmers and then store and market their crops gradually in order to maintain maximum prices. Bankhead, by contrast, wanted to make the existing AAA crop-reduction program mandatory through taxes on all cotton sold in excess of allotments. On February 2 President Roosevelt met with Smith to convince him to support Bankhead.[22] Hampton Fulmer, meanwhile, was already sponsoring the Bankhead program, which passed the lower house on March 19 with the support of all six Carolinians.[23]

To critics in the Senate who took House passage as an occasion to raise the issue of constitutionality, Cotton Ed Smith was quick to reply he was willing to "strain the Constitution" in order to provide relief that "85 percent of the cotton farmers believe is essential to their salvation."[24] Nevertheless, Smith labeled Secretary Wallace and his advisors "damned fool[s] away from home" and added, "I am no more in favor of this kind of legislation than you are except in this emergency."[25] In March the bill passed the Senate with both Smith and Byrnes voting in favor. House manager Hampton Fulmer was one of the four men who stood behind the president when he signed the Bankhead Cotton Control Bill into law.[26] Three weeks later Smith, still the loyal Democrat, guided to passage in the Senate the Kerr-Smith Tobacco Control Bill, a companion measure to the Bankhead Act.[27]

Smith reverted to his accustomed obstructionism in June 1934 on the question of approving Rexford G. Tugwell's nomination as undersecretary of agriculture. Publicly, Smith opposed elevating this urbane economist and agriculture "planner" because Tugwell was not a farmer. Privately, Smith was in battle with the administration over the distribution of patronage in South Carolina. Smith was piqued by several slights that culminated in the spring of 1934 when Roosevelt refused to appoint Smith's nominee, Reuben Gosnell of Spartanburg, United States marshal for the western district of South Carolina. Smith retaliated by refusing to allow his committee to hold hearings on Tugwell's nomination. On June 8 Smith was forced to surrender after Roosevelt had Majority Leader Robinson threaten Smith with a motion to discharge Smith's committee from further consideration of the Tugwell nomination.[28]

In 1936, an election year, congressional Democrats planned to avoid divisive legislation. They reckoned without the United States Supreme Court, which, on January 6, 1936, in the *Butler* case, voided the AAA's processing taxes. Claiming vindication, Smith denounced critics of the Court, whose carping about *Butler,* he warned, threatened to undermine the Constitution—a possibility he termed "the most dangerous thing that could happen in America." The only policies necessary to stabilize agriculture, Smith insisted, were currency inflation and agricultural banking.[29]

Roosevelt had little sympathy for Smith's Populist schemes. The president wanted immediate repeal of the Bankhead and Kerr-Smith acts, followed by the restoration of crop control under the guise of soil conservation. This scheme would allow the government to pay farmers for reducing soil-depleting crops such as cotton and for planting soil-building crops such as lespedeza. Money for benefit payments would come directly from congressional appropriations instead of processing taxes. The resulting Soil Conservation and Domestic Allotment Act of 1936 passed the upper house on February 15 with Smith and Byrnes voting yea. Both men took the floor in debate for the measure, and Smith even helped guide it through the Senate, although he concealed neither his displeasure with the bill nor his preference for currency inflation and agricultural banking. On February 21 the lower house passed the bill with no South Carolinian in opposition.[30]

By 1937 the South Carolinians were less united in support of far-reaching agricultural legislation. Agricultural prosperity had not returned to South Carolina, despite four years of the AAA. Nevertheless, forecasts in the spring of a bumper fall harvest and low prices prompted Roosevelt to urge a new and permanent agricultural adjustment program combining soil conservation, crop reduction, and parity. In response, Senator Smith scoffed at the forecasts and declared the impossibility of having his committee conclude hearings on a bill in time to act that year.[31] To bring Smith on board, Roosevelt continued a generous crop-loan program that pegged the price of cotton at twelve cents a pound. A partially placated

Smith then agreed to make agriculture the first order of congressional business in 1938. Between August 1937, when Congress was scheduled to adjourn, and January 1938, when the second session of the Seventy-fifth Congress would begin, Smith's committee would conduct hearings throughout the farm belt to learn what programs farmers wanted in a new AAA.[32]

After Congress adjourned in August 1937, the agriculture situation deteriorated. The September United States Department of Agriculture (USDA) estimate of the cotton crop was 16 million bales, the fifth largest in U.S. history. Cotton futures in New Orleans dropped nineteen points in twenty minutes when the estimate was announced. The October estimate was even worse: 17.5 million bales, the second largest crop in history.[33] Roosevelt and agriculture secretary Wallace decided to call Congress into special session in November to pursue new agricultural programs. This development would leave Smith's Agriculture Committee little time to whip the administration's farm bill into shape, especially since Smith was busy lobbying for a plan of his own. Smith wanted to scrap the crop-reduction plan so that American farmers could presumably recapture the world's cotton market. He also wished to use tariff revenues for equalization payments to balance the price a farmer received for his cotton and the price he paid for his supplies.[34]

Two weeks later Senator Smith sent half of his Agriculture Committee south, the other half west, to sample public opinion. October 19 found the southern group in Columbia before a large audience of farmers. Three basic positions emerged: Smith's plan was presented; a delegation of farmers from Calhoun County recommended a combination of Smith's plan and the Roosevelt administration's program; and South Carolina commissioner of agriculture J. Roy Jones presented the Roosevelt administration's plan for crop reduction, parity, and soil conservation. To Smith's chagrin, the audience voted ten to one in favor of the administration's program.[35]

Others in the South Carolina delegation were as disaffected as Smith. Taylor raised the question of constitutionality and attempted to amend the bill so that only those farmers participating in crop referenda would be subject to their provisions.[36] McMillan went even further. He insisted the compulsory features of the legislation were "certainly against the principles of our form of government" and added he did not believe "liberty-loving people" in South Carolina would be willing to submit to "straight-jacket methods emanating from Washington."[37] The Charlestonian further argued that crop reduction would seriously injure industries whose existence depended upon a large crop, such as gins, compresses, cotton merchants, steamship lines, dock facilities, and cotton oil and seed mills, many of which were located in McMillan's district. The only farm program that suited McMillan was the Smith plan with no limitations on production.[38] Accordingly, McMillan and Taylor voted against the Agricultural Adjustment Bill of 1938. Their apostasy was balanced by Hampton Fulmer's efforts on behalf of passage; an appreciative Roosevelt presented him one of the pens used to sign the legislation into law.[39]

The political landscape and economic configuration of South Carolina account for votes on farm legislation by the congressional delegation. Seven of the *ABCDs* were involved: *a*ncestors, *b*lacks, *c*onservatism, *c*ontrasts, *c*otton, *D*emocracy, and *D*epression. So were three *Ps*: *p*arochialism, *p*ragmatism, and *p*olitical effect. To vote consistently for New Deal farm legislation, as did Byrnes, Fulmer, Gasque, Mahon, McSwain, and Richards, kept faith with *a*ncestors such as Sen. James Henry Hammond who first proclaimed to the nation in 1857 that "cotton is king." Voting yes preserved the livelihood of *c*otton farmers, a majority of the state's citizens, who were in the throes of economic *d*epression in 1933. It strengthened an economic way of life that doubled as an instrument of racial control by keeping *b*lacks as landless tenants and whites as landowners. Furthermore, it supported the efforts of the leader of the *D*emocratic Party, Franklin D. Roosevelt. Moreover, *p*arochial South Carolinians were flattered that the national government finally was taking notice of the plight of their state and its localities. As *p*ragmatists, many of them were fond of programs that worked, or at least appeared to; and, although pre-Depression agricultural prosperity would not return until World War II, commodity prices at least were higher than they would have been without the AAA. Finally, Palmetto congressmen, cognizant of the popularity of the AAA, were careful not to jeopardize their seats in Congress by voting against it.

But two congressmen who were motivated primarily by *c*onservatism—McMillan and Taylor—were willing to take that risk. Neither man relished "straight-jacket methods emanating from Washington." In supporting voluntary but not mandatory acreage reduction, both men reflected their belief in individualism. McMillan's voting also mirrored the *c*ontrast between Charleston and the rest of the state; restricting production of cotton would help farmers outside the port city but unintentionally harm its gin operators, mills, and shippers whose livelihood depended on a large crop and cheap commodity prices. Conservatism certainly influenced Senator Smith, who endorsed historically popular schemes for raising agricultural prices such as currency inflation and agricultural banking while opposing revolutionary ones such as acreage reduction. He also resented not being consulted on agricultural matters by the Roosevelt White House. Nevertheless, out of loyalty to party, Smith never actually voted against the AAA.

Because South Carolina was a land of cotton mills as well as cotton farms, the congressional delegation also supported efforts aimed at industrial recovery. All eight men endorsed, at least in principle, the National Industrial Recovery Act, which contained both a public works program to stimulate the capital goods industries and a program allowing businesses to ignore the antitrust laws and restrain production in order to raise prices. In return, the act required businesses to agree to abide by wage, hour, and working-condition codes. Only Taylor voted against the measure on final passage because of his professed dislike for the bill's taxes on excess profits and capital stock to fund the public works program.[40]

Second only to recovery in agriculture and business, the congressional delegation was preoccupied with relief for the unemployed. As conservatives, they wished to promote "the good order and the harmony of the whole community," many of whose members lacked food, clothing, and shelter. Also as conservatives, they feared failure to act might invite violent revolution. Congressman Fulmer put it clearly when he told an audience of law students at the University of South Carolina that the national government had an obligation to spend "billions of dollars" to "prevent starvation" and "save this country from revolution, putting the burden of payment on the rich."[41] Consequently, the eight Carolinians voted for the Emergency Relief Act of 1933, which created the Federal Emergency Relief Administration to dispense $500 million to the states for relief work. They also supported the Home Owners Loan Act, authored by Byrnes, to guarantee defaulted home mortgages. In February 1934 seven of the eight South Carolinians (Taylor was paired) voted with the majority in favor of funding for the Civil Works Administration. In January 1935 the eight lawmakers supported the $4.8-million Emergency Relief Appropriation Bill that returned unemployables to state jurisdiction while simultaneously providing 3.5 million jobs in work relief and public works.[42]

Political considerations occasionally moderated the support of at least one Carolinian for relief spending. By mid-1934 Chairman McSwain of the House Military Affairs Committee was at odds with the administration. The specific point of contention was McSwain's desire for the Army Air Corps to become a separate branch of the armed forces and to expand from 1,800 planes to 4,400 planes in order to make American air strength "the equal or superior of any other nation."[43] McSwain was clearly a man ahead of his time; many in the administration were not. Secretary of War George Dern called McSwain's claim that air power would decide the outcome of the next war "romantic," while members of the Army General Staff dismissively labeled a "bugaboo" McSwain's prediction that America would someday suffer an attack by air. McSwain struck back by having a subcommittee investigate War Department spending since 1926. Dern then apparently worked through Roosevelt and Harold Ickes of the Public Works Administration to silence McSwain by curtailing funds and approvals for PWA projects in Greenville, McSwain's hometown. Greenville applied through the PWA for a post office, public swimming pool, airport, and stadium, all of which the PWA delayed.[44]

McSwain did not forget this slight in public works allocations. He tried to amend the $4.8-billion Emergency Relief Appropriations Bill of 1935 to force the president to enumerate beforehand where the government would spend every cent of public works money. The amendment failed by a vote of 127 to 278, with McSwain's five South Carolina colleagues voting against him.[45]

Despite McSwain's obstinacy, relations between congressman and chief executive were never seriously strained. For one thing, Roosevelt remembered McSwain was one of the parents of the Tennessee Valley Authority. In fact, McSwain's efforts on behalf of TVA were unremitting: he introduced the bill that became the House version of TVA; he protected it during hearings before his Military Affairs Committee; he managed the bill on the floor of the House; he headed the House conferees in their deliberations with senators; and he successfully lobbied the House to accept the conference report. When Roosevelt signed the measure into law, McSwain was among the nine men who stood behind him at the ceremony.[46]

Support for relief measures fell off sharply in FDR's second term. In April 1937 Roosevelt asked Congress for $1.5 billion for the Works Progress Administration through fiscal year 1938. Byrnes attempted to reduce the appropriation by a third and add a 50-percent matching requirement for local sponsors. Byrnes was miffed by an earlier presidential promise to request no more than $1 billion. In addition, he believed the national economic emergency essentially had ended: unemployment was down, income and prices were up, and the nation's economic output actually exceeded its predepression level.[47] Just as irritating was the sectional impact of the WPA, whose dollars went overwhelmingly to urban areas in the North. For example, South Carolina's $23.6 million in WPA funds paled beside New York's $620 million. Beyond that, Roosevelt appeared to Byrnes to be using such funds to aid urban political machines, thus increasing the popularity of the Democratic Party in the Northeast while also increasing the influence of elements too liberal for Byrnes on race, labor-management relations, and economics. In short, it appeared to Byrnes his beloved Dixie was being slighted in its share of WPA dollars and it soon would be ignored in the councils of the Democratic Party.[48] Apparently, Southern nationalism emanating from the Confederate War was never far below the surface in the senator's personality.

Realizing the Byrnes proposal would cripple the WPA, Roosevelt and Harry Hopkins, director of the Works Progress Administration, began to marshal the opposition. Byrnes was able to get his amendment through the Appropriations Committee but not the full Senate, which accepted the argument of New York senator Robert Wagner that the South was a greater beneficiary of New Deal dollars than the North, when all New Deal expenditures were taken into consideration. Byrnes was not surprised at the outcome. "You cannot hope to beat a Santa Claus who comes every day," he confided to a friend.[49]

Three weeks earlier the House of Representatives passed the appropriation, despite determined efforts by Gasque, Mahon, Richards, Taylor, and McMillan to amend it after the Byrnes fashion. McMillan, in particular, was angered that WPA employment created an agriculture labor shortage in the Palmetto State. Only Fulmer among the South Carolinians declined publicly to oppose the appropriation; he paired uncommitted.[50]

In 1939 Byrnes resumed his role of thrifty Southern nationalist. Roosevelt in January requested an additional $875 million for the WPA in the current fiscal year. The economy-minded House responded by giving the president only $725 million. The six South Carolina congressmen, motivated by the negative impact of the WPA on the availability of farm labor, and fearful that the lion's share of the appropriation would be spent in the North, supported the reduction. In the Senate, Byrnes teamed with

Vice President Garner and Sens. Pat Harrison of Mississippi and Alva Adams of Colorado to pass the House version. Smith also lent a hand by supplying the one-vote margin that killed the McKellar Amendment to restore the $150 million.[51]

Voting patterns on relief measures clearly indicate 1937 was a watershed. In fact, support from Byrnes for all administration measures dropped from 96 percent in Roosevelt's first term to 57 percent in his second; from Fulmer, 92 percent to 69 percent; from Thomas McMillan, 83 percent to 20 percent; and from Gasque, 83 percent to 56 percent. Richards's support wavered less: 83 percent (1933–1936) to 75 percent (1937–1939). The irascible Smith never offered more than tepid allegiance: 68 percent for the first administration, 50 percent for the second. Taylor, the most consistently conservative of the group, dropped from 71 percent in FDR's first term to 40 percent in his second. Even the newly elected congressmen in 1937 and 1939 felt less obligation to support the administration. Although Bryson and Mahon were loyal 80 and 73 percent of the time, respectively, Congressmen Hare and John McMillan offered only 60 percent of their votes or pairs.[52] Some historians have suggested Roosevelt's New Deal was really two New Deals: one in 1933, another in 1935, and each intellectually and economically different from the other. This perception was certainly not shared by the South Carolina congressional delegation, which considered the radical departure (and hence a Second New Deal) to come in 1937 and not in 1935.

The reasons for the shift in 1937 are not hard to find. To begin with, the second Roosevelt administration did not start auspiciously. On February 5 the president called congressional leaders and cabinet members to the White House and abruptly distributed copies of a bill that would allow him to add as many as six justices to the Supreme Court. Since 1935 this body had declared unconstitutional several New Deal measures.[53] This audacious proposal stunned Capitol Hill and the nation. In a letter to the editor of the *Chesterfield Advertiser,* Cotton Ed Smith warned of a conspiracy to destroy what he viewed as "the Southern way of life." After court packing, he predicted, Roosevelt would demand and receive antilynching and civil rights legislation, which would encourage African Americans to demand social equality. "It is the most dangerous thing that has ever occurred," Smith stormed. Joining Smith in opposition to court reform was Congressman Thomas McMillan.[54]

Despite the fact that Byrnes was not invited to the meeting at the White House on February 5, Roosevelt was nonetheless counting on

Byrnes to help lead administration forces in the upper house. Byrnes did not disappoint him. The senator still favored recovery and reform legislation that was struck down by the high court. Like many of his colleagues, he believed the four conservative justices on the court acted "in a very partisan spirit" and based their opinions on what Byrnes called "personal philosophies and political opinions."[55] Too, Byrnes was motivated by personal loyalty to Majority Leader Joe Robinson, who seemed certain to realize a lifelong dream of being appointed to the high court as one of the new justices, and by friendship with Sen. Pat Harrison, who would consequently realize his own ambition of becoming majority leader in the Senate once Robinson was elevated to the bench.[56]

The week following the bill's introduction in the Senate, Byrnes and Roosevelt met in an hour-long conference at the White House to discuss strategy. Among other things, the two men agreed the eloquent Byrnes should take to the airwaves to make the case for the plan.[57] On February 17, in a national radio address, Byrnes argued that most corporations forced retirement by at least age seventy, a policy also advocated over the years for federal judges by at least two chief justices. He insisted defeat of the plan would thwart the mandate given Roosevelt by forty-six states in the 1936 presidential election. But the crux of the matter for Byrnes was simply how soon the country could again enjoy the benefits of programs such as AAA and NRA. Joining Byrnes in support of the plan were Congressmen Hampton Fulmer and Allard Gasque.[58]

It quickly became apparent that court expansion was more popular in the nation's capital than in the Palmetto State. Fearful an enlarged Supreme Court would rule in favor of equal rights for African Americans, the Ku Klux Klan circulated broadsides warning: "Communism Must Be Destroyed. Hands Off the Supreme Court." Other South Carolinians called Byrnes a traitor and suggested that Byrnes change his name to Judas Burns.[59] In response, Byrnes persuaded the South Carolina legislature in mid-March to adopt a resolution, albeit weak, in support of court reform.[60]

Although publicly supportive of the plan ("Why compromise when we have the votes to win?" he responded to a *New York Times* reporter on April 15), Byrnes from the start privately urged Roosevelt to compromise on the number of new justices. The senator's hand was strengthened in April when the Supreme Court upheld the National Labor Relations Act and again in May when conservative justice Willis Van Devanter announced his retirement. Indeed, only minutes after Van

Devanter's announcement, Senators Byrnes and Harrison were in Roosevelt's office to urge retreat. "Why run for a train after you've caught it?" Byrnes asked the president.[61]

The court-expansion plan was a long shot from the beginning. By summer its only chance of success lay with Majority Leader Robinson, who was using his long-standing friendship with wavering senators to line up essential support. In early July, according to Alabama senator John Bankhead, forty-seven senators opposed court packing, forty-seven supported it, and the vote of John H. Overton of Louisiana hung in the balance.[62] On July 14, 1937, Robinson died suddenly of a heart attack in Washington, and with him died any chance of success.

Saddened by the death of close friend Joe Robinson, Byrnes was at the same time angry at Roosevelt for not fighting a smarter fight for court reform. Conventional wisdom in Washington held that Robinson "had worked himself to death fighting a lost cause for an ungrateful President."[63] Very likely, Byrnes agreed; certainly, he retained a residue of resentment toward Roosevelt. Beyond personal bitterness, Byrnes was concerned about political damage done by the 168-day court-packing campaign. Not only had the protracted squabble delayed consideration of other important measures by the Senate, but it had also destroyed New Deal momentum, exposed FDR's vulnerability, alienated public opinion, and splintered the New Deal coalition. Byrnes believed all of this could have been averted if Roosevelt simply had retreated in May as Byrnes had advised when Justice Van Devanter retired.

Byrnes's anger and resentment toward Roosevelt turned into a feeling of betrayal during election of the new Senate majority leader. Two men emerged as candidates: Alben Barkley of Kentucky and Pat Harrison of Mississippi. Supporting Barkley were liberal New Dealers and those with less seniority who had come to the Senate on Roosevelt's coattails in 1932, 1934, and 1936. Backing Harrison were less ardent New Dealers, including Byrnes, and conservative Democrats such as Cotton Ed Smith. Byrnes, after being offered the support of Vice President Garner and Senator Bankhead should he himself decide to enter the contest, ultimately let his friendship with Harrison govern his decision. He agreed to serve as Harrison's campaign manager.[64]

On July 15, 1937, Byrnes went to the White House to remind the president of Harrison's commendable New Deal record and to ask Roosevelt not to meddle in the Senate's internal affairs. The president made no promises. The next day someone leaked to the press a copy of FDR's controversial "My Dear Alben" letter, in which he obliquely expressed his preference for Barkley. The president then used patronage and threats to withhold WPA grants to secure Barkley's election.[65]

For the Carolinians, Roosevelt's refusal to condemn sit-down strikes added a sense of mistrust to feelings of anger, resentment, and betrayal already present. The sit-down, which was the preferred tactic of many locals in the new Congress of Industrial Organizations (CIO), involved a de facto takeover of a manufacturing plant by workers who simply sat down at their machines and refused either to budge or to allow production to continue until management acceded to their demands. A refusal to denounce such action not only struck at the common law doctrine of sanctity of private property, but it also seemed to be a toleration of the kind of social disorder that so plagued European nations (notably Germany and Italy) in the 1920s that their middle class retreated to fascism for protection.[66] To conservatives from an agrarian culture, it clearly indicated the New Deal was turning too far to the left.

Any lingering doubts to the contrary were dispelled by the administration's decision to allow consideration of an antilynching bill, sponsored by liberal Democrats. Actually, the measure first appeared in 1935. A Southern filibuster followed immediately. Byrnes claimed to speak for the "liberal" South of the 1930s; he denounced lynching as murder but pronounced the bill flawed and unconstitutional.[67] Far more passionate were the hate-filled outbursts of his colleague. "Nothing to us is more dear than the purity and sanctity of our womanhood," roared Cotton Ed Smith, "and so help us God, no one shall violate it without paying the just penalty which should be inflicted upon the beast who invades that sanctity."[68] In what was possibly his most embarrassing speech on the floor of the Senate, Smith moved quickly from decrying Reconstruction as an "orgy of corruption" to a lengthy description of a beleaguered South that had been victimized since 1876 by greedy Yankees and wicked Republicans. Through it all, Smith emphasized, the South's only friend had been the national Democratic Party, "our 'pillar of a cloud' by day and our 'pillar of fire' by night." But now in 1935, with the introduction of antilynching legislation by, of all people, two Democrats, how could Southerners ever again "dare to raise our voices on behalf of the national Democratic Party when they have betrayed us in the midst of an overwhelmingly so-called 'Democratic Administration'"?[69]

What might have seemed to some observers the ramblings of an embittered old Bourbon were more likely carefully chosen words designed to serve notice on the Roosevelt White House. Smith had willingly supported his last piece of New Deal legislation. His world was changing in ways he did not favor, and he partially blamed Roosevelt. He had never before seen a government "pouring so much priming in the pump that the people are drinking the priming and the pump hasn't hit a lick."[70] Born in an era when cotton was king, white was supreme, and farming was the dominant way of life, Smith was being forced to legislate for an urban nation in an industrial age that was beginning to demonstrate concern for the rights of minorities. Unable to change, Smith clung to the only standard he believed would remain firm—the national Democratic Party, which allowed the white South to have a free hand in racial matters in return for its Democratic solidarity. In 1933, for example, Smith admitted that while he might dislike the New Deal, he felt obligated to support it because of party loyalty. By the spring of 1935, however, even the national Democratic Party was welcoming African Americans into membership and championing antilynching legislation. Smith believed these actions absolved him of any further obligation to support his party.

His colleagues in the lower house felt similar absolution after the antilynching bill reappeared on the Senate floor in 1937 and 1938. Again both Smith and Byrnes participated in the filibuster with a vengeance. On one occasion Smith became so overwrought he seized a book that lay on the adjoining desk of Sen. Josiah Bailey of North Carolina, hurled it to the floor, and stamped it repeatedly.[71] Even the normally rational Byrnes was less restrained. He charged that the motivation for the bill was purely political: Northern Democrats were simply pandering to the wishes of Northern blacks who had deserted the party of Lincoln for the party of Roosevelt. White Southerners should "realize now the change that has taken place," Byrnes warned. "The Negro has not only come into the Democratic Party, but the Negro has come into control of the Democratic Party."[72]

Thus, only a few months into Roosevelt's second administration, the Carolinians in Congress were determined to assert their independence and create the condition of presidential-congressional antagonism that has so often prevailed in American politics. The race issue, Southern nationalism, and to a lesser extent residual conservatism, were fracturing the New Deal coalition. Roosevelt was also confronting a burgeoning parochialism among congressmen who exhibited skepticism toward, if not outright hostility to, programs to provide governmental aid for sections and interests other than their own. An enlarged Republican contingent in Congress, coupled with a growing conviction among voters that the worst of the economic crisis had passed, gave these formerly supportive congressmen a sense of safety in numbers when they opposed additional New Deal measures. Finally, demographics played a role. The percentage of congressional districts in urban areas that sent Democrats to Congress grew from 29 percent in 1931 to 46 percent by 1937. Inevitably and increasingly, the New Deal was having to assume a Northern and urban focus with policies that favored industrial unionists, the urban unemployed, and hyphenated Americans. Naturally, these policies invited opposition from many white, rural, native-born, Southern Democrats in Congress, among them eight South Carolinians.[73]

Votes on reform legislation in the second Roosevelt administration reflect this disaffection. In 1937 Roosevelt's Fair Labor Standards Bill was introduced imposing a national minimum wage of forty cents per hour and a maximum workweek of forty hours. Over the years industry had steadily moved from North to South to take advantage of the latter's lower wages, which would have been erased by the labor standards bill. Byrnes was quick to damn the measure, arguing that the farmer would suffer because higher wages in industry would increase the cost of what he purchased without increasing the price of agricultural commodities. Privately, Byrnes warned a state legislator that the minimum wage "would have to be paid to every negro working in any store as well as to the white employees." In the lower house all of the South Carolinians except Richards publicly opposed the bill. They claimed that without a wage differential, Southern industries could not compete with those in the North.[74] To the Carolinians the factors of race, Southern nationalism, cotton, and residual conservatism overcame party loyalty.

Opposition to the measure was easier for Cotton Ed Smith, who had long since divorced himself from party. Apparently paranoid in his advancing years, he claimed to have "uncovered" nothing less than a conspiracy against the South and the Southern Democracy. Smith began his oration against the bill with his customary review of the Civil War, Reconstruction, and Redemption, when the South's only friend was the Democratic Party. In recent years the South prayed for a Democratic president who would recognize "the problems and burdens peculiar to the South" and would offer the region "an opportunity to express herself once again in the councils of the nation." But what happened? Roosevelt entered office with an antilynching bill in hand—a measure that, to Smith's fevered mind, constituted a "blistering commentary on the depths to which a desire for election can sink an individual." Smith at this point in his harangue had to pause and compose himself. "I feel so intense about this matter," he explained angrily, "that it is difficult for me to approach the subject with any degree of so-called conservatism." The second part of the perceived conspiracy was the abrogation of the Two-thirds Rule in the national party convention in 1936, which deprived the South of its influence in selecting the nominee. "Antilynching, two-thirds rule, and, last of all, this unconscionable . . . bill," he shouted. "Any man on this floor who has sense enough to read the English language knows that the main object of this bill is, by human legislation, to overcome the splendid gifts of God to the South."[75]

A similar reaction greeted reforms in housing and government reorganization. In 1937, inasmuch as many of the beneficiaries would be African American, Senators Byrnes and Smith and Congressmen Mahon, McMillan, Richards, and Taylor unsuccessfully opposed the Wagner-Steagall Housing Bill that would create a United States Housing Authority with power to lend $500 million for low-cost housing.[76] In 1938 McMillan, Richards, Taylor, and Smith voted against an administration measure authored by their colleague Byrnes to allow the president to abolish or consolidate departments in order to make the increasingly chaotic federal bureaucracy more efficient, effective, and economical. Conservatives in Congress viewed the bill as an extension of Roosevelt's attempt to aggrandize the executive branch, which they said began with the court-packing scheme a year before.[77]

Contrast these votes with support given reform legislation during the first Roosevelt administration when party loyalty was still strong and before race, Southern nationalism, and conservatism drowned out other factors. All eight South Carolinians supported the Banking Act of 1933 to stabilize the nation's banking system. Byrnes, in fact, helped author the measure and was one of the four senators responsible for developing the strategy that ensured its speedy enactment.[78] Byrnes also helped develop and implement the strategy for passage of the Securities Act of 1933, which removed unethical marketing practices from the securities market. The following year, with no opposition from the Carolinians, the lower house passed the Securities Exchange Bill creating the Securities and Exchange Commission to regulate sales in the securities market. In the upper house Byrnes helped the bill's sponsor, Sen. Duncan Fletcher of Florida, report the bill to the Senate. Smith favored the bill, though he was absent when the vote was taken. Both Byrnes and Smith also voted for the Reciprocal Trade Agreement Act to allow the president to circumvent tariff barriers through trade agreements with individual nations. The House passed the measure with no opposition from the six South Carolinians, who, because of respect for ancestors, opposed protection and supported free trade.[79]

Midway through his first administration, Roosevelt asked Congress for a new banking act to strengthen and overhaul the Federal Reserve System, a public utility holding company measure to minimize such control in the field of public utilities, the National Labor Relations Bill to encourage collective bargaining and outlaw unfair labor practices by business, and a Social Security bill to establish old-age pensions, unemployment insurance, and care for the blind, the crippled, and dependent children. Of the eight Carolinians, only Smith, whose loyalty to party had already become a casualty of the antilynching campaign, offered much opposition. He tried to amend the old-age pension scheme of Social Security into oblivion and pronounced the holding company bill "an encroachment of States' rights and on the privilege of the individual."[80] This was the same Senator Smith who prior to the introduction of the antilynching bill was willing to "strain the Constitution" to pass agricultural legislation.[81]

Fortunately for Roosevelt, until the mid-1930s the 1.7 million citizens of South Carolina could not afford the luxury of such philosophical debate over the Constitution. During the Hoover administration unemployment and privation reached staggering proportions. In Columbia, the state's second largest city with 50,000 residents, the city dump was home to 100 of the city's estimated 12,000 unemployed who scrounged for scraps of food and lived in abandoned automobiles or shipping crates.[82] The South Carolina Constitution authorized pensions only for Confederate veterans and their widows, which shifted the burden of relief for the unemployed to the counties. Trapped in a nineteenth-century mentality of rugged individualism, county relief councils initially were reluctant to venture beyond the traditional almshouses and poor farms. Even after President Hoover signed the Emergency Relief and Construction Act in 1932 to empower the Reconstruction Finance Corporation (RFC) to lend $300 million to states and localities for relief, the $6 million in federal loans to South Carolina meant only pennies per person each week to those most in need, one-fourth of the state's entire population.

A few Carolinians did receive more. Richland County Relief Administrator Jack D. Wootin frankly admitted that he targeted relief allocations to persons who had been "the backbone of their section" and whose "courage and ambition should be maintained."[83] If Wootin was typical, pre–New Deal relief officials were determined to restrict aid as much as possible to the unemployed middle class and thus ensure that the Depression did not upset the existing class structure. Obviously, it was time for the federal government to intervene in the interest of fairness and sufficiency for all.

Gov. Ibra C. Blackwood. Courtesy, South Caroliniana Library, University of South Carolina.

BELOW: Sens. James F. Byrnes (front, left) and Alva Adams of Colorado stroll arm in arm. Courtesy, James F. Byrnes Collection, Special Collections, Clemson University Libraries, Clemson, S.C.

United States senator Ellison D. Smith. Courtesy, South Caroliniana Library, University of South Carolina.

BELOW: Sens. James F. Byrnes (right), Alva Adams of Colorado (center), and Carter Glass of Virginia prepare for Congress to adjourn, June 16, 1938. Courtesy, James F. Byrnes Collection, Special Collections, Clemson University Libraries, Clemson, S.C.

ABOVE: James F. Byrnes relaxes in his Washington apartment, his wirehair terrier, "Whiskers," by his side, ca. 1943. Courtesy, James F. Byrnes Collection, Special Collections, Clemson University Libraries, Clemson, S.C.

James F. Byrnes with friend and elder statesman Bernard M. Baruch. Courtesy, James F. Byrnes Collection, Special Collections, Clemson University Libraries, Clemson, S.C.

Secretary of Agriculture Henry A. Wallace (left) and Sen. "Cotton Ed" Smith confer in Smith's office, ca. 1938. Courtesy, South Caroliniana Library, University of South Carolina.

A typical SCERA-sponsored adult education class in a South Carolina textile mill. Courtesy, South Caroliniana Library, University of South Carolina.

Father, mother, and six children attend an SCERA-sponsored adult education class. Courtesy, South Caroliniana Library, University of South Carolina.

In May 1933 the unemployed from all social classes found reason to take hope. Roosevelt's first Congress enacted the Emergency Relief Act to provide $500 million in grants (not loans) to the states for relief. To head the Federal Emergency Relief Administration (FERA), which would administer the program, Roosevelt chose Harry Hopkins, who had served as relief director for New York while Roosevelt was governor. As an example of federal-state cooperation under the FERA, each state and locality set up relief administrations that were appointed by, and were responsible to, the governor of the state. In June 1933 Governor Blackwood appointed Malcolm Miller of Columbia to head the South Carolina Emergency Relief Administration (SCERA). In most instances Blackwood appointed the former county RFC administrators as county SCERA administrators. The SCERA would use FERA grants to provide jobs, funds, food, and clothing to those in need. Since the actual administration of relief was handled at the county level where administrators preferred work relief to the dole, work for employables was administered more efficiently and more generously than was aid to unemployables.[1]

In August 1933 SCERA work relief meant the difference between survival and starvation for thousands of South Carolinians. Miller's early efforts included sewing-room, public-library, playground-supervision, and day-nursery projects. By September 24 sewing rooms in Richland County alone had produced 23,588 shirts and dresses and 331 quilts, all of which were either sold in retail relief outlets or distributed to the destitute. Richland's public library project mended 708 books, and women on its public nursery project cared for 5,062 children. Because more than 200 South Carolinians had died of malaria since October 1932, 15 county relief administrations concentrated on swamp drainage to eradicate the disease.[2]

However, these early efforts made only a dent in the level of misery and privation. By October more than 23 percent of the state's 1.74 million citizens were in relief families. The national average was about 10 percent. South Carolina's high percentage derived partly from its having the highest percentage of its population under sixteen years of age (40.9 percent) of any state in the nation.[3] Another factor was the large number of African Americans formerly employed in menial or laboring jobs. Forty-six percent of the population, but 55 percent of relief families, were black. A final factor related to geography. Needs were most acute in midland counties of Calhoun and Richland, piedmont counties of Fairfield, Chesterfield, Kershaw, McCormick, and Oconee, and low-country counties of Georgetown, Jasper, Allendale, Beaufort, Hampton, Bamberg, Colleton, Dorchester, and Berkeley. These mostly rural areas suffered from a high rate of tenancy and a sick King Cotton on poor and eroded farmland. In these seventeen counties 30 percent or more of the population was on relief. The counties of textile mill concentration in the upcountry—Anderson, Pickens, Greenville, Spartanburg, Cherokee, and York—had less than 14 percent of their population on relief.[4]

Aware that the FERA would not be able to carry the nation through the critical winter of 1933–1934, Roosevelt created the Civil Works Administration (CWA) in November. The CWA was a federal operation with subdivisions on the state and local levels. In South Carolina, Miller became CWA state administrator, while county relief administrators doubled as CWA county administrators. State and county CWA personnel drew federal salaries apart from SCERA salaries and were responsible to Hopkins instead of Governor Blackwood. County administrators were responsible for initiating CWA projects and submitting them to Miller, who in turn sent them to Hopkins for final approval. CWA policy required projects to be on public property, of "social and economic value," and work not usually required of state and local government (i.e., routine maintenance). Hopkins relaxed the last requirement because the Depression made it impossible for South Carolina's state and local governments to properly maintain their schools, sewer systems, and public buildings.[5]

In November 1933 Miller opened the CWA in South Carolina by allotting employment quotas to each county administrator based on county population and relief needs. Richland County with 5,124 CWA workers had the largest quota; Marion County with 331, the smallest. Each county administrator was required to fill at least half of his quota with employables from the relief rolls. The other half came from the unemployed not on relief. They worked a thirty-hour week and received from forty cents an hour for unskilled labor to $1 an hour for skilled labor. The first projects consisted of draining swamps and constructing or repairing roads, ditches, sidewalks, water systems, and sewage systems. CWA employment rolls grew from 42,000 on November 28 to 66,951 on December 10. Soon the CWA in South Carolina was spending more than $1 million a week, four times as much as the SCERA.[6]

In March 1934 Roosevelt phased out the CWA for fear the cost would become excessive and reliefers would continually look to the federal government for a job. In spite of its duration of only four months, the impact of the agency in South Carolina had been profound. Nearly a third of the $11 million allocation and half the man-hours went to highway projects designed to give every family access to a paved road. One-sixth of the funds and the man-hours went for swamp drainage in the effort to eradicate malaria. Lesser amounts went for improvements on public facilities. The agency aided nearly 95 percent of those 413,877 citizens eligible for relief. Fifty-five percent were black. Ten thousand were women who worked on landscaping, light construction, and clerical projects. Moreover, the CWA hired 450 teachers in 42 counties to teach the "3 Rs" to more than 9,000 illiterate adults. In a letter to President Roosevelt, one former illiterate reflected the appreciation of all South Carolinians for the CWA. He wrote formally but simply, "We thank you for the New Deal. Whereas we were disheartened, we now work with a song."[7]

The demise of the CWA did not spell the end of work relief in South Carolina. Hopkins established the Emergency Work Relief Program within the FERA to complete the unfinished CWA projects and to undertake new ones.[8] Like the CWA, this program was predominately blue collar. Between April 1, 1934, and July 1, 1935, when the emergency work program was phased out, SCERA workers constructed or repaired more than 2,200 miles of highway, 116 miles of sidewalks, 315 bridges, 2 courthouses, 500 school buildings, 47 miles of sewage lines, 1,150 miles of drainage ditches, 45 athletic fields, 24 swimming pools, and the Charleston yacht basin.[9]

One South Carolina project—the reconstruction of Charleston's Dock Street Theater—received national attention. On February 12, 1736, Charleston open the first theater in America where an actress named Monimia dazzled audiences with George Farquhar's *Recruiting Officer*. After a sale and two fires, in 1806 the theater gave way to the Planters' Hotel, which soon became famous for its punch. In 1835 the hotel was remodeled but then slowly deteriorated until 1918 when it was scheduled for demolition. A group of Charlestonians concerned about preserving the city's architectural heritage organized to persuade city council to seal and preserve the building pending its eventual restoration to its antebellum grandeur. This effort at organization was a catalyst to the formation in 1920 of the Society for the Preservation of Old Dwellings (SPOD), which would direct Charleston's preservation efforts throughout the twentieth century.[10]

The 1920s and early 1930s were not kind to the hotel-theater. Under the leadership of the colorful and indefatigable Susan Pringle Frost, the SPOD ignored the hotel-theater and busied itself with preserving the Joseph Manigault House and Heyward-Washington House while also persuading city council to create a historic district and enact a zoning ordinance that would protect historic structures from external architectural alterations not in keeping with the building's style. Susan Frost was Charleston's first modern businesswoman, first woman in the port city to drive her own automobile, and well-known former suffragette who once picketed the White House. Her primary concern as a preservationist was halting the vandalization of Charleston by wealthy Northerners, who were purchasing for their own homes, businesses, and museums the priceless woodwork, ironwork, and ornamental plaster from old houses in the port city. The sealed Planters' Hotel was safe from such vandals; other precious historic structures were not.[11]

When the New Deal came, Charleston preservationists were ambivalent. On the one hand, they vigorously opposed its efforts at slum clearance, low-cost housing, and land inundation by such hydroelectric projects as Santee-Cooper because of the attendant demolition of historic structures, landmarks, and monuments. On the other hand, they applauded efforts by the SCERA emergency work program, and later the Works Progress Administration (WPA), to reconstruct the Dock Street Theater as part of the larger effort to preserve and restore the Planters' Hotel. Begun in 1935, the two-year undertaking eventually cost $350,000. The Charleston architectural firm of Simons and Lapham, preservation specialists, directed the efforts.[12]

The exterior of the four adjacent buildings in the theater-hotel complex required little alteration: the brickwork and cast-iron balcony were repaired, new window sashes and frames installed, the rusticated brownstone columns and carved mahogany brackets restored, and the exterior walls color washed. The interior, however, was either restored or gutted and then completely rebuilt. Workers added a grand ferroconcrete stairway, patterned after the original of wood, and Adam woodwork and ornamental plaster taken from Charleston's Mitchell King Mansion (ca. 1805). In the process of restoration, workers distributed more than a hundred truckloads of wooden rubble to the poor for firewood. The reconstructed theater occupied nearly half of the complex's interior; a renovated and restored lobby, dining room, kitchen, bar, courtyard, apartments, and lecture room–recital hall with magnificent Palladian window occupied the other half. Despite painstaking research, the architects were unable to locate interior drawings of the original theater. Thus, they built a theater after the fashion of Restoration London with tiers of elegant boxes and a "pit" of rough benches. Natural cypress woodwork, sand-finished plaster, and red velvet stage curtains gave a warm tint to the interior.[13]

The second opening night—November 26, 1937—was as much gala as its predecessor two centuries earlier. In attendance, besides Harry Hopkins from Washington, were Charleston's elite, including the Burnet Maybanks and the DuBose Heywards. The Charleston String Symphony performed Mozart's *Eine kleine Nachtmusik;* the Society for the Preservation of Spirituals sang selections; Harry Hopkins formally presented the key to the theater-hotel to Mayor Maybank; and Charleston's own theatrical troupe, the Footlight Players, performed *The Recruiting Officer.*[14]

The reconstruction of the theater was a powerful stimulus to the performing arts in Charleston for several years thereafter. In 1938 the facility hosted three additional plays by the Footlight Players, several productions by touring companies from as far away as England, and a foreign film series. The Rockefeller Foundation pledged $15,000 to underwrite the cost of operating the facility for three years. Until his death in 1940, DuBose Heyward presided over a group headquartered there for the encouragement of aspiring young playwrights. After his death, the theater continued Heyward's efforts by offering annually a cash award of $500 for the best new three-act play written by a member of the group. Also in 1938 the theater's general manager opened a school to train young people in the theatrical arts of speech and acting. The next year he added classes in stagecraft, makeup, and dancing. By 1947 these students had even organized a successful touring Shakespeare company. Throughout the period, community organizations such as the Charleston String Symphony and the Dramatic Society of the College of Charleston used the facility for local events.[15]

The SCERA also undertook a few professional projects. In October 1934, for example, the Richland County relief orchestra opened its seven-month concert season in the Columbia High School auditorium.[16] Workers in each county ERA also conducted surveys to determine such facts as the condition of school buildings.[17] Women were used to aid county home demonstration agents. They visited rural families to give instructions on domestic arts such as canning vegetables and fruits, preserving potatoes with lime, making peanut butter, even fashioning garments and rugs from artistically dyed sacks.[18] SCERA women also administered a school lunch program that reached 126,244 children in 1934 alone. A touching letter from one young recipient expressed appreciation: "I'm so glad you started lunches at our school. [My brother] Jim and me have to take it by turns at home; one morning he has breakfast and the next morning I eat. But like I told Jim this morning; he won't have to be hungry long, cause at 12 o'clock he'll get a bowl of hot soup."[19]

Lads like Jim benefited in other ways too. By October 1933 South Carolina suffered from a curtailment of local education funds that forced the closing of several hundred rural schools. Hopkins responded by authoring the SCERA to spend more than $750,000 to employ approximately 3,350 teachers in 900 rural schools. Meanwhile, the FERA's emergency education program commenced with the hiring of 588 teachers (increased to 800 by April 1934) to provide literacy training, adult education, kindergarten care, worker education, vocational education, and vocational rehabilitation. So popular did this program become that teachers found themselves conducting classes in churches, private homes, and in one instance at the end of a row of cotton where a plowman stopped his mule to receive a lesson. The SCERA's third education program—the college-aid program—paid nearly 1,200 needy college students between $10 and $15 a month for "socially desirable work," which usually included surveys, record filing, and research.[20]

Yet the SCERA's emergency work program was never as important in terms of number of people aided and amount of money spent as the SCERA's direct-relief program.[21] One essential feature was commodity distribution. In 1933 each county established at least one garden worked by reliefers. By May 1935 these county gardens covered nine square miles. The FERA also purchased cattle from the drought-stricken Midwest in the summer of 1934 and shipped 100,000 head to the SCERA, which pastured them in Richland, Fairfield, and Newberry Counties. In the autumn the SCERA set up ten canneries to slaughter and can the beef. The canneries produced 135 to 175 two-pound cans of stew beef and hamburger per head of cattle. The blood and viscera went into fertilizer for use on the county-relief gardens. In addition to the cattle, the FERA sent the SCERA more than 14 million pounds of other meats, 3.5 million pounds of flour, 2 million pounds of butter, 2.7 million pounds of potatoes, and lesser quantities of lard, rice, cheese, milk, sugar, and fruits.[22]

The FERA and SCERA programs ended in South Carolina in December 1935 after serving for two and one-half years. The cost of the SCERA's direct- and work-relief programs totaled $36.6 million, to which CWA programs provided an additional $11 million. This $47.6 million was 9 percent of New Deal expenditures in South Carolina by 1939. Recognizing the acuteness of poverty in the Palmetto State, Hopkins required South Carolina to contribute only 2 percent of the total funds spent by the SCERA and only 6 percent of those spent by the CWA, the smallest percentage of any state. Delaware, for example, provided 60 percent of its state ERA funds.[23]

Although few South Carolinians failed to appreciate the benefits of the SCERA, many were provoked by the favoritism, administrative laxity, and politics that seemed to pervade it. Occasionally, complaints to the SCERA provoked nothing more than laughter. One woman receiving SCERA aid inquired of the agency: "Please find out if my husband is dead, as the man I am now living with can't eat or do anything until he knows for sure." Another complained, "I am very annoyed to find that you have branded my oldest child as illiterate. It is a dirty shame and a lie, as I married his father a week before he was born."[24]

More frequently, SCERA officials received angry letters levying specific charges that were often true. Complaints mushroomed under the CWA. L. E. Jaeckel, secretary of the Heath Springs Chamber of Commerce, groused to the CWA in Washington that Lancaster County relief officials were intentionally sabotaging the CWA because they believed that "lousy ex-servicemen who are already living off the government" were its chief beneficiaries. Jaeckel also complained that Lancaster's wealthy Hough brothers were on the CWA payroll. Furthermore, small Lancaster communities such as Heath Springs were discriminated against in relief appropriations in favor of the city of Lancaster, which "has been spending money like water." Moreover, he insisted, "It is common knowledge that the male employees of the county [CWA] office are throwing booze parties on their earnings." Finally, Jaeckel voiced what would be a standard complaint: "The apportioning of Government provisions is ruining the negro element which refuses to do any form of labor."[25]

Not surprisingly, South Carolinians began to complain to their congressmen. Grievances included wages set too low for a level of skill, blacks receiving the same wages as whites, the number of blacks on CWA payrolls, people obtaining jobs they did not need, the CWA employing too many skilled workers from outside the county that sponsored the project, and, most of all, the necessity of political connections to get work.[26] Complaints were often selfish. One former bookkeeper and cashier for an oil company wrote to Congressmen Fulmer, "I was assigned as a laborer in a ditch with negroes, under a nineteen year old foreman, while [more desirable] places are being filled by direction of the local administration with men who say themselves that they do not have to work."[27]

By late January 1934 the volume of complaints was large enough for the congressional delegation to ask Harry Hopkins for a complete investigation. In February, Hopkins sent in field agent Lorena Hickok, whose cursory investigation angered the congressmen. The only irregularity she reported was the padding of a CWA payroll by a timekeeper, which led to his arrest and imprisonment. Congressman McMillan complained to Hopkins that Hickok's itinerary included nothing more than "a day or two in Columbia," followed by a "hurried visit to Greenwood and then to Charleston for a day," before concluding with "a visit to friends in Bennettsville." McMillan added angrily that "the money spent might as well have been thrown away."[28]

Complaints increased when the emergency work program replaced the CWA. Unfortunately, many of the complaints were valid. Favoritism on the county level was rife. When complainants came to the county offices, they were unable to obtain personal interviews with county administrators. Then, when complainants appealed to Malcolm Miller, he upheld the county administrator and referred the appeal back to the county office.[29]

The situation exploded in South Carolina in early June 1934 when 1,800 unemployed in Richland County met in Columbia's Township Auditorium to denounce the administration of relief. They demanded Miller's resignation, charged that the unemployed needed political connections to secure relief, and complained that several ERA officials had recently purchased new automobiles and vacationed at the seashore. A subsequent meeting of 200 of Greenville's unemployed also demanded Miller's resignation. Hopkins declined a request by Congressman Fulmer for a thorough investigation, adding that Miller was not only "one of the best administrators in the United States" but also a victim of political and personal antagonism.[30]

Miller's critics were not impressed. From articles in newspapers and newsreels in theaters, they concluded that relief efforts in other states were more generous, efficient, and equitable, and they were determined to have it so in South Carolina. On June 18, 1934, the unemployed in Allendale County petitioned Governor Blackwood to remove Miller because of favoritism, nepotism, and "disregard for the helpless fallen citizen." The petition also demanded the removal of the county adminis- trator for issuing "moldy meal and moldy butter and only these two articles for many weeks." Finally, the petition demanded an outside investigation of the county administration because "any person raising a word of PROTEST is promptly cut off" by the "SWIVEL CHAIR EMPLOY- EES."[31] By the day of the petition threats to do bodily harm to Miller and to ransack his office had reached such proportions that he seriously con- sidered moving the SCERA office from Columbia to Charleston.[32]

Sensing political opportunity, Ben E. Adams of Columbia arranged a statewide convention of unemployed citizens to discuss the unfair administration of relief. Adams was editor of the *Carolina Free Press* in Columbia and a candidate for the state legislature; he would later become an ally of Gov. Olin Johnston and a Grand Dragon of the Ku Klux Klan in South Carolina. At the June 29 meeting many of the more than 600 delegates booed both Governor Blackwood and Malcolm Miller when they rose to speak. Adams then led the convention in a resolution to give unemployed citizens representation on county relief councils that advised county relief administrators. Blackwood consented and began making the appointments in July.[33]

The conventions, petitions, and pressure from lawmakers finally forced Hopkins to launch a full-scale investigation of the SCERA. The results were frightful.[34] The absence of effective management was appar- ent everywhere. The state administrator did not sufficiently control the county units, which pursued policies independent of the state office. The SCERA's organizational structure of twelve divisions proved unwieldy, and lack of cooperation within it led to duplication and omission. One division, for example, was responsible for swamp drainage; another, for purchasing land for rural rehabilitation. When swamp land was drained, its value increased. Yet the rural rehabilitation division did not cooperate with the division draining swamps to purchase swampland scheduled for drainage.[35]

Another problem was personnel. When the SCERA began in South Carolina, first-rate administrators considered it temporary and shied away. As the SCERA expanded, it did not adjust salary scales accordingly. Two administrators performing the same function often drew different salaries, which negatively affected morale. Furthermore, lack of experience led SCERA personnel to adhere blindly to FERA suggestions when experimentation would have helped. Finally, the SCERA had not completed its technical staff. For instance, no home economist was available to advise local home-demonstration assistants.[36]

Disregard for accepted business practice was rife. Administrators did not provide privacy when interviewing prospective clients. Nor did they make thorough financial investigations of clients' backgrounds, which allowed people with money to draw relief. Each of the twelve divisions had its own record-keeping system. The SCERA was not careful in gathering and reporting statistics, and it neither appreciated nor employed uniform budget standards.[37]

Worse yet were county relief offices. Staffed by the politically well-connected, they made no effort to dispense work relief according to occupational skills. Their faulty statistics were as common as their faulty budgeting. For instance, the monthly county relief budget represented a rough estimate at best. Usually estimates were low, forcing administrators to overdraft when money was available or to suspend projects and reduce wages during the last week of the month, which threw clients out of work and resulted in protests. In one case where the estimate was too high, the accounting procedures were so inadequate that the county administrator was unable to account for the unspent surplus. Moreover, county administrators exercised "proprietary views of their positions" and appointed "their relatives, former private employees, their plantation workers, even, as they hire their own teams of mules and rent from themselves their own private quarters for relief purposes."[38] In one county the administrator's brother-in-law, who was also the work-relief engineer, rented to the county administration his own engineering equipment. Even so, the investigators concluded, "These things are usually done with the best intentions." Most county administrators "are conscientious, hard-working, sincere," but "incompetent."[39]

The investigation left Hopkins with no choice but to help Blackwood remove Miller, who was thus elevated to the position of FERA field representative for the six-state district stretching from Alabama to Oklahoma. Blackwood promoted F. M. Baker from assistant to director. In

October 1934 Baker began reforming the SCERA by directing that each relief household could have only one member on work relief.[40] Within a month the state agency was functioning more smoothly.

Yet no state director was able to deal successfully with race, labor relations, and state politics. The race question remained a minor annoyance, not emerging as a major cause of white opposition to the New Deal until after the demise of the SCERA. Nevertheless, in January 1934 complaints to congressmen over African American employment on CWA projects prompted Congressmen Fulmer to wonder publicly whether discrimination in favor of blacks was not an official CWA hiring policy. Two months later whites living along the Columbia-Winnsboro road insisted they should have preference in employment and refused to allow African American CWA workers to resurface the highway. After pressure from a Richland legislator, the CWA abandoned the project entirely.[41]

Despite complaints like these, African Americans remained on relief rolls. In March 1935, from a state population 45 percent African American and 55 percent white, the relief force was 49 percent African American and 51 percent white. Moreover, in urban areas, African Americans outnumbered whites on relief 53 percent to 47 percent. In their relative autonomy, county administrators determined who received relief. Their criteria usually were need, prevailing racial attitudes, political and social standing, and closeness of kin to administrative personnel. On all counts except need, the African American stood at a disadvantage. Nevertheless, the percentages of African Americans on relief in March 1935 in ten South Carolina counties chosen at random may suggest that need was paramount with several county administrators.[42]

TABLE 3.1 Relief in South Carolina in March 1935

| COUNTIES | POPULATION PERCENTAGE | | RELIEF PERCENTAGE | |
	WHITE	BLACK	WHITE	BLACK
Aiken	56	44	64	36
Anderson	72	28	66	34
Berkeley	32	68	33	67
Chester	48	52	48	52
Florence	55	45	61	39
Horry	76	24	82	18
Jasper	32	68	39	61
Laurens	58	42	56	44
Marlboro	42	58	46	54
Richland	48	52	46	54

On the basis of population alone, African Americans were overrepresented in the counties of Richland, Anderson, and Laurens, equally represented in the counties of Berkeley and Chester, and underrepresented in the counties of Marlboro, Aiken, Jasper, Florence, and Horry.[43]

Nevertheless, statistical comparisons do not prove racial discrimination was absent or even substantially reduced. The FERA's investigation of the SCERA in 1934, for example, revealed faulty statistics; SCERA figures may have indicated more African Americans on relief rolls than were actually there. In addition, conditions found in Calhoun County must have existed elsewhere. In allotting money to relief clients for food purchases, the Calhoun relief administrator set as a rule of thumb $1 per adult and 75 cents per child for white families, and 75 cents per adult and 50 cents per child for black families. Blacks also received the lower paying, unskilled jobs in work relief. Furthermore, for the 1933–1934 school year, the FERA allowed the SCERA to use $341,603 to employ public school teachers; African American teachers received aid in only thirty-four of the forty-six counties, and only $52,290, or 9 percent of the total, at that. In this instance, long-standing policies dictated the discrimination. First, the FERA earmarked the $341,603 for extending the school term to its normal length. Since terms were shorter in African American schools than in white ones, African American teachers received less of the money. Second, FERA money did not become available until after many of the black schools had closed. Finally, the FERA stipulated that salaries to teachers had to be the prevailing wage, which was lower for black teachers.[44]

Labor relations also posed problems. The SCERA established a policy of giving relief to any person in need. In many cases, relief payments were made to strikers. Manufacturers claimed that granting relief to strikers contradicted the SCERA's alleged neutrality in industrial conflicts. Union leaders, on the other hand, tried to persuade the SCERA to provide relief only to union members when strikes occurred. In reality, the attitude of county ERA personnel usually dictated the extent of SCERA neutrality. For example, during a textile strike at Belton in 1934, the ERA supervisor who worked 300 strikers on an ERA project was also mayor of the town and owner of the largest department store, which missed the mill's weekly payroll of $8,500. He worked the strikers unmercifully to force them back to the mill.[45]

The most important influence on relief policies was politics. In January 1935, when Olin D. Johnston became governor, state National

Emergency Council director Lawrence Pinckney reported to Washington, "The opinion is general that unless applicants for relief—either work or direct—belong to a certain [local political] faction or clique, it is very difficult for them to obtain results."[46] Pinckney did not add, but could have, that most of these factions were loyal to Senator Byrnes. To counteract the power of local politicos, Johnston appointed a new state relief council under Ben Adams. Trouble broke out immediately. The members of Governor Blackwood's council, led by Mayor Ben Hill Brown of Spartanburg, refused to resign, claiming incorrectly that Hopkins and not the governor had appointed them. Johnston then traveled to Washington, where he and Hopkins finally agreed the governor would abandon the plan for a new council and simply appoint a new state director.[47]

Johnston's choice was political ally Miller C. Foster of Spartanburg, who challenged Congressman John J. McSwain in the 1934 Democratic primary. Foster set out immediately to make reductions in local administrative personnel and make new appointments on the basis of merit. Local politicians, possibly encouraged by Senator Byrnes, blocked Foster at every turn. The frustrated director resigned in disgust.[48] To replace Foster, Johnston chose Col. J. D. Fulp of Greenwood, superintendent of Bailey Military Institute and one of Johnston's former teachers. Fulp began to consolidate the forty-six county administrations into nine district administrations in order to weaken the influence of local politicians. Probably on advice from Byrnes, Hopkins intervened to halt Fulp's reforms. He ordered Fulp to effect administrative cost cuts without instituting the district plan. Fulp traveled to Washington to plead his case. Hopkins agreed only to let the SCERA establish disbursement districts to handle purchasing and to pay salaries and expenses for the county offices. Although this arrangement removed finances from local control, county administrators still chose work projects, decided who should be employed, and determined who should receive direct relief.[49]

In March 1935 the Johnston forces struck back. In the South Carolina House of Representatives they pushed through a resolution praising the governor "for his efforts to bring about a fairer distribution of relief funds in South Carolina."[50] Opponents successfully struck from the resolution a section condemning county administrations and praising Fulp's district plan. Rep. Ben Adams charged on the floor of the House that "certain influences in Washington, but emanating from the State" (presumably Byrnes again) thwarted Fulp's designs.[51] The next day his *Carolina Free Press* entered the fray with an article charging that Byrnes, Mayor

Burnet Maybank of Charleston, and Charleston ERA administrator E. P. Grice, with permission from Harry Hopkins, were conspiring "to block every effort to oust the 'political mismanagers' who have been wasting relief money." It was clear to Adams that Byrnes and Maybank "have their own political appointees in office and what happens to the needy is of small moment compared to the welfare of their own political machine."[52]

Meanwhile, in May 1935 Roosevelt created the Works Progress Administration (WPA) under Harry Hopkins to substitute work relief for the dole. Hopkins appointed Lawrence M. Pinckney, state NEC director and ally of Senator Byrnes, to head the WPA in South Carolina. The WPA, unlike the SCERA, would be a federal agency with state and local subdivisions answerable to Hopkins and not to the several governors. Significantly, Hopkins did not appoint J. D. Fulp. Hopkins probably believed that the bifurcation of the Democratic Party in South Carolina into Johnston forces and anti-Johnston forces, resulting from Johnston's unsuccessful attempt to seize control of the State Highway Department, necessitated the appointment of a man not involved in the highway department controversy. Pinckney appeared to meet this qualification. Too, no legislator in Washington was more powerful than Byrnes, to whom Pinckney was loyal.

Nevertheless, Hopkins must have appreciated that Pinckney was from Charleston, an avowedly anti-Johnston city where voter fraud denied Johnston the governorship in 1930. Thus, on July 8, 1935, as a conciliatory gesture, Hopkins allowed Fulp to abolish the county relief administrations in favor of ten district administrations in the expiring SCERA.[53] Three months later Hopkins called a halt to the SCERA's work program. He allowed the SCERA to use its November grant to establish a Temporary State Department of Public Welfare under Fulp to distribute direct relief and care for the unemployed. The SCERA's administrative structure crumbled rapidly, although as late as May 1936 the SCERA still had auditors and statisticians completing their work.[54]

By contrast, state politics did not affect the Civilian Conservation Corps (CCC), which came to life in March 1933 and quickly became the most popular of all New Deal agencies in the state. The CCC selected unemployed males between the ages of seventeen and twenty-five, usually unmarried and from relief families, for six-month stints in CCC camps performing conservation work. On March 31 and October 1 of each year, a new enrollment period began as replacements filled the vacancies left by departing campers. Each camper earned $30 a month,

$22 of which the CCC sent to his family. The War Department furnished officers to run the camps; the Departments of Agriculture and Interior formulated the work programs; the FERA and later the State Department of Public Welfare certified and enrolled the youths; and CCC director Robert Fechner furnished administrative supervision.[55]

Recruiting began in April 1933 to fill South Carolina's initial quota of 3,500 boys. Each youth chosen from among the 8,000 applicants spent two weeks in a "conditioning camp" at Fort Moultrie, Benning, or McPherson before posting to one of the seventeen camps. Each camp contained about 200 boys, supervised by an army captain and two junior officers. Salaried technical personnel to direct the work included a project superintendent, several foremen, clerk-stenographer, mechanic, and blacksmith. Ideally, camp buildings included officers' quarters, recreation building, education building (containing classrooms, library, and workshops), administrative building, mess hall, and four barracks. Each barracks slept fifty boys in beds arranged head to foot in two rows in order to check the spread of germs from close body contact. In reality, many auxiliary buildings and most initial barracks were tents with wooden floors and potbellied stoves. Each tent slept from six to twelve boys on cots. Eventually, the tents gave way to wooden huts arranged in eight rows with six huts to a row.[56]

Life in the camps was a welcome change from poverty. The boys awoke at 6 A.M., dressed in their government-issue underclothes, shoes, and blue denim work fatigues, and breakfasted from 6:30 to 7:30. At 8:00 A.M. they boarded trucks to begin their eight-hour day that was punctuated at noon by an hour's rest for lunch. The workday ended at 5 P.M. with dinner served an hour later. After dinner the young men enjoyed outdoor recreation or amused themselves by shooting pool or playing Ping-Pong in the recreation hall, reading in the library, or improving their education through the CCC-sponsored education program. The latter offered academic subjects and instruction in such areas as radio repair, forestry, clerical work, first aid, mess management, agriculture, landscaping, and electrical wiring. As one camper quipped, the courses provided instruction in "everything from Homer to cucumbers."[57] Before taps was sounded each evening, campers often gathered to harmonize on old favorites such as "In the Evening by the Moonlight" and "My Bonnie Lies over the Ocean." One camper commented of his mates, "A trained ear might not be colossally impressed . . . but we love to sing. Yes, sir, we are a singing company."[58]

Ideally, each boy received 3,800 calories a day in three well-balanced meals. Breakfast included oatmeal, meat, potatoes, and eggs. Lunch and dinner offered meats, vegetables, bread, and dessert. Actually, lunch was occasionally cold, since it was served away from the camp, while dinner might consist of leftovers if the camp steward had budgeted his food allowance incorrectly. Yet food was plentiful if not always varied, and the boys were appreciative. No work was scheduled for Saturday and Sunday, and the young men could leave camp on Wednesday and Saturday nights.[59] Lectures in camp on etiquette and the perils of drunkenness, coupled with columns in camp newsletters condemning public cursing and littering, were designed to temper boorish behavior when campers went into nearby towns. Twice-monthly dances in the camp's recreation hall offered opportunities for fellowship with young ladies from the area. One camp newsletter was careful to remind dancers that "most after-dinner prosposals of marriage are 2 percent pure love and 98 percent [pure] alcohol."[60]

Appreciation by CCC alumni for the camp experience is universal. Ellison E. Jamison of Woodruff remembers simply, "It was the best experience I ever had; I wouldn't trade it for anything." They recall with fondness the beltline, a gauntlet new recruits had to run as their initiation into the corps. They remember the excitement of intercamp baseball games. Many recollect seeing their first "talkie" movie on a Saturday evening in a town near camp. All remember colorful personalities, ranging from a camp commander who bought his whiskey by the barrel, to an artful camper who "pinched" fruit from the mess hall to share with his tentmates. L. T. Fulmer of Aiken County recalls being so homesick that he spent his first paycheck on stamps and stationery and wrote to everyone he knew. With his second paycheck he purchased a twenty-two-caliber bolt-action rifle for hunting small game on weekends. This prized possession has since been passed on to son and grandson. Because of the bonding both with fellow campers and the CCC, they remember rivalry with other New Deal agencies. For example, they referred to WPA workers simply as "one, one, and one"—one going to the bathroom, one coming from the bathroom, and one working.[61]

By 1939 the CCC had employed 31,823 boys and 4,340 technical personnel at the camps. Monthly enrollment, on average, was about 5,000; the number of camps, 30. The camps were scattered through the state in national forests, national parks, forest protective associations, soil conservation districts, state forests, and state parks. By July 1937 the

CCC had built 1,420 miles of truck trails and 5,429 miles of fire breaks. It had improved and thinned 49,495 acres of forest, completed 115,580 man-days of nursery work, and spent 119,687 man-days in forest-fire control. By July 1938 the CCC had spent more than $36.4 million, making the agency one of the most heavily funded of New Deal operations in the Palmetto State.[62]

South Carolina's modern system of state parks owes its beginning to the CCC. The state had no state parks until 1933 when the general assembly enacted a law authorizing the State Commission of Forestry to develop and operate such a system. A lack of funds for state park development made federal aid imperative. The CCC agreed to furnish labor and materials; the National Park Service offered technical and professional advice; and individuals and localities offered the land. By 1938 the state boasted fourteen state parks whose facilities were enjoyed the previous year by an estimated one-fourth of the population. The parks were especially beneficial for people who lacked access to private facilities and for organizations such as 4-H Clubs and Future Farmers of America.[63]

The CCC's greatest impact was not on the land but on the boys and their families. The $22 a month that the families received helped provide the necessities of life and represented the fruits of honest labor rather than a dole. For the boys, the CCC provided work when no other work was available; it fed, clothed, and housed them; it taught them skills and lessons of cleanliness and safety that carried over into private life; and most of all it taught them respect for one another and for life itself. One South Carolina camper summed up his CCC experience by remarking that a man's highest calling is service to country and fellow man. "We used the Civilian Conservation Corps as a medium for this kind of service," he added proudly.[64]

The existence of the CCC, SCERA, and CWA kept the wretched conditions of 1932 at bay until the recession of 1937. By then more permanent strategies to combat unemployment and human misery had been devised. The era of temporary relief was ending; that of permanent protection was in sight.

RELIEF | 4
THAT LASTS |

The New Deal relief program in South Carolina was not confined to the SCERA, CWA, and CCC, whose efforts were stopgap and whose contributions were mostly transitory. Although dissimilar in objectives, the Works Progress Administration (WPA), Home Owners Loan Corporation (HOLC), Federal Housing Administration (FHA), and Social Security program tendered relief every bit as vital. In addition, their contributions were more enduring and, in the case of Social Security, their programs were more permanent.

The most revolutionary of the new programs was Social Security, which the state began to plan for in 1935. First, a temporary welfare department was established to administer Social Security. Then, Governor Johnston appointed a nine-member Social Security Committee to formulate administrative plans. In early January 1936 the two houses of the legislature appointed a standing Committee on Social Security that began to confer with John G. Winant, chairman of the national Social Security Board. Meanwhile, proponents were busy drafting legislation. Both the South Carolina Association for the Blind and the South Carolina Crippled Children's Clinic drafted legislation for their respective areas. These bills went to the national Social Security Board for review before being introduced in the state legislature.

This hard work and planning initially went for naught. The proposals clashed with the traditional reluctance of legislators to tax. In addition, opponents located a state constitutional provision that prohibited state relief payments and pensions to anyone except Confederate veterans and their widows. First, voters would have to amend the constitution to authorize aid for dependent children, the blind, the aged, the unemployed, and crippled children.[1]

The inability of the legislature to act left South Carolina embarrassed. By July 1936 only five other states had failed to enact old-age pension plans; only fourteen lacked aid-to-the-blind plans; and only two—South Carolina and Georgia—had no plans for aiding dependent children.[2] At least South Carolina did pass the Unemployment Compensation Act to provide unemployment compensation at 50 percent of a worker's weekly wage to a maximum of $15 a week for those employed twenty or more weeks a year. But even this law was conservative. Twenty-five states taxed employers working five or fewer employees, not eight or more employees. Nearly thirty states began unemployment benefits in January 1938, rather than in July 1938.[3]

In 1937 the legislature completed South Carolina's participation in Social Security after voters approved an amendment authorizing aid to the aged, the blind, and dependent children.[4] The South Carolina Public Welfare Act of 1937 was passed to create a permanent public welfare department to administer federal-state Social Security programs. The state's appropriation of $1.5 million would be matched by more than $1 million in federal funds and $200,000 in county funds.[5] In early summer the Board of Public Welfare, elected by the legislature and composed of a chairman and one member from each congressional district, selected a state welfare director, Thomas H. Daniel, who immediately began to organize the state agency. It did not open for business until the Social Security Board approved its plan for administering the Social Security programs on August 3.

Social Security contained ten separate assistance, welfare, health, and insurance programs. The Social Security Board administered the old-age insurance program; the South Carolina Unemployment Compensation Commission administered the unemployment compensation program; and the state Department of Public Welfare administered four of the eight remaining programs.[6] The three major Social Security programs administered by the state welfare department were aid to the needy blind, old-age assistance, and aid to dependent children.[7]

Old-age assistance consumed approximately 70 percent of welfare department expenditures under Social Security. Aid to dependent children accounted for another 20 percent; aid to the needy blind, less than 5 percent. No one grew rich from any of the three programs. For instance, under the Social Security Act, the federal government agreed to match old-age assistance programs up to $30 a month per person; the conservative South Carolina Public Welfare Act of 1937 set the maximum monthly assistance per person at only $20, which meant a federal contribution of $10. Equally painful, the state welfare department underestimated by 66 percent the number of elderly persons eligible for old-age assistance. To compensate, the department in 1938 had to reduce monthly aid per person by nearly 50 percent.[8] Not until the summer of

1939 were both the Social Security program and the State Department of Public Welfare functioning smoothly.[9]

Roosevelt wanted Social Security and the state welfare departments to provide permanent cradle-to-grave assistance in place of the never-popular dole under the FERA. Having realized, too, that Social Security would be slow getting started and continuing high unemployment in 1935 necessitated a federal work-relief program, he set up the Works Progress Administration to undertake the same types of projects as the expiring SCERA and the former CWA. The SCERA, and later the state welfare department, certified reliefers as eligible for the WPA, and state WPA director Lawrence M. Pinckney hired from this pool of potential workers.

WPA guidelines were lenient. WPA projects needed sponsors, usually localities or state agencies, willing to assume a small percentage of the project cost. Sponsors furnished the materials, equipment, and supplies, amounting to less than 20 percent of the total project cost, while the WPA furnished the labor. The WPA also required the projects to be on public property, have lasting value, produce no labor shortage in private employment, and offer guarantees of completion. A 40-hour work-week and a 130-hour work month were the maximum for workers.

Since the Public Works Administration (PWA) and WPA carried out similar projects, the WPA agreed to undertake projects costing $25,000 or less; the PWA, projects costing more than $25,000. Wages differed according to national wage region and wage classification. The lowest wage in South Carolina was $19 per month for an unskilled manual laborer, while the highest was $64 per month for a professional nonmanual worker. In 1936 the WPA transferred South Carolina to a new wage region and instituted a prevailing wage scale for each county. The lowest paid worker in fourteen South Carolina counties then received $21 a month, while the lowest paid worker in Richland and Charleston Counties received $33.60 a month. By June 30, 1939, the Palmetto WPA had employed a workforce of approximately 67 percent unskilled, 15 percent semiskilled, and 17 percent skilled/professional/technical workers.[10]

Lawrence Pinckney was a fortuitous choice for the position of state WPA director. A successful Charleston banker, real estate broker, and insurance executive in his early sixties, the patrician Pinckney enjoyed instant social acceptance by virtue of his presidency of the South Carolina Society of the Cincinnati and his membership in the Carolina Yacht Club and Charleston Country Club. He was also adept politically. As former chairman of the Charleston County Democratic Executive Committee and four-term city councilman, he knew well how to negotiate the complicated maze of state and local politics.[11]

Although Roosevelt did not confirm Pinckney's appointment until July 19, 1935, the state director began work as soon as Hopkins nominated him in May. Pinckney selected Columbia for the director's office and persuaded the City of Columbia and Richland County to share the rent. The state office had four sections—Operations, Finance, Women's Work, and Employment—with a state director and assistant director over each. Pinckney early established the policy of making promotions from within each section in order to combat the morale problem that had plagued the SCERA. He then created four district offices at Columbia, Florence, Charleston, and Greenville with a district director over each and with subdivisions corresponding to the four state sections. He also obtained free office space in each of the district cities.[12]

From the very beginning the WPA targeted the state's infrastructure. That the program included few frills guaranteed public acceptance. One basic need was an improved highway system, especially farm-to-market roads. By July 1938 the WPA had added 100 miles of paved roads, 3,476 miles of unpaved roads, 380 new bridges, 125 improved bridges, and 1,851 new culverts. By July 1939 WPA expenditures in South Carolina for highways, roads, and streets totaled 28.6 percent of all WPA expenditures in the state. When the WPA ended in July 1943, the agency had constructed or improved 1,138 bridges and viaducts, 11,699 culverts, and more than 10,000 miles of highways and streets. The latter figure becomes more significant when one considers that South Carolina's state highway system totaled only 6,000 miles in 1933 and 9,680 miles in 1941. Of the $109.3 million spent by the WPA in South Carolina on construction projects, nearly one-third went for highways and streets.[13]

Another basic need addressed by the WPA was education. By 1935 South Carolina's education problems were legion. Illiteracy was high, reaching 55 percent among adult African Americans in some counties. In addition, the Depression forced school districts to halt not only new construction but also routine maintenance. In 1935 more than 1,200 schools used homemade benches instead of desks. More than 700 schools lacked toilet facilities; more than 1,800 schools, a water supply. Sixty-one percent of the exteriors and 20 percent of the interiors of wood-frame schools for African Americans were unpainted or unfinished. Only 20 percent of black classrooms and 30 percent of white ones had standard fenestration. Moreover, the median school property value was only $59 per white child and $5 per black. The school property value per child reached the national average in only 5 percent of the white schools and in none of the black schools. Furthermore, more than 500 schools were fire hazards, and more than 900 African American schools were located in tenant shacks, lodge halls, or churches. Nor were the Depression, racism, and taxpayer indifference to the education of blacks and lower-class whites the only reasons for the impoverished condition of the state's schools. The state constitution drastically limited the capacity of school districts to borrow and required them to bear the entire cost of school construction.[14]

Here the WPA made a difference. Within three years the agency constructed 228 new schools and made additions or improvements to 632 others. When the WPA ended in July 1943, it had built, added to, or improved 2,179 schools. Moreover, federal money brought larger build-ings, since the low bonding capacity of school districts in rural areas had kept school buildings small. Equally significant were the repairs. WPA workers built thousands of desks to replace benches, added athletic fields that had been rare in the hilly piedmont, constructed 5,659 school toi-lets, landscaped school grounds, removed fire hazards, improved ventila-tion by adding or altering windows, and painted interiors and exteriors. Understandably, the impartial South Carolina Appraisal Committee noted in 1938 that the WPA had "contributed to the development of the educa-tion facilities of the state unparalleled in its history." With Works Progress assistance, each child finally could attend a school that was "adequate, safe, and comfortable."[15]

Nor was WPA aid for education confined to the elementary and sec-ondary level. WPA workers built a variety of new buildings for state col-leges and universities. WPA teachers provided literacy training for 53,357 illiterate adults. Vocational educators hired by the WPA taught courses in gardening, canning, pruning, and equipment repair to farm-ers; secretarial skills to secretaries; and housekeeping to domestics. By March 1938 the adult education program had reached an estimated 10 percent of the state's population.[16]

Established in June 1935 and affiliated with the WPA, the National Youth Administration (NYA) aided youths between the ages of sixteen and twenty-four in three ways: a school-aid program, a placement and counseling service, and a work program for unemployed and out-of-school youths from relief families. The NYA was headed in South Carolina by Professor Roger Coe of Presbyterian College, who was assisted by a ten-member NYA advisory board. When the academic year opened in September, he organized the school-aid program for high school and college youths. Although not limited to students from families on relief, the program provided money to students who could not remain in school without financial aid. Coe assigned quotas to 35 colleges and universities and approximately 700 high schools. School officials agreed to certify needy students and to supervise their work. The NYA required each high school recipient to work twenty-four hours a month at twenty cents an hour on "socially desirable projects" designed by the school principal and approved by Coe. These projects included cleaning school buildings, assisting in cafeterias and libraries, repairing classroom equipment, and providing clerical aid for teachers and principals. College students earned their stipends working in libraries, museums, and administrative offices. By March 1938 the NYA in the Palmetto State had paid nearly $1.1 million in wages to 19,303 high school and college students.[17]

The work of the Women's and Professional Division of the WPA was just as visible. Women usually averaged about 36 percent of the WPA workforce in South Carolina. More than 80 percent of these women were sole supporters of families. Women performed a variety of tasks. Some women helped with education, school lunch, and health projects. Others served as housekeeping aides who rendered assistance in parental and child care, sick care, and housework to underprivileged or incapacitated homemakers. Nearly 3,000 worked in WPA sewing rooms, which by March 1938 had produced more than 2.1 million garments for distribution to the destitute. Several hundred worked on the statewide library project, where they mended and bound library books. Other women supplemented library staffs to extend the hours of service. Still others worked on the thirty-two WPA library trucks that served as circulating libraries in thirty-six counties and circulated more than 4 million books from January 1936 to March 1938.[18] The WPA also employed women on the thirty-eight land beautification projects that landscaped and beautified 796 acres of public grounds by February 1937.[19]

Other projects in the Women's and Professional Division were not gender based. The South Carolina Writers Project, headquartered at the University of South Carolina under the supervision of Mabel Montgomery and Assistant Director Louise Jones DuBose, hired unemployed professionals of both sexes as researchers, writers, typists, proofreaders, and editors. By April 1942, when the project closed, WPA writers had produced twenty-three publications, including the *History of Spartanburg County, Palmetto Place Names, South Carolina Folk Tales,* and short biographies of Thomas Green Clemson and John C. Calhoun. The South Caroliniana Library indexed, cataloged, and deposited all manuscripts produced by the project.[20]

The most ambitious undertaking of the Writers Project was the 600-page *South Carolina: A Guide to the Palmetto State.* Under the supervision of the talented poet, sociologist, and amateur historian Louise DuBose, research and writing began in 1936 and was completed in 1940. Publication followed in 1941. The first section of the *Guide* contained nineteen essays on the state's natural and popular history, minorities, economy, education, religion, society, and cultures. Detailed descriptions of the state's twelve most important cities and towns followed in alphabetical order from Aiken to Sumter. The final section contained twenty-one scenic tours throughout the state to interest tourists and residents alike. The local scholars who worked on the project found Federal Writers Project (FWP) headquarters in Washington to be both helpful and irritating. On the one hand, FWP headquarters were so impressed with the essay on Charleston that they sent copies to other state projects for use as a guide. On the other hand, they winced at terms such as "War for Southern Independence" for the Civil War and complained about the class consciousness that pervaded some of the essays. Consequently, they edited with a heavy hand and even chose to write three of the nineteen essays in section 1. In all, despite its white, lowcountry, middle- to upper-class bias, the work was scholarly, readable, at times fascinating, and able to "capture the spirit of time and place."[21]

Also under the auspices of the Writers Project was the Historic Records Survey, directed by Dr. Anne K. Gregorie. Her credentials were even more impressive than DuBose's. The first woman to receive a Ph.D. in history from the University of South Carolina, she taught at colleges in Arkansas and Alabama and authored a published biography of Thomas Sumter and three entries in the *Dictionary of American Biography* before overseeing the Records Survey. The project began in 1935 to locate, transcribe, and preserve public records in the forty-six counties. Project workers compiled, copied, and abstracted coroners' records, estate inventories, deeds, wills, court minutes, and epitaphs. They also inventoried church records and private manuscript collections of historical significance. The project eventually published fourteen of the forty-six county inventories in the *Inventory of County Archives of South Carolina.* Each volume contained a brief history of the county and a description of the provenance of the records. With racism and sexism so rampant, it is not surprising to find that records of black churches, public manumission records, and dower books were neglected. Nevertheless, currently located in the Search Room of the South Carolina Department of Archives and History, the work of the survey serves each day as an invaluable primary source for scholars and genealogists alike. Also useful to both groups are Dr. Gregorie's subsequent published works, for which the Records Survey served as a catalyst: *Records of the South Carolina Court of Chancery, 1671–1779; A History of Sumter County; The History of Christ Church Parish, 1706–1959;* and ten years of the *South Carolina Historical Magazine,* which she edited from 1948 to 1958.[22]

No less appreciated were WPA music and art projects. The former furnished musicians to public schools to provide music instruction to underprivileged students. By July 1939 these musicians had conducted 29,857 classes for 20 percent of the state's population. The music project also assembled unemployed musicians into orchestras to provide free concerts for an additional 18 percent of the state's population. The South Carolina Art Project was more restricted in scope, since art galleries were less mobile than orchestras. Artists were commissioned to develop and operate five galleries at Florence, Columbia, Greenville, Walterboro, and Beaufort, and construct scenery for the Dock Street Theater in Charleston. By February 1937 the first three galleries had staged eighty-five exhibitions attended by 33,663 South Carolinians.[23] Other WPA artists provided art education in the public schools of Columbia, Beaufort, Greenville, and Walterboro. These artists also produced signs and posters for schools and civic organizations.[24]

At least one piece of New Deal art stirred controversy that raged for two years. In 1938 Vermont artist Stefan Hirsch painted a triptych mural titled "Justice as Protector and Avenger" for the federal courthouse in Aiken. At 12 feet, 6 inches by 12 feet, 10 inches, the work was overwhelming in effect. However, federal district judge Frank K. Myers objected to Hirsch's depiction of "Justice" as vengeful and ordered the work covered with a curtain. Local white residents applauded his decision. They complained that Hirsch's "Justice," a dark-skinned, barefooted, and highly symbolic figure, was a mulatto. Also objectionable were the seeming portrayal of a prisoner being released from jail by a corrupt lawyer, the "too-modern" format, and the "extravagant" $2,200 artist fee. In 1940 the Section of Fine Arts in the U.S. Treasury Department, which commissioned the work, tried to broker a compromise whereby Hirsch would lighten the skin pigment of "Justice" in return for Myers dropping his opposition to displaying the mural when court was not in session. Myers balked; Hirsch refused to return to Aiken; and the mural remained concealed.[25]

With some justification, the public perception of the WPA in South Carolina was of public building construction and infrastructure improvement. By July 1943 the tally included 1,267 noneducation buildings (courthouses, municipal buildings, and jails), 69 water and sewage treatment plants, 232 miles of water mains, 340 miles of storm and sanitary sewers, and 122,932 sanitary privies. Many areas that struggled with an antiquated water or sewage system, or simply did without, were able to install modern plants. Those communities for which the WPA made additions or improvements were able to serve more customers while they enjoyed increased revenue and even qualified for cheaper fire insurance rates. In addition, the WPA continued on a massive scale the swamp drainage program begun by the SCERA. Evidence of achievement in this area was a report in 1937 by the State Board of Health indicating a 16-percent decrease in cases of malaria from the preceding year.[26]

Impressive as these accomplishments were, there were always critics. Lawrence Pinckney's job was fraught with headaches, some of which were unavoidable. Inefficiency on the part of the director in the Greenville district and a personality clash with another of the division directors forced Pinckney to remove both men within the first six months.[27] The public records projects encountered difficulties when clerks of court in several counties diverted WPA employees from repairing and copying public records to routine office duties. Pinckney closed two public records projects when the clerks refused to comply. Local sponsors of construction projects insisted that they and not Pinckney should select both the workforce and the project supervisors. Pinckney drew the line at their request to select the employees but allowed them to name the supervisors. On one occasion, when the supervisor proved incompetent and the sponsor declined to remove him, Pinckney suspended the project.[28] Occasionally, tennis courts and sewer systems were inadvertently constructed on private property, and project foremen had to be dismissed for misuse of funds.[29]

Owing to the Southern proclivity for violence, Pinckney's subordinates found their jobs hazardous and nerve-racking. For instance, in the winter of 1936 Irene Allen of Anderson County supervised a WPA sewing project at Pelzer. When the sponsors of the project became delinquent in paying the rent and providing fuel, Allen coerced the workers into paying twenty-five cents every two weeks for fuel. With the rent still unpaid, Allen asked permission to move the project to nearby Williston. Mrs. J. H. Harrison, assistant district director for women's work, refused permission until the rent could be paid. After Allen disobeyed Harrison and commandeered a truck before daybreak one morning in order to move the project physically to Williston, Harrison had no choice but to discharge her. What happened at the termination interview is conjecture. According to Allen, Harrison insulted and kicked her. According to Pinckney, Allen pulled Harrison from the car and physically attacked her, dislocating several of her fingers, repeatedly striking her in the face, kicking her several times, and dragging her over rough pavement "with the result that Mrs. Harrison received several cuts." Needless to add, Pinckney and Hopkins ignored Allen's pleas for reinstatement.[30]

As always, there were political complications. Workers discharged by the WPA frequently complained to their congressmen, who wrote Pinckney to request an explanation. Pinckney and his staff were forced to spend hours investigating each complaint before replying by personal letter to each lawmaker.[31] Even more time-consuming were controversies such as the Alice Norwood Spearman affair. The *Atlanta Georgian,* an anti–New Deal newspaper in the Hearst chain, charged that in the summer of 1935 communism was taught in an SCERA project supervised by Alice Norwood. The paper misquoted and misinterpreted her remarks to a reporter to say that she not only taught pupils in her adult education classes to overthrow their oppressive capitalist overlords but also distributed communist literature advocating violent revolution. Norwood's travels in Russia in 1931 and 1932 during a European tour lent credence to the charges.

The article was read on the floor of the South Carolina House of Representatives, prompting the Speaker to appoint a special committee to investigate. After lobbying by Pinckney, whose WPA absorbed both the SCERA education program and Alice Norwood, a majority of the committee issued a report exonerating the WPA, declaring that the intent of the charge was to embarrass the New Deal and Senator Byrnes, and asking Pinckney to make a thorough administrative investigation. A minority report, the work of Ben Adams, requested a thorough legislative investigation. Adams, a partisan of Governor Johnston and an irreconcilable foe of the relief administration in South Carolina since 1933, shared Governor Johnston's irritation at the appointment of Pinckney, which excluded Johnston from control of the WPA.[32] Pinckney's subsequent investigation found that Alice Norwood, who was currently the WPA superintendent of workers' education, had not advocated communism, although she had advocated and practiced the free discussion of all topics in the classroom. Pinckney issued a statement denying the charge and explaining the circumstances, and the furor subsided.

Yet, Alice Norwood soon became a liability. She violated Pinckney's requirement that WPA personnel secure his permission before granting interviews to the press. She also failed to inform her superior when two participants in the education project charged her with teaching communism. The coup de grace was a private warning from a friend to Senator Byrnes about Alice Norwood telling a convention of African American school teachers meeting in Mullins that "the Negro should work for social equality as was their due," a statement that was bound to inflame white passions.[33]

Her marriage to John Spearman of the Resettlement Administration (USDA) gave Pinckney an opportunity to dismiss her, since government regulations prohibited both parties in a marriage from working for New Deal relief agencies.[34] The matter of her pending dismissal simmered as the South Carolina Federation of Labor held its twenty-second annual convention in Spartanburg in June 1936. Pinckney's mentor, Byrnes, was then seeking renomination to the Senate against fellow Democrat Thomas P. Stoney of Charleston. Dowell Patterson of Charleston, a former president of the state labor federation, was supporting Stoney; John A. Peel of the United Textile Workers was supporting Byrnes. Governor Johnston, who had little interest in the outcome of the Democratic primary, nevertheless wished to replace Pinckney because the WPA director was not giving Johnston "all the [WPA] appointments he wanted."[35] Thus, a coalition of Governor Johnston, Dowell Patterson, and Labor Commissioner John Nates hatched a plan to have the convention resolve in favor of Pinckney's removal.

Patterson and Nates led the fight against Pinckney on the convention floor; Johnston lobbied textile delegates behind the scenes. Nates outbid Peel for textile labor support by promising factory inspectorships in South Carolina's Department of Labor to textile labor delegates. Patterson, meanwhile, castigated Pinckney for cutting off the salary of Alice Spearman, whom he described as a longtime friend of organized labor in her role as superintendent of the workers' education program. In fact, Patterson claimed, so devoted was Alice Spearman to organized labor she was continuing as superintendent without pay. With Nates's promises and Patterson's oratory, the motion to remove Pinckney carried.[36]

Because Byrnes was an easy winner in the Democratic primary, Pinckney remained as WPA director. Alice Spearman, who refused to resign, was removed in October. In November, in an attempt to salvage something from the abortive coalition, a delegation including Nates, Alice Spearman, Patterson, and Secretary Thomas Crenshaw of the state labor federation conferred in Washington with Nels Anderson, WPA director of labor relations. The delegation requested that Pinckney be ordered to appoint a friend of organized labor to replace Alice Spearman, hoping that Pinckney would resign rather than comply.[37] Byrnes warned Harry Hopkins of the political factionalism at the root of the protests. Byrnes added of Patterson: "When he is not trying to give Pinckney trouble, he is devoting his time to denouncing Jim Farley and me. . . . Anything that Patterson and Crenshaw are connected with could not have merit in it."[38] Hopkins forwarded the letter to Anderson, who allowed Pinckney to appoint whomever he pleased to replace Alice Spearman.[39]

Actually, Pinckney's greatest difficulties stemmed from economics, not politics. This was especially true in his relations with farmers. The root of the problem lay in an inability or unwillingness to pay a decent wage for agricultural labor, the bulk of which was African American. From the beginning farmers such as David R. Coker of Hartsville complained, "The economic machinery of the South is being badly upset by the WPA. Farm labor is rapidly becoming scarcer. . . . It is also becoming demoralized because there are so many on work relief . . . who are doing very little work."[40] Robert Quillen of Fountain Inn added, "When the government pays $50 a month for easy work and short hours, what colored boy will be so foolish as to follow a plow from sun to sun for six bits or a dollar."[41]

In 1937 the agricultural labor shortage was especially acute. In January the South Carolina legislature petitioned Congress to request that relief authorities discourage farm laborers from seeking WPA employment.[42] In February a meeting of landowners in Marlboro County passed a resolution opposing all WPA projects that employed farm laborers.[43] In the summer the chief of police in Anderson invoked a vagrancy law from the old Black Code to force anyone not permanently employed (including WPA workers) to take a job picking cotton or be jailed and then hired out to a cotton farmer. Other South Carolina towns quickly emulated

Anderson. Finally succumbing to the pressure, Pinckney decreed that a WPA employee refusing to accept farmwork would be dismissed. Yet this action did not quiet the refrain that Pinckney heard throughout the New Deal: "Farmers cannot compete with WPA wages."[44]

Nevertheless, most of the vocal critics would agree that the WPA made essential contributions to South Carolina. It accounted for more than one-tenth of all New Deal expenditures. The $95 million paid in wages by 1943 kept hundreds of thousands of Carolinians from starvation. New highways, bridges, buildings, parks, playgrounds, sewage and water systems, and airports served as constant reminders of its impact on the state's landscape.[45] Equally significant was its impact on culture and society. The education program reached one person in ten; the recreation program reached an estimated half the population; and hundreds of thousands enjoyed the art exhibitions, concerts, and library privileges. Robert Armstrong Andrews, director of the South Carolina Art Project, reported South Carolina's "tradition of culture" was neither dead nor alive but rather "asleep" prior to the New Deal. Certainly the art project stirred and aroused that tradition. New art groups sprang up; attendance and membership at Charleston's Gibbes Art Gallery mushroomed; and the new galleries in Greenville, Columbia, Florence, and Beaufort became permanent. So did art classes in several public schools. Not only did native artists and art students have opportunities to exhibit their work, but they also could learn lessons from contemporaries whose works traveled among galleries in the WPA National Exhibition Service. In short, the South Carolina Art Project bought art to the masses for the first time in history.[46]

The steps to eradicate illiteracy and provide school children with adequate facilities were investments in the state's most valuable resource—its people. The WPA also cushioned the effects of setbacks such as the drought of 1936 and the recession of 1937–1938. For example, when farmers in Union, Cherokee, and York Counties ginned only 40 percent of their normal poundage of cotton in 1936, Pinckney expanded his WPA rolls to include nearly 4,000 farmers from this drought-stricken area. Then when South Carolina began to feel the effects of the recession, WPA rolls were increased from 15,771 in September 1937 to 50,718 by December 1938.[47] Without doubt, the WPA not only "supplied useful work to a veritable army of unemployed," but it also enriched society and culture in ways that "could not and would not have been secured for many years, if at all."[48]

Less in amount but greater in lasting impact was New Deal relief for home owners. In 1933 an estimated one-tenth of all nonfarm home owners in South Carolina were an average of two years behind in their mortgage payments and nearly three years behind in taxes. Congress responded with the Home Owners Loan Act to establish a Home Owners Loan Corporation (HOLC) that would exchange guaranteed HOLC bonds for mortgages in default. The HOLC then negotiated more favorable terms with the borrower, which in South Carolina meant monthly payments of $7.91 per $1,000 lent.[49] On July 15, 1933, the HOLC opened three district offices in South Carolina with state headquarters in Columbia under General Manager D. S. Matheson. By August the corporation had approved 476 mortgage loans totaling $600,000, although a delay in getting HOLC bonds from Washington prevented the loans from being closed. Finally on September 9, the HOLC closed its first loan of $1,288 to A. C. McFarland of Richland County.[50]

Unfortunately, like all New Deal programs, this one was plagued by administrative difficulties, and criticism mounted. Especially annoying to home owners was the length of time (in one instance, more than six months) it took to approve a loan. State NEC director Pinckney attributed the slowness to the "considerable lack of executive ability" at the state and district levels that bred "a serious lack of efficiency."[51]

Nevertheless, in three years of lending beginning in June 1933, the HOLC received more than 10,000 applications, negotiated nearly $14 million in loans, and saved more than 10 percent of the state's nonfarm homes from foreclosure. In addition, HOLC loans stabilized land values and helped save lenders such as banks, building and loan associations, trust companies, and life insurance companies. The loans also kept private interest rates low, while the HOLC's assumption of delinquent taxes on its properties aided state and local treasuries. Finally, HOLC loans to borrowers who wanted to remodel or repair their dwellings stimulated the housing construction industry.[52]

The Federal Housing Administration (FHA) complemented the efforts of the HOLC. The National Housing Act of 1934 created the FHA to offer insurance for bank loans negotiated by middle- and low-income families for the construction of new houses and the modernization of old ones. The act was designed to encourage private home ownership and stimulate recovery and employment in the building construction industry. Title I FHA funds insured loans for repair and modernization of existing dwellings; Title II insurance covered mortgages on new homes. By July 1939 the FHA in South Carolina had insured nearly 9,600 Title I loans totaling $3.7 million. However, Title II loans initially were not popular with bankers who in the 1920s learned the folly of tying up large amounts of capital in long-term real estate loans. Thus, in 1935, the FHA insured only 118 mortgages under Title II totaling only $442,609. Bankers gradually fell in line as the general economy improved, and by June 30, 1939, Title II insurance covered 2,848 mortgages totaling more than $10.8 million. Through June 1939, Title I, Title II, and the FHA's program for multifamily dwelling insurance, which covered one sixty-two-family dwelling, insured nearly 12,500 loans and mortgages amounting to nearly $14.8 million. It is no exaggeration to say that the HOLC and FHA saved private home ownership and the industries dependent upon it in the Palmetto State.[53]

CHANGING THE FACE OF THE PALMETTO STATE | 5

In June 1933 President Roosevelt signed the National Industrial Recovery Act containing a public works program of $3.3 billion administered by a new Public Works Administration. Roosevelt designed the PWA to serve as an engine of business recovery by stimulating those industries that were involved in public works, such as lumber, cement, steel, and construction. A secondary advantage would be relief for the unemployed, since PWA projects had to employ a certain percentage of workers from local relief rolls. From 1933 to 1939 the PWA spent nearly $36 million in South Carolina, about 7 percent of the $533 million spent by New Deal agencies there. The agency literally changed the face of the Palmetto State. Its visible legacy a half century later included hundreds of low-cost housing units to replace urban slums, miles of modern highways, a host of schools, courthouses, hospitals, post offices, and administrative buildings, a thriving shipyard, a number of new sewage and water systems, and two huge hydroelectric projects.[1]

The president selected Secretary of the Interior Harold L. Ickes to head the program. For each state Ickes chose a PWA advisory board to approve local requests for projects. South Carolina's three-man advisory board consisted of state senator Tom B. Pearce of Columbia as chairman, Mayor Burnet R. Maybank of Charleston, and L. P. Slattery of Greenville. Senator Byrnes had recommended Pearce and Maybank because of their political connections and public stature. L. P. Slattery of Greenville was the brother of Harry Slattery, noted conservationist and personal assistant to Ickes. J. L. M. Irby of Laurens became the state PWA director and chief engineer.

Governmental units such as municipalities initiated projects and applied to Ickes through the advisory board and Irby. The PWA awarded the recipient a grant of 30 (later 45) percent of the cost and usually a loan of the remainder. The recipient advertised for sealed bids, which were opened in the presence of a PWA representative. The lowest bidder won the contract and had to agree to hire a certain percentage of workers from the relief rolls. The required percentage varied from time to time, and Ickes and Roosevelt were lax in forcing contractors to obey the percentages. Through 1936 only about a third of all PWA project workers in South Carolina came from the relief rolls. The first wage scale for South Carolina ranged from 40 cents an hour for unskilled labor to $1 an hour for skilled labor, which the PWA scrapped in 1935 in favor of the prevailing wage. The initial workweek of 30 hours soon increased to a work month of 130 hours and finally to a workweek of 40 hours.[2]

PWA projects were of three classes: federal projects, nonfederal projects, and housing projects. Federal projects (repair and construction of federal property) required no local sponsors and were funded entirely by the PWA. Nonfederal projects (work on state and local property) required local sponsors and were funded by the grant-loan system. Housing projects were federally funded and consisted of slum clearance through the construction of low-rent multifamily dwellings.

The largest beneficiary of Class I, or federal-project, funds was the state highway system. Working in conjunction with the Bureau of Public Roads and the state highway department, the PWA sponsored 179 highway projects at a cost of $5.5 million by July 1939. Actual work did not begin until mid-October 1933. By November 1934 the work was employing an average of 4,300 men per month. However, the election of Olin D. Johnston in 1934 signaled the beginning of a two-year fight over control of the state highway department that would temporarily halt federally financed construction and contribute to the state's unemployment burden.[3] During the 1934 gubernatorial campaign, Johnston attacked the state highway department as a corrupt political machine, vowing to remove its chief commissioner, Ben M. Sawyer. When the highway commissioners and the legislature declined to approve Johnston's reorganization scheme, the governor called out the National Guard and seized control on October 28, 1935. Despite repeated assurances to Washington that his action would not imperil the highway construction program, legal action in the state courts tied up hundreds of thousands of dollars in highway money from November 1935 until mid-April 1936.[4]

The PWA had greater success at the Charleston Navy Yard. Established in 1901 on approximately 2,000 acres of land along the Cooper River, the facility barely survived the disarmament and isolationist fervor of the 1920s. Intercession on its behalf by the state's congressional delegation kept the yard open, although as late as 1930 it employed only 400 workers. In 1933, when Navy Department officials once again recommended closing the facility, Mayor Maybank and Senator Byrnes interceded with Ickes to save it. The first PWA project, begun in 1933, was construction of the gunboat *Charleston* at a cost of $4 million. From 1933 to 1936 a monthly average of 500 men worked on the *Charleston.* Byrnes obtained additional PWA funds for three Coast Guard cutters, four Coast Guard harbor craft, and the destroyers *Sterrett, Hilary P. Jones,* and *Roe.* By 1936 these ships had consumed nearly 4 million man-hours of work; two years later, ship construction involved 1,600 workers, a four-fold increase over 1930. Other federal projects employed 1,700 workers to repair and improve dock and yard facilities and construct a galvanizing plant, new wing of the naval base hospital, new officers' quarters, and dry dock—all at a cost of $2 million.[5]

Wartime and postwar events proved the wisdom of Ickes's decision to save the facility in 1933. During the war the Yard served as a primary production facility for destroyers, nineteen of which had been launched by May 1943 to join the successful effort to neutralize the German U-boat menace in the North Atlantic and make possible a cross-channel invasion of fortress Europe in June 1944. Because of the shortage of white males in the wartime workforce, thousands of black males and women of both races got jobs there, gained confidence in their ability to work as productively as white males, and destroyed forever the distinction between male jobs and female ones, white jobs and black ones. Although discharged from the Yard at war's end, these new workers let their wartime experience be a primary catalyst for struggling to achieve racial and gender equality in the 1950s and 1960s.[6]

The PWA housing program, although less important financially, represented a radical departure for the federal government. Never before in peacetime had the government assumed responsibility for seeing that its citizens had decent housing. Plagued with substandard housing, Charleston and Columbia were the first two cities in South Carolina to request PWA funding. A national survey classed 32.4 percent of all Columbia dwellings as crowded, nearly twice the national average. Only two-thirds of the dwellings in the capital city had electricity. The national average was more than 90 percent. Only 62.1 percent of Columbia's houses had indoor water closets, against a national average of 82.7 percent. Charleston fared no better. A local survey disclosed that one dwelling in four lacked electricity, more than one in five lacked running water, and one in two lacked indoor toilets. Nearly 38 percent needed major repairs.[7]

Therefore, it is not surprising the PWA awarded two of its first fifty-one low-rent projects to Columbia and Charleston. In August 1935 Ickes announced that the PWA would construct low-rent housing for African American families in Columbia at a cost of $450,000. The city objected so strenuously to the exclusion of whites that Ickes increased the allotment to $706,000 and divided the project into forty-eight units for whites and seventy-four for blacks. University Terrace, as the project was called, would maintain segregation by allotting the units on its lower terrace to blacks and those on its upper terrace to whites.[8]

The Charleston project was larger but also more strenuously opposed. In September 1935 the PWA announced plans to spend $1.5 million for construction of 291 units for African Americans. Low-rent housing for whites, the agency said, would be considered at a later time.[9] This announcement sparked "considerable resentment" among whites.[10] Black-property landlords even tried to persuade city council to turn down the proposal altogether.[11] But Mayor Maybank was quick to defend public housing. Selfishly, he reminded whites, "When we help the negroes living in the slums we help ourselves. . . . [because] your wash, your family's wash, goes into their houses."[12] Privately, however, Maybank urged the PWA to relent. In March 1936 Ickes agreed to divide the project into Cooper River Court for blacks and Meeting Street Manor for whites. A wide avenue separating the projects maintained racial segregation.[13]

In 1937 Congress passed the Wagner-Steagall Housing Act to set up the United States Housing Authority (USHA) with $500 million for loans to municipal housing authorities. Both Charleston and Columbia applied for USHA aid. By November 1939 the USHA had approved five Charleston projects with 728 dwelling units, including Robert Mills Manor, Robert Mills Manor Extension, Anson Borough Homes, and two unnamed sites.[14] Columbia was also a beneficiary, receiving $1.5 million for 200 dwelling units each at Gonzales Gardens and Calhoun Court. Later, the USHA earmarked $1.6 million for two projects in Greenville and Spartanburg to accommodate 350 low-income families. By 1940 more than 1,800 families were discovering for the first time what an "American Standard of Living" in decent, modern housing really meant.[15]

Nonfederal PWA projects requiring local sponsors who would plan the project, accept the 30-percent grant, assume the 70-percent loan, and contract with the lowest bidder, had the greatest impact on the Palmetto State. By August 1939 nonfederal projects amounted to nearly $80 million, federal projects to approximately $21 million, and housing projects to $2 million. Nonfederal public building projects accounted for $18.2

million of the nearly $80 million. The results were eighty-seven education buildings, ten city halls and courthouses, eleven hospitals and buildings at eleemosynary institutions, and five administrative buildings. Sewage, waterworks, and related construction accounted for $15.3 million. Included were thirty-three sewage systems and forty-seven water systems. Nonfederal highway projects accounted for $5.1 million, and heavy engineering structures and miscellaneous undertakings totaled $1.5 million.[16]

The PWA's greatest effort was in hydroelectricity. Approximately half of nonfederal PWA expenditures ($39.5 million) went toward the development of hydroelectric power at the Buzzard Roost project in Greenwood County and the Santee-Cooper project in the lowcountry.[17] In 1933 Greenwood County took advantage of a national rivers survey by the Corps of Engineers designating Buzzard Roost on the Saluda River as an excellent site for a dam and applied to Ickes for a loan and grant of $2.8 million for construction of a hydroelectric complex. The proposed dam, 85 feet high, 2,000 feet long, and 800 feet thick at the base, would create a lake with a 300-mile shoreline. Construction was expected to provide employment for an estimated 500 men. The complex would sell electricity to towns and municipalities in Greenwood, Laurens, and Newberry Counties, which in turn would retail it to users.[18] Letters of endorsement from Congressman McSwain and Senators Byrnes and Smith accompanied the application to Washington.[19]

In June 1934 the PWA approved Buzzard Roost, beginning a struggle over public power that would rage in and out of the courts until 1938. Duke Power Company lodged a protest at once, contending that construction would jeopardize the schools, hospitals, and orphanages subsidized by the Duke Endowment in both Carolinas. The company was careful not to mention that the Duke Endowment held only one-eighth of the total shares of stock issued by Duke Power Company. Nor did the company acknowledge that in 1933 only $490,588 of the more than $4 million in dividends from the power company went to the endowment. Nevertheless, George C. Allen, chairman of the Duke Endowment and president of Duke Power Company, threatened to warn all recipients of the Duke Endowment that "this great philanthropy by Mr. Duke" was jeopardized by "unfair competition" from the PWA.[20] Musing over Duke's high rates and huge dividends, Ickes opined, "Charity covers a multitude of sins."[21]

The Duke interests seemed to know that their philanthropic arguments would go nowhere, especially since Buzzard Roost would deprive Duke of less than one-third of 1 percent of its business. Thus, pressure was exerted where it could do the most good—on Sen. James F. Byrnes, whose position was delicate. Prior to 1931 Duke Power Company retained the firm of Nichols, Wyche, and Byrnes to handle its business in Spartanburg County. When Byrnes resigned to go to the Senate, the firm of Nichols, Wyche, and Russell continued to represent the company. Byrnes could not afford to offend his former partners and political allies, nor could he incur the wrath of powerful Duke interests. At the same time, he could not risk angering the voters of Greenwood County.

Byrnes maneuvered skillfully. In June 1934 Pres. Bennette E. Geer of Furman University wrote Byrnes that the Duke Foundation had promised a "nice slice for Furman" of approximately $350,000. Could not Byrnes use his influence to make Ickes more favorable to the Duke position?[22] Byrnes wired Ickes, but only to request a hearing for Geer and other Duke representatives. Byrnes added confidentially that he still favored the project.[23] Byrnes then wrote Geer that he requested the hearing and he personally knew little of the Greenwood project, although his Senate office staff "on one or two occasions" helped lobby the PWA on behalf of the grant and loan. Feigning innocence, Byrnes lamented that he "did not know that [his] office had been quite as active as it had been in this matter."[24]

This strategy worked beautifully. Geer replied by return mail: "Bless your heart! I have never once thought that you have done anything in connection with the Greenwood County Project other than what you should do. . . . I can assure you that there has not [been] one word of criticism from your [Duke Power Company] friends in Charlotte. They understand."[25] Two weeks later state senator W. H. Nicholson of Greenwood County asked Byrnes to testify for the project at a hearing requested by Duke before the electric power board. Not surprisingly, his secretary advised Nicholson that Senator Byrnes "has gone away for a much needed rest and does not expect to return to the city [Spartanburg] for some time."[26]

In July 1934 the electric power board accorded Duke its hearing. Duke engineers argued that the PWA underestimated the cost of Buzzard Roost. Duke lawyers maintained that most of the electricity would go to Greenwood Mills, whose owner, J. C. Self, was in the forefront of the struggle. Duke officials charged that competition from the government was unfair and unlawful. Recipients of the Duke Endowment added that competition from the government would leave orphans hungry, the sick unattended, and schools unendowed. The board was unimpressed, however, and the PWA gave the project final approval.[27] Byrnes then wrote to state senator Nicholson to take credit.[28]

Duke's only recourse was legal action. After the South Carolina Supreme Court upheld the constitutionality of an act creating a finance commission in Greenwood County to issue revenue bonds to cover the PWA loan, Duke sued in federal court where *Duke Power Company et al. v. Greenwood County et al.* would consume three years of litigation. The constitutionality of fifty-two other public hydroelectric projects hinged on the outcome. [29]

Both sides were ably represented. Former cabinet member and presidential hopeful Newton D. Baker headed the team of lawyers for Duke. Counsels for the county and for Ickes included noted government lawyer Jerome Frank and state senator W. H. Nicholson. Plaintiffs argued that the project created unfair competition for Duke and permitted the PWA to engage in unconstitutional business endeavors. Defendants countered that the major objective of Buzzard Roost was to hasten business recovery and stimulate employment under the general welfare clause of the Constitution. They contended further that Duke lacked standing to sue, since a power company could not suffer injury from lawful competition.[30]

Both sides also lobbied behind the scenes. Duke apparently solicited editorials from the friendly publisher of the *Greenville Piedmont* and persuaded railroads under whose bridges the proposed dam would back water to inflate the estimated costs of elevating those structures. Daniel T. Duncan, chief PWA engineer at Buzzard Roost, countered by organizing a whispering campaign to discredit federal district judge H. H. Watkins, whose decisions were favorable to Duke. Duncan reminded Mayor Maybank of Charleston that earlier in his career Watkins represented a Duke subsidiary and served as a trustee of Furman University, a frequent recipient of Duke Foundation money. Subtly, Duncan suggested to Maybank that the *Charleston News and Courier* might need this information to "clarify the facts with the public."[31] Meanwhile, state senator Nicholson applied political pressure. He introduced a bill that would empower the state Public Service Commission to reserve all power sites for public projects. Growled Nicholson, "If the authority of the president [of the United States] is broken down, I actually believe the power companies are going to take charge of this country."[32]

In December 1937 the case finally reached the United States Supreme Court as a companion case to *Alabama Power Company v. Ickes.* Jerome Frank, Att. Gen. Homer Cummings, and Sol. Gen. Stanley Reed filed briefs for respondents in both cases. On January 3, 1938, Justice Sutherland reasoned in the Alabama case that competition per se was the traditional American way and did not constitute a recognizable injury, which meant Alabama Power Company had no standing to sue. The decision in *Duke Power Company v. Greenwood County* was thus a foregone conclusion. Justice Sutherland simply upheld the circuit court decision that also denied standing to sue. Greenwood County was now free to proceed with the project, which would be completed in July 1940 at a cost of more than $5.2 million.[33]

When the decision was announced, the citizens of Greenwood were ecstatic. Sirens screamed, firebells rang, and little boys shooting firecrackers ran from neighborhood to neighborhood. The next evening, more than 1,500 citizens jammed into the local high school auditorium to celebrate. To the strains of "Happy Days Are Here Again," the crowd heard Governor Johnston offer congratulations, PWA board member Maybank herald the defeat of the "power trusts," and state senator Nicholson announce the dawning of a new day "for those who love freedom and the rights of the individual."[34]

South Carolina's other hydroelectric project, Santee-Cooper, was much larger in scope. In fact, it became the largest PWA construction project and created the largest man-made lake in the Atlantic states. For nearly 150 years South Carolinians tinkered with Santee-Cooper schemes of one sort or another. Before the Revolutionary War, adventurers dreamed of a canal connection between the Santee River, a 538-mile-long river system that emptied into marshes and sandbars on the Atlantic Coast fifty miles above Charleston, and the Cooper River, which emptied into the harbor at Charleston. Such an artery of transportation would support Charleston's bid to become the commercial capital of the Southeast by funneling trade to and from both Carolinas through the port city. Completed in 1800, the Santee Canal became a major highway for moving cotton bales to Charleston and manufactured goods from the port city to the interior. At mid-century, however, it was abandoned, a casualty of faulty design, periodic droughts, and competition from railroads.[35]

There the matter rested until the 1920s, when the Columbia Railway and Navigation Company, owned by Thomas Clay Williams, resurrected and expanded the dream of a canal to include the generation of electricity by channeling water from the Santee down the 75-foot gradient to the Cooper. The New York engineering firm Murray and Flood not only encouraged Williams but also built Lake Murray above Columbia on a tributary of the Santee River to produce hydroelectricity and control the flow of water to the Santee-Cooper basin. Meanwhile, the International Paper Company purchased Columbia Railway and Navigation Company and its plans to improve inland transportation and generate hydroelectricity. In 1929, before construction of a dam could begin, the Depression struck and forced the indefinite postponement of the project.[36]

Since private financing was out of the question, proponents lobbied for federal funds. In 1932, at the Chicago convention, Burnet Maybank and state senator Richard M. Jefferies of Colleton County tried without success to commit Roosevelt to a loan from the Reconstruction Finance Corporation to the Columbia Railway and Navigation Company. The project, they argued, would aid rural electrification, attract industry, and stimulate employment. It would also eradicate malarial hazards, aid in land reclamation, help eliminate flooding in the lowcountry, and provide recreational facilities. In November 1933 the Columbia Railway and Navigation Company applied for $24 million in PWA funds. The state advisory board endorsed the application.[37] In January 1934 Governor Blackwood led a delegation to Washington on behalf of the project. After Washington officials explained PWA policy of making loans for public, not private projects, the delegation called on South Carolina congressmen to introduce legislation setting up a corporation similar to TVA for public development of the Santee-Cooper basin. Senator Byrnes responded that TVA transcended state boundaries while the Santee-Cooper project would not. He pointed out that the government had a history of investing in the nitrate plant at Muscle Shoals on the Tennessee River. Byrnes added that the creation of TVA had been a campaign promise in 1932. He then advised the delegation to have the state legislature create a public service authority that could qualify for PWA funds.[38]

This remained the only option. PWA lawyers helped draft a bill that was introduced in the state legislature by Senator Jefferies and Rep. James S. Glymph of Oconee to create the South Carolina Public Service Authority.[39] Similar to the federal TVA, this state body would undertake improvement of navigation on the two river systems, generation and sale of hydroelectric power, drainage and reclamation of swampy lands, and reforestation of river watersheds. All of this would be accomplished by the construction of dams, canals, and power plants.[40]

Immediate opposition came from wealthy Northerners who hunted in the South Carolina lowcountry or owned power company securities.[41] One selfish investor complained to Byrnes that his "only source of income" was $200,000 in power company stock, which would devalue if Santee-Cooper were constructed.[42] Duke Power Company officials assailed the estimated cost as too low by at least one-half. They also insisted that competition from Santee-Cooper would adversely affect private utilities. State legislator Wyndham M. Manning of Sumter, a future gubernatorial candidate, alleged that Santee-Cooper would destroy the lumber industry in the lowcountry. Other legislators charged that the Public Service Authority would become a "vast political machine."[43]

Proponents of the project were more persuasive. Maybank asserted that localities would not suffer if private utilities declined, since localities received so little in taxes from utilities and paid such high rates for electric power. Favorable testimony by TVA director Arthur E. Morgan swayed many undecided legislators. So did lobbying by Congressman John E. Rankin of Mississippi, a noted advocate of public power, who criticized the "gigantic octopus of the power trust" in South Carolina.[44] House sponsor Glymph reminded his colleagues of the need for rural electrification, electricity for industrial expansion, and alleviation of unemployment. In April the legislature passed the bill, and Governor Blackwood appointed the seven members of the South Carolina Public Service Authority, which included Maybank as chairman. Jefferies, the Authority's general counsel, immediately filed application for a PWA grant-loan of nearly $36 million.[45]

Delays followed as the finance, engineering, and legal divisions of the PWA investigated the project's feasibility. In December 1934 Byrnes began urging lower echelon PWA officials, who had come before his Senate subcommittee requesting funds, to speed up the inquiry and persuade Ickes (who liked neither Byrnes nor Santee-Cooper) to look kindly upon the project.[46] Ickes favored small projects over large ones and thought Santee-Cooper too expensive and environmentally destructive. Byrnes, on the other hand, viewed Santee-Cooper as a way of giving South Carolina her "fair share" of relief and recovery money, and as partial repayment for his loyal support of the New Deal. Also apparent to Byrnes were the opportunities for dispensing patronage that Santee-Cooper would create. Consequently, Byrnes took pains to remind Ickes of the benefits that would accrue to South Carolina, adding that opposition centered around hunting-club aristocrats who "fear that as a result of this great development, there will be fewer ducks for them to kill."[47]

Although he was unable to speed up the process, Byrnes managed to keep in touch with the engineering division, the last to report. In early July 1935 he learned the assessment would be favorable. Aware that Ickes might try to delay the project, Byrnes asked the president to call Ickes for a copy of the report. A week later Roosevelt sent Byrnes a copy. The report estimated the total cost at $37.5 million. The PWA would provide a grant of $16,875,000 and a loan of $20,635,000. Final approval of the application awaited the outcome of a test suit in state courts to confirm the right of the Public Service Authority to issue revenue bonds.[48] In September 1935 the South Carolina Supreme Court in *Clark v. South Carolina Public Service Authority* ruled in favor of the project.[49]

A month earlier the *Charleston News and Courier* carried a feature article headlined: "Santee Dam Plan Called Big Bluff, Byrnes Politics." In the article, officials of the Carolina Power and Light Company assailed the project as propaganda for the senator's reelection campaign, adding that after the election the public would hear no more of Santee-Cooper. Nevertheless, the company added, should the project prove a reality, Carolina Power and Light company would join other private utility companies in opposing it in federal court.

In the meantime, Morris L. Cooke, rural electrification administrator, wrote the president to complain. Santee-Cooper, he argued, was in essence a private undertaking, since its advocates were only interested in having the PWA bail out the Columbia Railway and Navigation Company, which was selling its license to construct the hydroelectric complex. Conservationists and sportsmen re-entered the fray. Jay Darling, formerly of the USDA Biological Survey, charged that the project would upset the delicate ecological balance in the lowcountry. Garden clubs nationwide wrote the president in opposition. Finally, several engineers said the project was geologically unfeasible. Succumbing to this pressure, Roosevelt asked Ickes to select a board to study these concerns.[50]

This carping criticism and delay were more than Byrnes could endure. He wrote the president to refute Morris Cooke's allegations point for point.[51] He then unsuccessfully pressed Ickes to select the investigating board from among PWA engineers, who would be more amenable to political pressure than army engineers Ickes had in mind.[52]

On September 11, 1935, the senator wrote Roosevelt again to remind him that conservationists opposing the project were "being misled by men who are members of the Santee Gun Club, but who are more deeply interested in public utilities than they are in the gun club."[53] On September 18 Byrnes wrote Hopkins for help: "I know that the Santee-Cooper Project is a PWA project. I know, however, that you may have an opportunity to talk to the Chief about it and I want you to do so."[54] Throughout August and September, Byrnes badgered Roosevelt to make an appropriation to start the project. The president finally surrendered and approved $500,000 in a grant of $225,000 and a loan of $275,000.[55]

The feasibility study remained. Ickes appointed four noted geologists who visited Santee-Cooper reservoir sites and examined borings by PWA engineers. In October the board conducted a hearing in Columbia where sportsmen and conservationists insisted Santee-Cooper would imperil every fish in, and every migratory duck on, the Santee River.[56] In reply to a reporter's question, the chairman said he "hoped to file a report before the end of the year." Irritated at this prospect of further delay, Byrnes fired off a letter to Roosevelt to request a "prompt report by the commission." For good measure, Byrnes complained that the niggardly allotment of only $500,000 was a source of embarrassment to the Public Service Authority.[57]

On November 4, more promptly than anticipated, the board released its report, concluding that Santee-Cooper was "feasible from an engineering standpoint," while "its effect on wildlife would not be sufficiently grave to justify a refusal to proceed."[58] Then in December, Byrnes was pleased to learn that Ickes approved a $5.5 million loan for the Santee-Cooper and that Hopkins agreed to furnish $4.5 million in labor.[59]

Meanwhile, the private power companies went to court to stop the project. In December 1935, in federal district court in South Carolina, the South Carolina Electric and Gas Company, Carolina Power and Light Company, and South Carolina Power Company challenged, among other things, the constitutionality of government funding for public hydroelectric projects. They were able to secure a temporary injunction prohibiting construction. Since suits involving TVA and Buzzard Roost were already pending and would serve as precedents for Santee-Cooper, both sides then agreed to delay the Santee-Cooper case. In March 1937, after *Ashwander v. Tennessee Valley Authority* only indirectly upheld the TVA, the power companies felt strong enough to press the issue again in Santee-Cooper. Armed with testimony from an impressive array of engineers, lawyers, and geologists, the power companies began by challenging the National Industrial Recovery Act (NIRA) provision allowing the PWA to fund public hydroelectric complexes. They further insisted that no market for Santee-Cooper power existed, competition afforded by Santee-Cooper was unconstitutional, and the project was unfeasible from an engineering standpoint. Yet in late summer 1937, district court judge J. Lyles Glenn of Chester decided these arguments were not sufficient to warrant a permanent injunction.[60]

The power companies appealed to the Fourth Circuit Court in January 1938. There, they insisted the Santee-Cooper project would disrupt the navigability of the lower Santee River. The court decided the power companies would suffer no injury from disrupted navigation, since navigation on the river was already practically nonexistent. The Buzzard Roost decision by the U.S. Supreme Court in January 1938 made appeal of the circuit court decision in Santee-Cooper practically useless. On May 23 the high court refused to review the case, thus removing all legal obstructions.[61]

Finally, five years after creation of the PWA, the South Carolina Public Service Authority could let contracts and proceed with construction. The immensity of Santee-Cooper is best appreciated by comparing the initial $31-million PWA grant-loan for the Public Service Authority to the approximately $12.5-million state budget of 1939. Initial work on the project included the purchase of property and the relocation of 901 families and more than 6,000 graves. Swamps were then drained and mosquito-control efforts implemented to stamp out malaria. Land clearing by WPA workers for the 155-square-mile Lake Marion, 95-square-mile Lake Moultrie, and the 7-mile-long diversion canal between the two followed. Nearly 9,000 men cleared and disposed of the timber; another 7,300 men worked on the excavation and construction of the navigation lock, hydroelectric station, and 50 miles of dikes and dams. By the completion of the project in 1942, the cost had risen to nearly $65 million, making Santee-Cooper the most expensive PWA project on the East Coast.[62]

The effects of Santee-Cooper on the Palmetto State were enormous. The project stimulated recovery in construction and allied industries, and it employed thousands of South Carolinians at a time when jobs were scarce. However, the effects would have been greater had the project commenced in 1935–1938, when unemployment was high and industry lagging, rather than in 1939–1942, when wartime production was putting idle machinery into operation and idle workers on payrolls. Obviously, suits by the private power companies caused the delay.

Nevertheless, benefits extended beyond employment. Electricity generated by Santee-Cooper not only encouraged expansion of the service sector and location of new industry in the lowcountry, but it also aided powerfully in rural electrification. In 1935 only 2 percent of farms in South Carolina had electricity. By 1959 more than 74 percent received Santee-Cooper power. Gone were oil lamps, smokehouses, spring houses, and hand labor. In their place were electric lights, home appliances, refrigeration, incubators, milking machines, electric hand tools, and indoor plumbing.[63]

In addition, Santee-Cooper improved public health and recreation. By 1941 mosquito-eradication efforts had reduced deaths from malaria by 66 percent. In 1937 five counties surrounding what would become Santee-Cooper reported 1,300 cases and one-third of the state's malarial deaths; by 1948 they reported none. This decline was fortuitous, since thousands of sportsmen have flocked to Santee-Cooper every year since its completion for good hunting and some of the best fishing in the United States. National tournament anglers and amateurs alike know well what "Goin' to Santee" means.[64]

Despite Santee-Cooper's silting of Charleston Harbor and an inconsequential impact on inland navigation, on balance the project was beneficial. In fact, it could well be true that the PWA's hydroelectric projects, public buildings, roads, housing projects, and water and sewage systems have provided the most lingering visible presence in South Carolina of any New Deal agency.

HOORAY FOR THE NRA | 6

By the time of the New Deal, the textile industry in the upcountry was a culture all its own. In company with large landowners, many mill owners lived a charmed life of wealth, privilege, and power. They usually determined who served in local government, influenced the selection of the county's legislative delegation, and maneuvered behind the scenes to guide community decision making. Churches, civic clubs, and cultural organizations vied for their membership, since mill-owner generosity could build a new church sanctuary, complete a Community Chest campaign, or sponsor a concert series.

Yet the textile depression in the 1920s made the life of a mill owner stressful. In 1926 mill owners created a trade association, the Cotton Textile Institute, to tackle the problem of domestic overproduction and promote textile recovery. In 1930 this body tried to persuade mills to limit weekly production to 105 hours through the introduction of two weekly shifts of 55 and 50 hours respectively. The 12 percent of the mills who refused to cooperate rendered ineffective the efforts of the other 88 percent. By 1933 even many of the 88 percent occasionally ignored their pledge. Included among them was the progressive and respected Walter Montgomery, whose Spartan Mills in Spartanburg was operating two 55-hour shifts for a total of 110 hours. By 1933 most manufacturers were willing to give any plan that promised recovery through mandatory restrictions on production a chance to work.[1]

Textile workers in South Carolina were equally distinctive. With them the paramount issue next to bread-and-butter ones was race. Poor as they might be, they at least ranked above blacks so long as blacks were excluded from semiskilled and skilled jobs inside the mills. Before 1915 an unspoken contract inhered between many mill owners and their workers: the latter would not join national unions if the former made no attempts to integrate the workforce. In 1915 part of the contract was codified when workers lobbied for and won a law barring African American workers from all but menial jobs in mills. This agreement had nothing to do with local, homegrown unions, however. Workers had a history of forming them and striking to redress grievances such as the stretch-out and wage cuts. In the late 1930s a CIO drive to organize workers foundered partly because of CIO support for biracial unionism.[2]

Other factors retarded but did not prevent periodic unionization. National unions were Northern based and often run by hyphenated Americans of recent vintage; South Carolina workers were Southern, WASP, and nativist. Most manufacturers owned from one to three mills; a successful strike against one operator had little effect on the industry statewide. Management usually found ways to manipulate labor legislation; local sheriffs were often allies of management; and the structure of law enforcement at the state level was designed for union busting. Too, a one-party political system prevented labor from playing Democrat against Republican. Like most Carolinians, many mill workers were deferential; they deferred to their employers who in turn showed their commitment to equality by coming to the shop floor each day dressed in ordinary clothes to converse with each employee. Moreover, workers who organized could be evicted from mill housing where one in six white Carolinians resided in 1920, thus losing any benefits of life in a mill village. These included shopping in a company store, studying in a company-sponsored school, receiving medical care from a company nurse or clinic, playing in a company recreational building, picnicking in a company park, worshiping in a company-sponsored church, and burial in a company cemetery. Workers seldom needed to venture beyond the boundaries of their mill village because the mill was happy to furnish cheap electricity, water, coal, and free membership in mill scout troops, ball teams, women's clubs, and garden clubs.[3]

Mill-owner paternalism bred a measure of dependency but never servility. Mill workers were able to create a rich culture that gave them dignity, expression, and meaning. They found a hero in Cole Blease, an enemy in would-be reformers, a daily modus operandi in individualism and egalitarianism, a comfort in family, sustenance for the soul in fundamentalist evangelical churches, an opportunity for management in teaching new employees the routine of textile manufacturing, and an economic worldview in "moral economy," a concept that entailed "a certain balance between effort and reward, a certain opportunity for individual progress and family stability, a certain sense of belonging and group support and fairness in labor relations."[4] In particular, management kept wages halfway decent and work pace slow in return for high worker productivity and obedience. They also recognized the importance of mill-family cohesion in several ways. Fathers, for instance, retained a measure of control and influence over family members in the work setting as though they still worked on the farm from which they came. Moreover, workers were able to integrate home life and work by having family members visit them in the mill during the workday for a family conference or lunch, by working hard to "get ahead" in the morning in order to take time off in the afternoon to run errands, and by ending work early enough in the afternoon to accompany wife and children to a baseball game.[5]

Of all Southern mill workers, South Carolina's were the most politically empowered. Traditionally voting in large numbers, as early as 1902 they elected a textile labor organizer to the state legislature before electing Cole Blease to the governor's mansion in 1915. Over the years their legislators introduced bills to outlaw lockouts (unsuccessful), mandate biweekly paychecks (successful), and require payment in cash instead of scrip or tokens (successful). Their political clout often kept governors neutral in labor disputes so long as their unions were local and homegrown and not national and Northern based. Recognizing their political weight, management often caved in on matters such as length of the workweek so long again as unions remained local and homegrown.[6]

Much changed in the 1920s and early 1930s. First-shift workers typically worked ten hours a day, Monday through Friday, and five hours on Saturday morning. Second-shift workers labored eleven hours a day, Monday through Friday. Beginning in 1925 some mills cut wages as much as 50 percent, although a 10- to 25-percent reduction was more common. In 1931–1932 the average annual wage declined nearly 20 percent from $616.28 to $495.18. In 1928 a University of South Carolina study estimated the weekly subsistence wage for a family of five to be $21, or about $1,000 a year. Cotton mill workers earning the average of 28 cents an hour were $4.20 a week and more than $200 a year below the subsistence wage. Obviously, several members of each family had to work to make ends meet.[7]

Also in the 1920s, mills hired efficiency experts to calculate the most efficient workload. The result was usually the hated stretch-out, an increase in machine load per worker. Hot Carolina summers rendered the stretch-out especially pernicious. Often, female workers on the first shift fainted from their heavy work load in the oppressive heat. When asked how he felt after tending the maximum number of machines for eleven to twelve hours, one worker responded simply: "Tired. Tired and weary—like all the others."[8] In the eyes of mill workers, manufacturers were violating "moral economy." Once again strikes by homegrown unions broke out to roll back the pay cuts, speedups, and stretch-outs. Some were successful, others not. Therefore, labor also wanted a New Deal, but unlike management's, theirs would restore a living wage and slower work pace.[9]

President Roosevelt responded to employer needs and employee wants with the NIRA of 1933, a measure aimed at restricting production, stimulating employment, increasing wages and profits, shortening hours, and protecting labor's right to bargain collectively with employers. Government would allow business to restrain production and raise prices in return for adherence to codes of fair competition. These codes promised higher wages, shorter hours, better working conditions, and collective bargaining. The National Recovery Administration (NRA), set up by Roosevelt under the direction of Gen. Hugh Johnson, supervised the drafting of codes for each industry. Each code, once approved by the NRA and President Roosevelt, set up a national authority, which, in turn, could establish state and local authorities. The code authorities investigated and handled complaints and violations. If the authority proved unable to persuade the violator to comply, the state NRA compliance director, assisted by local and state adjustment boards, investigated and ordered compliance.

The summer of 1933 was the heyday of the NRA. While General Johnson was busy overseeing the drafting of several hundred codes of fair competition, the NRA devised a blanket code called the President's Re-employment Agreement (PRA), which required a workweek of forty hours, a minimum weekly wage of $14, and an agreement not to raise prices more than the increase in the cost of production. An employer signing the PRA followed its provisions until the NRA could formulate a code for his industry or trade. All businessmen who signed either a specific code or the PRA, and all consumers who pledged to patronize only businesses that endorsed the codes, proudly and prominently displayed the emblem of industrial recovery—the Blue Eagle. On July 21 General Johnson telegraphed both W. E. DeLoache of the Columbia Chamber of Commerce and C. S. Lamon of the State Merchants Association to request that everyone in South Carolina cooperate in the effort to win acceptance of the codes. DeLoache wired back, "Columbia will cooperate 100 percent on this request or anything that Franklin D. Roosevelt wants."[10]

Employers quickly fell in line. On July 27 Columbia merchants voted without dissent to sign the blanket code. The next day, merchants in Greenville, Bishopville, Cheraw, and Laurens followed suit. On August 1 Greenville staged a New Deal parade and pageant, complete with a mock trial and execution of "Old Man Depression." Employers throughout the state began receiving copies of the PRA, which they signed and returned to Washington. On August 1, the day the PRA took effect, Blue Eagle emblems began arriving from Washington. Meanwhile, on July 30, Columbia businessmen began purchasing full-page newspaper advertisements to broadcast their support. The advertisements featured portraits of Roosevelt, the Blue Eagle emblem, and comments such as "We're Back of the Man of Action" and "The Undersigned Food Dealers Pledge Their Loyal Support to President Roosevelt in His Determined Effort to Bring about National Recovery."[11]

Meanwhile in Washington, General Johnson asked three men— George Sloan of the Cotton Textile Institute, Thomas Marchant of the American Cotton Manufacturers Association (ACMA) in the South, and Ernest Hood of the National Association of Cotton Manufacturers (NACM) in the Northeast—to select prominent textile manufacturers to make up the Cotton Textile Industry Committee (CTIC) that would write the textile industry's code of fair competition. Marchant was a native of Greenville, president and treasurer of Victor-Monaghan Mills, vice president of the Wallace Manufacturing Company, and a director of the Piedmont Manufacturing Company and the Aragon-Baldwin Cotton Mill chain. Among the ten Southerners he selected for the CTIC was R. E. Henry of Greenville, president of the Aragon-Baldwin chain and president and treasurer of both Dunean Mills of Greenville and Watts Mills of Laurens.[12]

On June 19, 1933, Marchant, Henry, and the other members of the CTIC submitted their draft to Hugh Johnson. A week later Johnson conducted four days of hearings on the proposed code at the Commerce Building in Washington. Senator Byrnes, who appeared as a witness to support the code, warned that the industry would not realize the benefits of higher wages, shorter hours, and increased employment if manufacturers were free to stretch out workers. He suggested that Johnson appoint a committee to investigate the stretch-out and to recommend maximum workloads per worker. In response, Johnson appointed an investigating committee that later became the textile industry's first labor board.

The proposed textile code was comprehensive. It required a minimum wage of $12 per week in the South and $13 per week in the North, excluding learners, cleaners, and outside employees. It established a forty-hour workweek and imposed a restriction on production of eighty hours per week. The code forced each mill to report to the code authority every four weeks on hours, wages, number of spindles and looms in place, and number of spindles and looms in operation, and it abolished child labor under 16 years of age. Each mill was required to accept Section 7(a) of the NIRA, which allowed workers to organize and bargain collectively, and no mill could increase the machine load per worker that prevailed on July 1, 1933. The Cotton Textile Institute was designated to serve as the code authority responsible for compliance. So favorable was the code to industry that one New Deal historian insisted manufacturers "whom the NRA was supposed to be regulating" were "the one group that most clearly seized power."[13]

On July 9, 1933, President Roosevelt approved the cotton textile code, which became NRA Code Number One. Two days earlier the Cotton Manufacturers Association of South Carolina (CMASC) met in annual convention in Spartanburg. Pres. Samuel M. Beattie warned that the certainty of increased production costs and injection of organized labor into industrial relations would demand "intelligence, courage and character of the highest order to keep the situation sane and reasonable." Nevertheless, he expressed hope that all association members would cooperate and help render "the new order of things" successful.[14] Marchant also attended the meeting to explain the code and lobby for its acceptance. The CMASC issued a public statement vowing to uphold the code "100 percent."[15]

General Johnson appointed the national committee to investigate the stretch-out. Columbia University professor and Wall Street lawyer Robert Bruere represented the public and served as committee chairman; Bennette E. Geer, president of Furman University and former president of Judson Mills in Greenville, represented manufacturers; and George L. Berry of Tennessee, president of the International Pressman's Union, represented labor. Byrnes tried unsuccessfully to persuade Johnson to replace Berry with a cotton textile worker. Electing to concentrate on mills in South Carolina, the committee came to Spartanburg on July 13 and to Greenville on July 14 to hear testimony. Byrnes accompanied them to help interrogate witnesses.

At neither hearing was there unanimity. One Spartanburg worker testified that a recent stretch-out at Saxon Mills not only was accompanied by a discharge of workers but also created such unbearable working conditions that workers could not even stop for a drink of water. Samuel M. Beattie of the CMASC countered that the stretch-out was the inevitable consequence of progress. It neither reduced the number of jobs nor overloaded workers, first because the installation of new and more efficient machinery usually accompanied the stretch-out, and second because the mill added unskilled workers to relieve the stretched-out skilled worker of his menial duties. Contradicting Beattie, one witness at Greenville pointed to the F. W. Poe Manufacturing Company, which had reduced wages 55 percent since 1929. The mill granted a 10-percent pay increase in early 1933 but then laid off sixty-one men and stretched out the remaining workers in order to pay for it.[16]

In the face of such contradictory testimony, the committee found it impossible to restrict the stretch-out. Desirable workloads, the committee found, varied from mill to mill and even day to day because they depended upon such factors as coarseness of the weave, quality of the cotton, strength of the yarn, humidity inside the mill, and condition of the machinery. Thus, the committee concluded the stretch-out was "sound in principle" although subject to abuse.[17] The report recommended that each mill have a committee containing labor and management that would set the workload for the mill. Above the mill committees would be both a state board and a Cotton Textile National Industrial Relations Board (CTNIRB) to hear appeals.[18]

General Johnson was delighted with the report. On August 2, 1933, he announced that the stretch-out committee of Bruere, Geer, and Berry would become the Cotton Textile National Industrial Relations Board with authority to settle stretch-out disputes and other labor-management conflicts that arose in the textile industry. The CTNIRB, also known as the Bruere Board, then selected nine state boards. South Carolina's textile board contained Dean H. H. Willis of the Clemson Textile School as chairman and neutral member, textile engineer J. E. Sirrine of Greenville to represent management, and Earl Britton of the International Typographical Union to represent labor. In November, Furman B. Rogers of the UTW replaced Britton. Just like its parent CTNIRB, the South Carolina textile board, or Willis Board, would settle labor-management disputes arising in the state's textile industry. The Willis Board also selected local mill committees. After this textile board structure was complete, President Roosevelt abrogated the provision of the textile code requiring mills not to increase their July 1, 1933, workloads. Presumably, mill committees and their parent and grandparent boards would settle work-load disputes.[19]

After July 17, 1933, when the code took effect, most mill owners began complying with NRA requirements. All mills reduced production to two 40-hour shifts. Mills in Columbia and Rock Hill increased their weekly payrolls by $9,000 and $10,000 respectively. By June 30 textile manufacturers in South Carolina had already replaced all but 95 of the 1,356 youths under 16 years of age who were working in 1932. By July 17 child labor had been abolished. In addition, employment climbed dramatically—from 67,004 in November 1932 to 80,154 by November 1933, an increase also indicative of renewed prosperity. The upturn in the economy between the spring and fall of 1933 accounted for a 25-percent increase in the annual value of the state's textile product from $134 million in November 1932 to $168 million by November 1933.[20]

Nonetheless, some features of the code proved troublesome. Elliott White Springs, president of the Springs chain, found the provision requiring monthly reports on spindles and looms especially annoying. Springs, a Princeton graduate, former World War I fighter pilot, novelist, and poet, was in the process of reorganizing the ten mills in the Springs chain and was constantly shifting sides and looms from plant to plant. On December 20 he reported to George Sloan of the code authority that his auditor, "after working for nearly two months" on machinery reports, "has developed spots before his eyes, and has gone to a sanitorium for a rest."[21]

Other manufacturers were concerned with the increased cost of production. They were able to absorb the increase of 8 cents a pound on manufactured cotton caused by the change in wages and hours. They were less able to absorb the 4.2-cents-per-pound processing tax levied by the AAA. In fact, this increased cost of 12.2 cents per pound severely restricted the market for cotton goods. In September 1933 some South Carolina mills closed for a week in order to balance orders and inventories. On December 2 the NRA approved a code-authority request for a 25-percent curtailment of textile production for the month of December.[22]

Labor's initial reaction to the textile code was equally ambivalent. On July 17, 1933, when the code reduced the workweek to forty hours, more than 1,500 textile workers in Greenwood held a street dance to celebrate. One newspaper reporter noted, "Some of them just cannot help thinking maybe there's a trick in it."[23] Code wages of $12 a week were an added blessing. Meals for a family of four in a mill village at Columbia cost only $3 a week, leaving $9 for rent and other necessities. Smith's Slaughter

House sold bacon for 5 cents a pound, a picnic ham for 30 cents, a side of fatback to season homegrown vegetables for 30 cents, and a "streak of lean" higher on the hog for 55 cents. The company store in the village sold a 25-pound bag of flour for 35 cents. Never mind the monotony of biscuits, pork, and vegetables; with code wages mill workers finally could make ends meet.[24]

But problems remained. Although the code established a $12 minimum weekly wage, it did not require mills to increase the pay of skilled workers making more than $12 a week before the code. As a result, the code lessened the differential between skilled and unskilled wages. Moreover, until the Bruere and Willis Boards began to function, mills felt at liberty to stretchout workers. Beginning in late July 1933, strikes caused by the stretch-out idled about 3,500 workers in six plants. These strikes were brief, unsuccessful, and nonunion. Bruere and Geer, already in South Carolina in July and August to explain the code to manufacturers, said the strikes would "defeat the very purpose of the recovery act and the code by hindering the increase in purchasing power."[25]

Yet, the strikes indicated that textile workers in South Carolina were stirring. Armed with Section 7(a) of the NIRA as incorporated in the textile code, organizers from the United Textile Workers (UTW) descended on the Palmetto State.[26] On July 25, 1933, at a labor rally of 400 workers on Dreyfus Field in Columbia, organizer Paul W. Fuller dubbed the National Industrial Recovery Act labor's "Declaration of Independence" and called nonunion workers "slacker[s]" who violated "the spirit of the law."[27] At another rally three weeks later, Fuller labeled the NRA "a bridge over the deep chasm of misunderstanding, low wages, bankruptcy, and low standards of living."[28] Responding with cries of "Hooray for the NRA," workers rejuvenated old locals and organized new ones. Local 1771 in Columbia, formed on July 29, had 1,500 members at year's end. By mid-September 75 percent of the state's textile mills had UTW locals.[29] These workers considered UTW membership a patriotic duty because the NIRA seemed to encourage it.

As the textile boards began to function in October 1933, two distinct viewpoints emerged. Alarmed by the code's reducing the differential between skilled and unskilled wages, and a lack of protection from the stretch-out, workers turned to the labor movement for protection. They would remain pacified only so long as textile boards kept them informed about pending investigations of alleged violations, and manufacturers raised skilled wages, halted the stretch-out, honored wage and hour requirements, and bargained collectively. Manufacturers, for their part, would submit to wage and hour restrictions and self-government under the auspices of the NRA only so long as such measures fostered prosperity. To them, the NIRA was a recovery and not a reform measure. Moreover, they looked askance at restrictions on the stretch-out, which they regarded as efficiency and progress in manufacturing. Most of all, manufacturers preferred control to contractual agreements, and they planned to resist any attempt by workers to bargain collectively.

The textile boards and the code authority could not reconcile these opposing viewpoints. The Bruere and Willis Boards tried to distinguish between "complaints" and "disputes." The two boards investigated and mediated "disputes." But "complaints" alleging violation of the code were usually referred directly to the code authority or returned with complicated instructions on how to lodge a formal complaint with the code authority. In either case, the complainant often did not hear from the boards again. The code authority—in reality, the manufacturers' trade association—received complaints from the boards and then asked manufacturers concerned to explain the matter. In December 1933, for example, the code authority contacted Elliott Springs regarding alleged discrimination against union men and existence of child labor in his mills. Springs replied that one of his overseers had, in fact, threatened to fire any worker who joined a union. Springs denied any violation of the code because "the statement was made in the barber shop on Saturday night, and the overseer in question was arrested for drunkenness about half an hour later" and was discharged from the mill at once.[30] As for the charge that he employed child labor, Springs replied that since most workers lacked birth certificates, he had no way of determining their ages. "The code authority . . . won't let me look at their teeth," Springs added wryly.[31]

With this, as with most complaints, the code authority accepted the mill owner's explanation and dismissed the complaint. Unfortunately, the complainant received no notification of any action taken. He concluded that the overseer's remarks reflected company policy and that the NRA never investigated such incidents. Worker confusion and animosity toward the boards, the NRA, and textile manufacturers were the inevitable result.

Perhaps most destructive of worker respect for the state textile board was the belief that its chairman, H. H. Willis, was not impartial. On November 14, 1933, John A. Peel of Greenville, vice president of the UTW, complained to Senator Byrnes: "I have talked to Prof. H. H. Willis personally and over long-distance telephone in regards to several situations in South Carolina, where the employer is violating from one to every section of the Cotton Code, and each time Mr. Willis says, "I want to talk with Mr. Geer" [of the Bruere Board], and each time there is nothing that can be done. . . . Now if Mr. Willis is going to take his orders from Mr. Geer then the manufacturers have two representatives on the [Willis] Board, the public one, and Labor one."[32]

The Bruere and Willis Boards were no more successful in settling disputes than in handling complaints. An examination of sixteen disputes settled by the Willis Board and four settled by the Bruere Board uncovers the major weakness in the New Deal program for industrial harmony: the absence of any coercive power to force compliance with code provisions and board decisions in an environment of inflated worker expectation and heightened management apprehension. The first dispute arose from Horse Creek Valley in Aiken County. Among the mills there were the Langley, Bath, and Clearwater plants of Aiken Mills and the Graniteville, Warrenville, and Vauclause plants of Graniteville Manufacturing Company. The six mills employed approximately 4,000 workers. A strike at one mill would likely affect three mills and possibly all six.

Moreover, Aiken County was located across the Savannah River from Augusta, Georgia, where the UTW had long been active. In July 1933, before Roosevelt approved the textile code, UTW organizers from Augusta combed the Horse Creek Valley for recruits. To management, their inducements were often provocative. One UTW notice, for example, promised that collective bargaining would further reduce the eight-hour workday mandated by the code. On July 13 Manager G. A. Franklin of Aiken Mills warned Gen. Hugh Johnson that "unless some steps can be taken to curb the activities of the originators of this Notice, serious trouble" would result when the mill began operating under the code four days later.[33] Aiken County mill owners began the NRA experiment fearful that Section 7(a) would imperil the prosperity of their mills.

A month later a delegation of workers called on management at the Bath and Langley plants of Aiken Mills to discuss allegations of a stretch-out and discrimination against union workers. Management declined to meet with the delegation. In October the UTW ordered a strike at Aiken Mills, claiming that management refused to bargain collectively after having discharged workers because of union membership. According to management, however, the strike began when gun-toting union workers shut off the power at the Bath plant after beating an overseer.[34]

Gov. Ibra Blackwood immediately sent highway patrolmen to maintain order. Some strikers agreed to return to work pending an investigation by the Bruere Board, but others vowed to continue the strike. UTW members from Augusta then crossed the river to help picket the Horse Creek Valley mills. After pickets and highway patrolmen clashed in a battle of rocks and tear gas, Blackwood sent in a company of National Guardsmen. A subsequent clash left a mill foreman seriously injured and twenty-two pickets arrested, several of them for carrying arms. By October 31, 1933, the strike idled workers in five of the six valley mills. All five mills continued to operate, but with a small workforce and constant picketing. The pickets were angry at the governor for sending National Guardsmen, angry at other workers who refused to strike, and angry at the mill for the alleged stretch-out, refusal to bargain, and discrimination against union members.[35]

At this juncture the Bruere Board intervened. Ignoring striker grievances, it decreed that they should return to work and management should reinstate them without regard for union membership or strike participation. Not eligible for reinstatement were strikers who had destroyed property or committed acts of violence. The Willis Board would oversee all reinstatements. Needless to say, the decision was a defeat for the strikers, the UTW, and the textile code. Not only were worker grievances not addressed, but the decree required the mills to rehire strikers only "as rapidly as . . . work is available," rather than immediately.[36]

Four months later twenty-five workers testified before the state senate that the mills in Horse Creek Valley were violating the spirit of the settlement. Strikers applied for their old jobs, but the mills offered them unskilled work instead of their former positions. Strikers who earned between $12 and $16 a week before the strike were offered jobs sweeping floors at from $8.40 to $9 a week. Men who refused to accept the demotion claimed the mills pressured the Aiken County ERA to deny them relief. One former striker testified that the mills that employed more than 300 spare hands to avoid having to rehire the strikers in skilled positions. In addition, Aiken Mills refused even to place 19 of the 750 former strikers on the employment eligibility list.[37] Labor was growing discouraged.

The second dispute involved Musgrove Mill in the Hamrick chain in Cherokee County. State senator Waite C. Hamrick owned the chain— made up of Alma, Hamrick, Broad River, Limestone, Vogue, and Musgrove mills—operated by his two sons, Waite, Jr., and Lyman. In late December 1933 workers began complaining to the Bruere Board that management at Musgrove was firing workers because of UTW affiliation. The complaints also alleged that the mill was violating the maximum hours provision of the code by starting the production machinery fifteen minutes early each day and forcing workers to begin work at that time. Bruere called in the Willis Board, which investigated the charges on February 20, 1934, and rendered a decision on March 23. The board decided the mill had, in fact, violated the hours provision by starting the machinery too early. In the matter of discharges because of union affiliation, the mill alleged that the four workers in question performed unsatisfactory work, although the Willis Board determined their work had been satisfactory. The board thus recommended the mill reinstate the four men, since "there appears to have been some lack of fact or judgment" in their dismissals.[38]

When management received the decision in March, they had no jobs available for the four men at Musgrove. They could have implemented the decision by shifting four less senior workers at Musgrove to other mills in the chain. Instead, they offered the four union men jobs at other mills, "so that the workers would not feel that they had won their point in the hearing," according to Furman B. Rogers of the Willis Board.[39] The four unionists refused the offer. On May 14, after Rogers persuaded Waite Hamrick to reinstate them at Musgrove, the four men unwisely asked Hamrick for back pay. He allegedly responded by closing the mill, claiming that a shortage of orders rendered further operations unprofitable. Rogers warned, "The belief is general among the employees that the shutdown was put into effect as a reprisal on the part of Dr. Hamrick against the union because these members asked for back pay."[40]

Nevertheless, after a visit to Hamrick in mid-July, Bennette Geer of the Bruere Board assured Bruere the Musgrove Mill was "broke" because it manufactured "a kind of goods for which there is no market." Hamrick, he added, "would be glad to run the mill if he had any business."[41] On the other hand, several workers in the Hamrick chain informed the Willis Board that Hamrick was transferring orders normally filled at Musgrove to other mills in order to keep Musgrove closed. Another worker claimed that Lyman Hamrick, superintendent of Musgrove, vowed to keep the mill closed until the workers either abandoned the union or starved. Finally, on July 25, 1934, Waite Hamrick appealed the March decision of the Willis Board to the CTNIRB. When Roosevelt abolished the textile boards in September, both parties were still filing briefs.[42] Mutual distrust had trumped industrial harmony.

The Musgrove dispute highlights the other glaring weaknesses of this system of industrial cooperation. First, the procedure was slow and cumbersome. The CTNIRB received the complaints in December and January; the Willis Board did not decide the case until March; Hamrick did not begin to implement the decision until May; and the issues of the shutdown and back pay remained unsettled in September. Second, the Willis Board lacked machinery to enforce its decrees, depending instead upon the good faith of manufacturers. In addition, the board was indecisive and vague. For example, rather than stating that Hamrick had discriminated against the four unionists, the board merely suggested that he acted from "lack of fact or judgment." Hamrick could claim legitimately that the workers were not entitled to back pay because the board had not specified discrimination. Fourth, the three members of the Willis Board did not cooperate and exchange information. For example, Willis did not learn that the issue of back pay was involved in the shutdown until Bruere sent him a copy of a letter from Furman B. Rogers, labor representative on the Willis Board, in late June. Finally, board procedure was tailor made for a manufacturer who chose to delay. Not until July, four months after the Willis Board decision in March, did Hamrick begin the motions of appealing the decision to the CTNIRB.

The NRA was no more successful with other industries in South Carolina. Lumber, for example, was a seasonal industry, employing workers who divided their time between cotton field and sawmill. Only five to twenty-five workers labored in a majority of the state's 800 sawmills and lumber companies and earned only 10 cents an hour for seven to nine hours of work a day, three to five days a week. Moreover, the market for products was predominantly local, since many customers were farmers who purchased lumber for farm repairs. Limited capital and credit forced most sawmillers to pay expenses after the product was sold.[43]

Then came the code, written by large manufacturers such as the Louisiana Central Lumber Company and administered in the South by the Southern Pine Association, which served as the code authority and which contained no representatives of the small South Carolina companies. The code required a minimum workday of eight hours and a minimum wage of 24 cents an hour. Large lumber companies with regional or national markets could fix prices and compensate for increased cost of production resulting from higher wages and shorter hours. Marginal operators with local markets could not. To offset the code requirements, they had to double the price they charged for rough lumber from $10 to $20 per thousand feet, which partially destroyed their market.[44]

Many of these marginal operators complained to a sympathetic Congressman Hampton Fulmer, who operated a small sawmill on his farm near Orangeburg. Fulmer wired General Johnson that trouble was inevitable unless the code could be modified to recognize the needs of the small operator. In early 1934 E. W. Watson of Windsor protested to Fulmer not only that he was unable to obey the wage provisions of the code but also that large lumber companies in Aiken and Augusta kept spies in his mill to keep them informed of code violations. Fulmer offered sympathy and advice. "If I were you," he wrote to Watson, "I would operate your mill on a commonsense basis, being just as fair to the hands who work for you as you possibly can, in line with prices you receive for your lumber."[45]

C. C. Sheppard, an executive with the Louisiana Central Lumber Company and a member of the lumber code authority, obtained a copy of the letter. In a March 1934 hearing before the NRA, Sheppard charged that Southern congressmen, specifically Fulmer, were advising their constituents to disobey the lumber code. An angry Fulmer retorted that Americans soon would "find this country in a hell of a fix" if the NRA did not start using "a little common sense."[46] Finding comfort in Fulmer's remarks, operators in South Carolina considered themselves free to conduct business as usual.[47]

Compliance was just as spotty in other industries. Each industry code, once approved by the NRA and President Roosevelt, set up national, state, and local code authorities to receive and investigate complaints and then order compliance where necessary. An array of local and state compliance boards, headed in South Carolina by NRA compliance director Lawrence M. Pinckney, assisted the code authorities. Lacking coercive powers, compliance boards often felt their efforts were wasted because manufacturers ignored their rulings. Not surprisingly, within six months Pinckney was complaining to Washington that many local compliance boards had simply "ceased to function."[48] The state code authorities were no more successful. Not only were two of the three members of one industry code authority charged with code violations, but members of code authorities often were not familiar enough with their own codes to know when violations occurred. From a survey of Spartanburg businesses in March 1935, Pinckney determined that 70 percent of employers were openly violating their codes. He also discovered that some local code authorities were advising members of their industry "not to pay any attention to the codes, but to go ahead and operate as they see fit."[49] No doubt, many of these were fertilizer plants, cottonseed oil mills, and tobacco manufacturers who traditionally hired unskilled black laborers and balked at paying them code wages.

Not all businessmen even chose to sign a code. Thomas Waring, editor of the *Charleston Evening Post,* was afraid that code setting for his industry was merely the first step toward control and censorship of the press by the federal government. Not only did he regard preservation of freedom of the press as a "duty [publishers] owe to the public . . . whose interests they are deeply obligated to serve," but he also professed to see a burgeoning "autocracy" in the NRA. Waring's fears were not unfounded. Because the goverment could influence the content of a newspaper code, it had the capacity to muzzle radical journalists, whose operations were usually hand to mouth, by threatening to mandate high wages and impose expensive building requirements for newspaper offices and plants. Likewise, it could influence the message of conservative journalists by imposing restrictions on advertising. Therefore, Waring pleaded with his fellow newspapermen not to draw up even a voluntary code. When they disregarded his wishes, he refused to sign, although he did obey the code requirement of a forty-hour workweek and $13 minimum weekly wage. Waring understood correctly that attorneys for the NRA were so concerned about possible contravention of the First Amendment guarantee of freedom of the press that they would not take legal action against publishers such as he.[50]

Clearly, industrial cooperation among government, management, and labor under the NRA was not bringing industrial harmony to South Carolina. Employers felt threatened; workers felt cheated; worse was to come.

ABOVE: A pilgrimage to Columbia by four thousand African Americans in the SCERA-sponsored adult education program, April 1935. Courtesy, South Caroliniana Library, University of South Carolina.

Exterior of the reconstructed Dock Street Theater in Charleston. Courtesy, South Carolina State Museum, Columbia.

ABOVE: A presentation of *The Recruiting Officer* by the Footlight Players at the Dock Street Theater in November 1937. Courtesy, South Carolina State Museum, Columbia.

First Sgt. Willie Sullivan, CCC Camp, Rodman, ca. 1939. One camper wrote that Sergeant Sullivan, who supervised work details, punished campers with extra work when they missed adult education classes. "We like him notwithstanding," the formerly illiterate camper wrote. Wil Lou Gray Papers. Courtesy, South Caroliniana Library, University of South Carolina.

Camp buildings, CCC Camp, Rodman, ca. 1939. Courtesy, South Caroliniana Library, University of South Carolina.

Adult education class, CCC Camp, Rodman, ca. 1939. Courtesy, South Caroliniana Library, University of South Carolina.

July 1936 issue of *South Carolina Newsview,* featuring the work of local WPA artist Corrie Parker McCallum. Courtesy, South Carolina State Museum, Columbia.

Artist Laura Glenn Douglas of Winnsboro displays her Federal Art Project (WPA) paintings. Courtesy, South Carolina State Museum, Columbia, and Isabelle T. Morrison, Washington, D.C.

Mural by Stefan Hirsch, "Justice As Protector and Avenger." Federal Courthouse, Aiken. Courtesy, South Carolina State Museum, Columbia.

Mural by Alice R. Kindler, "American Landscape." Ware Shoals Post Office. Courtesy, South Carolina State Museum, Columbia.

Buzzard Roost. TOP: Excavations underway for the construction of the spillway, June 1938. BOTTOM: Site of dam with initial excavation, August 1938. Courtesy, South Caroliniana Library, University of South Carolina.

Buzzard Roost. TOP: Construction of the dam and power plant, April 1939.
BOTTOM: Excavation for the levee, January 1940. Courtesy, South Caroliniana
Library, University of South Carolina.

Buzzard Roost. TOP: Relocation of a railroad bridge, February 1940.
BOTTOM: Levee completed; lake filling, July 1940. Courtesy, South Caroliniana
Library, University of South Carolina.

Buzzard Roost. TOP: Aerial view of dam and power plant. BOTTOM: Aerial view of lake with dam in foreground. Courtesy, South Caroliniana Library, University of South Carolina.

Graniteville Manufacturing Company, Warren Division, Warrenville. Courtesy, South Caroliniana Library, University of South Carolina.

Mill village, Graniteville Manufacturing Company. Courtesy, South Caroliniana Library, University of South Carolina.

Community gardens for workers at Joanna Cotton Mills in Goldville, ca. 1934.
Courtesy, South Caroliniana Library, University of South Carolina.

White House reception for Troop 75 (Boy Scouts of America) from the mill village at Goldville, ca. 1932. Note Pres. Herbert Hoover in the center of the group. Courtesy, South Caroliniana Library, University of South Carolina.

The Orr Rifles (men's baseball team) from Orr Cotton Mills, Anderson, ca. 1932. Courtesy, Lowenstein Corporation Records, Special Collections, Clemson University Libraries, Clemson, S.C.

Girls' basketball team from Orr Cotton Mills, Anderson, ca. 1932. Courtesy, Lowenstein Corporation Records, Special Collections, Clemson University Libraries, Clemson, S.C.

Until outlawed by the NRA, the employment of children in cotton mills such as this one at Newberry was not uncommon. Courtesy, South Carolina State Museum, Columbia.

Union parade at Saxon Mills, ca. 1935. Courtesy, South Caroliniana Library, University of South Carolina.

THE GENERAL TEXTILE STRIKE OF 1934 AND ITS AFTERMATH | 7

The halcyon days of the previous summer gave way to disenchantment in the winter and spring of 1934. In February, UTW vice president John Peel complained to Byrnes that he was "sick and tired" of touting the NRA's concern for textile workers, "only to learn that [textile workers] have no rights whatever, and that the same methods and practices of the past still prevail."[1] In April, at the gathering of labor representatives in Greenville to create the South Carolina Federation of Textile Workers (SCFTW), international UTW president Thomas F. McMahon acknowledged that manufacturers throughout the state were guilty of Section 7(a) violations. "We have a ten-inch sheaf of cases in this state alone," he charged.[2] A month later, the SCFTW held its first annual convention in Columbia. Two thousand delegates assembled to hear the invited speaker, H. H. Willis, declare his board's diligence in trying to settle labor-management disputes impartially. After several angry delegates disputed this assertion, the convention adopted a resolution demanding removal of Willis and Bruere from their respective boards and replacement by "fair and impartial" men.[3]

Textile executives in South Carolina were also disenchanted. In the January 1934 issue of *Manufacturers Record,* Thomas M. Marchant lamented the "shortage of profitable orders" in the textile industry. Apparently, the New Deal was doing little to bring prosperity. The price of goods increased as soon as Code Number One took effect, but the slowness of the NRA to get other industries under codes meant consumers did not have additional income to meet the rise in textile prices. In addition, Marchant criticized the AAA cotton processing tax, which manufacturers had to absorb and which exceeded the combined sum of existing taxes.[4] In his presidential address to the American Cotton Manufacturers Association in Charleston, Marchant also pointed to the erosion in manufacturer confidence caused by pending New Deal legislation such as the Wagner Bill.[5]

These same business leaders blamed the New Deal for the rise of organized labor. With costs fluctuating and purchasers scarce, they wanted a free hand to keep labor costs as low as possible. They complained that collective bargaining threatened to transform the cost of labor from a variable factor into a fixed one. Collective bargaining also flew in the face of fifty years of tradition that let manufacturers operate their plants as they pleased. Even though the NRA never compelled South Carolina mill owners to honor the code requirement of collective bargaining, which was one reason they did not openly desert the industrial recovery program, the mere presence of organized labor in strength was irritating.[6]

Another reason manufacturers continued to support the New Deal was the ability of the code authority to recommend restrictions in production to balance orders with inventories. Because the textile economy slumped in the fall of 1933, the NRA sanctioned a 25-percent curtailment of production for December. During the winter and spring of 1934, orders were few and inventories still large. On May 22 the code authority recommended and the NRA sanctioned another 25-percent curtailment to last for ninety days.[7]

During the first curtailment higher code wages since July averted worker unrest. By May 1934, however, conditions had changed. Provoked since 1933 by the manner of code enforcement, inept handling of disputes, and frequency of code violations, labor was also suffering a decline in real earnings because of inflation. Moreover, a familiar pattern in labor-management relations was emerging: manufacturers responded to reduced profits by instituting the stretch-out; workers countered by unionizing; management discharged union members on grounds of incompetence; workers then struck; management employed strikebreakers who were met with acts of violence; and the end result was more violence, intimidation, evictions, and blacklisting of strikers.[8] To no one's surprise, when Thomas McMahon of the UTW threatened to call a national textile strike to accompany the curtailment in the spring of 1934, J. A. Frier, president of the South Carolina Federation of Textile Workers, stated publicly that labor would follow McMahon "100 per cent."[9]

Even so, the cutback came on June 4 as scheduled and without incident. Most mills achieved the thirty-hour week by operating eight hours a day Monday through Wednesday and then six hours on Thursday. As the summer wore on, labor began to suffer a string of defeats. When the spring curtailment took effect, more than 2,000 workers were striking Belton Mills, Piedmont Manufacturing Company owned by CMASC president Samuel Beattie, and Victor-Monaghan Mills owned by Thomas

Marchant of the code authority. Labor's losses began on June 20 when union men lost a battle of rocks and picker sticks to nonunion men in an attempt to close the Orr Cotton Mills of Anderson. Then on July 16 the Piedmont Manufacturing Company reopened with the aid of strike-breakers. Governor Blackwood sent troops to protect them, despite complaints from labor leaders. Shortly thereafter, Marchant announced that Victor-Monaghan would reopen on July 23 on his terms. Finally, when the Willis Board decided a case at Cowpens Mill in favor of the union, the mill responded by discharging all of the officers and many of the members of the UTW local. The mill thumbed its nose at attempts by the Willis Board to have the men reinstated. By midsummer 1934 textile workers in South Carolina were spoiling for a fight.[10] Their respect for and faith in the compliance boards had nearly disappeared.

In July 1934 the SCFTW held its quarterly convention in Spartanburg and pledged total support to McMahon "should [he] feel it necessary to call a general strike."[11] In mid-August, at the UTW annual convention in New York, delegates from South Carolina helped generate a groundswell for action. J. A. Frier of Columbia stirred the gathering with lurid descriptions of stretch-out abuses, the major grievance in his state.[12] He was tired of the national union ignoring the stretch-out in favor of cooperation with the NRA. By an overwhelming margin the convention voted a nationwide strike to begin September 1. The announced goals were higher wages for restricted hours of production, union recognition, elimination of the stretch-out, and rehiring of fired union workers.[13] The unstated goal was to force the government to choose "between upholding the grievances of the workers or maintaining the power of the cotton textile industry."[14]

The UTW set up a strike council of ten men, including C. W. McAbee of Spartanburg, vice president of the SCFTW. It divided the East into four regions with John Peel of Greenville as regional director for the Deep South. On his return to Columbia, SCFTW president Frier advised workers throughout the state to conduct an orderly walkout on September 1, post responsible pickets, and refrain from any disturbance that could justify the use of troops.[15] On September 1 the UTW telegraphed Governor Blackwood that the strike, resulting from "abuses no longer bearable," would begin at 11:30 P.M.[16]

Because September 1 was a Saturday and September 3 Labor Day, the strike would not become effective until September 4. Yet, several mills that refused to close on Labor Day were struck on September 3.

More than 2,200 strikers closed the five Columbia mills and staged a parade down Main Street in New Brookland (later West Columbia). They carried signs reading "New Deal" and "Roosevelt Our Greatest Leader." These placards advertised worker support for the New Deal, implied that workers were loyal and manufacturers were disloyal to it, and affirmed workers' faith in the good will of the NRA to compel management to obey the code. Pickets were also posted at Dunean Mills and Victor Mills in Greenville County and at Pacific Mills in Spartanburg County. Governor Blackwood sent National Guard units to these three mills at once "as a precautionary measure against possible violence."[17]

Blackwood's action posed an obstacle that strike leaders knew they would have to confront: a state law enforcement structure designed to protect the mill owner. To maintain order during an industrial disturbance, the governor could deploy National Guardsmen, highway patrolmen, and constables. The constabulary was the investigative arm of the executive, in which the governor could commission "constables without compensation" for temporary duty. Mill owners paid their salaries and reimbursed the state for any ammunition and equipment used. Constables took their orders from mill owners.[18] Blackwood further aided manufacturers by placing the National Guard under the direction of the county sheriff, who was often a friend of management.[19] Finally, at mill expense, the sheriff could deputize as many special deputies as necessary.[20]

On September 4 the second largest strike in American history to that point began in earnest. The Associated Press estimated there were 27,000 strikers in South Carolina; J. A. Frier said the number was 46,000. Labor developed a new weapon called the flying squadron. As many as 1,000 strikers would form a gigantic motorcade and descend on mills that remained open. One of these closed Victor Mills and Franklin Mills at Greer and then Appalache Mill at Spartanburg. Blackwood answered with troops and constables.[21] Meanwhile, President Roosevelt telephoned Senator Byrnes for information on conditions in South Carolina. The senator, who sympathized with the strikers, believed the stretch-out and discrimination against union labor were widespread. Byrnes made three recommendations: (1) abolish the boards, (2) empower U.S. attorneys, in addition to the attorney general, to bring suits against manufacturers who discriminated against union members, and (3) use federal power to mediate the strike in order to avoid prolonged conflict.[22]

On September 5 the president set up the Board of Inquiry under New Hampshire governor John G. Winant to investigate causes of the strike and recommend solutions. The strike continued because Roosevelt declined to mediate. One flying squadron of 625 men in 105 cars and 3 trucks struck Greenville, where they confronted more than 400 National Guardsmen who had been ordered to "shoot to kill." Luckily, the confrontation was peaceful. Most of the members of the flying squadron were from Spartanburg County, where 13,000 of the county's 14,000 textile workers closed 26 of the county's 30 mills. Another flying squadron of 100 men from Columbia closed the three mills in Lexington County. A third squadron struck Chester, where Elliott Springs closed two of his mills, neutralized the squadron by allowing it to use a company field for a rally, and then telephoned Blackwood for troop protection. By the end of the second day, approximately one-half of 80,000 textile workers in South Carolina were on strike. Twenty-one National Guard units confronted them.[23]

On the third day management's control of law enforcement collided with the militant tactics of the flying squadrons and created a tragedy of unprecedented proportions. Dan Beacham, mayor of Honea Path in Anderson County and owner of Chiquola Mills, swore in 130 special deputies to protect the mill and loyal workers. Beacham was described by Greenville labor lawyer H. P. Burbage as "one of those sanctimonious sons-of-bitches that carries a Bible under one arm and shoots a forty-five at people who demand their rights" with the other.[24] When a flying squadron descended on Honea Path to aid pickets at Chiquola, several of Beacham's deputies were armed and inside the mill. When pickets clashed with nonstrikers who were entering the mill, a fistfight broke out. The special deputies opened fire, leaving six strikers dead and fifteen seriously wounded, one of whom died two days later. Secretary of Labor Frances Perkins issued an immediate statement decrying the violence and labeling the practice of arming management "hazardous, to say the least."[25] Ten thousand people attended the funerals, where the Reverend James Myers of New York, industrial secretary of the Federal Council of Churches, called the slain men "instruments of Jesus Christ in His work of love." Pronouncing union membership "a test of Christian character," he exhorted workers everywhere to "hold up these fallen comrades as examples of Christian unselfishness."[26]

Meanwhile, on the same day of the Honea Path slayings, the flying squadrons began to meet limited success elsewhere. They were able to close one mill in the Springs chain but unable to close three others because of troop protection. Those mills remaining open resembled armed camps. At Ninety Six Cotton Mills in Greenwood County, National

Guard units mounted a machine gun on the roof, trained it on the strikers, and advised them that the governor's orders were "shoot to kill." A hundred special deputies with fire hoses kept the pickets at Ninety Six a distance of thirty feet from the mill fence. Apparently, few more mills would close. Remaining open were Greenville County plants employing more than 11,000 workers, most of the Springs chain (7,000 workers), at least half the mills in Anderson and Greenwood Counties (10,000), and all of the plants in Horse Creek Valley (3,500).[27]

On September 7 Governor Blackwood issued a proclamation demanding dispersion of groups engaged in "unlawful obstruction, combination, and assemblage." This declaration of martial law disbanded the flying squadrons, and the strikers settled down for a long siege. Those in Columbia staged a rally where a sympathetic Baptist minister based his sermon on the first stretch-out recorded in history—the Egyptian Pharaoh forcing the Hebrews to gather their own straw for bricks. The UTW suggested that Roosevelt authorize the Winant Board to mediate the strike, although Thomas Marchant of Greenville bluntly told Winant that the manufacturers planned to fight the strike to the end.[28] On September 9 J. A. Frier of the SCFTW vowed that "The automobiles will roll again next week" in defiance of the governor's proclamation, but John Peel overrode Frier's decision for fear of more bloodshed.[29]

As the second week of the strike dawned, nearly 400,000 textile workers were on strike nationwide, 43,000 of them in South Carolina. Blackwood had committed 43 of his 47 National Guard units, totaling nearly 2,000 men and officers. Frequent rallies boosted striker morale, and the strike held its own.[30] During the third week of September 17 to 21, it began to wilt. On September 17 three mills reopened, and the number of South Carolina strikers declined to approximately 37,000. Meanwhile, the Winant Board was completing its report, which was released on September 20. It recommended appointment of an impartial Textile Labor Relations Board (TLRB) to replace the Bruere and Willis Boards that would, in turn, create a Work Assignment Board to examine the stretch-out and investigate wages and hours to determine if manufacturers were obeying the code. Roosevelt then appealed to strikers to return to work and let implementation of the Winant Report settle the dispute. On September 22 the UTW claimed an "overwhelming victory" and called off the strike.[31]

Striking workers knew better. They had exhausted their stockpile of supplies; hunger was forcing them back into the mills. Because of overstocked inventories, mill owners could afford to operate indefinitely on a part-time basis with strikebreakers. In a public statement the day after the strike ended, W. P. Jacobs of Clinton, secretary-treasurer of the Cotton Manufacturers' Association of South Carolina, stated that most mills probably would not reopen before "determining the desires of the workers to return to their jobs."[32] In other words, a lockout would leave workers hungry enough to accept management's terms. Gradually, mills reopened, although James C. Self did not resume operations at Greenwood Mill until October 29 and Mathews Mill until December 10. Two and one-half months after the strike, the UTW charged that twenty-six mills in the South were refusing to rehire former strikers; fifteen of these were in South Carolina.[33]

Not only did the settlement result in a loss of jobs, but implementation of the Winant Report again left labor holding the bag. The investigation of wages and hours revealed that management was obeying the code, although the report admitted textile workers were the lowest paid in any industry. The three-man Work Assignment Board containing E. R. Stall of Greenville as management's representative concluded the stretch-out was the exception rather than the rule. The board suggested that setting workload standards would be unwise and recommended instead the creation of a permanent work assignment board to set workloads for individual mills. John Peel wrote the chairman of the Work Assignment Board, "If the manufacturers had been given the right to write the report they could not have made it more favorable to themselves."[34]

This "overwhelming victory"—in reality, a shattering defeat—cost the union movement dearly. Workers left the UTW, never to return. They chose, instead, to channel their energies into electing a friend of labor, Olin D. Johnston, governor of South Carolina. They had gambled on the national government and lost; it sided with mill owners. An observer noted at one local in Spartanburg, "Members just met, idled away their time as in a social club, and then drifted back to their homes."[35] A few other locals decided to maintain their national affiliation but look to their own interests first. In November 1934, for example, the president of local 679 in Columbia stated his members would give the UTW "full support" unless "national demands do not come up to what we wish."[36]

Nevertheless, the 1934 strike was not a complete debacle for labor. Its gain was abolition of the Bruere and Willis Boards with the appointment of a Textile Labor Relations Board (TLRB) empowered to settle industrial disputes and, unlike the earlier boards, to investigate complaints of Section 7(a) violations. Unfortunately, because the TLRB lacked power to enforce its decisions, labor once again grew disillusioned. For instance, the board's first business was to settle cases of alleged discrimination against workers stemming from the September strike. The board did not ask mills to hire strikers whose jobs had been taken by strikebreakers, but it did demand that mills not discriminate against strikers once additional jobs became available. Discrimination would be an NIRA violation. The Clinton Cotton Mills, in reopening after the strike, rehired all strikers except four officers of the UTW local. On December 7, 1934, the TLRB gave the mill one week to rehire the men before the TLRB would request that the NRA compliance division remove the mill's Blue Eagle. When the mill refused, it lost its Blue Eagle. Before the Justice Department was able to take legal action forcing compliance, the U.S. Supreme Court struck down the NRA in the *Schechter* decision.[37]

Three other disputes at mills owned by the Bank of Boston at Pelzer, Walter Montgomery at Spartanburg and Gaffney, and the Hamrick family in Cherokee County speak volumes about the effectiveness of TLRB mediation and the variety of factors that affected settlements. The five-month dispute at the Pelzer Manufacturing Company in 1935 had all of the elements of volatile confrontation: the presence of two armed camps made up of a tiny UTW local fighting to stay alive and a goodwill association determined to kill it, allegations of firings because of union membership, threats against a mill superintendent's life, a strike that idled one-third of the mill's 1650 workers despite the efforts of John Peel to avert action, evictions of strikers from company housing, invasions by strike sympathizers from other localities, strikebearers in abundance; local law enforcement that sided with management, numerous fistfights, several arrests on charges of assault and battery, a five-minute gun battle that consumed 500 rounds of ammunition and left one strike sympathizer dead and twenty-two other persons wounded, and intervention by a state governor sympathetic to labor.[38]

Despite minimal hope of success, TLRB mediators plunged in to end the matter harmoniously. Bad luck seemed to dog them. Their initial investigation of labor's charges ended inconclusively from simple lack of evidence, thus inviting labor's distrust. Their success in persuading the mill superintendent to submit the charge of discrimination to arbitration and refrain from evicting strikers evaporated when a striker threatened his life and convinced him to settle the dispute with a minimum of outside interference. Throughout the dispute management had the upper hand; there was never a dearth of local men willing to serve as strikebreakers. Oddly, despite or perhaps because of the casualties, the gun battle was actually a catharsis. TLRB mediator J. L. Bernard was able to arrange a conference between strikers and management that framed a settlement. It called for re-employment of strikers as work became available, an investigation of charges of violence with the understanding that strikers who engaged in such would not be rehired, and an investigation of the original charges of discrimination with the understanding that workers discharged because of union affiliation would be re-employed. Provision 3 of the settlement benefited labor, while provisions 1 and 2 benefited management.[39]

Here again bad luck dogged the TLRB. As so often happened, the aftermath of the settlement worked against the strikers. Within the next twelve months, the mill rehired fewer than forty of them to full-time positions. A few others were given part-time work. A larger number were deemed guilty of "acts of violence," denied employment, and promptly evicted from their houses. To union members, the divine always seemed to be in the TLRB decision, the devil in its implementation.[40] Once again they beheld a government siding with management.

The year 1936 witnessed a rash of small strikes. Two of these occurred in mills owned by Walter S. Montgomery of Spartanburg, by all accounts a reliable and responsible manufacturer. At Spartan Mills, Montgomery rehired all 900 workers after the September 1934 strike without discrimination against union members. In November 1934 he discharged two members for organizing a short-lived strike, although the local union, as well as the SCFTW, refused to support them because their loose talk and aggressive actions alienated other workers. So highly was Montgomery regarded by employees that the local union president informed a TLRB mediator, "Any statement made by Mr. Montgomery could be absolutely relied upon."[41]

Labor-management relations were less harmonious at Montgomery's Gaffney Manufacturing Company. In December 1934 the shop committee charged him with violating Section 7(a) by refusing to negotiate with them. TLRB mediator J. L. Bernard found that Montgomery disliked the personnel on the shop committee because he believed they broke faith with him in the September 1934 strike. Bernard worked out a compromise whereby a worker could complain to Montgomery via a three-man committee from the worker's department and thus circumvent the shop committee.[42] Then in April 1936 workers at Gaffney struck because of a stretch-out of spinners. Montgomery promised the new workload would be temporary; he also offered to furnish as many helpers as each spinner needed to tend the extra sides. The spinners, however, feared the new situation would be permanent, and the strike continued. Montgomery then agreed to a compromise on the stretch-out by paying for a time study to set each worker's machine load, although he rejected the union demand of outside arbitration of grievances he and his workers were unable to settle.

A month later workers at Spartan Mills struck because Montgomery allegedly transferred orders to that plant from Gaffney. He broke off negotiations at Gaffney long enough to crush the Spartan strike. TLRB mediators persuaded Montgomery to re-employ all but 33 of the 925 Spartan workers. He also agreed to drop riot charges against the 33 and help them find work elsewhere.[43]

Having settled the Spartan strike, the mediators persuaded Montgomery to let them intervene at Gaffney. The only impediment to settlement was Montgomery's refusal to re-employ a striker who directed the beating of an overseer. TLRB mediators prevailed upon Lawrence Pinckney of the WPA to employ the striker on a local WPA project; the union local voted to remove the man from the union shop committee; and Montgomery and the local then agreed to a settlement. Montgomery re-employed all of the strikers, and the TLRB established a suitable workload for each worker. When the subsequent time study revealed that Montgomery had overloaded spinners, he agreed to hire spare hands to clean the sides, a task that normally consumed 35 percent of a spinner's workday. This episode illustrated the likelihood of TLRB success when labor and management cooperated.[44]

Similarly, lack of cooperation yielded negative results. In the mills of the Hamrick chain, according to preliminary TLRB reports, Production Manager Lyman Hamrick was "not consistent in his decisions effecting disciplinary infractions" and seemed "to have gathered around him a number of low grade overseers," some of whom were accused of "heavy drinking, wife beating, and immoral conduct."[45] The 2,225 workers seemed to have little respect for top management and even less for their overseers. The Hamricks, in turn, blamed outside interference for their lack of profitability. Equally critical of the American Cotton Manufacturers' Association, Cotton Textile Institute, and NRA, they were determined to operate "as they see fit" and close the mills in the face of a strike rather than "submit to operations on any set of rules by any outside source."[46] This was a recipe for ugly confrontation and TLRB failure.

In May 1935 the TLRB began investigating the Hamrick chain for alleged discharges of union men who refused to comply with a stretch-out. In August, Alma Mills in the chain increased weekly hours to fifty-five, the maximum allowed under state law. Walter Montgomery, chairman of the print cloth group of cotton manufacturers, wanted all mills to continue the forty-hour requirement in the defunct NRA code, despite the recent *Schechter* decision. He and TLRB mediators George Kamenow and Yates Haefner pleaded with the Hamricks but to no avail. Finally, they at least were able to coax owner Waite Hamrick to adjust pay upwards for the additional hours. The workers, in turn, agreed to the increase in hours with the stipulation that it be temporary. Then, because an overseer forced a spinner to hire a helper at her own expense, workers at Hamrick Mills in the chain voted to strike. Governor Johnston persuaded the workers to postpone the action pending further TLRB investigation.[47]

Meanwhile, mediator George Kamenow worked through state UTW leaders to remove a major obstacle to settlement. In late November members of the four UTW locals in Cherokee County were scheduled to elect a president of the Cherokee County Textile Council. Pres. S. O. Neal, who was seeking reelection, led the strike faction; his opponent, J. H. Palmer, the antistrike faction. Neal reportedly was fomenting hatred against the Hamricks as a means of securing reelection. Kamenow convinced John Peel and state textile organizer Gordon L. Chastain to use their influence to elect Taylor Best instead of either Neal or Palmer, thus removing the strike as an issue in union politics. Kamenow also persuaded Lyman Hamrick to decrease the workweek to forty hours unless the workers voluntarily requested overtime.[48]

Harmony prevailed for two months until 400 of the 425 workers at Alma Mills struck because of a stretch-out in the weave room. Waite Hamrick admitted he made "a few minor changes" in the weave room "to the extent that we can operate on a 'live and let live' basis."[49] Kamenow tried to convince workers to postpone action, but he found them "so prejudiced against the Hamricks for what they consider inhuman treatment that nothing I could do or say could defer the strike action." Kamenow called on Waite Hamrick, who insisted he "would handle matters his own way."[50] Waite Hamrick then departed for a vacation in Florida.

After waiting a month to let passions cool, Kamenow brought Lyman Hamrick and the union shop committee together. Their discussions yielded a settlement under which the workload for weavers favored the mill while the grievance procedure favored the workers. To Kamenow's dismay the union rejected the proposal; Kamenow believed the schedule at Alma was actually less than at neighboring mills. The Hamricks then attempted to reopen Alma. Only five workers reported for work and the mill closed again. Next the Hamricks resorted to strikebreakers from Atlanta, who tried to pass the pickets by posing first as federal agents and then as special deputies sent by the governor. A telephone call from union members to Governor Johnston brought genuine special deputies who ushered the strikebreakers out of Gaffney.[51] Meanwhile, workers at two other mills in the chain struck in sympathy with strikers at Alma. Finally, after the Hamricks insisted on reaching a temporary cease-fire with striking workers without TLRB mediation, Kamenow and Harding simply gave up and reported ruefully to Washington, "Trouble here is not settled but postponed for the time being," an observation that would prove accurate.[52]

The disputes at Pelzer, Spartanburg, and Gaffney offer a glimpse at the variables affecting TLRB effectiveness. Where workers were cooperative, both with management and with the TLRB, mediation was successful. Where workers were uncooperative or where internal union politics were complicated, as in the Hamrick chain, the TLRB failed. The presence of goodwill associations, whether company unions or not, made effective TLRB mediation impossible. Mediators were successful in profitable mills such as the Gaffney Manufacturing Company, but unsuccessful in marginal ones such as those in the Hamrick chain. Finally, and most important, the TLRB succeeded at mills of cooperative owners such as Walter Montgomery but failed at mills owned by men who distrusted outside interference and mediation.

When the *Schechter* decision struck down NRA codes in May 1935, South Carolina textile manufacturers reacted with mixed emotions. Although happy to be free of government-sanctioned collective bargaining, they were reluctant to part with wage-and-hour regulations. For years they had tried voluntarily to restrict production in order to alleviate cutthroat competition; *Schechter* opened the door for a return to unrestrained competition and overproduction. Also, if manufacturers deserted code wages and hours, workers would flock to the UTW for protection. Consequently, on June 7, 1935, the American Cotton Manufacturers

Association met in special session in Charlotte and called on members to continue the wage-and-hour provisions of the code. The association also set up its own Southwide committee to pressure defectors. W. P. Jacobs of Clinton was committeeman for South Carolina. A month later the Cotton Manufacturers Association of South Carolina vowed to support code wages and hours "100 percent."

Apparently, the return of prosperity to the textile industry in the last half of 1935, coupled with mill-owner fear of unrestrained competition and unionism, had a salutary effect. By November 1936, a year and a half after *Schechter,* 193 of the 220 textile mills in South Carolina continued the forty-hour workweek, while 210 of the 220 paid code wages. In fact, 105 of the 220 plants paid wages from 5 to 10 percent above code requirements. As late as 1938, when Congress passed the Fair Labor Standards Act setting a minimum wage and maximum hours, the 90,000 textile workers in South Carolina averaged 15 cents above the minimum and already worked a forty-hour workweek by state law. Thus, wages and hours was not an issue with textile workers after *Schechter.*[53]

Collective bargaining was an issue. Therefore, in June 1935 Congress enacted the National Labor Relations Act to restore the right to unionize. A National Labor Relations Board (NLRB), upon petition from workers, was empowered to order an election to determine the workers' bargaining agent. The act also outlawed unfair labor practices such as restraining workers from joining unions, fostering company unions, discriminating against workers who filed complaints, and refusing to bargain with a union. Until April 1937, when the Supreme Court upheld the act in *National Labor Relations Board v. Jones and Laughlin Steel Corporation,* the NLRB operated in limbo, since few expected the court to uphold the act. Mill owners simply allowed elections ordered by the NLRB and then refused to bargain until the new union local filed a complaint. When faced with an NLRB cease and desist order, the mill owner secured an injunction against further NLRB action and allowed the government to pick and choose which suits it planned to carry to the Supreme Court as test cases. Labor, in turn, was reluctant to use the NLRB until the Supreme Court acted.[54]

This reluctance, coupled with the weakness of organized labor in South Carolina as a result of the 1934 strike, accounted for only two NLRB cases before 1937. The first involved Clinton Cotton Mills, which openly refused to negotiate with a union local and discharged its members from employment after signing a closed-shop agreement with the

Clinton Friendship Association, a company union. Defendant in the second case, Wallace Manufacturing Company of Jonesville, followed a similar pattern of unfair labor practices. The NLRB ruled in favor of labor in both instances, and the mills finally complied after the *Jones and Laughlin* decision.[55]

Nineteen thirty seven was a watershed in labor-management relations not only because of the *Jones and Laughlin* decision. Organized labor also became more assertive as the AFL-CIO rupture signaled the beginning of a new campaign to unionize Palmetto textile workers.[56] The CIO-affiliated Textile Workers Organizing Committee (TWOC) opened its drive under state TWOC director Paul R. Christopher. He divided the state into four districts supervised by six individuals: Greenville (Elizabeth Hawes), Horse Creek Valley (Furman Garrett), Cherokee (H. K. Hammett and Charles Puckett), and Columbia (Ralph Simmerson and Owen Brewster). The TWOC followed a policy of not requiring dues from a local union until after the union won a contract. Workers first signed cards empowering the TWOC to bargain for them, followed by a request for an NLRB election to choose their bargaining agent. Then came collective bargaining, a contract, and certification of the local with a requirement of monthly dues of 50 cents per member.[57]

With this inducement, TWOC began its campaign at a rally in Columbia on April 17, 1937. There, organizer Elizabeth Hawes called John L. Lewis "the Moses to lead you out of the wilderness."[58] Two days earlier, 95 percent of the 1,100 workers at Marlboro Mills in Bennettsville signed TWOC pledge cards. On April 23 the mill recognized the TWOC as the workers' bargaining agent, making Marlboro the first mill in the South to do so. Contract negotiations began at once, and after a short-lived strike the union and management came to terms. [59]

This initial flurry of success was deceiving. By the time of Pearl Harbor, TWOC campaigns to organize the Palmetto State had failed utterly. Eight months into the drive, the TWOC could boast only one local and one contract, both at Marlboro Mills. Another year passed before the union was listed as bargaining agent for 8,000 workers in 13 mills, leaving 82,000 workers in 223 mills unrepresented. Moreover, terms of subsequent contracts were paltry. The contract with Pacific Mills in Columbia contained a 12½-percent hourly wage *decrease;* the one with Columbia Duck Mills, a 10-percent wage *decrease.*[60]

Reasons for TWOC failure are not hard to find. Among the least important factors were worker individualism and deference to management, continuing internecine warfare between AFL and CIO affiliates, and faltering economic conditions in 1937–1938 that rendered textile employment precarious. Major factors were racism, the inability of the AFL and later the TWOC to appreciate the depth of worker concern over the stretch-out, traditional affection for homegrown unions and hostility to nationals, the inability of state TWOC leaders to win other constituencies to their cause, the legacy of the disastrous General Textile Strike of 1934, and hostility from manufacturers. The first factor, racism, was paramount. Criticism of enlightened TWOC racial policies forced supporters to defend with metaphors and arguments that were seldom convincing to workers. The *Una News Review,* for example, tried unsuccessfully to defend TWOC biracial unionism by using anatomy for illustration: white and black labor should be as separate as "fingers on a hand": but in dealings with management, "a clinched fist."[61] Calling the hubbub over racial equality "irrelevant" because "Wade Hampton's red shirts settled that question satisfactorily many years ago," a TWOC newspaper advertisement professed to believe "the enemies of labor have a negro in the woodpile and know a vote for the TWOC will bring him out." To the organizer who placed the advertisement, the issue was simple: "We didn't bring the negroes . . . into this country, we don't employ them, we don't pay them, we don't sleep with them, so why should we get excited about them."[62] Unfortunately for the TWOC, a number of textile workers did get sufficiently "excited about them" to avoid union membership.[63]

In addition, textile workers in South Carolina had a history of grievance expression by means of homegrown unions that even governors, manufacturers, and the general public respected. The formation of unions by outsiders was another matter. Foreign (i.e., Northern) names such as Gorman, McMahon, and Hillman did not resonate melodiously. Therefore, Governor Blackwood felt free to use the weight of his office to help break the General Textile Strike of 1934. Moreover, South Carolina in the 1930s was a land of powerful constituencies, a combination of which was necessary to effect change. Among these were the county-seat elite, planter aristocrats, editors, Baptist and Methodist denominations, influential Democratic politicians, lowcountry, upcountry, Charleston, textile manufacturers, small farmers, bourgeoisie, and textile workers. Prohibition, for example, was adopted because influential politicians, mill owners, preachers, women, and the press coalesced behind it. Similarly, organized labor lost the 1934 strike because all of the constituencies except textile workers were either hostile or neutral toward job actions that were perceived to be directed by outsiders. In short, the failure of other constituencies to come to labor's side, plus the partiality of the federal government toward textile manufacturers during and after the strike, quickly convinced workers of their powerlessness so long as they flirted with national unions organized by the proverbial outside agitators. Thus, they avoided TWOC affiliation.

Perhaps most crucial was mill-owner opposition. In this highly competitive industry, manufacturers were determined to control labor costs. Carl Gibbs, a former textile worker and UTW member in Spartanburg County, remembers that manufacturers found myriad ways around the National Labor Relations Act. "If you mentioned the word 'union,'" he recalls, "you lost your job." Manufacturers simply fired the worker for incompetence after finding his work unsatisfactory, or eliminated his position by reorganizing his department.[64] In some localities union busting was more blatant. In Anderson County, when union leaders begged protection from the local sheriff for a TWOC organizer threatened by company thugs, the sheriff simply responded that the National Labor Relations Act "did not affect Anderson."[65] Moreover, manufacturers always had a large pool of available labor to replace workers discharged for union activity.

The Hamrick chain seemed to be in the vanguard of this antiunion effort. Indeed, Gaffney came to be known in labor circles as "the roughest place this side of Harlan County [, Kentucky]."[66] As a result of unsuccessful strikes at Alma, Limestone, and mills in the Hamrick chain, UTW locals in Gaffney became inactive. In late 1937 the TWOC moved into Gaffney and, according to testimony before the NLRB, the Hamricks moved against them. Top management allegedly met with five mill supervisors to encourage both the formation of company unions and destruction of the TWOC. This task was to be accomplished peacefully, if possible, but otherwise if necessary.[67]

Shortly thereafter, workers formed the Square Deal Club at Alma, the Free Fellowship Club at Limestone, and the Good Fellowship Club at Hamrick. Management aided these company unions with funds and the use of mill property for meetings. When union evangelist Dr. Witherspoon Dodge visited Gaffney in May to address a TWOC gathering, about forty members of the Square Deal Club, armed with hose pipes and rocks, broke up the gathering and physically assaulted one of Dodge's companions. He complained to two policemen standing nearby who claimed they "never seed what happened." The company unions then forced members of the TWOC to sign cards revoking the authority of the TWOC to bargain for them. In late May the Hamricks closed the mills and reportedly denied TWOC members credit at the company store until they joined company unions.[68]

In June the Hamricks allegedly sponsored a religious revival where preachers stressed that CIO meant "Christ Is Out." Management warned that TWOC promises were the "evil tongue" spoken of in the Bible. One of the evangelists, appropriately named Paul, was described by C. W. Whittemore, the NLRB trial examiner, as "a loose-lipped moronic youth" who earned only $10 a week as a laborer in the Hamrick chain but who "thanked God and Mr. Hamrick for that much" and was confident "that neither he nor his fellow workers deserved more." A millennialist, Preacher Paul "led religion-drunk 'prayer bands' from one company house to another," warning that the millennium was fast approaching. For evidence he pointed to the book of Revelation, which associated the end times with the appearance of chariots, devils rising from the sea, and a "mark of the beast" on people's foreheads. "The devil," Preacher Paul told Whittemore, was "John L. Lewis." The "mark of the beast" was communism. What about the chariots, Whittemore asked? "Automobiles," Preacher Paul answered. To Whittemore's bemused observation that automobiles had been present for forty years, Preacher Paul shot back, "A thousand years are but a day in the sight of the Lord."[69] Considering the tendency of many Southerners then to accept biblical literalism, Preacher Paul's message no doubt resonated throughout the mill community.

Meanwhile, supervisors continued to warn union members that attendance at TWOC functions would bring immediate discharge from the mills. When the mills reopened in July, most union members discovered their jobs no longer existed. At Limestone about fifty members of the company union blocked TWOC men from entering the plant. Overseer White, when asked by men in the company union if they should bar TWOC members from the mill, allegedly replied, "You are yellow sons-of-bitches if you don't hold them out." Mill policemen reportedly arrested union members on trumped-up charges, which provided the Hamricks with grounds for dismissal.[70]

In December 1938 an NLRB trial examiner heard the case in Gaffney. The mill filed exception to his report of April 1939, and the NLRB ordered new hearings for December. "It is heart-rending," trial examiner Whittemore wrote, "to see one witness after another" take the witness stand, "start to tell his story," catch Hamrick's glance, "and then stutter his or her answers until courage returns."[71] In May 1940 the NLRB issued a cease and desist order based on the trial examiner's report; the board also ordered the Hamricks to reinstate those workers discharged for TWOC affiliation. Unfortunately for the TWOC, the victory was a hollow one; the TWOC was not able to establish strong locals in the Hamrick chain.

By 1939 South Carolina textile manufacturers were convinced the New Deal had brought too much reform and too little recovery. The NIRA was able to reduce overproduction, which did contribute to a temporary and modest improvement in profits. Yet, with the exception of mid-1933 and the period from mid-1935 to mid-1937, the industry continued to encounter hard times. In the summer of 1933, before the textile code and the processing tax took effect, garment manufacturers, anticipating a rise in prices, bought heavily. Orders continued into the autumn but then diminished. Periodic curtailment of textile production sanctioned by the NRA depleted inventories but did nothing to stimulate orders.

Then in mid-1935, without help from the New Deal, the textile economy rebounded and orders increased. The Supreme Court's invalidation of the cotton processing tax in the *Butler* decision of January 1936 further increased profits by reducing costs, as did action by the federal government to lessen the impact of competition from the Japanese. In particular, under pressure from Senator Byrnes in May 1936, the president increased tariffs on Japanese textiles.[72] The Cotton Manufacturers Association of South Carolina labeled this action "one of the most constructive steps taken by the Federal Government" during the New Deal.[73] Manufacturers had good reasons to rejoice. Of sixteen representative textile mills in South Carolina, only three were paying dividends in 1933, while the stocks of six were not even being quoted. By August 11, 1936, the stocks of ten were unavailable for purchase, all sixteen were paying dividends, and the average per-share value had increased from $36.50 in 1933 to $85 in 1936. Total dividends for the sixteen mills rose from $226,000 for the year ending February 1933 to $1.4 million for the year ending August 1936. In fact, the demand for textiles was so great during the last half of 1936 that some South Carolina mills had to refuse orders.[74]

Then came the recession of 1937. Demand fell off, and by December one labor leader reported that one-fourth of the state's textile workers were idle, while the other three-fourths were only working part time. By April 1938 more than two-thirds of the mills were operating only six to twelve days a month. Several employing more than 10,000 workers were closed indefinitely. The recession ended in the summer of 1938, but the industry continued to experience hard times. Not until the war years would cotton manufacturing in South Carolina prosper as it had before the mid-1920s.[75]

Although war cured many of the ills plaguing the cotton mill owner, the New Deal was at least a palliative for his workers. NRA codes, the National Labor Relations Act, and the Fair Labor Standards Act brought a minimum wage, a forty-hour workweek, the abolition of child labor, and a guarantee of collective bargaining. Only the latter would prove to be a hollow gain. By 1980 only 6.7 percent of the labor force was unionized, the second smallest percentage in the nation. Clearly, the New Deal was a dawn, not a noon, of a new day for organized labor in South Carolina.[76]

AGRICULTURE | 8

One winter's day in January 1936, two farmers who met on the streets of Columbia began to complain about life on the farm. "I know there's money in farming," joked the first, "because I started when I was just a boy putting it in there."

"Yes," replied the second farmer, "and you never knew how to take any of it back until Franklin D. Roosevelt came along and showed you how."[1]

Both men enjoyed a rise in the price of agricultural commodities under the New Deal. Both remembered well when cotton prices plunged from 37.93 cents per pound in 1919 to 16.62 cents in 1920 to 6 cents in early January 1933, if a buyer could be found. At that time agricultural conditions were so harsh a cotton farmer needed an additional 7.2 cents per pound to enjoy the same purchasing power he had known in the 1909–1914 period. More pathetically, annual gross farm income in the cotton belt declined 71 percent from $735 per family in 1928–1929 to $216 in 1932–1933.

Although manufacturing employed about half as many people in South Carolina as farming in 1932, the value of manufactured products was three times greater ($195 million versus $63 million). In addition, gross farm income before expenses totaled $46 million, while industrial wages alone amounted to almost that much. The low paid, poorly nourished, and stretched-out industrial worker was well off, indeed, compared to the farmer.[2] King Cotton in the fields was not only sick, he was nearly dead.

Several historic factors combined to depress farm income in the Palmetto State. Farmland there was not as fertile as farmland in other states. On a descending land-grading scale of from one to five developed by the USDA, South Carolina had no grade one farmland, little grade two, and an abundance of less fertile land in grades three through five. Loose soil, a high annual rainfall on sloping land that allowed rapid water runoff, an absence of frozen land in warm winters to prevent soil leaching, and an abundance of row crops with a dearth of broadcast crops such as legumes, all contributed to erosion and infertile soil. Consequently, South Carolina farmers bought more fertilizer per capita than farmers in any state except Georgia. Nevertheless, fertilized land in South Carolina yielded only 14.7 bushels of corn per acre to Iowa's 54.8, only 12.2 bushels of wheat to New York's 23.8, and only 22 bushels of oats to Ohio's 37.2.[3]

Income was also low because farms were too small to be profitable and produced labor-intensive cash crops whose market price was subject to dramatic fluctuation. Of the 157,931 farms in 1930, nearly two-thirds were smaller than 50 acres, and nearly one-fourth were less than 20 acres. In 1929 the average farmer produced only 6.4 bales of cotton. At 16 cents a pound, he grossed only $480. With an 8-cent cost of production, his net income was $240. In 1932 the average market price of cotton was below the cost of production, and so the farmer lost $19.20 simply by planting a crop.[4]

Widespread tenancy contributed to low per-capita farm income. The highwater mark for farm tenancy in South Carolina was 1930, when more than 65 percent of the state's farmers were share croppers, share tenants, or cash renters. Under a share cropper–landowner contract, the share cropper furnished labor and half the fertilizer, while the landowner provided land, fuel, house, work stock, tools, seed, and half the fertilizer. With the share tenant–landowner arrangement, the share tenant furnished labor, work stock, tools, seed, and feed for the stock, while the landowner supplied land, fuel, house, and all the fertilizer. Both the share cropper and the share tenant divided the crop equally with the landowner. In a cash renter–landowner agreement, the cash renter furnished labor, work stock, feed for the stock, seed, tools, and all the fertilizer; the landowner provided a house and land. The cash renter received all of the crop and paid the landowner an annual rent. In 1930 approximately 31 percent of all farmers were share croppers; 23 percent, share tenants; and 12 percent, cash renters.[5]

Thus, for two-thirds of the state's farmers, life was exceedingly hard. In 1929, for example, when cotton netted the average farmer about $240, only those who owned their land actually received that sum. Share croppers and share tenants got only $120. So meager was the typical tenant's portion that one of them opined in 1939: "Thank Gawd, dere won't be no landlords up dere before Jesus's seat, and dat's what will make hit heaben."[6] At the same time, when the price of cotton fell below the normal cost of production, as in 1932, the farm owner discovered that proceeds from the sale of the crop would not cover the tenant's living expenses for which the landowner cosigned at the country store.

Desperate by March 1933, landowners and tenants alike greeted the new president with high hopes. Roosevelt responded immediately by having Congress pass the Agricultural Adjustment Act, which encouraged those growing seven basic commodities, including cotton and tobacco, to restrict production by "renting" cropland taken out of cultivation to the secretary of agriculture in return for rental or benefit payments. Any farmer signing crop-reduction contracts was eligible for parity payments that would supplement the price he received for his commodity and guarantee the same purchasing power he enjoyed from 1909 to 1914 (for cotton) or 1919 to 1929 (for tobacco). The act also created an Agricultural Adjustment Administration (AAA) to administer the program.[7]

Predictions in the spring of 1933 of a bumper crop in cotton demanded immediate action. Congressman Hampton Fulmer urged Secretary of Agriculture Henry A. Wallace to reduce cotton acreage through a program of carryovers. For example, a farmer producing ten bales of cotton in 1933 would be permitted to market only seven bales in both 1933 and 1934. He would thus "carry over" into 1934 three unmarketed bales and plant only enough cotton to yield four bales. In May, Wallace decided, instead, to have farmers agree to plow up 10 million acres of cotton in return for rental payments. Farmers in South Carolina would be expected to plow under 30 percent of their estimated 1.77 million acres of cotton. After each farmer calculated his average yield for the five-year base period (1928–1932), the AAA graduated payments for acres of cotton destroyed from $7 to $20, depending on average yield per acre. For example, a farmer destroying one acre of cotton that averaged 220 pounds, the approximate yield for South Carolina, received $14.[8]

Wallace also announced that the campaign to persuade farmers to sign crop-destruction contracts would begin on June 26, 1933. Dr. W. W. Long of Clemson College, state director of the Agricultural Extension Service, would be its director. Each county agent, who would direct AAA programs in his county, began appointing local committees, ranging in size from three men in Georgetown County to sixty-seven men in Spartanburg County, to urge farmers to sign contracts. Also helping with the campaign would be teachers and inspectors in the state agriculture department. After publicly expressing hope that this campaign would "meet the largest possible degree of co-operation by the cotton planters of

South Carolina," Governor Blackwood proclaimed the week of June 26 to July 1 Cotton Acreage Reduction Week.[9]

The campaign began with the same excitement that would characterize the NRA program two months later. Senator Smith buried his opposition to crop reduction and took to the hustings to plug the theme: "If you do not plow up your cotton now, it will plow you up in the fall."[10] W. W. Long, who accompanied Smith, observed that in twenty-five years of campaigning he had "never seen farmers more enthusiastic or more nearly unanimous than they seemed today" in support of "the Roosevelt plan."[11] Meanwhile, county AAA committeemen were conducting meetings in schools, churches, country stores, and private homes. As a show of support, David R. Coker of Hartsville, the state's best-known farmer, announced he was destroying part of his crop without awaiting AAA approval of his contract.[12]

After the campaign ended on July 12, 1933, county agents began checking contracts before forwarding them to Washington for final approval. Because a few obviously fraudulent production estimates delayed the county agents beyond the July 18 deadline, the AAA declared all contracts previously approved by county agents effective immediately without final action by Washington. More than 68,200 contracts were negotiated with farmers planting more than 70 percent of the state's cotton acreage. They agreed to plow up 424,000 acres of cotton, 24 percent of the crop. On July 25 South Carolina agriculture entered a new era as the first cotton stalks were turned under.[13]

Yet crop reduction did not prove to be an immediate panacea. Cotton prices, which increased to nearly 10 cents a pound in the early summer, sank again in August and September. Moreover, NRA codes were increasing other prices the farmer had to pay. In response, farmers held conventions to demand redress. On September 12, 1933, at a gathering in Columbia summoned by Governor Blackwood, Rep. Neville Bennett of Marlboro County called for a "blue eagle on the farms" with a guaranteed price of 18 cents for cotton.[14] Instead, the Columbia convention endorsed a federally guaranteed cotton price of 15 cents, currency inflation, and immediate payment of 1933 rentals.

Ten days later, the Roosevelt administration received these resolutions and others from a general cotton conference in Washington. The president's long-range response was to inflate the currency through gold purchases. His immediate answer was an offer to lend farmers 10 cents per pound on their 1933 cotton so they could store it and await better prices. Only farmers agreeing to sign 1934 crop-reduction contracts would be eligible for loans made by the Commodity Credit Corporation, set up in October 1933. Farm discontent subsided for the moment.[15]

Meanwhile, tobacco farmers were also bemoaning hard times. The 23,000 of them were mostly concentrated in the Pee Dee, a district named for the rivers that drained it, containing the counties of Darlington, Florence, Dillon, Horry, Marion, and Williamsburg. In the 1920s tobacco growers fared better than cotton farmers. In 1929, for example, the average tobacco farmer in South Carolina grossed $100 more than his counterpart in cotton. From 1929 to 1932, however, the state tobacco crop dropped in value from $12.7 million to $4.1 million as acreage decreased and prices fell.

Secretary Wallace had not announced a reduction plan for tobacco when markets opened in Georgia on August 1, 1933, with the new leaves selling for an anemic 10 cents per pound. The following week the same price prevailed in South Carolina. With tobacco selling at below the cost of production, Congressman Gasque of Florence wired Wallace for immediate assistance. On August 27 a Florence convention appealed for AAA action to peg the price at 23 cents per pound. Delegates presented the resolution to Wallace at Hartsville, where the secretary was conferring with David R. Coker and Senator Smith. On August 31, two days after North Carolina markets opened with low prices, Tarheel farmers asked Gov. J. C. B. Ehringhaus to proclaim a marketing holiday. He complied and requested the same of Governor Blackwood. On September 1 Blackwood closed all tobacco markets until further notice.[16]

At this juncture Wallace took action. He first announced that the AAA would offer a crop-reduction plan for tobacco in 1934. He hoped the predicted shortage a year hence would stimulate higher prices on the 1933 crop. A series of meetings on September 4 between AAA officials and tobacco growers in the Carolinas and Virginia fleshed out the details of the 1934 plan, which included a 30-percent acreage reduction and parity payments. County agents in the Pee Dee quickly began the sign-up campaign, and Governor Blackwood proclaimed a two-day business holiday there so businessmen could help collect signatures. More than 90 percent of tobacco growers agreed to reduce their 1934 acreage.[17]

Unfortunately, Secretary Wallace's announcement and the ensuing sign-up campaign did little to raise prices. The AAA Tobacco Section had no choice except to present tobacco buyers with an agreement pledging them to purchase a specified quantity of tobacco at a minimum price. In late September, after proposals and counterproposals proved unacceptable to both sides, Wallace threatened to license buyers and compel them to pay a minimum price. The tobacco companies surrendered, agreeing to purchase at least as much tobacco as they processed during the fiscal year ending June 30, 1933, at an average price of 17 cents. The agreement was retroactive to September 25, when Governors Blackwood and Ehringhaus ended the tobacco holidays in the Carolinas and reopened their markets. At an average price of 12.59 cents per pound, the 1933 crop brought $10.3 million, the best yield since 1929.[18]

By December 31, 1933, all South Carolina farmers had ample reason to praise the AAA. Not only was the return on tobacco the best since 1929, but the cotton crop was 64 percent more valuable than in 1932. In addition, the AAA made $4.7 million in benefit payments to cotton farmers, which made up 4.9 percent of total farm income. Dr. W. W. Long estimated that AAA action actually added more than $21 million to their income because cotton would have sold for 5 cents a pound without it.[19]

On January 8, 1934, the second crop reduction drive began when the extension service mounted a campaign to have cotton farmers sign contracts for both the 1934 and 1935 crops. A total of 71,562 South Carolina farmers did so, covering nearly 90 percent of the state's cotton acreage. More than 15,000 additional signers in 1935 brought coverage to more than 96 percent. Under the terms of these contracts, a farmer would reduce his acreage 35 to 45 percent in 1934 and 25 to 35 percent in 1935. He would receive rental payments to a maximum of $18 per acre. He would also be granted a parity payment of 1 cent per pound in 1934 and 1.25 cents per pound in 1935 on 40 percent of the base-period production.[20]

Despite these generous terms, many cotton farmers refused to sign but benefited from the rise in price caused by those who did. In February 1934 the South Carolina legislature petitioned Congress to consider a compulsory reduction program. Congress responded two months later with the Bankhead Cotton Control Act. The law covered the 1934 crop and would cover the 1935 crop if two-thirds of all farmers voted to comply. Under the law the AAA allotted to each farmer so many bales, or fractions of bales, which he could market tax free with tax exemption certificates. Farmers who had already signed acreage-reduction contracts received tax exemption certificates approximating the poundage of their allotted acreage. All cotton marketed above the bale allotment was subject to a tax of 50 percent of its market value. The AAA allotted South

Carolina farmers about 600,000 bales from the national allotment of 10 million bales.[21]

Administering the AAA and Bankhead programs was not a simple task. Each contracting farmer automatically became a member of his county production control association, which elected a county committee of three men. This committee, with help from the county agent, divided the county into communities of about 300 farmers and appointed three-man community committees. Community committeemen secured the farmer's signature on the acreage-reduction contract and then checked compliance after the farmer had planted. The county committees reviewed the contracts, ordered adjustments when required, and forwarded their approval to the AAA in Washington. A South Carolina board of review, appointed by extension service director W. W. Long, compared acreage with USDA estimates and then ordered the county committee to bring contract estimates into line with those of the USDA, if necessary.

A similar method of implementation prevailed under the Bankhead bale control program. Community and county committeemen secured, checked, and adjusted each farmer's application for tax exemption certificates and channeled the application to the South Carolina allotment board, which was headed by farmer and state legislator Neville Bennett. The allotment board computed the county's and each farmer's share of the 600,000-bale allotment and then sent each farmer his tax-exemption certificates.[22]

Surprisingly, with two-thirds of South Carolina farmers classed as tenants, few of the public complaints arising from the administration of the crop-reduction program involved the tenant-landowner relationship. This was owing to tenant quiescence, favoritism shown landlords by the local press, and AAA foresight in prearranging the division of benefit payments between landlord and tenant. According to the 1934–1935 contracts, for example, cash renters received the entire payment—parity plus rental. "Managing share tenants," who were defined as tenants that furnished labor, equipment, and stock and who managed the farm, received half the rental payment and two-thirds of the parity payment. Other share tenants and share croppers received only a share of the parity payment equal to their share of the crop.[23]

Nevertheless, a number of South Carolina landowners did cheat the system. Some refused to divide parity checks with tenants. Others kept the tenant share of money for payment of past debts, real or imaginary, or for payment of current or future living expenses. Many others circumvented the contract requirement that they not reduce their number of tenants by evicting them before signing the contract. A few landowners even exploited the SCERA requirement that a tenant secure landowner permission before applying for relief work, forcing the tenant to pay them a portion of relief wages as a condition for permission.[24]

The administration of the Bankhead program was even more problematic. Following an initially favorable public reaction to compulsory crop control, the allotment board assigned each farmer his bale allotment. Farmers who had already signed crop-reduction contracts received tax-exemption certificates first. Those who had not signed were granted certificates from the residue of the county's allotment, usually less than what farmers under contract received. In addition, large farmers apparently acquired bale quotas first, with small farmers receiving proportionally less. Furthermore, different bale apportionments to neighboring counties could cause two adjacent farms to receive different allotments, even though their base production was approximately equal. Accordingly, for six months nonsigners and small farmers groused at the unfairness of the Bankhead program.[25] As with many New Deal programs, the divine was in the plan; the devil, in the implementation.

Nevertheless, gradual improvement in agricultural prices made cotton farmers anxious to sign new crop-reduction contracts and reluctant to scrap the compulsory Bankhead program. The total value of the state's lint cotton both in 1934 and 1935 was nearly double the 1932 figure. In addition, AAA parity and rental payments accounted for 8.6 percent of total farm income. The Commodity Credit Corporation also made loans and granted subsidies to cotton farmers on warehoused cotton to help peg the minimum price for the staple at above 12 cents per pound.[26]

Tobacco farmers also prospered under AAA guidance. In the spring of 1934 they honored contracts by planting only 70 percent of their former acreage. In May they began receiving price adjustment payments on their 1933 crops to compensate for losses sustained before manufacturers consented to a minimum purchase agreement. Later in 1934, after community committeemen checked each tobacco farmer for compliance, the farmer received his rental payment for 1934 of $17.50 per acre removed from production, plus a parity payment of 12.5 percent of the crop's net market value.[27]

Yet Congress did not trust the voluntary program for tobacco any more than the one for cotton. In June 1934 they passed the Kerr-Smith

Tobacco Control Act with poundage quotas and a tax on the excess. Farmers were receptive to compulsory control, especially after South Carolina's tobacco market opened on August 9 with leaves selling for 22 cents per pound, or nearly double the 1933 price. In fact, the average price for the 1934 crop was a respectable 21.6 cents per pound. Tobacco benefit payments of nearly $2 million helped make 1934 the best year since 1927. Small wonder that 18,332 South Carolina tobacco farmers voted to continue the Kerr-Smith program; only 223 farmers voted no.[28]

The year 1935 was an even better one for tobacco. Contracts called for a 15-percent reduction in acreage with rental payments of $17.50 per acre. Parity payments would be 6.25 percent of the net market value of the farmer's crop. The Kerr-Smith compulsory reduction program also continued in effect. In July, South Carolina tobacco farmers voted 18,745 to 466 in favor of continuing AAA production controls for another year. "Man," said one South Carolinian, "I hope I never have to grow another crop of tobacco without a contract. I can see my way out now."[29] The nearly 85 million pounds of tobacco on markets in 1935 averaged 18.56 cents a pound and sold for nearly $16 million, the highest sum since 1921.[30]

On January 6, 1936, the agricultural picture darkened. The Supreme Court in the *Butler* decision struck down the acreage-reduction program and the processing tax. Farmers in South Carolina were alarmed. Wade Stackhouse of Dillon wired President Roosevelt to suggest a constitutional amendment giving Congress control over agricultural production. Clemson president E. W. Sikes predicted that before farmers in South Carolina "go back to the old system, you'll see them put up the damndest fight anybody ever put up."[31]

Congress answered with the Soil Conservation and Domestic Allotment Act. Under its terms, farmers reduced a percentage of soil-depleting crops such as tobacco and cotton and planted instead soil-conserving crops such as grasses and legumes. Payments to farmers for diverting land to soil-conserving crops stood at 5 cents per pound for cotton and 3 to 5 cents per pound for tobacco, depending on the type. Diversion payments would average $10 an acre. The maximum acreage a farmer could divert was 35 percent of his cotton base and 30 percent of his tobacco base. South Carolina farmers who participated in the program submitted conservation plans, had their farms checked for compliance by community committeemen, and then applied for funds.[32]

Conservation, the name if not the real purpose of the new program, was sorely needed. The saying had become common that general erosion wrought more devastation in South Carolina than General Sherman. In 33 of the 46 counties, erosion was so serious that farmers were abandoning 12,000 acres of land each year. In 14 piedmont counties, more than 50 percent of farmland was so eroded as to be classed as worthless. Gullies averaging 500 feet in length scarred the countryside.

Nor was conservation a new initiative in 1935. It began in 1933 with FDR's creation of the Soil Erosion Service in the Department of Interior. This agency quickly initiated two soil-conservation projects to demonstrate conservation methods and educate farmers. The South Tyger River project embraced 125,000 acres in Spartanburg County, and the Fishing Creek project contained 52,000 acres near Rock Hill.[33] The South Tyger River project was significant enough to receive constant attention from the press. The project area was thirty-five miles in length and varied in width from four to eight miles. With manual labor supplied by the SCERA and CCC, the Soil Erosion Service demonstrated the advantages of tractor terracing, gully treatment, strip cropping, cover cropping, and reforestation. Most farmers were eager to emulate these innovations. One farmer admitted that "those 'book farmers'" in the Soil Erosion Service "have certainly taught me a lot more than I ever learned through experience."[34]

In 1935 Roosevelt renamed the Soil Erosion Service the Soil Conservation Service (SCS) and transferred it to the Department of Agriculture. By 1936 the SCS boasted five demonstration projects in the Palmetto State, ranging in size from 25,000 to 100,000 acres. By October 1936, 95 percent of the farmers within the projects were following SCS-prescribed practices. In addition, the SCS had educated more than 90 percent of farmers living within a 25-mile radius of each of the projects on the benefits of erosion control.[35]

Meanwhile, in 1936, South Carolina farmers began marketing crops under the new soil conservation and domestic allotment program. They were not unhappy with receipts. The cotton crop brought more than 12 cents per pound and yielded $52.2 million. The return on the tobacco crop was a respectable, if not spectacular, 19.38 cents per pound, more than a cent above the 1935 price. Yet a drought-stricken smaller crop brought $2 million less than in 1935. Conservation payments totaling nearly $8 million were also welcomed additions to the incomes of nearly 72,000 farm families. Representing more than 5 percent of total farm income, these payments covered 538,241 diverted cotton acres and 17,189 diverted tobacco acres. They reflected soil conservation measures undertaken on farms containing more than 75 percent of the state's total cropland. In particular, South Carolina farmers terraced 30,847 acres and planted more than 700,000 acres of soil-conserving crops and grasses.[36]

Nevertheless, many farmers realized that a noncompulsory program of diverted acreage would not sustain commodity prices. Tobacco growers from Virginia to Georgia lobbied their legislatures to enact interstate compacts renewing the stricter production-control program struck down by *Butler.* In March, after the Virginia legislature acted favorably, Sen. Paul Quattlebaum of Horry introduced a bill in the South Carolina Senate to allow a three-man tobacco commission, appointed by President Roosevelt, to set state quotas. The opposition was led by Sen. Henry K. Purdy of Jasper County, whose announced philosophy, "If I want to starve to death, it's nobody's business but mine," won a few adherents.[37] A larger part of the opposition, however, was rooted in historic distrust of interstate action without the cooperation of all parties involved. Gov. Eugene Talmadge of Georgia already had refused to call the Georgia legislature into special session to consider the plan, and without Georgia the efforts of Virginia and the Carolinas would be fruitless. Accordingly, the Quattlebaum Bill failed, and with it the effort at stricter crop control.[38]

As a result, tobacco and cotton faced an uncertain future. In 1937 the tobacco crop of 101 million pounds sold for 20.83 cents per pound and yielded $21.8 million, making it the first crop in history to exceed 100 million pounds and the first to gross more than $21 million. Unfortunately, cotton fared very poorly. USDA predictions of a bumper crop so depressed the market that South Carolina farmers received only $44.3 million for their 985,000 bales, putting the average price at only 9 cents per pound. In September one schoolteacher recorded that cotton farmers in her locality adjacent to the Pee Dee were "expressing feelings of resentment towards Roosevelt because of the price of cotton."[39] By October 1937 these cotton growers had sobered enough to demand another compulsory control program.[40] Congress responded in 1938 with a new Agricultural Adjustment Act. This law continued the 1936–1937 soil-conservation program with diverted acreage. It also redefined parity payments and authorized Commodity Credit Corporation loans under certain market conditions. Moreover, it allowed the secretary of agriculture, with the consent of two-thirds of the farmers of a given commodity, to impose marketing quotas on each farmer if crop estimates indicated that the commodity would exceed the "normal supply."[41]

Since projected cotton and tobacco acreage in every state in 1938 exceeded the normal supply, Secretary Wallace established marketing quotas for the two commodities and scheduled the referenda for March 12, 1938. In South Carolina more than 96 percent of cotton farmers and 89 percent of tobacco farmers voted in favor of marketing quotas. The resulting cotton and tobacco crops were smaller than those of 1937, when marketing quotas had not existed. Although the 1938 cotton crop sold for an anemic 8.96 cents per pound, AAA payments of about $12 million actually made 1938 profitable. Thus, in the December 1938 cotton referendum 88 percent of cotton farmers cast ballots in favor of marketing quotas for 1939.[42]

Tobacco farmers did not fare as well. The 1938 crop brought only $19.3 million, nearly $2 million less than in 1937. Accordingly, when they voted on 1939 marketing quotas, farmers remembered the record crop with higher profits in 1937, plus what many farmers considered to be "rank favoritism in the administration of the law" in 1938.[43] The vote in South Carolina was 15,759 for continuation and 10,585 against it, about 1,850 votes shy of the necessary two-thirds. Since the national average in favor of continuation was only 56.9 percent, tobacco farmers in 1939 planted their crops without marketing quotas.

Cotton farmers lived to appreciate their vote; tobacco farmers, to regret theirs. The 1939 crop of 871,000 bales sold for a somewhat healthier 9.5 cents per pound, producing a gross income of $41.3 million. The largest tobacco crop in state history (117 million pounds) sold for 8 cents a pound less than in 1938. Consequently, in October 1939 nearly 90 percent of tobacco farmers voted in favor of marketing quotas for the next three years. Two months later 96 percent of cotton farmers followed suit. As the war years began, in spite of the inability of the New Deal to restore pre-Depression commodity prices, South Carolina farmers were solidly wedded to the New Deal's program of crop reduction, conservation, and price supports.[44]

Programs in rural rehabilitation, rural electrification, tenancy reduction, and farm credit supplemented programs of conservation and income enhancement. Farm credit received immediate attention in March 1933, when President Roosevelt set up the Farm Credit Administration (FCA) with twelve district offices to coordinate the lending activities of the several federal agricultural loan programs. district three contained South

Carolina, North Carolina, Georgia, and Florida. The district office, headed by former state treasurer Julian H. Scarborough, was located in Columbia. The FCA negotiated long-term and short-term loans. Long-term loans (twenty to thirty years) were usually made to refinance farm mortgages; by December 1935 long-term loans totaling more than $21 million had gone to nearly 13,000 South Carolina farmers. Short-term loans, by contrast, were made for seed, feed, livestock, and farm improvement. By 1940 the FCA had closed nearly 76,000 loans, totaling $25 million. By that time all FCA loans in South Carolina amounted to more than $61 million, a sum greater than the value of the state's cotton crop in any year of the New Deal.[45]

The Farm Credit Administration helped farmers who owned property that could be pledged as collateral; the rural rehabilitation program aided those less fortunate. Rural rehabilitation began in 1934 under the Rural Rehabilitation Division of the SCERA, providing the destitute landless farmer with loans for seed, fertilizer, farm equipment, and livestock. If his land was unproductive, the division purchased better land and moved him to it. By January 13, 1935, the division had relocated about 4,300 South Carolina farmers and provided loans for more than 7,300 of them. Nevertheless, class considerations partially gutted the rural rehabilitation program. The South Carolina Rural Rehabilitation Advisory Committee, dominated by large farmers, imposed a ceiling of $500 for each rehabilitation loan. The average ceiling in other states ranged between $2,500 and $3,000.[46]

In April 1935 the Resettlement Administration (RA) under Rexford Tugwell absorbed the rehabilitation program. During the next four years nearly 16,000 South Carolina farm families received $8.6 million in rural rehabilitation loans for seed, fertilizer, livestock, and equipment. By following a prescribed farm-management plan, clients in 1939 increased the average net worth per family from $441 to $556. Most of the increase came from production for home consumption, especially in canning, poultry raising, and dairy farming. The RA's Rural Rehabilitation Division also offered a farm-debt adjustment service, which negotiated substantial reductions in the debts of nearly 1,500 South Carolina farmers.[47]

Rural resettlement was the most ambitious but least successful aspect of rural rehabilitation in South Carolina. The RA's Rural Resettlement Division, and afterward the Farm Security Administration (FSA), relocated families from marginal land to productive farmland, either on scattered farms or in resettlement communities. This effort reduced farm tenancy, rested worn-out cropland, and reduced tenant migration from farm to city and, inevitably, to urban relief rolls. In addition, emphasis on self-sufficiency to supplement commercial farming not only reduced each tenant's overhead but also aimed to re-create an America of Jeffersonian yeomen. In particular, resettled farmers raised vegetables, grains, chickens, and hogs in addition to cotton, while each resettlement community contained necessary facilities such as a cannery, shop, cotton gin, warehouse, feed mill, grist mill, store, and filling station, all managed cooperatively.[48]

Twelve resettlement communities were planned for South Carolina; six eventually began, and three became significant enough to elicit statewide notice. Ashwood Plantation on 11,500 acres in Lee County contained 160 farms for whites. Orangeburg Farms, with 67 farms on a 6,400-acre tract in Orangeburg County, was originally planned for blacks until an outcry from white farmers caused the FSA to add several families of white tenants in what the FSA called a "protective belt" between local whites and resettled blacks. Allendale Farms in heavily black Allendale County was an all-black project of 118 farms, a community of 11,334 acres. This resettlement effort in South Carolina eventually cost more than $3.6 million and involved 464 farms on more than 40,000 acres of land.[49]

The devil with rural resettlement was in the implementation. Problems encountered at Ashwood Plantation are typical. So many clients lacked either the expertise or the desire to become efficient farmers that twenty of the first seventy arrivals had to be evicted. Second, the Rural Resettlement Division divided the community into farms too small to be economically viable. As James M. Eleazer, the project manager and former county agent of Sumter County, explained: "You can't turn a mule around in twenty acres, let alone grow cotton." Furthermore, the RA did not provide trained personnel to operate processing equipment such as the cotton gin. Instead, it selected three untrained clients for the task.[50]

The same dependence upon amateurs was evident in the Ashwood cooperative, which farmers formed in September of 1936 to direct production, processing, and marketing at the plantation. By October 1938 the cooperative, which was managed by inexperienced personnel, had lost money. Although operating in the black by October 1939, the cooperative was in the red again by December 1940, having lost money on the store, warehouses, sweet potato hotbed, livestock operations, and grist and feed mill. By 1944 the Farm Security Administration disbanded Ashwood and its sister projects and placed the small independent farms under the guidance of the county rural rehabilitation agent. Most of the owners eventually sold their farms to agribusiness.[51]

The final segment of rural rehabilitation began in 1937 with the passage of the Bankhead-Jones Farm Tenancy Act to authorize FSA farm-purchase loans to tenants. The duration of each loan was forty years; the annual interest, 3 percent. Secretary of Agriculture Wallace appointed a committee for each county to approve applications, supervise farm purchases,and ensure that tenants bought good land. Again, class considerations dominated. In publicizing the loan procedure, the county committees in South Carolina that stressed the FSA preferred tenants who already had stock and tools and possibly a down payment. Accordingly, in 1937 only 2,250 tenants from a state total of 102,926 (1 in 50) made application for purchase loans. Even so, the federal appropriation for the 1938 fiscal year was sufficient to cover only 160 loans in 16 counties. In fact, the appropriations through June 1940 allowed only 870 additional loans in South Carolina, which aided less than 1 percent of the state's tenants. The Bankhead-Jones program made hardly a dent in farm tenancy in the Palmetto State.[52]

More enduring were the achievements of the Rural Electrification Administration, which Congress created in 1935 to make loans for construction of rural distribution systems. With only 3,700 of nearly 168,000 farms electrified by 1934, rural South Carolinians were eager for the REA to begin. Private power companies neglected rural areas. In fact, their control of the South Carolina Public Service Commission kept that public agency from pressuring private utilities to extend service to rural areas.

In February 1935 the state legislature overcame power-company opposition and created the South Carolina Rural Electrification Authority (SCREA) to construct and operate electric distribution systems. The agency was authorized to purchase electricity from private or municipal power companies at a wholesale rate set by the Public Service Commission and then sell it to rural consumers at a rate sufficient to liquidate costs of construction and operation. Until 1939 the SCREA, Aiken County Cooperative, and Greenwood County Finance Board (overseer of the Buzzard Roost project) were the only agencies to borrow from the federal REA. SCREA projects proceeded too slowly to suit rural dwellers, who created eight additional cooperatives that eventually surpassed the SCREA in rural electrification.[53]

Not surprisingly, private power companies, after letting the SCREA finance surveys to determine optimum distribution routes, hastened to construct the most profitable lines. Sumter County agriculture agent J. M. Eleazer recalled heading a delegation of Sumter County farmers who pleaded with the Public Service Commission to pressure the Carolina Power and Light Company to extend rural lines, only to be told the proposed extension was unprofitable. Later, the farmers appealed to the SCREA, whose survey of Sumter County was still incomplete when Carolina Power and Light began erecting poles.[54] In order to protect the SCREA, the legislature passed a law regulating extension of private power lines into rural areas. Even so, the farmer benefited as much from competition between the SCREA and private power companies as from the law. In 1936 alone, private power companies constructed 1,200 miles of rural lines, or about one-fifth of the total private power lines in existence in rural areas by December 1939.

By World War II, South Carolina farmers had good reason to appreciate the REA. In 1934 only 2 percent of them had electricity; by 1940 the figure had risen to 14.5 percent.[55]

The New Deal left its mark on South Carolina agriculture. In 1932 the farmer was unencumbered by federal regulation and at the mercy of market forces; by 1939 he had swapped some of his freedom for higher profits. The following chart depicting the ten-year price of cotton and tobacco in South Carolina shows the salutary effect of acreage reduction and production control after 1932.

Tobacco prices showed a general increase under AAA control and a decline in 1939, when tobacco farmers sold without marketing quotas. Cotton prices also showed a general improvement under AAA guidance

TABLE 8.1 **Effect of Acreage Reduction and Production Control**

YEAR	COTTON (CENTS PER POUND)	TOBACCO (CENTS PER POUND)
1930	9.73	12.03
1931	6.08	9.14
1932	7.37	11.14
1933	10.99	12.59
1934	12.62	21.60
1935	11.82	18.56
1936	13.17	19.88
1937	9.02	20.83
1938	8.96	22.23
1939	9.50	14.55

and a drop in 1937, when cotton farmers disregarded acreage limits set by the conservation program. Better prices were supplemented by benefit payments, which totaled nearly $50.5 million by 1939. Better commodity prices also meant a decline in farm bankruptcies from thirty-one per thousand in the 1933 fiscal year to three per thousand in the 1939 fiscal year. The number of forced farm sales dropped more than 78 percent between March 1932 and March 1938.[56]

Nevertheless, although South Carolina farmers were more prosperous during the New Deal than during the early 1930s, they were far less prosperous than in 1910–1914 and often less so than in 1929. At no time during the New Deal did their total cash income approach the $132 million received in 1929. The highest cash income during the New Deal was $116 million received in 1937. At no time during the New Deal did the price of cotton equal the 15.97 cents per pound received in 1929. Furthermore, the value of farm real estate climbed from 57 percent of the 1910–1914 value in 1933 to only 89 percent by 1940. Finally, as late as 1939, a cotton farmer's purchasing power was still only 60 percent of that in 1909–1914. In short, World War II, and not the New Deal, brought higher prices that ushered in agricultural prosperity.[57]

Farm owner and tenant in Chesterfield County show off their field of cotton. Courtesy, South Caroliniana Library, University of South Carolina.

Farmhands picking cotton. Courtesy, South Caroliniana Library, University of South Carolina.

Tobacco field in the Pee Dee. Courtesy, South Caroliniana Library, University of South Carolina.

Tobacco being carried on sleds from the field to the curing barn where the leaves were tied onto sticks before being flue-cured. Courtesy, South Caroliniana Library, University of South Carolina.

Upcountry rural homestead with eroded fields. Courtesy, South Caroliniana Library, University of South Carolina.

Upcountry rural homestead showing the beneficial effects of erosion-control measures. Courtesy, South Caroliniana Library, University of South Carolina.

Large gully in Spartanburg County resulting from soil erosion, ca. 1935. As much as thirty-two tons of dirt and organic matter drained weekly from such gullies. One gully of only an acre in size could ruin forty acres of farmland. Courtesy, South Caroliniana Library, University of South Carolina.

Erosion-control measures for large gullies included sloping the sides with a bulldozer, constructing check dams on the interior, and planting vegetation such as kudzu, shown here. Courtesy, South Caroliniana Library, University of South Carolina.

Typical lowcountry tenant cabin. Courtesy, South Caroliniana Library, University of South Carolina.

A mother of fourteen children, grandmother of fifty-six grandchildren, from the small-farmer class relaxing at the end of a workday, July 1937. Courtesy, South Caroliniana Library, University of South Carolina.

A prosperous farmer and his wife relaxing on their front porch at the end of a workday. Courtesy, South Caroliniana Library, University of South Carolina.

An FSA tenant-purchase client canning vegetables in an effort to become self-sufficient, ca. 1939. Courtesy, South Caroliniana Library, University of South Carolina.

Gov. Olin D. Johnston. Courtesy, Elizabeth Johnston Patterson.

BELOW: Gov. and Mrs. Olin D. Johnston pose for a photograph with President Roosevelt at the Governor's Mansion in Columbia on December 5, 1938. Courtesy, South Caroliniana Library, University of South Carolina.

Gov. Burnet R. Maybank. Courtesy, South Caroliniana Library, University of South Carolina.

BELOW: Modjeska M. Simkins. Courtesy, South Caroliniana Library, University of South Carolina.

John H. McCray. Courtesy, South Caroliniana Library, University of South Carolina.

SCPDP delegation to the Democratic National Convention in Chicago, July 1944. Osceola McKaine is front row, third from left. To his left is John H. McCray. In the second row between McKaine and McCray is Levi Byrd. Courtesy, South Caroliniana Library, University of South Carolina.

African Americans in Columbia line up to vote in the August 10, 1948, Democratic primary. Courtesy, South Caroliniana Library, University of South Carolina.

(Left to right) John H. McCray, Pete Ingram, J. C. Artemus, and James M. Hinton pose for a photograph after casting the first black votes in the August 10, 1948, Democratic primary. Ingram was an executive with Pilgrim Health and Life Insurance Company; Artemus, a Labor leader and SCPDP treasurer. George A. Elmore, plaintiff in *Elmore v. Rice*, was the photographer. Courtesy, South Caroliniana Library, University of South Carolina.

THE NEW DEAL IN POLITICS AND PUBLIC OPINION IN SOUTH CAROLINA
1933–1939

The New Deal brought a minirevolution in politics and public opinion. It launched the political careers of several Palmetto politicians, many of whom participated in government until near the end of the century. It also changed the focus of the average citizen. Before 1933, conversations among whites at ball games, country stores, barber shops, coffee klatches, and churchyards were filled with topics of local or state interest: Blease, bootleggers, Confederate dead, Big Thursday, the Free City of Charleston, and the boll weevil. With the advent of the New Deal, topics of national interest were added: Roosevelt, parity, collective bargaining, public welfare, and Social Security. In the process FDR became one of the most popular figures in the annals of the Palmetto State.

After an inauspicious beginning, the distribution of federal patronage bound to the New Deal the very men whose opinions carried weight in every locality. In February 1933 state Democratic chairman Claud Sapp announced that a special patronage committee consisting of the Democratic National Committeeman and Committeewoman, state party chairman, and the two United States senators would oversee the distribution of patronage in South Carolina. Postmaster General James A. Farley would referee all disputes. Unwisely, Sapp also cautioned that office seekers should be willing to contribute money to help retire party debt. No sooner had he made this announcement than he had to deflect charges that appointees would be purchasing their offices. The *New York Times* and several South Carolina newspapers failed to see any difference between "Pay-For-Your-Pap" Sapp and state Republican boss "Tieless Joe" Tolbert, who required Republicans holding federal appointments during the 1920s to tithe a portion of their salaries to the national party. However, the kiss of death for the patronage committee was the refusal of Senator Smith and Congressman McMillan to be bound by its rulings.[1]

With the patronage committee dead, the question of federal appointments caused less squabbling because plums were available in a quantity scarcely dreamed of before 1933. Besides the usual jobs in the post office, the congressional delegation for the first time had to select supervisory personnel for CCC camps, fourteen RFC counsels, more than a hundred HOLC counsels and appraisers, the PWA board, PWA engineers, appraisers and counsels for the farm credit agencies, and a host of stenographers, registrars, office managers, and clerks. Apparently, Byrnes and Smith agreed to divide appointments belonging to senators, and each senator, in turn, bargained with the six congressmen over other appointments. For example, in the Fourth Congressional District, Smith named the HOLC appraiser for the Greenville office; Byrnes chose the general counsel, general appraiser, county counsel, and county appraiser in Spartanburg County; and McSwain selected not only the attorneys and appraisers in Union and Laurens Counties but also the office manager and attorney in Greenville County. These arrangements assured harmony among lawmakers.[2]

Far more important, the appointees were community leaders useful in influencing public opinion. Former Richland legislator James H. Hammond, for example, became attorney for the HOLC in Richland County. In return, at the annual convention of the South Carolina Bar Association in 1937, Hammond used his influence to pass a resolution endorsing Roosevelt's court-packing scheme. Former Congressman Frank Lever, who, at the behest of Senator Byrnes, became public relations officer for district three of the FCA, showed his appreciation in 1938 by leading the fight against anti–New Dealers at the state party convention.

Distributing federal judgeships, attorneyships, marshalcies, and collectorships was not as easily settled. The most coveted appointment in South Carolina was collector of internal revenue. Byrnes and Smith agreed on Robert M. Cooper, state finance director for the 1932 campaign and a former state senator from Lee County. Postmaster General Farley preferred the Democratic national committeewoman, Maria Croft Jennings. Smith opposed Jennings because of her previous support for Edgar Brown against him in the Senate primary of 1926. Finally, in June 1933 President Roosevelt named Cooper to the post but placed Jennings as registrar of the Federal Land Bank in Columbia over the objections of Byrnes and Smith.[3]

Smith's frustration in the tug-of-war over patronage escalated; that of Byrnes remained minimal. In June 1933 Byrnes secured the appointment of his former law partner, Cecil Wyche, as U.S. attorney for the western district of South Carolina. Smith claimed appointment of the marshal for the district and nominated Reuben Gosnell of Greenville, a former prohibition agent whose reputation was sullied by the shooting of a bootlegger under suspicious circumstances. Accordingly, Roosevelt refused to confirm Gosnell's appointment. In March 1934, when the federal district judgeship for the eastern district fell vacant, Byrnes recommended Frank K. Myers of Charleston, father-in-law of political ally Burnet Maybank. Smith, in turn, recommended five men for the judgeship. Roosevelt delayed filling the vacancy, although rumors were rife that the appointment would go to Myers. Later that spring the president elevated Rexford Tugwell from assistant secretary of agriculture to undersecretary of agriculture. Smith, whose Senate committee had to approve the appointment, delayed confirmation. According to Harold Ickes, President Roosevelt acknowledged at a Cabinet meeting that he was being forced to trade Rexford Tugwell for the "favorite murderer [Gosnell] of Senator Smith." Ickes added wryly of Gosnell, "This man is said to have a homicide record, but aside from that seems to have a very good reputation."[4] Roosevelt appointed Gosnell but also selected Myers to the judgeship over Smith's five nominees. On June 12 Smith allowed his committee to report Tugwell's nomination to the Senate.[5]

After the 1934 Congress adjourned, Roosevelt named Claud Sapp as U.S. attorney for the eastern district. The appointment had to be interim because Smith objected to Sapp and vowed to oppose this breach of senatorial courtesy. Although Farley was responsible for Sapp's appointment, Byrnes approved it, which would plague him in 1936. Former Charleston mayor Thomas P. Stoney, who craved the attorneyship, claimed that Byrnes treated him "extremely badly" by endorsing Sapp and decided to even the score by opposing Byrnes for the Senate in 1936.[6] In 1935, with Smith still not reconciled to Sapp's nomination, Roosevelt allowed Congress to adjourn without submitting Sapp's name for Senate approval. In the spring of 1936 the pending retirement of Judge H. H. Watkins of the western district turned Smith's attention to a richer trophy. McSwain, who was retiring from Congress, wanted the judgeship and was endorsed by Senator Smith. Byrnes proposed Cecil Wyche. Fully aware of the dangers inherent in a patronage battle with Smith during a renomination campaign, the junior senator persuaded Judge Watkins to postpone his retirement for six months. Byrnes was renominated; Watkins then retired; and McSwain died. To continue in opposition to Byrnes would have been dangerous for Smith, who faced reelection in 1938 and would need help against Gov. Olin Johnston. Accordingly, Byrnes and Smith reached an agreement giving the federal judgeship to Wyche, the U.S. attorneyship in the western district to another Byrnes nominee, Oscar Doyle, and the U.S. attorneyship in the eastern district to Sapp.[7] In 1938 Byrnes supported Smith for renomination to the senate.

Smith suffered several rebuffs in distributing patronage; Byrnes was seldom turned down. His appointees were always willing to contact newspaper editors or speak a kind word on behalf of the New Deal. Therefore, public opinion of the New Deal fluctuated as the junior senator's support for it waxed and waned. Like Byrnes, South Carolina enjoyed a honeymoon period with the New Deal until 1937, after which the relationship became a marriage of convenience.

In March 1933 few Carolinians disagreed with an editorial in the *Columbia State* titled "Safety Depends upon Backing Roosevelt."[8] It did not bother most of them not to fully comprehend New Deal concepts such as parity, industrial planning, regional revitalization, or budget deficiency theory. Their faith was in Roosevelt, whose self-assurance, determination, willingness to improvise, penchant for action, and promise of a brighter future won their confidence. L. T. Fulmer of Aiken County recalls, "Roosevelt was a hero for everybody; he made things happen." To criticism that Roosevelt stretched the Constitution and trampled on states' rights, B. W. Gettys of Kershaw County responds: "Roosevelt was doing something to help people out. You tend to overlook a lot when you're hungry. Our backs were to the wall." Only in such an environment of complete trust could a South Carolina newspaper acknowledge that America had finally found what she needed—"an honest, wise man with dictatorial powers."[9]

Yet, despite the overwhelming popularity of Roosevelt, no Democratic newspaper anywhere in America would assault the New Deal as early or forcefully as the *News and Courier* of Charleston and the *Horry Herald* of Conway. Editor H. H. Woodward of the weekly Conway paper was a social Darwinist/classical economist who championed reductions in taxes and spending, opposed secondary education at public expense, and believed in "natural laws" such as supply and demand and survival of the fittest. On March 23, 1933, he publicly expressed skepticism of relief expenditures because recipients soon would clamor for permanent aid. That summer he denounced regulation of agriculture and industry because of the conflict with "natural economic laws." He even opposed the popular CCC because of its cost and its contradiction of self-reliance.[10] His tirades reflected the uneasiness of the small-town elite, a class of substantial property owners who controlled commerce in county seats. Some were bankers; others were gin and warehouse owners; still others were wealthy merchants. Often they owned a farm or two, which were managed and worked by hired hands. They also controlled local politics. All were interested in sound money, cheap labor, low taxes, and social stability, which were threatened by New Deal programs. In fact, if the small-town elite had not been able to control local New Deal agencies, their opposition would have become more vocal and more public.[11]

Criticisms levied by William Watts Ball of the *News and Courier* were no less trenchant. He professed a belief in "aristocratic" and "limited government" after the fashion of the Founding Fathers. So wedded was he to an agrarian past that he thought the proper solution to economic depression was self-sufficient farming by the unemployed. During the early days of the New Deal, he kept his silence, although he did manage an occasional editorial lament of the trend toward the centralization of powers in the federal government. By May 6, 1933, he was confiding to a friend that "the multifarious things that the federal government is undertaking" left him "confused and baffled."[12] Within days, bafflement turned to indignation. "The revolution proceeds," he wrote to another friend, in "the abdication of Congress." Ball could not foresee a successful conclusion to the New Deal "without reducing statehood close to impotency—without destroying the nature of the republic as we have known it."[13] Consequently, in May 1933 *News and Courier* editorials began to express opposition to relief expenditures, forsaking the gold standard, and centralizing power at the federal level. In June, editorials criticized agricultural subsidies, government-business partnership through the NRA, and government intrusion into business with the FDIC. As Ball's biographer noted, "In the summer of 1933 *The News and Courier* declared war on the New Deal."[14] Ball became the first publisher in the South to don his armor.

Fortunately for the New Deal, such conservative ideology was a luxury few South Carolinians could afford in 1933, and Ball's admonitions went unheeded. The *Columbia State* thought Ball's rantings silly and said so. The overwhelming majority of South Carolinians found their sentiments well expressed in an editorial that appeared in the *State* on January 1, 1934, titled "Thank God for Roosevelt"—a glowing tribute to America's "Providential Leader."[15] They were also quick to contrast March 1933 and March 1934. "A year ago," wrote David R. Coker of Hartsville, "all was confusion and fear. Now . . . practically all industry is operating and at a profit, while most farmers have made some money."[16] A poll by the *Literary Digest* in July showed 84 percent of all South Carolinians in favor of the New Deal. The *State* was certain Roosevelt's popularity was much greater, judging from the likenesses and photographs of him prominently displayed in homes and businesses.[17] In fact, one traveler in the upcountry noticed Roosevelt portraits occupying "the place of honour over the mantel" of every mill house. "I can only compare this to the Italian peasant's Madonna," she concluded.[18]

A better indication of FDR's immense popularity was the outcome of the 1934 elections. The pro–New Deal Olin Johnston, who during the campaign lavished praise upon the NRA, organized labor, and rural electrification, won the governorship.[19] In the six congressional primaries, all of the candidates ran as New Dealers. Congressman Gasque went so far as to proclaim FDR the greatest president since George Washington. Other incumbents waved letters of appreciation from Postmaster General Jim Farley for their loyal support of the New Deal.[20]

Nineteen thirty five was a year of much hubbub but little change in public opinion. Olin Johnston was sworn in as governor and became the New Deal's staunchest defender. As went Johnston, so went most of his following. A branch of the American Liberty League was established in South Carolina in February, though its attraction beyond Main Street was negligible. In June, Senator Byrnes addressed the graduating class at the University of South Carolina and suggested a constitutional amendment to legalize the NRA. His suggestion sparked a three-month debate over states' rights that allowed the typical white Carolinian to pay his respects to his ancestors by opposing the amendment, and to his children by supporting the rest of the New Deal. In September an irritated Byrnes suggested that South Carolinians had "heard more about 'States' Rights'" since July "than we have heard since 1861."[21] Misjudging the depth of anti–New Deal sentiment in this debate, former United States senator Blease maneuvered to oppose Byrnes for the Senate in 1936. The Liberty League, it was rumored, would finance his campaign.[22]

Also funded by the Liberty League was the Farmers' Independence Council of America, one of whose founders was the Northern-born Stanley F. Morse of Edgehill Plantation at Stateburg in Sumter County. In speeches, press releases, and publications, he and the Council assailed New Deal agricultural programs with disparaging terms such as *regimentation, unsound, subversive, un-American, socialistic, communistic, dictatorship, dole, political machine, Russian collective farms, unbalanced national budget, crisis for American liberty,* and *national interference* in state and local affairs.[23] Turning a deaf ear to Morse, farmers sided with David R. Coker, who wrote, "Generations of tariff discrimination have enabled the North and East to fatten at the expense of the agricultural sections of the country, particularly the South. The Roosevelt administration has been the first to put in effective measures towards the equalization of agriculture with other sections of the national economy."[24]

The event in 1935 that overshadowed all others was a visit to South Carolina by Huey Long, one of Roosevelt's implacable foes. Long hoped to generate support in South Carolina for "Share Our Wealth," his plan for taxing the rich to help the poor. In particular, he wanted to organize Share Our Wealth clubs on college and university campuses. The incentive he offered was a proposal for a federally financed college education for all qualified students. Invitations to address the South Carolina Federation of Textile Workers, coinciding with invitations to address the annual Junior-Senior Law School banquet and the Clariosophic Literary Society at the University of South Carolina, offered the Louisiana Kingfish an opportunity to organize support simultaneously in both textile and college circles.

When plans for Long's visit to Columbia on March 23 were announced, the reaction at once was praise for Roosevelt and damnation for Long. Influenced, no doubt, by the generosity of the PWA toward the University of South Carolina, the faculty and administration resolved that the invitation did not have their blessing. The state legislature officially deplored the visit. The *State* editorialized that "no Republican" anywhere in America was "a more bitter enemy of President Roosevelt." The Columbia paper was certain that "until men gather grapes from thorns and figs from thistles," South Carolina could "not expect good to come through Long or from his welcome."[25]

When the Kingfish arrived in Columbia, state legislators conspicuously absented themselves by attending the Azalea Festival in Charleston, where Senator Byrnes and Harry Hopkins were honored guests. A telephone conversation on the morning of March 23 between Long and university president Leonard T. Baker dissuaded the Kingfish from addressing the Clariosophic Society. Instead, Long invited all interested Carolina students to his midday luncheon at the Columbia Hotel, where he plugged the education features of Share Our Wealth. He then called at the statehouse to confer for an hour with a reluctant Gov. Olin Johnston. The governor allowed Long the use of the south corner of the statehouse grounds for a speech to 5,000 curious spectators. But to emphasize his own continuing allegiance to Roosevelt, Governor Johnston sat in the audience and not on the platform containing Long, a few textile labor leaders, and state representative Ben Adams of Columbia, a radical for all seasons. Long's speech included his usual attacks on Roosevelt, the New Deal, and the wealthy. Little applause, student heckling, and student banners reading "Too Much Hooey" and "We Love Our President" greeted Long's address.

This hostile reception made this visit Long's first and last attempt to expand Share Our Wealth onto college campuses. Nevertheless, Long protégé Gerald L. K. Smith remained behind to organize Share Our Wealth clubs in textile communities. His success, too, was limited. Unknown to Smith, UTW organizers followed him from village to village distributing anti-Long propaganda supplied by Senator Byrnes. The Long visit was actually counterproductive; South Carolinians embraced their besieged president even more ardently.[26]

Roosevelt's popularity continued in 1936, as reflected in the overwhelming victory of Byrnes in August and Roosevelt in November. The biggest news story prior to the election was removal from command of Gen. Johnson Hagood of Allendale by Secretary of War George Dern. The previous year, while testifying before a subcommittee of the House Appropriations Committee, Hagood scoffed at inadequate appropriations for the military. In disgust, he noted it was "harder for me to get 5 cents to buy a lead pencil than to get $1,000 to teach hobbies to CCC boys."[27] Since the hearings were closed, Congressman McMillan of Charleston, who sat on the subcommittee, ordered the stenographer to disregard the comment for the moment and asked Hagood if he wanted his remarks printed. Unwisely, the general answered yes, and he then proceeded to label WPA funds "stage money" and "easy money."

In January 1936 Hagood wrote letters to several congressmen urging an increase in appropriations for the military and the elevation in rank of four Army friends. When Chief of Staff Malin Craig privately reprimanded Hagood for the letters, the general began having second thoughts about his earlier remarks, which were scheduled for publication in February 1936. Unfortunately, the Government Printing Office had released advance copies of the testimony. Hagood at once wired Byrnes that "no criticism [of the New Deal] could have been intended, as I am personally a staunch advocate of the administration."[28] The War Department was understandably upset, since Army criticism of the New Deal might invite civilian criticism of the military. On February 24 the secretary of war, acting on the advice of Chief of Staff Craig, removed Hagood from command of the Eighth Army Corps.[29]

The Hagood affair quickly blossomed into a national cause célèbre with repercussions in the Palmetto State. The American Liberty League issued a statement charging that Hagood's removal was "not surprising," since "suppression of free speech" was one of the "universal weapons of dictatorship."[30] The Liberty League also distributed a pamphlet about Hagood's dismissal titled "The Story of an Honest Man." In South Carolina, former senator Blease, with eyes fixed on the Senate seat held by Byrnes, called the matter a "damnable outrage" and added, "Summons a man to appear before a committee, place him on the stand, ask him questions and then expect him to lie—That's not South Carolina blood and especially a Hagood."[31] Senator Smith labeled the removal "perhaps the greatest instance of ingratitude" in governmental history.[32] The *Charleston News and Courier* laid blame squarely on Roosevelt. Mail received by Byrnes revealed indignation throughout South Carolina.[33]

Byrnes knew the Hagood affair could derail his bid for reelection. With Representative McSwain, he appealed to Dern and then to General Craig, who agreed only to consider restoring Hagood to active duty "after a reasonable time."[34] Byrnes also pleaded with Roosevelt, who sided with the military. In the meantime, the War Department issued a statement in response to the newspaper criticism, asserting that Hagood's record as a general officer had been marked by irresponsible statements and a lack of self-control. For example, Hagood once had publicly called the Army bureaucracy "top-heavy and extravagant."[35] Finally by April, with public opinion turning against the general, Byrnes arranged a compromise: the War Department would appoint Hagood to command the Sixth Army Corps, headquartered in Chicago, and Hagood would serve one day as corps commander before requesting transfer to Charleston, where he would await retirement. Both sides complied, and the Hagood affair was soon forgotten.[36]

Meanwhile, Democrats in South Carolina were making ready for the forthcoming Democratic primaries. In May 1936 Col. William C. Harllee of Dillon and former mayor Thomas P. Stoney of Charleston announced they would oppose Byrnes. The wickedness of the New Deal would be the only issue in their campaigns. Stoney was angry at being excluded from dispensing patronage in Charleston, which was controlled by Mayor Maybank, and failing to receive a U.S. attorneyship. Colonel

Harllee blamed Byrnes for not securing his promotion to general in the Marine Corps. Deciding that a three-way split of the anti–New Deal vote was suicidal, Blease bowed out.

Byrnes worried little about this opposition. Neither man had a large statewide following or financial support, and the New Deal continued popular. Byrnes warned Edward Hutton of the American Liberty League to "mind his own business and let me alone and let South Carolina politics alone."[37] So powerful and popular was Byrnes that he was invited to keynote the state party convention on May 20. After his address, which was a warm endorsement of the New Deal, the convention voted unanimously to instruct the South Carolina delegation to support Roosevelt for a second term.[38]

The race for the Senate, better known as South Carolina's traveling political roadshow that would make stops at all forty-six county seats, where each candidate in turn would speak from the same platform, began in Lexington on June 9. Stoney led with an attack on Byrnes and the New Deal. "Byrnes went to Washington as a Democrat," he acknowledged, "but the G-Men . . . got hold of my little friend Jimmie. They bumped him on the head and knocked him out, and now he is headed for that kind of government that Russia and Germany seem to like."[39] Harllee professed concern that the New Deal was deviating from states' rights and Jeffersonian Democracy. On June 13 at Edgefield, Stoney tried without success to inject the race issue; he criticized Byrnes for failing to sponsor legislation to segregate whites and blacks in Washington theaters. Byrnes continued to ignore his opponents and supported the New Deal with his parable of a man whose wife was ill and required costly medical attention that the husband could not afford. The husband had two choices—either save his wife by plunging into debt, or let her die. He went into debt to save his wife and paid the debt when she recovered.[40]

Byrnes interrupted his campaign for two weeks to attend the national party convention in Philadelphia. As in 1932, the South Carolina delegates were conspicuous. Governor Johnston seconded FDR's nomination; Byrnes helped write the platform and seconded the nomination of Vice President Garner. But Cotton Ed Smith eclipsed everyone. Delayed by having attended the funeral of Sen. Duncan Fletcher of Florida, Smith did not arrive in Philadelphia until the convention was in progress. He was already piqued at not being selected for a convention committee. As he took his seat, the Reverend Marshall L. Shepard, an

African American from Philadelphia, rose to open the session with prayer. This was the last straw for Smith, who already believed a conspiracy was afoot to degrade Southern Democrats and foster the African American in the Democratic Party. The senator walked out, taking Burnet Maybank with him as far as the door. Although Smith returned after the prayer, he walked out permanently when black Congressman Arthur Mitchell of Illinois addressed the convention.[41] Smith issued a statement to the press, claiming race relations in the South made it impossible for a white Southerner "to recognize and accept the Negro as an equal political factor." Political equality would lead to social equality, which would bring "intermarriage" and "the mongrelizing of the American race." Smith concluded he could no longer support a "political organization that looks upon the Negro and caters to him as a political and social equal."[42]

Fortunately for Byrnes, South Carolina's reaction to Smith's walkout was mixed. The Beaufort City Council telegraphed to Smith its "congratulations and sincere admiration."[43] Five newspapers, including the *Charleston News and Courier*, applauded Smith's "fearlessness" and "honesty" and sneered at "social equality," "political equality," and "cheap politics." Others such as the *Columbia State* and *Florence Morning News* deplored the walkout. When the *News and Courier* persisted in its warnings of black rule, the *State* commented abruptly, "It seems to us impossible for any intelligent and sincere person to believe in that ghost." Presciently, the *Marion Star* interpreted the walkout as the opening volley of Smith's reelection battle for the Senate in 1938, when he would ride the white horse to victory over Olin Johnston.[44]

Regardless of motive, Smith's walkout threatened to overturn what Byrnes had spent years building—a South Carolina Democratic Party moderate on national issues and free of race baiting and the "politics of color." Five days after the convention ended, Byrnes "leaked" a story to the press that he kidded Sen. Carter Glass of Virginia, an opponent of the New Deal, for not walking out with Smith during the prayer. Glass replied: "God knows I stand in need of prayer. I wish every Negro in the country would pray for me."[45] The implication was obvious: Glass, who shared Smith's conservative racial views and Stoney's and Harllee's opposition to the New Deal, saw no need for bolting the convention simply because of participation by African Americans. Nevertheless, postcards bearing postmarks from Charleston, Stoney's hometown, flooded the state to advertise "a vote for Roosevelt and Byrnes means that the day is coming when dirty, evil-smelling negroes will be going to church with you, your sister, your wife or your mother. . . . All under Roosevelt laws."[46]

Fortunately for Byrnes, the race issue did not take hold in 1936. African Americans were not clamoring for membership in the state Democratic Party, and whites continued to control the patronage. Governor Johnston, whose political future lay in supporting the New Deal, took steps to quiet racial tensions among his followers.[47] Most newspapers that trumpeted the race issue were already against the New Deal, a fact not lost on undecided voters.[48]

On August 25 Byrnes was victorious by a vote of 257,247 to only 25,672 for Stoney and 12,551 for Harllee. Byrnes carried every precinct except one. In the autumn, counties held Roosevelt-for-Reelection rallies; the state party raised more than its quota for the national victory fund; and major dailies (excluding, of course, the *News and Courier*) gave the Republican Party its customary drubbing. On election day in November, Roosevelt carried the Palmetto State with 98.5 percent of the popular vote. Victory celebrations in Columbia that evening spilled over into Main Street, resembling Time Square on New Year's Eve.[49]

Confidence and optimism characterized South Carolinians at the end of 1936. A Democrat would be in the White House for four more years. Cotton brought an average price of more than 13 cents a pound, its best during the New Deal. Prosperity was also returning to textile country; employment and earnings were up, and demand was so great that mills were having to refuse orders. When the *Columbia State* professed its eagerness to begin Roosevelt's "Second New Deal," no doubt the paper had in mind a fine tuning of a state and national economy already on the road to recovery, not the revolution in separation of powers, race relations, and industrial relations that followed. Indeed, by 1939, after two years of political turmoil, the typical white South Carolinian differentiated between Roosevelt and the New Deal. He continued to regard the president with admiration and affection, but like his congressmen in Washington, he began to distrust at least a part of the New Deal as too Northern, too radical, and too minority oriented.

It all began with FDR's court-packing scheme, which stunned many South Carolinians. Within a month of his February 5, 1937, proposal, the critics were out in force. In the interest of judicial efficiency, the daily *Spartanburg Herald* and the weekly *Marion Star* and *Winnsboro News and Herald* favored the measure. Most other papers were opposed. Even the *State*, which approved the goal of obtaining favorable court decisions but disapproved the means, spoke of feeling "shame" and "humiliation" over the proposal.[50] Opposition soon crystallized in other quarters. The president of the South Carolina Bar Association stated that the proposal was "the beginning of the end of constitutional government as we know it."[51] Several Charlestonians formed a Supreme Court Security League pledged to defeat the court-reform legislation.[52] Prominent businessmen vented their anger in letters to Senator Byrnes, who supported court reform but whose mail ran heavily against the legislation. One lumber manufacturer complained, "I have been an ardent supporter of President Roosevelt until his attempt to pack the Supreme Court in order to be able to resurrect NRA and force upon industry regulations inimical to prosperity."[53] Greenville realtor H. D. Burgiss feared "this apparent assumption of dictatorial power" would be "just one long step towards Hitlerism or Fascism or the like."[54]

Nevertheless, there is good reason to believe that opposition of Main Street was not shared by the average citizen. One Gallup poll estimated 76 percent of all South Carolinians supported court reform. Moreover, former representative Frank Lever and Public Service Commissioner W. J. Cormack were convinced the average South Carolinian stood with the president. Wrote Cormack, "In recent months I have talked to the farmer in the field, to the worker in the shop, to the small storekeeper, to the textile operative, to the filling-station attendant, and to every other class and occupation of the average man; and I know this: there is an universal dissatisfaction with the Supreme Court as it is now constituted. The average man cannot see why there should be such a close division of Constitutional interpretation; and, whether true or not, they think the reactionary majority of the court cannot inhabit [sic] their minds from their earlier training and associations, and can only see property rights and view with disdain . . . 'human rights.'"[55]

Without the support of the average voter, the state legislature certainly would not have gone on record in favor of court reform. On February 10, five days after Roosevelt sent his court-reform bill to the United States Senate, state representative J. E. Leppard of Chesterfield and state senator Edgar Brown of Barnwell introduced resolutions in the South Carolina House and Senate endorsing the court-reform proposal and requesting the congressional delegation in Washington to vote for it.[56] The forces for the resolution, led indirectly by Senator Byrnes, were able to muster the votes. Collector of Internal Revenue Robert Cooper was his liaison with the legislature; former law partner Sam Nichols handled communications between Byrnes and Governor Johnston; and former law partner Donald Russell was his liaison with John Peel, who controlled labor representatives. Byrnes sent copies of his speeches on behalf of court reform to each legislator. Meanwhile, Johnston's floor leader, Caston Wannamaker, marshalled the governor's forces, while Congressman Fulmer lobbied the lower house on behalf of the resolution. In early March the House and Senate adopted a concurrent resolution stating court reform was "desirable and proper" because it was "designated and calculated to restrict the excessive powers of the United States Supreme Court and to enhance the powers of the people through their elective legislature and the Executive."[57] On March 12 Byrnes and Fulmer proudly inserted the resolution into the *Congressional Record.*[58]

Nevertheless, an increasing number of South Carolinians were growing wary of the unfolding Second New Deal, and Roosevelt's refusal to denounce sit-down strikes by the CIO did nothing to allay their fears. Press opinion in South Carolina was practically unanimous against the sit-down, even among New Deal organs such as the *Spartanburg Herald.* The *Daily Mail* of Anderson, for example, portrayed the CIO as Communistic, a haven for "foreign radicals and negroes," and synonymous with "flagrant disregard for law."[59] Businessmen joined the outcry. Harry M. Arthur of Union, a banker and a delegate to the Philadelphia convention, warned Byrnes that "while South Carolina gave Franklin Roosevelt the greatest majority of any state, the people are beginning to believe that he is deserting them for a cause the people down here do not believe in."[60]

More than any other factor, fear that Roosevelt wished to elevate the African American politically and socially fed apprehensions that he was deserting white South Carolinians for "alien" causes. As early as 1935 the *News and Courier* warned that African Americans were taking control of the Democratic Party. After the Philadelphia convention several more papers joined the chorus. The *Walterboro Press and Standard* sneered, "The Democratic party has showered favors upon the negro race, far above what the Republican party ever did."[61] A. G. Kennedy of Union warned Byrnes in June 1937: "Please watch Roosevelt, John L. Lewis and Jim Farley. The Triumvirate would gladly sell and sacrifice the entire white population of the South and put the Negro over us politically and economically if by so doing they could carry the Negro vote in America."[62] Blease, in an address to Greenville Young Democrats, denounced "so-called Democrats and foreigners and pap-suckers calling themselves

Democrats" who were supporting the antilynching bill.[63] The anxiety felt by men such as Kennedy and Blease, coupled with both a weariness of federal spending and bewilderment at a business recession in the midst of programs that were supposed to guarantee prosperity, promised to make 1938 an uncertain year for the popularity of the New Deal in South Carolina.[64]

Because the first order of congressional business in 1938 was the antilynching bill, the race issue remained a focus of attention. On January 12, 1938, the South Carolina House of Representatives adopted a resolution branding the measure "an insult to the Southern States."[65] Through January and February several newspapers remained convinced that the measure had administration backing because Roosevelt did nothing to keep it off the Senate agenda. The *Keowee Courier* worried that the New Deal aimed at both social and political equality for African Americans, since Eleanor Roosevelt seemed to delight in inviting them to the White House for tea.[66]

The race issue nearly wrecked the biennial state Democratic convention in the spring. Conflict loomed over state party Rule 32, which pledged a voter in the summer primary to support the national ticket in November. Party members, fearing a spokesman for racial equality or industrial unionism might be the national party's nominee in 1940, were determined to abolish Rule 32. The *Keowee Courier* mirrored this anxiety: "In the light of present conditions, with such a thing as a 'white man's party' nothing but a memory, we'd like to have the privilege to vote a national ticket just as we pleased."[67] A majority of delegates felt the same way: the convention tabled a motion pledging "unwavering faith" in President Roosevelt and voted to abolish Rule 32. It also adopted a platform urging the national Democratic Party to support the principle of white supremacy and rebuking national Democrats "who had so little regard for the rights of the South as to use every effort at their command to try to cram down the throats of the South an anti-lynching bill for political purposes."[68]

Obsession with race clouded the most dramatic Senate primary in the state's history, which pitted Cotton Ed Smith, the veteran of thirty years, against Gov. Olin Johnston and state senator Edgar Brown of Barnwell. Clearly, by 1938 Smith was the most conservative of the candidates. In December 1937 he joined ten other anti–New Deal senators to draft the Conservative Manifesto, a ten-point declaration for fiscal orthodoxy, tax revision, balanced budget, states' rights, and respect for both private property and private enterprise.[69] Johnston, by contrast, was liberal; Brown, moderate. The contest began in earnest on May 8, when Brown announced his candidacy as a New Dealer but not a "rubber stamp" or "yes-man" for the Roosevelt White House. Two days later Smith unveiled a platform containing his usual planks of tariff for revenue only, states' rights, and white supremacy. Finally, on May 16, from the White House steps in Washington after a conference with President Roosevelt, Johnston announced his candidacy on a record of "100 percent" support for the New Deal. He claimed to have Roosevelt's approbation.[70]

The traveling political roadshow opened on June 14 in Sumter, where all three candidates spoke in turn from the same platform. Brown promised to support the New Deal but vowed to follow the wishes not of Roosevelt but of the people of South Carolina. To say "tweet, tweet" whenever the president called would earn for South Carolina "bird seed and nothing more." Brown also attacked Johnston for trying to dominate the state legislature. The governor ignored Brown and focused on Smith, whom he portrayed as an obstructionist and an enemy of President Roosevelt. The senator was quick to deny the charge: "I have co-operated whenever I thought it was beneficial and right and opposed . . . when I thought it was wrong," he insisted. Labeling both opponents "coat-tail swingers," Smith added, "God knows what would happen if Roosevelt took off his coat." Smith questioned Johnston's "100 percent" New Deal-ism by asking if Johnston were 100 percent in favor of the antilynching bill and social equality for the African American. Here the senator served notice that the principle issue in his campaign would be white supremacy. Although insisting he loved blacks, Smith backtracked, "My love for them does not countenance political and social equality and I will never stand for it."[71]

From June 14 until President Roosevelt's visit to Greenville on August 11, the three candidates amplified the issues developed at Sumter. All three men used racial epithets freely. Brown reaffirmed his "wholehearted" support of the Roosevelt administration, denied that he was a "coat-tail swinger," charged that a senator was worthless if his only asset was an ability to "cuss niggers," blasted Smith for saying that a worker in South Carolina could live comfortably on a daily wage of 50 cents (which Smith had said only for illustrative purposes in arguing to retain the North-South wage differential), labeled Johnston "Machine-Gun Olin" for his attempt to control the highway department by force, and promised, if elected, to "bring home the bacon."[72] Johnston paraded his "100 percent" New Dealism, exploited Smith's 50-cents-a-day remark, charged that Smith was "trying to ride in [to the Senate] on a poor nigger," and called him a "termite working [from] within" and a "rubber head" who acted as an eraser of New Deal legislation.[73]

Neither Johnston nor Brown was able to best the old political thespian in debate. Smith called the charge that he said a South Carolinian could live on 50 cents a day a "damn lie" and flaunted a copy of the *Congressional Record* to prove it. To Brown's claim that he would "bring home the bacon," Smith retorted, "Yes, and he will put it in his own smokehouse." Smith suggested that if Roosevelt ever kicked backward toward his coattail, Johnston would be "crippled for life." "When God made Olin," Smith added, "he forgot to give him a brain" to think for himself.[74] Without question, the senator's most potent rhetorical weapon, the racist "Philadelphia Story" about his walkout from the Democratic National Convention in 1936, was polished to perfection. To an enraptured audience of one-horse white farmers, Smith would start to deliver what he called his "highbrow [speech] if there ever was a highbrow speech" reviewing the evolution of constitutional government. As he explained: "I started off on the Plains of Runnymede, got down through the battle of King's Mountain and was headed for the Civil War via the cussed protective tariff with a lot about the immortal John C. Calhoun. I felt somebody down in front was watching me. [All] of a sudden I looked down and there on the front seat was an old farmer with a torn black hat on his head and tobacco juice running down both sides of his mouth. I hesitated for a moment and looked at him. When I did he growled: 'Aw, hell, Ed, tell us about Philidelfy!'"[75] The audience would roar approval, and Smith would then recount his tale of the "slew-footed, blue-gummed, kinky headed Senegambian" who opened the Philadelphia convention with prayer. As "he started praying and I started walking," Smith added, "old John Calhoun leaned down from his mansion in the sky and whispered . . . 'You did right, Ed.'"[76]

Smith's prospects dimmed somewhat in mid-August. Against the advice of many of his counselors, the president had already marked for defeat in the Democratic primary several conservative senators, including Walter George of Georgia and Cotton Ed Smith of South Carolina. In midsummer Roosevelt went to Florida to indulge his favorite outdoor hobby, fishing. Rumors were rife that he planned whistle stops in Georgia and South Carolina on his return trip to Washington in order to campaign against the incumbents. Harry Hopkins, a close friend of pro–New

Deal gubernatorial candidate Burnet Maybank, feared that interference in the senatorial primary would adversely affect Maybank in the gubernatorial one. Asked by Hopkins to intervene, Byrnes warned the president of possible damage to Maybank and certain damage to the New Deal. He explained that if Roosevelt supported Johnston, who would likely find himself in a runoff against Smith, the Brown supporters would oppose the governor in the runoff. A defeat for Johnston would then be a defeat for Roosevelt and the New Deal.[77] Byrnes neglected to mention he was secretly supporting Smith in order to eliminate both Johnston and Brown as future opponents of his protégé, Burnet Maybank, who could take Smith's seat in 1944, when advanced age would almost certainly force his retirement. In addition, Byrnes realized the disadvantage of having two senators, Johnson and himself, from Spartanburg.[78]

On the afternoon of August 11, President Roosevelt stopped in Barnsville, Georgia, to campaign against Senator George. Later in the day Governor Johnston boarded the train and rode with Roosevelt to Greenville, arriving about 10:30 P.M. There a coterie of politicians, including Smith, Brown, Byrnes, and Maybank, scrambled aboard the train to be near Roosevelt when he addressed a crowd of some 25,000. The president gave a perfunctory greeting to Brown and said good-naturedly to Smith, "Well, here's the old pirate."[79] Flanked by Byrnes and Smith, the president then stepped to the rear platform to greet the crowd. After a welcoming speech by Governor Johnston, the president spoke briefly on the South's economic problems and concluded with two reminders. First, he planned to accept Governor Johnston's invitation to visit Columbia in the near future. At this point Byrnes motioned for the engineer to start the train. As the train began to move, Roosevelt, still holding the microphone on the rear platform, shouted his second reminder: "I don't believe any family or any man in South Carolina can live on 50 cents a day!"[80] As the train pulled away, the audience must have realized the president had demonstrated his opposition to Smith without specifically endorsing Johnston or Brown, both of whom used the 50-cents-a-day remark against Smith. Apparently, Roosevelt intended to endorse both Johnston and Brown and hope for a runoff between Johnston and Smith in which Brown's support would go to Johnston.

Byrnes quickly moved to repair the damage to Smith. In an effort to swell Smith's war chest, he warned wealthy financier Bernard Baruch, who was quietly supporting Smith: "Had the President remained out of South Carolina, Smith would undoubtedly have been elected. His success now, however, depends upon how many votes the President takes from him."[81] The next day Byrnes advised Baruch's secretary how best to aid Smith financially. In his letter Byrnes acknowledged he had already paid to have Smith's campaign literature distributed among war veterans, postmasters, and postal employees. In addition, Byrnes had given money to one sheriff, one U.S. marshal, and "two or three other persons" to hire poll workers for Smith and Maybank. The junior senator had also agreed to underwrite the cost of hiring poll workers in Charleston County, where vote tallies were traditionally subject to manipulation, and promised money to Smith through Collector of Internal Revenue Robert Copper to secure "some worthwhile people in two counties we deem important." Byrnes concluded, "We will be called upon for substantial help after [the first primary on] August 30th."[82] He was certain Roosevelt's promise to visit Columbia in the near future was an indication he would return to South Carolina during the runoff to campaign openly for Olin Johnston.[83]

The issues in the Senate primary remained the same after Greenville. What changed was the slate of candidates. On August 27, three days before the election, Brown withdrew from the race, saying he was the "third man" and realized it. No doubt aware that Roosevelt planned to campaign actively for Johnston in the runoff, Brown stepped aside to clarify differences between senator and governor and thus defeat Johnston, who had earned Brown's contempt during the bitter highway department struggle.[84] Brown knew that in a two-way race, many South Carolinians would perceive the major issue to be racial equality (Johnston) versus white supremacy (Smith).

Brown's action left Roosevelt in the lurch. The president issued a statement claiming Brown's withdrawal "clarified" the race, leaving voters to choose between one candidate who "thinks in terms of the past and governs his actions accordingly," and the other who "thinks in terms of 1938, and 1948 and 1958 as well."[85] Unwisely, Johnston telegraphed Brown to ask whether the Barnwell senator was a true New Dealer who intended to vote for Johnston or "only a stalking horse" for "Liberty Leaguers, Republicans, and Roosevelt-haters." Brown's public reply was devastating to Johnston. Brown claimed to be the only New Dealer in the race and called Johnston a demagogue of the Talmadge and Long variety. Consequently, Brown vowed, he would vote his conscience and "for the best interest of South Carolina Democracy," which served notice to his followers that he would vote for Smith.[86] Most of Brown's support, especially from the business community, went to Smith, who defeated Johnston on August 30 with 55 percent of the vote.[87]

Smith's decisive victory was more of a referendum on the New Deal than some pundits assumed but less of one than anti–New Dealers claimed. South Carolinians who voted for Smith did not vote against the New Deal of Roosevelt's first administration. Most were satisfied with the policies of the first four years. Votes for Smith were ballots against the New Deal of the second administration, containing the antilynching measure, the sit-down strike, and attempts to advance African Americans, all of which were interpreted as an insult to the white South. Smith cleverly designed his election-eve newspaper advertisements to capitalize on the popularity of Roosevelt's first administration and the unpopularity of his second. They stressed Smith's role in enacting New Deal farm legislation, his efforts in behalf of PWA and WPA, and his good relations with the AFL. His advertisements also stressed that the CIO, the favored labor organization of the second administration, supported Johnston and racial equality.[88]

Other factors crucial to Smith's victory were more local than national. First and foremost, Smith used race baiting as a smokescreen to cloud the ideological differences between senator and president. Of the eleven ABCDs, blacks was the most significant. This factor explains Smith's strong (though not majority) support from mill precincts in Spartanburg, Johnston's hometown.[89] Moreover, Governor Johnston's blunderbuss actions toward both the powerful highway department and the state legislature alienated many people and split the New Dealers in South Carolina into factions. For example, Fitz Hugh McMaster of Columbia, although a New Dealer, regarded Johnston as a "scoundrel," an "egotistical blind ass," and "such a fool that he does not understand the responsibilities of high office."[90] In addition, voters resented the meddling of Roosevelt, an outsider and Northerner, in their state's politics.[91]

No less important was the quiet, covert support given Smith by the junior senator, whose vast network of partisans throughout the state could influence election results in myriad ways. Noting that the "roll of officeholders in the state is four times as lengthy as was the roll of Grant's soldiers," whose votes in the early 1870s successfully maintained state and local Republicans in power, W. W. Ball of the *News and Courier* predicted accurately that the current "federal state machine," made up of "federal officeholders, WPA, the collectors of revenue, farm agents, [and] Santee-Cooper outfit," would support the candidate backed by the junior senator. "Byrnes, and not the president, controls the patronage in South Carolina," Ball explained. In fact, Ball was certain Roosevelt already had been warned, "You can't afford to interfere with Byrnes's plans in South Carolina. If you go out for this Johnston you will openly array the Byrnes gang including the federal machine in the state against you and they will beat you."[92] Roosevelt ignored this warning at his peril.

Despite the outcome, a vote for Smith in 1938 did not necessarily reflect wholesale disapproval of the New Deal. Roosevelt endorsed some policies that pleased, some that displeased, each person. The typical white South Carolinian, if asked his opinion of the New Deal, would have criticized the antilynching bill, sit-down strikes, probably relief spending, and possibly the Fair Labor Standards Act. The typical black South Carolinian would have condemned the flagrant discrimination against African Americans in the administration of all New Deal programs. Yet both of these individuals would have endorsed the New Deal if the alternative was no deal at all.

A breakdown of state population into economic interest groups reveals why the New Deal remained popular. Cotton farmers, cotton mill workers, and their families made up more than a million of the state's 1.7 million citizens. They appreciated the New Deal's attention to their needs. For farmers, the New Deal brought price supports, agricultural credit, a reduction in farm tenancy, soil-conservation measures, and rural electrification. For mill workers, there were better wages and hours, the right of collective bargaining, and an end to child labor. Yet, because of Smith's race baiting, the farm vote and part of the mill vote went to him in 1938.

By the same token, groups opposing the New Deal, which included Liberty Leaguers, Main Street, and political "outs" such as Stoney and Blease never were able to build a mass following. By 1940 Roosevelt's foreign policy brought many erring brothers, including Byrnes, back into the fold, and in the presidential election South Carolina gave Roosevelt more than 95 percent of its popular vote for an unprecedented third term. Jeffersonian Democrats, who supported Wendell Willkie and thus invited South Carolinians to vote against the New Deal without voting Republican, polled only 2,469 votes. In short, as the war years approached, South Carolinians still revered Roosevelt as a national messiah. But even national messiahs occasionally make mistakes.

A NEW DEAL FOR AFRICAN AMERICANS | 10

The New Deal was a mixed blessing for African Americans in South Carolina. Unaccustomed to government aid of any kind, they were overjoyed by the sudden economic opportunities afforded to all citizens. Like whites, they enrolled in the CCC, built schools for the PWA, dug ditches for the WPA, rented acreage to the AAA, continued their education with the help of NYA jobs, and received relief from the FERA. On the other hand, most government programs not only maintained segregation but also discriminated in terms of pay and frequency of employment. Some programs such as the AAA and NRA were even counterproductive. As a result, the New Deal did little to alter pernicious social and economic relationships and often deplorable conditions.

Politically and psychologically, however, the effects of the New Deal were beneficial. Initially, race relations seemed to improve. The exigencies of the Great Depression temporarily pushed racial issues aside, and the less virulent attitudes of Senator Byrnes prevailed until 1936. Racial politics did not resurface until the antilynching bill appeared session after session in the United States Congress, the national Democratic Party began to welcome blacks, and Cotton Ed Smith unfurled the battle flag of white surpremacy. But the same New Deal liberalism that, by 1938, encouraged whites to embrace racial politics also raised the consciousness of African Americans. Granted, the struggle for equality made few tangible gains in South Carolina before the 1940s. This reawakening of the 1930s actually began more than a decade earlier when World War I heightened expectations and the Harlem Renaissance spawned a more activist New Negro. It is also true that this consciousness raising would be limited largely to the small black bourgeoisie. Most of the isolated, illiterate, rural blacks, who in some counties made up more than 50 percent of the adult black population, could not yet envision a world of activism and equality.[1] Nevertheless, this reawakening has led one historian to suggest that the modern movement for equal rights "had its origin in the years of the Great Depression and the New Deal."[2]

At the outset of the New Deal, blacks were second-class citizens, if that. White control of the state was total, ranging from a monopoly on participation in the three branches of government to education, appropriations, and employment. Politically, blacks were largely disfranchised. After nine years of active political participation during Reconstruction, blacks gradually lost political entree through a combination of violence, fraud, and changes in election laws and procedures. In 1890 the Democratic primary—the only election that mattered in South Carolina—was closed to all but whites and a handful of blacks who could prove party loyalty since 1876. Through a combination of residency requirement, poll tax, literacy provisions, and an understanding clause, the 1895 state constitution eliminated all but about 5,500 black voters from participation in the general election. By 1900 blacks had effectively been removed from politics, and by 1930 far fewer than 1 percent of blacks were allowed to vote.[3]

Segregation by law, tradition, and custom accompanied disfranchisement. The assumption behind it was that blacks were inferior and would degrade white institutions and white society if the two races were allowed to intermingle. What had begun after the Civil War as de facto segregation was codified in the 1890s and early 1900s in education, transportation, accommodations, recreational facilties, penal institutions, and labor facilities. Interracial marriage was forbidden, and the militia, jury service, and police work were reserved for whites. Noted black educator and activist Dr. Benjamin Mays, who grew up in Greenwood County in the early 1900s, recalled that "black was black and white was white and never the twain did meet except in an *inferior-superior* relationship."[4]

Blacks were expected to address whites as "Mr.," "Mrs.," "Miss," "Cap," "Boss," "Sir," or "Ma'am," while whites addressed blacks by their first names or as "boy," "uncle," "girl," "aunt," or "nigger." This inferior-superior relationship required separate water fountains, restrooms, entrances, and exits in public places. It allowed whites to call at the front door of black homes, while forcing blacks to use the back door of any white residence. It required separate water containers, or at least separate drinking gourds, when blacks and whites worked together in construction or farm labor. It made walking down the street a humiliating experience for blacks, who had to be careful not to touch whites and to step off the sidewalk into the street if whites approached. In short, this inferior-superior relationship required that blacks be subservient, deferential, and cognizant of all whites as society's natural leaders.[5]

No doubt, many African Americans played the subservient role because of economics: blacks lived in poverty, and whites controlled their livelihood and thus could define their social status and political opportunities. Close to 80 percent of black Carolinians lived in rural settings where sharecropping, day labor, and domestic service predominated. As a result, in 1930 nearly 90 percent of rural blacks lived in unpainted dwellings whose value ranged from the equivalent of only seven bales of cotton for houses of landowners to five bales of cotton for those of tenants. Fewer than one-half of 1 percent of black farmers had telephones, electricity, indoor plumbing, or tractors.[6] Reading, writing, and keeping accounts were skills often reserved for white employers and farm owners. As Benjamin Mays pointed out, if the white landowner told John, the black tenant, that the latter "owed him so much, questions were not in order and no explanations were forthcoming." Or, if the landowner advised the tenant, "'We broke even this year; neither of us owes the other,' even if John knew he had cleared a hundred dollars, he would ask no questions, register no protest."[7]

Rural blacks learned early in life to rely on and look after one another. Lottie Cook Belton remembers that in Ridgeway during the late 1920s and early 1930s, several white businessmen routinely lent money to black landowners for seed, feed, and fertilizer. The borrower was required to put up his land and chattels as collateral. Her father, Richard Cook, was a black farmer who owned mules and wagons and often did contract work for one of the businessmen. One autumn morning after cotton had been selling below the cost of production, the businessman came to Cook's house with instructions; "Go down and break up Jubilee Williams." Cook realized that Williams, a black landowner, was in default on his loan and would have to forfeit all of his property, including even his household possessions. Although Cook had no choice but to comply with his employer's orders, he managed to store a wagonload of Williams's corn in his own cornhouse for Williams to retrieve later.[8]

Economic opportunities were little better in industry, trade, and commerce. Blacks traditionally labored at dirty, arduous, menial jobs that few whites wanted. Jobs in lumber, cottonseed oil, and fertilizer manufacturing were particularly unpleasant, and blacks made up from 75 to 80 percent of the workforce in these three occupations as late as 1940.[9] In the textile industry, the state's largest employer, blacks stoked furnaces, toted cotton, drove trucks, and cleaned bathrooms. Skilled and semi-skilled jobs were reserved for whites because state law prohibited blacks and whites from mixing in the textile workplace. Black workers made up only 5 percent of the textile workforce. Elsewhere in urban areas, blacks were common laborers or helpers to white tradesmen. The black bourgeoisie was tiny. Most members owned and operated businesses such as poolrooms, restaurants, or beauty parlors that catered only to blacks. In 1930 only thirteen black lawyers practiced in South Carolina, and the ratio of white to black doctors was twenty-two to one. With the exception of ministers, many of whom were not academically trained, teachers made up the largest segment of the black middle class. Yet discrimination in pay prevailed in education. The average salary for white male teachers was four times that of their black counterparts.[10]

Whites went to great lengths to maintain the colonial, nearly feudal, status of the African American. First, they resorted to terror and violence. Although the number of lynchings declined from fifty-one in the decade of 1890 to 1900 to seventeen in the period 1920 to 1933, the threat of rope and fagot was sufficient to make blacks "be careful and stay out of trouble" with whites.[11] Restricting public services to whites was designed to impress upon blacks their "nobodyness." In cities and towns, streets in white neighborhoods were paved; those in black neighborhoods, dirt. Black school systems were inferior in all respects, characterized by poorly trained and poorly paid teachers, dilapidated facilities, shorter school terms, and higher student-teacher ratios. Laboratories and libraries were almost nonexistent, and state appropriations were miserly.[12]

No less pervasive was cultural brainwashing by whites. Racist textbooks were supplied to black schools. Signs of "colored" and "white" labeled every public place. Racist jokes in white newspapers and by white speakers before black audiences were commonplace. Many whites refused to capitalize the "N" in "Negro" and tended to say "nigras" instead of "Negroes" when they did not simply say "niggers." The white community spoke approvingly of the Reverend Richard Carroll of Columbia, an accommodationist whose pronouncements seemed to concede black inferiority and endorse gradualism, self-help, conciliation, and industrial education. All of these examples were designed to stunt self-concepts, blunt aspirations, curtail ambitions, produce apathy, and promote a sense of powerlessness in the black community.[13]

Blacks responded in a variety of ways. No doubt, some did accept the subservient role, whether willingly or under duress. According to Benjamin Mays, they regarded the white man as "a little god—to be honored, revered, and idolized; or to be feared and obeyed."[14] Others simply feigned subservience. Still others resented the lot in life that an accident of birth assigned to them. In 1939 Walter Coachman of Bennettsville explained to a WPA interviewer, "I am a Negro. A mere whimsy of fate made me black and you white. It might easily have been the other way around. You were born with the blessings of Providence. Hands were extended to help you the day you were born, and you may go as far as your capabilities permit. But me? The cards were stacked against me the day I came into the world. I can go just so far—no further."[15] And yet, Coachman was content to demand nothing more than economic equality; social and political equality were beyond his aspirations.[16]

A few were more militant. World War I, the war to make the world safe for democracy, gave philosophical justification to black activism and opened up economic opportunities for blacks in war industries. Black emigration from South Carolina in the 1920s offered a safety valve for those who found life in the Palmetto State intolerable. The founding of organizations such as the NAACP in 1909 and the National Urban League in 1911 demanding fairer treatment for blacks gave black Carolinians a national podium to voice their grievances. The literary and intellectual Harlem Renaissance of the 1920s spawned a New Negro to compete with the accommodationist. The New Negro was race proud and resentful of racial insults. He was determined to have rights of citizenship enjoyed by other Americans. In reply to the accommodationist's assertion, "I know my place and I stay in it," the New Negro said, "The Negro who is constantly looking for his place can never assert his manhood."[17] The ratio in South Carolina of New Negroes to those who were, or appeared to be, accommodationists is unclear, although as late as 1928 Benjamin Mays admitted that the New Negro was a "rara avis."[18]

Whether rara avis or vulgaris avis, blacks in South Carolina quickly grew to appreciate the New Deal. The state's 13,000 or so black landowners were eligible for AAA benefit payments in the summer of 1933, and most took advantage of the program. By October, FERA relief payments were sustaining 28 percent of the black community. After relief payments gave way to WPA employment, blacks made up 40 percent of that agency's workforce. In the initial enrollment for the CCC in June 1933, 36 percent of the positions went to African Americans. By the time the New Deal ended, 26 percent of the campers and 23 percent of the camps were black. In 1939 black students made up 20 percent of NYA rolls. Although blacks never enjoyed New Deal aid in proportion to their population or need, they often fared better than blacks in other Southern states, as was the case with CCC enrollment. And the fact that they benefited at all was a departure from the recent past. Countless thousands of black Carolinians survived the 1930s literally because of the New Deal.[19]

Not only were black Carolinians recipients of New Deal aid, but they also participated in the implementation of at least one New Deal program. Administration of the AAA crop reduction program involved a cooperative effort by county agents, farmers who voted in referenda, and a host of local committees to encourage the signing of acreage reduction contracts and check compliance after farmers planted. Most counties had a black assistant county agent who was given the job of mobilizing the black community behind the AAA. For instance, James Dickson, assistant county agent for Richland, appointed several local committees of prominent black farmers to advertise the program's advantages. He then organized public hearings in schools, churches, and lodge halls to answer farmers' questions and stress the importance of 100-percent participation. He also traveled from farm to farm to pressure wavering producers. Finally, he collected the acreage-reduction contracts, checked them for accuracy, and turned them over to the white county agent for submission to Washington.

Black farmers also voted in large numbers in the cotton and tobacco referenda, and their votes were often decisive. In the 1938 cotton referendum, for instance, black farmers in Beaufort County cast at least 83 percent of that community's affirmative votes. In counties such as Beaufort, where black farmers outnumbered white ones, blacks even served as local committeemen to secure farmers' signatures on acreage reduction contracts and then checked for compliance after the farmer planted. As a result of widespread black voting in crop referenda and blacks' shouldering responsibilities as local committeemen, whites complained that blacks were "getting restless."[20] No doubt, these activities did give blacks a measure of self-confidence and a conviction that they could discharge the responsibilities of citizenship as well as whites.[21]

In education and health, blacks also benefited. Although a decent public school system for blacks was at least fifteen years in the future, black education made strides just before and during the New Deal through a combination of private Northern charity, local black generosity, and New Deal expenditures for capital improvements and programs under FERA, WPA, and PWA. Between 1926 and 1936 the percentage of high school seniors who were black rose from 0.3 percent of the total to nearly 12 percent of the total. Even per-pupil expenditures by the state increased for blacks nearly 43 percent between 1930 and 1940. The number of black college students more than doubled between 1928 and 1940, reflecting not only rising black self-confidence but also the impact of NYA aid. Advancements in health kept pace with those in education. As noted in chapters 3, 4, and 5, efforts in swamp drainage undertaken by FERA, WPA, and PWA in counties with large black populations significantly reduced deaths from malaria. Better water and sewage systems, courtesy of FERA and WPA, had a similar effect on deaths from typhoid and paratyphoid, which declined 70 percent and 77 percent respectively, between 1920 and 1940.[22] Certainly, the New Deal was a major contributing factor.

Economic stimulation helped reduce black unemployment. PWA purchases of lumber stimulated employment in an industry that was already the largest industrial employer of black workers. In 1930 approximately 88 percent of the lumber workforce was black. The diversion of cropland to forests in the late 1920s, and the promise of cheap power through Santee-Cooper in the late 1930s, created raw materials and future electric power for a pulp and paper industry that blossomed in the lowcountry between 1936 and 1938 and hired blacks in large numbers. The workforce in pulp and paper was approximately 25 percent black by 1940, and these workers took home nearly a half million dollars in wages annually.[23]

In addition, New Deal agencies furnished rural blacks with cash, a precious and scarce commodity before 1933. Its significance is difficult to overstate: the availability of cash gave tenants a measure of independence from the landowner, while the absence of cash had always contributed to the black man's semifeudal status. Dock Belton of Ridgeway remembers that prior to the AAA black sharecroppers never had cash because they stayed in debt to a landlord who "stood for" their purchases at the country store. "You're a bale shy of breakin' even," the sharecropper always expected to hear from his landlord at harvest time. Belton added of most black farmers, "If you had a quarter at Christmas time, you thought you were rich."[24] Another tenant, commenting on the availability of cash after 1933, said, "Seems like whites treat me better since the AAA. Tenants can now go to the government if they need something and the boss won't give it to them. They get it too." A white observer agreed: "The boss man used to arrange for them [black tenants] to trade somewhere and then pay the bill every month at *cash* prices and then charge them *times* prices. Now they let' em have cash—and if they don't they get it . . . from the government."[25]

Nevertheless, there were limitations to what the New Deal could do and would do for black Carolinians. Discrimination in all programs was rife. Black women, but not whites, constructed and maintained roads in the work-relief program. African Americans made up nearly 46 percent of the population and an overwhelming majority of the poor. Yet, they received about half as many CCC camp assignments and four-tenths as many NYA jobs as they were entitled to simply by virtue of population percentage. They were occasionally overrepresented in relative population on local relief rolls, partly no doubt to keep cheap black labor from migrating to other states. Whites were alarmed by an 8-percent decline in the black population in the 1920s, when 204,000 left the state. Yet even where blacks were overrepresented on relief rolls, individual black families received smaller relief payments than families of whites. Whites also received more than 95 percent of PWA appropriations for school construction before 1938. Their congressmen purposely exempted from coverage under Social Security and the Fair Labor Standards Act most jobs traditionally held by blacks.[26] As a result, in 1940 black businesses continued to be marginal enterprises that catered to a black clientele; black workers continued to occupy the lower-paying, unskilled, usually menial jobs. Clearly, economic advances and increased opportunity for blacks during the New Deal were absolute but never relative. In 1940 whites still controlled the economy, while blacks still struggled in a colonial status.

Some New Deal programs were counterproductive for blacks. The effects of the AAA and NRA were particularly insidious. Not only did increased costs associated with NRA codes force some black businesses into bankruptcy, but also many white employers either fired African American workers rather than pay them the same wage as whites or simply ignored the code requirement. In addition, jobs in agriculture and domestic service—traditionally black occupations—were not even covered by NRA codes. When the *Schechter* decision invalidated the NRA in May 1935, the black *Palmetto Leader* of Columbia predicted that blacks would "shed no tears," inasmuch as "many thousands of them lost their jobs they had for years, their employers being unwilling to pay them the wage prescribed."[27]

The negative impact of the AAA came in the form of tenant displacement. Landowners often complied with AAA acreage reduction by displacing black tenant families. Scores of tenants who remained, and many small black landowners as well, were unable to make ends meet on meager acreage allotments and forced to migrate to the North or to a nearby city. Between 1930 and 1940 the number of black farm operators decreased by 21 percent, from 77,425 to 61,307; the decline in white farm operators was only 5 percent, from 80,506 to 76,251. Similarly, the acreage in black farms fell 12 percent, from 3,171,976 acres to 2,781,837 acres, while white farm acreage actually increased 17 percent, from 7,221,137 acres to 8,456,860 acres. Coupled with an increase in the size of the average farm from 65.8 acres in 1930 to 81.7 acres in 1940, these figures indicate white landowners simply absorbed the land of former black tenants.[28] In light of black tenant displacement, as well as the increase in meat and grocery prices caused by restricted agricultural production, the *Palmetto Leader* was certain the "average [black] consumer" would "thank heaven" for the *Butler* decision invalidating the AAA.[29]

There is also reason to believe that white supervisors on WPA projects worked black laborers harder than white ones. On one farm-to-market road project in Charleston County that employed thirty-nine black laborers in 1938–1939, the white project superintendent suffered the disdain of the white community for accepting a job with WPA. Some local residents complained that the project was unnecessary. Others agreed, "The Negroes spend their time leaning on their shovels, the foremen sitting on their behinds." The white superintendent, who would have been unemployed but for the project, complained bitterly about his own predicament. "When a man reaches forty," he said, "its all over for him. Friends and politicians have made me promises but they were just talking, trying to let me down easy." He seems to have taken out his frustrations on the black laborers. Except for lunch, he allowed no breaks during the eight-hour workday for any reason. "They are supposed to take care of their bodily needs before they leave home," he said. He also refused to allow absences for illness. "If they are absent five days hand-running," he explained, "they are automatically released from the project."[30]

The New Deal not only accepted but also encouraged segregation. All alphabetical programs practiced it, and in those that benefited both races, patterns of discrimination remained. In administering the AAA, black assistant county agents answered to whites. Even in heavily black counties where blacks gained positions on AAA committees, a white county agent admitted, "I use them as little as I possibly can."[31] In the

CCC, black campers were under white camp commanders and project superintendents, but never were white campers under blacks. The same was true in work-relief projects under FERA and WPA. The PWA housing program had separate white and black projects. On at least one occasion the FSA was willing to create a "protective belt" of relocated white tenants in order to keep relocated black tenants from residing on land adjacent to white landowners. On WPA construction projects with integrated workforces, blacks called white supervisors "Cap" or "Boss," while whites called blacks any name they wished. Separate dippers hung on water jugs. Blacks rode in the bed of dump trucks; whites rode in the cab; and blacks and whites went their separate ways when the workday ended. In short, just as the New Deal did not alter the African American's relative economic status, neither did it improve him socially.

Paradoxically, this New Deal, which did so little to alter pernicious social and economic norms, was a major stimulus of black activism. The threat of congressional passage of an antilynching bill, which hung over the South throughout the New Deal, may have discouraged white violence against blacks. The decline of the black population in the 1920s from a majority to a minority of the state's citizenry perhaps diminished the seige mentality of the white community. The continuing threat of black emigration made whites more attentive to black grievances. Actions by the Roosevelt administration served notice on white Carolinians that blacks were henceforth to be considered as better than second-class citizens.

In particular, in 1936 FDR pledged that his America would be a land of "no forgotten races."[32] He insisted on black participation in that year's Democratic National Convention. Over the next four years he publicly denounced lynching, appointed the army's first black brigadier general, and worked for fuller black participation in defense employment and military training. He also supported a plank in the national party platform, calling for "complete legislative safeguards against discrimination in government service and benefits and in the national defense forces."[33] Finally, the right of blacks to vote in AAA referenda, serve on county AAA committees, and take advantage of alphabetical programs gave many of them a sweet taste of first-class citizenship, a draft of which they were determined to drink deeply.

In summary, the New Deal milieu not only encouraged what whites called a "black restlessness" but also gave rise to an activism with less fear of reprisals, especially among younger blacks not dependent on the white community for their livelihood. For many blacks, therefore, the New Deal completed what historians call "psychological emancipation."[34]

Even though the modern Civil Rights Movement in South Carolina dates from the 1960s, the decade of the New Deal was certainly a "prelude to revolution" for the black community's "talented tenth."[35] Black activism was apparent from at least 1934. In that summer a small group led by Dr. Robert W. Mance of Columbia attempted to register for the Democratic primary. State law, as noted earlier, restricted membership in the Democratic Party and the privilege of voting in the party primary to whites and those blacks who could prove their Democratic loyalty since 1876. Initially, the Mance group was allowed to register. But ten days before the primary—too late for them to seek remedial action in the courts—party officials demanded that they prove their Democratic loyalty since 1876 or be purged from the voting rolls. Unable to do so, Mance argued unsuccessfully that the requirement was unconstitutional because it was not uniformly administered; white women, in particular, were allowed to vote in the party primary in 1934, even though their Democratic loyalty extended only to 1920, the year of women's suffrage. Mance then sued for relief in state court, which did not consider the case until the primary election had been held. The court even salted the wound by claiming that Mance had not brought his suit within "a reasonable time before the primary is held."[36] Further salt was added when the Democratic Party simply dropped the loyalty requirement for blacks and restricted primary voting to white Democrats.

The introduction in Congress of an antilynching bill in 1935 prompted formation of a State Negro Citizens Committee under Dr. Mance and Modjeska M. Simkins of Columbia. The committee sent telegrams supporting enactment to President Roosevelt and the state's congressional delegation. The communication to Senator Smith requested that he act the part of a Christian lawmaker and not the part of a "barbarous and brutal . . . two-by-four politician."[37] Such activism was appropriate to the Simkins strategy of "strike the opposition as hard as you can, as fast as you can, in as many ways as you can."[38]

Nor were blacks willing to sit quietly while supervisory and professional jobs in New Deal relief agencies went exclusively to whites. In 1935, at a public forum hosted in Columbia by the WPA to explain its new work-relief program, Simkins and Mance quickly realized that professed white concern for "undeprivileged" blacks would relegate blacks to laboring jobs only. They protested strenuously. Complaining that all blacks, including even doctors, were "underprivileged," Dr. Mance warned, "You had better give my people some white-collar jobs, too."[39] In response, WPA officials agreed to hire blacks as teachers, health-care professionals, and academicians for the state history project. In Greenville, meanwhile, a group of black business and professional men successfully pressured the WPA to install sewage systems in African American districts.[40]

In 1936 a two-party system budded in black Carolina when a number of blacks once again tried to participate in the Democratic primary and succeeded in voting for Roosevelt in the general election. The Republican Party was no longer an option for many African Americans. The Tolbert faction was politically active only in election years, when "Tieless Joe" would assemble a delegation of "black and tans" and carry them to the Republican National Convention for sale to the highest bidder. If the Republicans won the general election, he would distribute patronage plums and then lie dormant for three years until the next election. The Hambright faction was "lily white" with no more than a token representation of blacks. Moreover, blacks by 1936 adored Roosevelt and wanted to share in his reelection victory. One registrar in Columbia observed, "They say Roosevelt saved them from starvation, gave them aid when they were in distress, and now they are going to vote for him."[41]

Blacks were no more successful in registering for the Democratic primary in 1936 than they had been two years earlier. Registering for the general election was another matter. A poll tax of $1 a year no longer proved to be a major impediment. Although the white chairman of the Charleston board of registrars hoped the poll tax "saves us from having a great big nigger vote," scores of black teachers, nurses, professors, doctors, dentists, pharmacists, lawyers, undertakers, ministers, and businessmen paid the tax and met the other voting requirements in order to declare their allegiance to FDR.[42] In fact, black registration during the summer before the general election in the fall was sufficiently large to warrant a *New York Times* article on August 23 proclaiming, "Negro Vote Jumps in South Carolina."[43] A white registrar in Sumter took note of the "big registration of darkies."[44] He was certain "'might' near all of them voted for Roosevelt, too."[45] Within two years, estimates of black registration in Columbia reached nearly 1,000 persons. Another 800 to 1,000 registered in Charleston. In rural counties such as Pickens, however, where the black middle class was negligible, fewer than ten African Americans were able to satisfy the voting requirements.[46]

The white response was predictable. Despite the fact that blacks had been a minority since 1923, voting-age blacks still outnumbered whites in nearly half of the forty-six counties.[47] Some whites feared that black voting portended a return to the bloodshed of Reconstruction. "We are coming on bloody times when he [the African American] becomes a part of our voting public," said former Charleston mayor Thomas Stoney.[48] A member of the Maybank Machine in Charleston was more cynical. Black voting would simply exacerbate electoral corruption, he argued. Leaders of the machine in Charleston "already have the poor whites to buy. The Negro vote would greatly increase the cost . . . [and] the machine could not bear it."[49] Accordingly, whites in heavily black counties repeatedly warned white registrars, "You better be careful the way you register up all those niggers."[50]

Whites also went beyond warnings. In Saluda a politically active black narrated the reprisals by whites against six of the eight blacks who registered to vote. Ford mechanic James Bush "got fired." School teacher Ella McGraw "was warned by the authorities that she had better not 'mess with such as that.'" One preacher, John Davis, was "warned." Another clergyman, John Williams, who worked during the week as a popular bank janitor and even claimed friendship with Saluda's mayor, lost his job at the bank. "The mayor said he was surprised," the black narrator said. "He said he'd always liked him [Williams], but right there he ruint hisself when he started foolin' with votin'."[51] Only one of the six registrants, a self-employed undertaker, escaped punishment. Thus, in spite of occasionally heavy black registration, black voting remained light, especially in rural counties. As late as 1940, not more than 1,500 blacks voted.[52]

Nevertheless, the fact that more blacks voted in 1940 than in 1930, coupled with a burgeoning black awareness of how their votes could influence elections, bespoke political maturity. Black leaders in Charleston were aware that in the 1910s Mayor John P. Grace inquired about the feasibility of courting the black vote in municipal elections. On being told that only 328 Charleston blacks were registered, he replied in disgust, "I'm sorry. I can't use 328. It will do me more harm than good."[53] By the late 1930s black activists in the port city were encouraging heavy black-voter registration in hopes that competing white factions would do what Mayor Grace had been unwilling to do: namely, to bid for the black vote by offering economic and political guarantees. These black leaders were only twenty years ahead of their time. After the 1960 presidential election, when black voters gave John F. Kennedy a victory in South Carolina, competing whites began to bid for the black vote.[54]

White pressure in Greenville was even more systematic than in Saluda, but black resolve there was also more determined. By the fall of 1938 blacks in Greenville were not politically energized. Only thirty-five were even registered to vote. Early the following year the city fathers rejected an $800,000 PWA grant for public housing and slum clearance favored by the black community. Leaders and members of several black organizations were so incensed that they stepped up plans for a voter registration drive already in its infancy. Sermons in black churches stressed the importance of voter registration. Personal visits to prospective registrants generated enthusiasm. Guides in front of the courthouse offered instruction on registration procedure, and activist Mary McLeod Bethune encouraged participants at a Greenville rally to "get representation." Led by local educator and Republican activist James A. Briar, the campaign enrolled approximately 350 voters. The aim of the campaign was to influence the municipal elections in the fall by electing a candidate who favored the housing project and construction of a public park for blacks.[55]

At this juncture the Ku Klux Klan, local police, and white press swung into action. Inflammatory newspaper accounts warned of 600 to 900 new black registrants flooding the polling booths. Fred D. Johnson, local KKK leader, publicly announced, "The white race is and should remain what God created it—supreme."[56] The July 7, 1939, edition of the *Greenville News* carried a Klan notice that read, "Fiery Summons—All Klansmen Are Called to Action."[57] With the approval of local policemen, most of whom were thought to be Klansmen, the KKK attempted to terrorize the black community. They beat up a war veteran who worked in the registration drive. They warned other campaign workers. Eight black homes were ransacked. Klan motorcades paraded through Greenville.[58] After publicly arguing with a Klansman in front of the county courthouse, a campaign worker was arrested for allegedly attempting to date a white girl. Another was jailed and twice terrorized there by Klansmen.[59]

In decades gone by, such pressure would have been sufficient to cower the African American community. In 1939 it retarded the registration drive but also emboldened many blacks. Fearful of damage to their persons and property, black businessmen and professionals armed themselves. Some even notified the Klan of their willingness to meet violence with violence. Although Briar was arrested and fined for carrying a concealed weapon, black registration continued into the 1940s "one or two at a time."[60] It also continued despite an announcement by city fathers that Greenville would use WPA money to construct two well-equipped playgrounds for African Americans. Nevertheless, blacks decided to place limits on their electoral activism. In the Greenville municipal elections of September 1939, only about fifty-four blacks voted, although this figure was more than 50 percent greater than the number of black registrants the year before.[61]

This spirit of political activism inspired the black middle class to become more assertive. Throughout the New Deal, the *Columbia Palmetto Leader*, edited by black attorney Nathaniel J. Frederick, spoke out eloquently against all visible forms of white racial oppression. The paper decried discrimination in education—$44.31 allotted to educate each white child but only $12.57 for each black child. It supported antilynching bills and attacked lynching as the product of "race hatred," "meanness," and the South's willingness to "allow mobs to take the place of its courts." Frederick demanded the right of blacks to vote in Democratic primaries and serve on grand and petit juries. When Olin Johnston and Ben Adams complained about the unfairness of state relief policies, the *Palmetto Leader* could not help wondering why they neglected to mention blacks. "The population of the state is about equally divided," the paper wrote, "but anyone with sense enough to change a fifty-cent piece knows that most of the money finds its way to the white side."[62]

Interestingly, the *Palmetto Leader*, which reflected the sentiments of black (and often Republican) Main Street, never wholly embraced the New Deal. To be sure, the paper admired Roosevelt. It often praised the "broad-minded, liberal and courageous man" in the White House. In 1938 a black ministerial group in Charleston echoed these sentiments in a telegram praising Roosevelt for appointing an administration "characterized by tolerance and fair dealing for all groups."[63] But the black business and professional community understood that the New Deal coalition rested on the goodwill of white Southern Democrats, all of whom were hostile to black aspirations. Consequently, the *Palmetto Leader* was frank to call FDR's Social Security Act racist because domestic servants, farm laborers, and casual workers—mostly blacks—were exempted from its benefits. The paper opposed SCERA aid to white strikers: "No one who can work . . . should be thus supported," the paper opined. It opposed Roosevelt's court-packing scheme because Southern racists would likely be Supreme Court nominees. It decried the nomination of

Hugo Black to the high court because of his former Klan membership.[64] Therefore, because of the prominence of white Southerners in the Democratic Party, a few African Americans were reluctant to join the stampede into it. As late as 1948 black activist Modjeska Simkins was a delegate to the Republican National Convention. Two years later she chaired the Richland County Republican Party.[65]

Middle-class blacks such as Simkins were as pragmatic as they were liberal. As early as the presidential election of 1932, the *Palmetto Leader* urged readers to divide their votes between parties. "Two markets are always better than one for healthy bargaining," the paper urged. "God help the nation, and God pity the Negro," Frederick added, if blacks should decide to restrict their support to one party. The *Palmetto Leader* warned both political parties in 1938 that they "must offer the Negro something more than oratory and empty promises to control his vote from now on."[66] Perhaps black activists also split their votes because of the negative economic impact of the New Deal on blacks in South Carolina. In addition to the rampant discrimination evident in all New Deal programs, the effects of the AAA and NRA were particularly resented.

The awakening of black Carolina even extended into the countryside. Historically, civil rights movements had centered in urban areas, where confident, race-conscious, and better-educated blacks were less dependent upon whites for their livelihood and better able to protect themselves through group solidarity and communication. The cities also had large black churches, colleges, and professional organizations that furnished leadership for black protest.[67] Consequently, Charleston, Columbia, Greenville, Spartanburg, Orangeburg, and Rock Hill were the centers of black activism in the 1930s. Nevertheless, the proverbial black telegraph that moved information from plantation to plantation in the days of slavery had become the black telephone by the 1930s.

Late in the decade, for example, farm laborer Buster Hubbard was interviewed for Ralph J. Bunche's *The Political Status of the Negro in the Age of FDR*. Although admitting he had never read a newspaper or listened to a radio, Hubbard quickly added that he knew all about President Roosevelt. "Swell man, Mistuh Roosevelt," he said. "He is Negro fren' 'cause mos' people out here is renters and Mr. Roosevelt 'low so much a year to rent crops and give us peas and food for cotton and all."[68] Another farmworker, Nero Brown, in reply to an interviewer's question about blacks discussing politics, answered, "Yes'm, 'specially we colored folks gits together and talks about Senator Smith. He's a mean white man to us colored folks."[69] Thad Gibson added, "Roosevelt has done more for colored people than any other president. . . . He give us our first school—a three-room WPA school. He give us teachers. . . . He give us food when we was hungry and our children hot WPA lunches in school."[70] Peter Epps, a farmworker for twenty years, cinched the matter; blacks, he said, "talked more politics since Mustuh Roosevelt been in than ever befo'."[71]

With some rural blacks awakened and many urban blacks protesting, key segments of the black community emerged to provide the future leadership for the civil rights movement of the next three decades. The NAACP would be their vehicle. Local branches had been established shortly after the founding of the national organization in 1909. Efforts before 1920 by the chapter in Charleston helped secure employment of black women in the Charleston Navy Yard and the removal of white teachers from black schools. Yet, the harsh economic conditions of the Great Depression depleted organization ranks. By 1930 chapters remained only in Charleston, Columbia, and Greenville to do little more than complain of police brutality and lynchings.

The reappearance of the antilynching bill during the New Deal inspired blacks to intensify their struggle for better treatment. In Columbia, NAACP chapters were formed at Benedict College and Allen University, whose members joined students from Claflin College in Orangeburg to participate in a nationwide antilynching demonstration on February 21, 1937. The following year members of Columbia's black middle class formed the Civic Welfare League to demand better housing, better law enforcement, playgrounds for black children, and black policemen. In 1938 seven African American clergymen telegraphed Roosevelt to oppose Olin D. Johnston's bid for a federal judgeship. His own racist actions and words in the 1938 senatorial primary, the telegram stressed, "wounded the sensibilities of approximately one-half of his constituency."[72]

Nineteen thirty nine brought the creation of the South Carolina Conference of the NAACP, a turning point in the struggle for black rights. The formative event occurred in the library at Benedict College in Columbia on November 10, when representatives of branches in Sumter, Greenville, Georgetown, Florence, Cheraw, and Aiken assembled at the instigation of Cheraw activist Levi S. Byrd. The executive board of the new state conference read like a *Who's Who* of the Civil Rights Movement from 1940 to 1970: Modjeska Simkins and the Reverend

James M. Hinton of Columbia, James A. Briar of Greenville, Samuel J. McDonald of Sumter, and Byrd. With "better leadership and more direction," wrote historian I. A. Newby, the new statewide organization was now able to become "more active, more persistent, and more concerned with real problems."[73] Leadership provided in the new conference by members of the Cheraw branch indicated its leftward turn, Cheraw's Rev. Alonzo Wright serving as first statewide president and Maggie Robinson as executive secretary. Five months earlier the Cheraw chapter adopted a document critical of attempts simply to obtain fairer treatment within separate but equal. "To be set aside as a subject group by social prejudice and government sanction," the manifesto proclaimed, "is to be robbed of the same native rights which others demand. . . . What the Negro needs is INTEGRATION, instead of SEGREGATION."[74] Within ten years membership statewide increased from 800 to 14,237. Within fifteen years the number of branches grew from eight to eighty-six.[75]

Like a mother who dies in childbirth, the New Deal ended the same year the statewide conference of the NAACP began. Just as the effects of the New Deal extend beyond the 1933 to 1939 period, so the effects of black protests in the 1930s transcend that decade. In fact, every gain realized in the 1940s and early 1950s had its origin in the activism of the 1930s. These include abolition of the poll tax and white primary, equitable salaries for black teachers, a separate law school and/or state support for black Carolinians in graduate studies outside the Palmetto State, a voice in Democratic councils, and, in the case of the Cheraw NAACP, integration in areas such as public education. These gains were made possible by the tremendous changes brought about by World War II and its aftermath. Nevertheless, it is possible to view the years 1933 to 1954 as a continuum partly inspired by the New Deal.

The first gain to be realized was the equalization of teachers' salaries. In late 1940, after the U.S. Supreme Court upheld NAACP suits to equalize teachers' pay in Maryland and Virginia, the NAACP in South Carolina worked with national counsel Thurgood Marshall to prepare a suit. Marshall outlined a blueprint that involved appointment of a steering committee to collect data proving discrimination, solicitation of funds to handle both legal expenses and salary support for teachers who lost their jobs in the effort, and identification of a suitable plaintiff. The most active member of the steering committee quickly became forty-eight-year-old Osceola McKaine of Sumter, who had fought as a lieutenant in

World War I and spent the next two decades as a businessman in Belgium before returning to Sumter in December 1940 after World War II broke out in Europe. With money derived from the sale of Belgian property before his departure for America, McKaine was free from white economic pressure and able to devote his days to data collection and war chest building. Equally important, he worked as associate editor and columnist for the *Charleston Lighthouse,* later to become the *Columbia Lighthouse and Informer,* where for three years he made salary equalization the paper's cause célèbre.[76]

By early 1943 the suit was a certainty. Data collection was complete, and a South Carolina Teachers' Defense Fund was in place. White opponents quickly swung into action, warning taxpayers that the state would have to raise $2.5 million in new taxes each year to fund equalization. Undeterred, the NAACP secured Charleston educators Malissa Smith and later Viola Louise Duval to bring the action. Harold C. Boulware of Columbia assisted Thurgood Marshall as counsel for the plaintiff. In the Smith case the Charleston School Board took evasive action and let community pressure frighten her into taking a job in New York. Duval was more persistent, braving hate mail, anonymous threats to her person and property, and even ostracism by fellow black teachers.[77]

On February 10, 1944, the case of *Duval v. Seigneus* came before federal district judge J. Waites Waring of the eastern district of South Carolina in Charleston. Marshall and Boulware had little hope of victory at this level, hoping instead to win on appeal to the U.S. Supreme Court. Before his appointment to the federal bench in 1941, Judge Waring had been a member of the Maybank Machine, city attorney for Charleston, and supporter of Senators Byrnes and Smith. He was also a member in good standing of the first families of blueblood Charleston. As the trial opened that winter morning, Marshall grew even more dismayed. Judge Waring asked counsel for the Charleston School Board to provide the date of the Norfolk, Virginia, decision requiring salary equalization. When Marshall attempted to answer, Waring cut him off with, "I didn't ask you, Mr. Marshall." A second request for the defense to ascertain the date of the Maryland decision drew the same attempt to speak by Marshall and the same curt response by Waring. After defense attorneys answered Waring's queries, he turned to a stunned Marshall and said: "Mr. Marshall, I don't want you to think I was being rude in not permitting you to answer those questions. I know you know the answers. . . . What I was trying to determine was how long it has been that the School

Board has known it must pay equal salaries to its teachers. This is a simple case and there isn't need to take up the court's time. I have a question for you—what kind of order do you wish entered? Do you want salaries equalized immediately? Do you want to give the Board some time to equalize?"[78] Based on Marshall's response to him, Judge Waring gave the city until September of 1946 to equalize teachers' pay. NAACP suits in other counties quickly brought them into compliance.[79] These suits sounded the death knell of educational inequality, although the final demise would be a long time in coming.

The second gain to be realized, opening the Democratic primary to black voters, was more valuable. Over time, politically empowered blacks would be able to use their voting prowess to wring economic and social concessions from the white power structure. The leaders in this campaign were mostly hardened veterans of the black protest movement during the New Deal who worked in occupations immune from white pressure: State NAACP president James Hinton, a Baptist minister and life insurance company executive; Modjeska Simkins, an alumna of Benedict College, NAACP state secretary, representative of the South Carolina Tuberculosis Association, and wife of a successful black merchant; physician Robert W. Mance; plumber Levi Byrd; John H. McCray, publisher and editor of the weekly *Columbia Lighthouse and Informer;* Osceola McKaine, newspaper columnist and well-to-do entrepreneur; and pastor E. A. Adams of Columbia. Every two years since 1934, many of them had attempted unsuccessfully to register for the Democratic primary. In 1942 America was at war and blacks were being asked to die for a nation and state that denied them the right to participate in the only election that mattered. A sense of urgency gripped the black community, and scores of would-be registrants flooded voter registration offices. Despite support from white doctor J. Heywood Gibbes and white lawyer R. Beverly Herbert of Columbia, who spoke at the State Democratic Convention in favor of opening the primary to black voters, the white power structure was unyielding.[80]

The black community remained determined. At a statewide meeting called in May by James Hinton after the State Democratic Convention adjourned, a South Carolina Negro Citizens' Committee (SCNCC) was created to oversee the campaign for an open primary. A month later Hinton met in Columbia with NAACP counsel Thurgood Marshall to plan strategy. The two agreed that black Carolinians would forego legal action until the U.S. Supreme Court decided the pending *Smith v. Allwright* case to open the white primary in Texas. In the meantime, black citizens would attempt to register in every primary election and fill out affidavits documenting what happened. The SCNCC also contributed financial support to the effort in Texas.[81] In a letter to Marshall, Hinton expressed the mood of black Carolina. "South Carolina is aroused as never before," he wrote, "and we expect great things from this awakening."[82]

Great things seemed to come in April 1944, when the U.S. Supreme Court struck down the white primary in *Smith v. Allwright.* Because Texas statutes regulated the white primary, the court ruled the primary was actually part of the state electoral process and violated the Fifteenth Amendment with respect to the exclusion of black voters. A delighted Osceola McKaine wrote, "Thank God South Carolina is still a part of the United States. Unless and until she once again secedes from the Union, she shall be compelled to obey the courts."[83] Unfortunately, the ingenuity of white South Carolina was equal to the occasion. As soon as the Supreme Court ruled in the Texas case, Gov. Olin D. Johnston called the legislature into special session to convert the state Democratic Party into a "private club" by repealing 150 statutes pertinent to the primary. The "private" Democratic Party then proceeded to exclude blacks from its "private" primary elections. The white voters of South Carolina were delighted enough with Johnston's "South Carolina Plan" to elect him to the U.S. Senate over the aging and frail incumbent, Cotton Ed Smith. Johnston, who lost when Smith played a race card in the 1938 Democratic primary, won with a race card of his own in 1944.[84]

However, this time black determination was more than a match for white ingenuity. First, blacks organized the South Carolina Progressive Democratic Party to give blacks a political voice until the white primary could be opened permanently. The party claimed an active membership of 45,000 and a sympathetic following of thousands more. It was born on May 23, 1944, at a convention in Columbia of 150 delegates from 38 counties. Thirty-four-year-old John H. McCray, whose *Lighthouse and Informer* was the semiofficial voice of the state NAACP and widely recognized as "the political bible of the new Negro voter in South Carolina," served as temporary and later permanent party chairman.[85] The distinguished orator and keynote speaker, Osceola McKaine, eighteen years McCray's senior, urged the convention to decide "here and now" whether black Carolinians "shall be free men or . . . spineless serfs." The loud response in favor of "free men" elicited his ringing conclusion: "On to the polls, on to congress, and on to yonder statehouse!"[86] With movement already afoot among white Democrats to bolt the national party and create a Southern Democratic Party pledged to anyone but Roosevelt, who was deemed too liberal on race relations, the SCPDP convention selected a delegation pledged to FDR to attend the National Democratic Convention in Chicago. McCray and McKaine would serve as cochairs.[87]

This action put national party leaders in a quandary. Anxious to dump Vice Pres. Henry Wallace from the national ticket, they wanted to avoid potentially damaging battles over credentials that might shatter party unity. Their hopes were dashed when Sen. Burnet Maybank, leader of the regular South Carolina Democratic delegation, announced to the Democratic National Committee, "As a Southern Democrat, I do not propose to be run out . . . by either the Negroes, the Communists, or Northern agitators," and John H. McCray responded, "Gentlemen, we are going to Chicago. Now if you care to, you can start talking from that point."[88] McCray eventually softened his position after the DNC promised unspecified efforts to integrate the South Carolina Democratic Party, protect black voters, and help finance PDP organizational efforts. Although the PDP delegation went to Chicago and joined the abortive movement to keep Wallace on the ticket, partly out of fear that South Carolina's James F. Byrnes might get the vice presidential nod, McCray accepted without challenge the DNC ruling to seat the regular Democrats.[89]

At home, PDP leaders plunged into a statewide black voter registration drive. White opposition was universal. In Marlboro County, black registrants were given the wrong voting cards. In Calhoun a white registrar spent nearly eight hours determining the fitness of five black teachers with respect to the literacy and understanding clause. In Chesterfield not only did a white registrar make black applicants wait in line at an unmanned registration table for seven hours, but countless other blacks waited for a registrar who never returned from lunch. Nevertheless, blacks persisted.[90]

Determined to act in all respects like a political party, on August 30, 1944, the Progressive Democrats named Osceola McKaine as their candidate for the U.S. Senate seat being vacated by Smith and sought by Johnston. McKaine became, in the words of his biographer, "the first African-American in the twentieth century to run as a Democrat [albeit a Progressive Democrat] for a major federal office in a southern state."[91] Not only would this campaign demonstrate the organizational and marketing abilities of blacks, it would also advertise the new party in the black community as a viable alternative to white political groups. McKaine campaigned with characteristic panoply and gusto. His rallies featured flags and bunting in abundance, songs, prayers, musical entertainment, and always remarks on the theme, "I have always stood for everything the New Deal and Franklin Delano Roosevelt stand for."[92] The white power structure took his candidacy seriously enough to allow him a fifteen-minute radio address over Columbia station WIS. No doubt, they concluded that black votes for him would simply reduce the already negligible Republican total.[93]

Election day was a disappointment. McKaine finished third behind winner Johnston and first runner-up Republican James B. Gaston. Nevertheless, he did garner more than 3,000 votes, and perhaps as many as 5,000 more were discarded or not counted. Whites had resorted to business as usual: white employers patrolled polling places to take down names of black employees who voted; white policemen at polling stations provided a menacing presence; and polling officials either did not display PDP ballots or gave blacks regular Democratic ballots.[94]

The intimidation and fraud perpetrated by whites in the general election of 1944 made blacks more determined than ever to open the regular Democratic primary. They did not know they had an ally in Judge J. Waites Waring of Charleston. In June 1947 Thurgood Marshall, on behalf of black Columbia merchant George A. Elmore, sued to have the "private" white Democratic primary declared unconstitutional. Judge Waring heard the case on the federal bench in Columbia. He ruled that "racial distinctions cannot exist in the machinery that selects the officers and lawmakers of the United States."[95] The following year the circuit court of appeals upheld Waring's decision, and the U.S. Supreme Court refused certiorari. *Elmore v. Rice* became the law of the land.[96] John McCray called the decision "the most eventful act in our history since Lincoln signed the Emancipation Proclamation."[97]

The aftermath was also eventful. Approximately 35,000 blacks voted in the statewide Democratic primary of 1948. In cities such as Greenville and Columbia, blacks were gradually integrated into the local party apparatus. Elsewhere, local party leaders sought to deter black participation by insisting that black voters swear an oath supporting segregation and states' rights, the code word for white supremacy. Black Democrats were quick to sue in federal court, and the oath had to be discarded as a prerequisite for voting. Blacks finally won the most basic right of citizenship.[98]

Judge Waring had one more prop of inequality to knock down. In the spring of 1938 the national NAACP persuaded C. Bruce Bailey of Columbia to apply for admission to the law school at the University of South Carolina. The board of trustees decided not to acknowledge the application, suggesting instead that the legislature create a separate law school for blacks at the South Carolina State College in Orangeburg. Bailey renewed his application in 1939 after the legislature failed to act. When the board again took no action, NAACP lawyer Thurgood Marshall began making preparations for a suit on Bailey's behalf.[99] This threat forced the state legislature in 1944 to authorize the creation, at least on paper, of graduate and professional schools at South Carolina State College in Orangeburg. Two years later the legislature funded the graduate school in education and provided money for blacks to pursue other graduate and professional studies out of state. Nevertheless, John Wrighten of Charleston brought a federal lawsuit when he was denied admission to the USC School of Law. On the same day Waring handed down the *Elmore* decision, he ruled that South Carolina must either close the white law school at USC or create a black one if USC declined to admit Wrighten. The legislature created a law school in Orangeburg to postpone the inevitable until the Civil Rights Act of 1964 finally dismantled segregation.[100]

The final gain—integration of the public schools—had its inception in the 1939 Cheraw manifesto and the NAACP organizational drives of the 1930s and early 1940s. After returning to Sumter in 1940, Osceola McKaine helped reorganize the local branch of the NAACP and served as the state conference's most effective public speaker and recruiter. At one of McKaine's rallies the Reverend Joseph A. DeLaine of Summerton in Clarendon County became a member and helped establish the Manning branch of the NAACP. There he confronted educational discrimination reminiscent of Third World countries. Only 13 percent of the public-school students were white, yet two-thirds of all education funding went to their schools. These were twelve attractive and fairly modern buildings, at least for the time and place. Blacks, on the other hand, attended classes in sixty dilapidated structures, many of them one-room shacks that served a student population living as far away as five miles. Whites had school busses; blacks had none.[101]

Aware that the U.S. Supreme Court was insisting upon a measure of equality within separate but equal, in 1947 DeLaine and several supporters approached R. W. Elliott, chairman of the county school board, to request a bus for black children. "We ain't got no money to buy a bus for your nigger children," was Elliott's blunt reply.[102] After unsuccessful appeals to the South Carolina Department of Education and even the U.S. Department of Justice, black parents in Clarendon conducted enough fund-raisers to purchase a bus. DeLaine also searched about for parents of black children who, with the assistance of NAACP legal counsel, were willing to bring suit in federal court. Eventually, twenty blacks stepped forward. First among them alphabetically was Harry Briggs, a filling station attendant in Summerton. Thus began the litigation the Supreme Court would know as *Briggs v. Elliott,* and the world would come to know as *Brown v. Board of Education of Topeka,* a companion case whose name became the umbrella designation for cases from South Carolina, Virginia, Delaware, the District of Columbia, and Kansas.[103] Legal scholars agree that "it is doubtful if the Supreme Court in its entire history has rendered a decision of greater social and ideological significance than this one."[104]

In November 1949 Briggs filed his suit to equalize education in Clarendon County. The following year his counsel, Thurgood Marshall, withdrew this suit in favor of another on Briggs's behalf to strike down segregation in education as a violation of the Fourteenth Amendment. In May 1951 a three-judge federal panel, which included J. Waites Waring, heard the case in Charleston. Joseph A. DeLaine was in the audience; Harry Briggs, at the bar. "They had come there on a pilgrimage," Judge Waring later wrote.[105] By a two-to-one vote the court decided against Briggs. Waring, of course, was the dissenter. Appeal to the U.S. Supreme Court, a remand and rehearing by another three-judge federal panel, and another appeal to the high court consumed the next two years. The Supreme Court heard arguments in December 1952 and rearguments in December 1953. Through it all, black Carolinians kept faith in the court. John McCray noted that South Carolina political leaders "have never acted decently until and unless they had the club of a policeman over their head. . . . And the only policeman they fear is the federal courts."[106]

On Monday, May 17, 1954—"Black Monday" to white Southerners—the new chief justice Earl Warren delivered the Court's unanimous opinion. "We conclude that in the field of public education the doctrine of 'separate but equal' has no place," Warren read. "Separate educational facilities are inherently unequal."[107] Local white pressure in Clarendon County forced DeLaine to seek pastorates in the North and finally in North Carolina, where he died. Briggs settled in New York. At least both men had the satisfaction of knowing they made history that day in May.[108]

No doubt, they and their black colleagues who lived through the New Deal and its aftermath had a profound appreciation for its impact. The New Deal fostered activism, organization, and political awareness among black Carolinians. Its agencies and programs fed, clothed, housed, and employed thousands. It ended what historian Harvard Sitkoff called the "'invisibility' of the race problem" and made civil rights "a part of the national liberal agenda."[109] It spawned hope; as Sitkoff noted, "Racial change began to seem a possibility."[110] Blacks could now fight "with expectation of success."[111] Nevertheless, in the short term the New Deal did little to relieve the African American's severe economic and social plight. The typical black Carolinian ended the decade of the 1930s essentially as he began it—an uneducated, isolated, functionally illiterate victim of economic colonialism, dependent upon the white man for employment and services.[112]

THE IMPACT OF
THE NEW DEAL IN
SOUTH CAROLINA

Units of Hitler's *wehrmacht* smashed through the Polish frontier on September 1, 1939, and shattered the fragile peace in Europe that had lasted
for only twenty years. Within a month, despite its neutrality, America
began shifting from a peacetime economy to preparation for war. The old
threats of unemployment and privation quickly gave way to threats of
fascism, militarism, and aggression. International heroes such as Winston
Churchill and Charles de Gaulle replaced national idols such as Lou
Gehrig, Shirley Temple, and other sports and screen figures.

These changes revitalized the economy of South Carolina. Indeed,
they ended the Depression. Six miles east of Columbia, for example, the
U.S. War Department reactivated and expanded the tiny World War I
training center, Camp Jackson, into a 55,000-acre induction and reception center rechristened Fort Jackson. More than $17 million in con-
struction work, a monthly payroll of more than $1 million, and 8,000
civilian employees stimulated the local economy as nothing had before.
Fort Jackson's 32,500 men and officers in January 1941 made the base
the fourth largest metropolitan area in the state. In 1940 alone, its presence increased the number of area jobs by 483 percent.[1]

Columbians were basking in relative prosperity in 1940, but they
recalled with ease, if not with pleasure, the bleak decade between the stock
market crash and the reactivation of Fort Jackson. As they mused about the
Depression, several nouns dominated their thoughts: hunger, poverty,
bankruptcy, foreclosure, crash, dust bowl, defeat, despair. Partly because
Columbians regarded Roosevelt as "the man of action," their mental image
of the New Deal evoked action verbs: *regulate* industrial output, *assure*
parity, *hire* the unemployed, *reduce* hours of labor, *improve* the quality of
life in retirement, *raise* wages, *tax* the wealthy, *save* banks, *eliminate* child
labor, *break up* the holding companies, *ameliorate* the ravages of poverty.
And yet, when they assessed the impact of the New Deal, action verbs
gave way to adjectives and antonyms: immediate versus long-term, transitory versus lasting, real versus apparent, significant versus minimal, visible
versus invisible, tangible versus intangible, beneficial versus detrimental.

By 1939 the immediate, tangible, visible, and beneficial impact was apparent everywhere. Hundreds of thousands of people saved from starvation, thousands of miles of highway, several hundred bridges, and numerous sewage and water systems were permanent reminders of relief programs that temporarily sustained one-fourth of the state's population. Extensive reforestation and a system of state parks served as lasting monuments to a CCC that trained 32,000 young men. Shorter hours, higher wages, and better working conditions reflected the impact of industrial reform. Hydroelectric projects, low-income housing, and a larger navy yard at Charleston remained as permanent contributions of the PWA. Weekly paychecks from the WPA, the state's largest single employer, bespoke the creation of thousands of jobs when none were available in the private sector. Terraces, more fertile farmland, price supports, farm credit, and rural electrification symbolized a revolution in farm life.

Less apparent at first glance was the immediate economic impact. Acting as an economic pump primer, the New Deal saved the state from economic collapse. From 1933 through 1938 federal expenditures in South Carolina totaled nearly $533 million. The largest single allocation (nearly $68 million) came through the AAA. Work programs (PWA, CWA, WPA) and lending programs (RFC, FCA, FSA, REA, PWA, HOLC) each accounted for approximately one-fourth of the expenditures.[2] A portion of these funds stimulated retail trade, which posted a 100-percent increase in 1933–1934. New motor vehicle registrations doubled in four years from about 17,000 in 1933 to 34,000 in 1937. A Columbia automobile dealer noticed in 1934 that cars were being given as Christmas presents for the first time in many years. Consumers spending New Deal money also stimulated the building construction industry, which posted a 348-percent increase in volume of business from $3.1 million in 1933 to $13.9 million in 1935. Insurance policies, which lapsed during the early Depression, were reactivated; premiums paid for life insurance increased 25 percent from $24.5 million in 1933 to $30.7 million in 1935. Dealers in luxury items even benefited from the influx of new money; Columbia florists, for example, estimated a 50-percent increase in business in 1934.

Consequently, the state posted an impressive gain in per-capita income. In 1930 South Carolina ranked forty-eighth with per-capita net income of $223. Although that figure rose to only $281 by 1940, placing the state forty-fifth, the percentage of increase was second highest in the nation. Twenty-eight states actually showed a decrease during the decade. In addition, the 1940 figure was 86 percent higher than the 1932 figure of only $151.[3]

Without question, New Deal money and New Deal legislation were responsible for saving the state's banking industry. In March 1933 money and banks were in short supply in South Carolina. Not only had more than 300 banks, nearly three-fourths of the total, suspended operations between 1921 and 1933, which tied up millions of dollars in liquidation proceedings requiring years to complete, but also an abysmal drop in personal income in the early Depression years depleted the currency supply. Deposits in the South Carolina National Bank, for instance, shrank by nearly 66 percent between 1930 and 1933. Even more irritating were periodic bank holidays brought about by mindless runs on banks by panicky depositors.[4] In October 1932, for example, the governor of Nevada declared a banking holiday that signaled the beginning of bank closings throughout the West. The trend spread eastward in February as governors in Michigan, Indiana, Maryland, Arkansas, and Ohio followed suit. By March 4, when Roosevelt took office, governors in thirty-five states had proclaimed holidays. Panicky depositors in South Carolina joined the rush to withdraw savings, thereby closing institutions that held more than 40 percent of all deposits.[5]

Roosevelt acted immediately to restore confidence in the nation's money supply and banking system. On March 5 he issued a presidential proclamation declaring a national banking holiday. Four days later Congress passed his banking bill, which validated the March 5 proclamation; provided for reopening sound banks, reorganizing marginal ones, and liquidating unsound institutions; empowered the Federal Reserve to issue new bank notes; and gave the president control over gold. The *Columbia State* echoed public sentiment in South Carolina with a March 6 editorial titled "At Last, Here Is the Leader."[6]

Roosevelt's proclamation automatically closed South Carolina's eighteen national banks but had no effect on more than a hundred state banks. Consequently, Governor Blackwood joined forty-seven other governors in declaring a banking holiday for state banks to last from March 6 through March 17.[7] In the interim the newly created State Board of Bank Control examined all state banks as a precondition for reopening, reorganizing, or liquidating. The eighteen national banks received similar scrutiny from examiners in the United States Treasury Department. Eventually, twenty-one state banks and three national banks were placed under conservators. Of these, ten state banks and two national banks were liquidated; nine state banks and one national bank were reorganized. These actions, coupled with assurances by President Roosevelt and Governor Blackwood, quickly restored public confidence. Two days after banks reopened, the South Carolina State Bank increased deposits by $500,000. In the next four years bank deposits increased by more than 177 percent against an increase in personal income of only 69 percent. This restoration of confidence would last for half a century until the banking crisis of the late 1980s.[8]

If the banking holiday put South Carolina banks on their feet again, the Federal Deposit Insurance Corporation helped keep them there. The Glass-Steagall Banking Act of 1933 created the FDIC to insure deposits at 100 percent of their value up to $5,000. The purpose was to instill confidence in the safety of deposits and remove any motivation for withdrawals during bank scares. By December 31, 1934, 97 of South Carolina's 134 commercial banks carried FDIC insurance, which protected $105.8 million of $114.2 million (more than 92 percent) in average monthly deposits. Evidently, the thirty-seven uninsured banks were small ones that either could not or did not choose to qualify for FDIC insurance. By December 31, 1938, the number of insured banks had risen to 131; the proportion of insured deposits, to 95 percent.[9]

The dearth of bank failures from January 1, 1934, to July 1, 1939, attests to the value of the FDIC. During those five and one-half years only the uninsured Fort Mill Savings Bank and the insured Palmetto State Bank of Lake City failed. Two bank closings in more than five years pales into insignificance beside the average of twenty-five bank failures per year from 1921 to 1933. Moreover, one of the failures was owing to unavoidable circumstances. In the autumn of 1934 a robber relieved the Lake City institution of $114,000. Unable to collect robbery insurance, the bank was forced into liquidation. On March 11, when stockholders announced immediate formation of the new Palmetto Bank and Trust Company from the old Palmetto State Bank, the FDIC offered to pay former depositors in cash. Depositors of all but $350 stipulated that their cash be transferred to new accounts in the Palmetto Bank and Trust Company. Obviously, protection of deposits by the FDIC worked a miracle in public attitude toward banks.[10]

This meteoric rise in both deposits and confidence naturally stimulated demand for new banks. South Carolina's 130 banks on June 30, 1933, increased to 172 banks by December 31, 1938. More impressive was the spread of national banks, partially reflecting heightened respect for the national government and its banking system. Eighteen closed in South Carolina for the 1933 banking holiday; thirty-five were prospering five years later.[11]

No one was more delighted to see the state emerge from the doldrums than Gov. Olin D. Johnston, who embarked on a "Little New Deal" of his own in 1935. Like FDR, Johnston exhibited concern for the forgotten white American, which in South Carolina meant the cotton mill worker. Not only did Johnston publicly defend the CIO, but he also aided evicted strikers by donating surplus military tents and foodstuffs. Where previous governors used the National Guard and martial law to crush strikes, Johnston used both to protect strikers and seal off mill precincts from strikebreakers. He often forced management to accept him as mediator and occasionally found state jobs for strikers whom mills refused to rehire.[12]

Moreover, in his inaugural and subsequent addresses, Johnston unveiled a program whose provisions for education, governmental reorganization, penal reform, labor relations, and Social Security reflected the liberal rhetoric of the New Deal then astir in America. He certainly deserves the title "Education Governor." At his urging, the legislature established a textbook rental system, extended the school term from six months to eight months, raised teachers' salaries from $66 a month to $90 a month, and required compulsory school attendance of those between seven and sixteen years of age.[13] In the area of labor relations, the state legislatures from 1935 to 1938 enacted and then liberalized workman's compensation, established an unemployment compensation program, and created a state department of labor that eventually was given power to arbitrate disputes and inspect factories. Added to these accomplishments were significant provisions for better wages, hours, and working conditions. South Carolina became the tenth state to establish sixteen years of age as the minimum age of employment. The state also required time and one-half pay for Sunday work in textile mills, established a forty-hour workweek for that industry, and mandated a maximum twelve-hour workday, fifty-six-hour workweek for employees in most other trades and industries. For women, the legislature imposed a maximum forty-hour workweek in garment factories and a maximum forty-eight-hour workweek in bleaching, dying, and finishing plants. Night work for minors under eighteen years of age was outlawed, and textile employers were required to post wage scales and deduct no more than 50 percent of a worker's weekly wage to cover delinquent rent.[14]

In other areas legislators were less responsive. Johnston presented a comprehensive package of requests for governmental reorganization: pooling of all state revenue into one fund; reduction in the number of highway commissioners; requirement that all state banks join the FDIC; creation of a single police force from the highway patrol and constabulary; and creation of a South Carolina Rural Electrification Administration. The lawmakers gave him the electrification administration but turned a deaf ear to his other requests. For penal reform, Johnston sought creation of a comprehensive probation system and funds to relieve prison overcrowding. The legislature ignored his first request but did give him $75,000 for construction of a women's prison near Columbia. Finally, at Johnston's urging, the legislature enacted laws to enable the state to participate in Social Security and passed an act to prevent misrepresentation in the sale of securities.[15]

The impact of the New Deal on alcoholic beverage control was also profound. Roosevelt's drive to repeal the Eighteenth Amendment, coupled with an aversion to the lawlessness bred by prohibition, gave South Carolinians the push they needed to consider reform. On April 13, 1933, after Congress repealed the Volstead Act, the state legislature legalized the sale of nonintoxicating 3.2 beer and wines and allowed on-premises drinking. A tax of 15 cents per gallon provided timely relief for a depleted state treasury. Three days later eighty cases of beer arrived at the Jefferson Hotel in Columbia and were sold within two hours.[16] The 1933 legislature also called for a convention that in November would consider ratifying the Twenty-first Amendment to repeal prohibition. Postmaster General Farley visited Columbia earlier that month to deliver Roosevelt's personal plea for ratification. Although local political leaders assured Farley of victory, voter participation in the special election to choose delegates was light; ratifiers, assuming repeal was certain, simply stayed home. The vote was 36,000 against repeal and 34,000 for it. Nevertheless, by December 5 three-fourths of the states had ratified the Twenty-first Amendment, and South Carolina drys were confronted by a fait accompli.[17]

Since a majority of citizens voting in the special election opposed repeal, the 1934 legislature passed no significant liquor legislation. Lawmakers raised the allowable alcoholic content of nonintoxicating beverages to 4 percent and scheduled an advisory referendum for August on legalizing, regulating, and taxing the sale of intoxicating beverages. Held in conjunction with the regular Democratic primary, the August vote of

158,000 in favor and 133,000 against was decisive enough to force the 1935 legislature to act. In May members authorized a system of private retail "package" stores that sold liquor by the bottle. With slight notification the 1935 law remained the centerpiece of alcoholic beverage control throughout the twentieth century.[18]

In other areas, however, the impact of the New Deal was minimal. State fiscal policy never exhibited, either in priorities or amount, prevailing New Deal liberalism. In 1933, at the same time the federal government was increasing spending on everything from relief to agriculture, the state legislature was reducing expenditures from its general fund by more than 35 percent. That fund paid for all major operations except highway construction, financed by the highway fund. Despite an increase in general fund disbursements by nearly 68 percent between fiscal 1935 and fiscal 1938, only in 1938 did appropriations exceed those of any year from 1929 to 1931.[19] Admittedly, a limited tax base and low per-capita income provided little public revenue during the 1930s. In fact, per-capita income was so low that by 1937 South Carolinians led the nation in percentage of income paid in taxes. In addition, a major experiment with deficit financing (the $65-million bond issue for highways in 1929) left the state determined throughout the 1930s to live within its means.

The New Deal certainly had little influence on the policies of Gov. Ibra Blackwood, South Carolina's equivalent of Herbert Hoover. More than three-fourths of his annual message in 1933 contained a request for a balanced budget, a sales tax to accompany elimination of the state property tax, and reduction in state aid to education. Only in general terms did he recommend a state relief program and rural electrification. The general assembly responded by enacting the lowest appropriation bill in eleven years, reducing teachers' salaries, and decreasing aid to education by 19 percent.[20]

The 1934 general assembly was almost as conservative. Blackwood met lawmakers in January with requests for economy and efficiency in government: a reduction in the amount of highway bonds issued, merging of all state supported colleges into one university system, and imposition of a sales tax coupled with elimination of the state property tax. In addition, he recommended a civil service commission, a commission (but not a department) of labor, and the Santee-Cooper project. To its credit the legislature passed the Santee-Cooper enabling act (which cost the state nothing) and fixed maximum interest on bank loans at 6 percent. The lawmakers also granted teachers a 10-percent pay raise, allowed NRA

code violators to be tried in state courts, and set up a mortgage conciliation board to reduce foreclosures by persuading lenders to refinance
obligations they held. On the other hand, the legislature broadened
exemptions and reduced taxes on income derived from dividends and
interest. Lawmakers also killed a compulsory school attendance bill, a
measure to raise the minimum work age from fourteen to sixteen,
anti–stretch-out legislation, and a proposal to establish a maximum forty-
four-hour workweek for women and minors in textile mills.[21]

Legislative liberalism under Blackwood's successor, Olin Johnston,
partly inspired by the New Deal, waned in 1939 as Roosevelt's program
lost impetus nationally. Burnet Maybank, inaugurated governor in January 1939, was no more successful than Johnston in attempts to pool all
state revenue and create a state police force. After sitting for a record 173
days, the general assembly reduced general fund appropriations from
$12.56 million to $12.55 million and shuffled priorities. The Social Security program was especially hard hit; aid for the aged, blind, and dependent children was reduced from $2.32 million to $1.75 million. In fact,
nine representatives, led by Jack Nathans of Charleston, waged an unsuccessful battle to repeal the Public Welfare Act of 1937 that created the
Social Security program.[22]

Judging by laws enacted from 1934 to 1939, the impact of the New
Deal on South Carolina was substantial; judging by proposals not
enacted, the impact was less pronounced. The legislature could have
enacted Johnston's entire reform program, including maximum funding
for education and Social Security, and financed it by diverting highway
funds. In addition, it could have enacted more swiftly several features of
his program that were finally adopted. In January 1935, for example,
Johnston recommended creation of a labor department that did not
appear until May 1936. In January 1936 he asked that the department be
empowered to arbitrate disputes, a request lawmakers did not heed until
May 1937, when the CIO threatened to make a shambles of industrial
relations. Furthermore, in declining to fund a temporary state welfare
department, the legislature in 1936 ignored the plight of legions of hungry people. The next year members enacted a weak Social Security program whose benefits did not begin to address the needs of dependent
children, the aged, and the needy blind.

Finally, much of the labor legislation of the 1930s was conservative in comparison to that of other states. By 1941 South Carolina was
not among twenty-six states (including four in the South) that enacted

minimum wage laws for women. Nor was it among nineteen states with laws limiting women to forty-eight hours of work per week. Although Louisiana and fifteen non-Southern states limited women to eight hours of work a day, and although five Southern and twenty-five non-Southern states restricted women to nine hours or less of work per day, South Carolina allowed women to work ten hours a day. South Carolina and Mississippi were alone among Southern states in not regulating the employment of minors under eighteen in hazardous occupations. Finally, South Carolina's workman's compensation law did not cover employees in establishments of fewer than fifteen workers, the largest such exemption in the country.[23] In short, South Carolina remained conservative throughout the 1930s, despite the presence of Johnston's Little New Deal.

Nor did the New Deal affect the predominance of legislative government in South Carolina. Traditionally, the South Carolina executive was weak. Simultaneous with Roosevelt's successful attempt to be strong, Governor Johnston attempted to exert greater executive leadership. He not only advanced his comprehensive program of reform but also attempted by use of force to control and reform the highway department. Here, the legislature balked, and the state supreme court ruled against him. Johnston took to the hustings in the summer of 1936 in an effort to secure legislators friendly to his programs. His forces gained strength in the House but failed to win the Senate, resulting in a stalemate. The legislature retaliated by stripping the governor of power to appoint the highway commission and the public welfare board. Johnston's legislative opponents also supported Smith in the 1938 primary. Having learned his lesson, Johnston respected legislative dominance in his second term as governor (1943–1945) and won enough support from formerly hostile legislators to defeat Smith in 1944.

Efforts in South Carolina to emulate the New Deal's policy of planning were also unproductive. Concepts such as industrial, agricultural, and regional planning gained so much popularity that in 1934 the National Resources Board began persuading state governors to create state planning boards. Governor Blackwood's planning board accomplished nothing and was replaced in 1935 by Johnston's board under Anderson publisher Wilton E. Hall. Underscoring its own lack of faith in planning, the legislature did not accord the board a permanent status until 1938. The initial purpose of the state planning board was to determine South Carolina's economic, social, and resource needs for the next half-century. The board was expected to outline potential and offer means of developing it. Although grandiose in purpose, state planning was meager in accomplishment. The board did not issue its first report until 1938. More than 200 pages long, with 8 chapters on the state's natural resources, society, and economy, it was elementary in the extreme. In sections on soil erosion and farm tenancy, for example, the statistical presentation was inadequate and the discussion of problems too brief. The seeker for solutions would have been better served by federal publications. In sum, the commitment to state planning in South Carolina during the New Deal was less than halfhearted.[24]

This lack of commitment was probably a result of the open wounds that remained from geographical factionalization. By the time of the New Deal, differing approaches to economic development fed the centuries-old animosity between upcountry and lowcountry. The fourteen textile counties of the northwest had a majority of the state's white population but elected less than a third of the state senate, which was controlled by Black Belt counties of the lowcountry. The greater economic and tax base of the upcountry allowed its counties to build paved highways and encouraged private investors to develop an adequate system of public utilities. Therefore, the concept of planning in the upcountry assumed a local and private mien.

In the poorer lowcountry, by contrast, planning for economic development was viewed in terms of state and later federal involvement. In the 1920s lowcountry political leaders such as state senators Edgar Brown of Barnwell and Richard M. Jefferies of Colleton sought economic development through the building of paved roads financed from a highway fund of gasoline taxes and license tag fees administered by a highway department run by their political cronies. In 1929 the state abandoned pay-as-you-go by floating a $65-million bond issue. The upcountry, led by Olin Johnston, opposed the bond issue and later the Highway Department because upcountry taxes to retire the bonds were used, in effect, to finance lowcountry roads. The upcountry also was cool to the creation of Santee-Cooper by the federal government, which symbolized additional taxpayer support for lowcountry industrial development.[25]

Silhouetted against this background of lowcountry-upcountry conflict came New Deal encouragement of state planning. A few South Carolinians such as David R. Coker were enthusiastic. He envisioned this as a means of appraising and publicizing the state's natural resources and economic opportunities to keep "our best people" from migrating "because of their ignorance of the opportunities at home."[26] Many, however, could see only negatives. Some upcountry leaders no doubt saw state planning as a means of further shifting their taxes to aid the low-country. The lowcountry, on the other hand, must have feared planning would become a vehicle for diverting highway funds to education and social services in the upcountry. Small wonder, then, that efforts at state planning came to naught.

So did all hopes that the New Deal would alter pernicious social norms such as class snobbery and sexism. For example, the textile worker and tenant farmer began and ended the 1930s on the bottom of the white social ladder despite New Deal attention to the plight of the working class. In 1935 an SCERA adult educator wrote condescendingly of white tenant farmers, "I think a *Birth Control Act* or *Sterilization Law* as well as *Compulsory* [School] *Attendance Law* for this class would not be too much."[27] More sympathetically, another bemoaned the lack of social mobility for young people from cotton mill villages. Pointing to a young textile worker who sang part time in a Spartanburg orchestra with a voice that "would be worth a fortune, if he were the son of a rich man," this sympathetic observer added, "If he could say that he had studied in New York or Paris, he would be able to demand a good position and salary. But what can a poor, ignorant, cotton mill boy who was born in poverty demand? He may cry out loud and long, but he is the only one who will hear the echo."[28]

As late as 1944 a Greenwood adult educator complained of the "silliest attitude on the part of *city* folk toward mill people," which was reflected by a refusal of the state federation of garden clubs to include a group from a local mill village. In fact, whenever mill village members attended a regional garden club function, women from the host club were prone to "just wonder [out loud] who those women are."[29] W. W. Ball of the *Charleston News and Courier* was partially correct in his observation to a friend: "The New Deal, in South Carolina, is entirely middle class—the laboring people, the really poor, have gotten nothing from it."[30]

Likewise, in spite of role modeling by women such as Eleanor Roosevelt, professional women in South Carolina began and ended the 1930s as intruders in a man's world. In 1929 one female adult educator complained, "I am just a woman and regardless of training, twelve months active work [each year], and long hours running into the night, I am not worth what men are to the state. . . . That is the penalty I must pay for being born [a woman] in the early eighties."[31] By 1941 little had changed.

Charlotte Stevenson, a social worker in the Richland County Department of Public Welfare, complained bitterly to friends that although she had scored "second in the state on the old Employment Office exam," she could "never get an offer" of promotion because of her gender. Of one man who received a promotion that she applied for, she wrote, "He doesn't have the qualifications, but he does wear pants." She mused in disgust, "I don't see why Negroes howl so about discrimination, and women say nothing."[32]

South Carolina also began and ended the 1930s with its political geography intact. The influence of ancestors, Baptists, blacks, cotton, conservatism, contrasts, Confederate War, Depression, and Democratic Party was unaffected by the New Deal. The issues of Blease and booze did suffer some diminution but did not disappear. Bleaseism, to the extent that it meant concern for the textile operative, was coopted and redefined by Olin D. Johnston to include activist government in the positive liberal state. Likewise, booze remained enough of an issue that dry wedding receptions were the general rule in many localities throughout the century.

In other ways, New Deal impact was ambiguous. Despite having saved and rejuvenated the state's banking industry, the New Deal had less effect on the larger economy in general because it did not bring sustained prosperity to cotton farmers, textile manufacturers, and mill workers. The textile industry experienced difficult times in every New Deal year except 1935 and 1936. Although various reforms brought an improvement in wages, hours, and industrial relations, the war years and not the New Deal brought back the level of prosperity enjoyed by the industry before 1924. The most that can be said for the New Deal is that it kept workers from starving and manufacturers out of bankruptcy long enough for them to take advantage of both wartime prosperity and the accompanying destruction of European and Japanese competitors. As a measure of industrial stagnation, the number of mills in South Carolina increased only slightly from 234 in 1932 to 236 in 1938, the number of spindles rising only from 5.68 million to 5.75 million. Although average daily wages increased 29 percent (from $1.98 in 1932 to $2.56 in 1934), they remained only slightly above starvation level until the TWOC and Fair Labor Standards Act applied pressure in the late 1930s.[33]

Perhaps with some justification, mill owners complained they were unable to increase wages and still operate at a profit. For the year 1935, for example, one industry spokesman calculated profits at only 0.88 percent of total revenues, wage costs consuming 25.57 percent. The industry was careful not to broadcast profit in terms of dollars, but it can be computed from state labor department statistics. If the figures of 0.88 percent and 25.57 percent are correct, a wage increase of only 10 cents a day for each worker would have consumed the total profits of the average mill. On the other hand, the average profit at each mill was a sum twelve times greater than an average worker's annual wage. Therefore, the major stockholder—in many instances the mill president who also drew a handsome salary from the mill—never lacked life's amenities.[34]

World War II brought brighter days. Without a substantial increase in capital investment, the state's annual textile product more than doubled from $383 million in 1941 to $787 million in 1945, after averaging only $236 million a year during the New Deal. Understandably, as late as 1939, mill owner J. C. Self of Greenwood confided to a friend that the "lack of business at a profit" continued to be his "worst headache." He concluded, almost pessimistically, "It looks to me like we are headed for the rocks, but let us hope for the best."[35] By contrast, during the war, profits increased so handsomely that W. J. Roddey, Jr., who lost a personal fortune during the Depression as president of the liquidated Central Union Bank, was able to recoup his wealth and status by operating a Rock Hill textile mill.[36]

Agricultural prosperity, which for six years eluded New Deal planners, also accompanied World War II and postwar demand for American agricultural commodities in a devastated Europe and Asia. Under the New Deal program of restricted production, the cotton farmer never enjoyed average annual prices comparable to those of the 1920s. The highest price paid for cotton during the New Deal was 13.17 cents per pound, while the lowest during the 1920s was 14.37. On the other hand, the price climbed during World War II from 17.9 cents in 1941 to 22.1 cents in 1945. In fact, the latter was more than double the average annual price during the New Deal. The value of cattle and calves declined during the New Deal from $11 million in 1930 to slightly more than $8 million in 1940, then shot up to $20 million in 1945 and $33 million in 1950. Dairy products fell in value during the New Deal from $4.2 million in 1930 to slightly under $4 million in 1940, then climbed to $8.4 million in 1945 and $11.4 million in 1950. Gross farm income from the sale of cotton averaged $604 per farm in 1925 and $607 per farm in 1930 before dropping during the New Deal to $327 per farm in 1935 and $445 per farm in 1940. It skyrocketed to $1,059 per farm in 1945 and $949 per farm in 1950.[37]

The low levels of price and income during the 1930s negatively, or at best neutrally, affected land values and farm debt. After a 43-percent decline in the 1920s, the average value of South Carolina farms increased only 2 percent in the 1930s before jumping 131 percent in the 1940s. The average value of land and buildings declined 44 percent during the 1920s and 17 percent during the 1930s; it increased 129 percent in the 1940s. One-fifth of all farms were mortgaged in 1920; approximately one-third were when the New Deal began and ended.[38]

The return of agricultural prosperity during and after World War II had important ramifications. Farmers first used a part of their extra income to mechanize operations. They had only 3,462 tractors in 1930 and 4,791 in 1940, an increase during the New Deal of only 38 percent. By contrast, 30,282 tractors were in use by 1950, an increase of 532 percent. The use of farm trucks increased only 18 percent in the 1930s but 260 percent in the 1940s. Farmers secondly spent their extra income in the 1940s to buy farmland. The number of farms owned by farm operators increased only 10 percent in the 1930s but 27 percent in the 1940s. Farmers used a third portion of their wartime and postwar income to make improvements to land and buildings. The average value per farm increased 130 percent from $2,461 in 1940 to $5,684 in 1950.[39]

If World War II and not the New Deal rejuvenated agriculture, then the question arises of why South Carolina farmers remember the New Deal so fondly. The answer is threefold. First, commodity prices from 1933 to 1939 were much higher than those in 1931–1932. Second, cotton farmers recognized that commodity prices would have been below the cost of production throughout the 1930s without the New Deal. Finally, AAA expenditures of nearly $68 million from 1933 to 1939 meant an average payment per farmer of approximately $77 per year. This figure is significant because the average annual farm income from cotton in 1935 was only $327.[40]

The New Deal was no more successful in shaping the configuration of agriculture in South Carolina in the last half of the twentieth century than it was in achieving sustained agricultural prosperity. Cotton, the dominant crop when the New Deal began and ended, was only the eighth most important crop by 1980.[41] More valuable than cotton were the two major field crops of tobacco and soybeans, plus dairy products, cattle and calves, eggs, hogs, and wheat. In fact, in the four decades following World War II, cotton farmers reduced their cotton acreage by more than 90 percent from 1 million to only 97,000 acres. The cotton fields of 1945 had become soybean fields, pastures for beef and dairy cattle, and pine forests to serve the pulp and paper industry by 1985. Tenancy had practically disappeared by 1985. So had horse-and-wagon agriculture. The advent of mechanization in the 1940s and 1950s displaced tenants, created agribusiness with large farms worked by wage laborers, and produced a dependence on machinery to meet seasonal peaks in agricultural activity. The approximately 75 percent of South Carolinians who lived in rural settings in 1940 declined to 46 percent by 1980.[42]

Because the New Deal did so little to bring about these changes, it was the end of one era in South Carolina agriculture, not the beginning of another. Increased competition from cotton growers on more productive lands in California, Arizona, and Texas—not the New Deal—hastened the decline in cotton production. Mechanization in the 1940s and 1950s, more so than the New Deal, spelled the end of farm tenancy and the rise of agribusiness. The increasing postwar profitability of livestock and pulp and paper accounted for the diversion of cotton fields to soybeans, pasturage, and pines. Construction of the interstate highway system in the 1950s and 1960s, not the New Deal, enticed Northern and European industries, particularly in durable goods such as fabricated metals and electrical machinery, to relocate to urban areas in South Carolina, thus accelerating diversified industrialization and urbanization.

Some historians have demonstrated that the New Deal revolutionized agriculture in the South in terms of "land consolidation, mechanization, the introduction of new crops, and the displacement of a large segment of the rural work force."[43] However, in at least three of the four ways mentioned, the idea of a revolution in agriculture seems to have more validity for other Southern states than for South Carolina. The number of tenants, for example, had been declining since the early 1920s, when the agricultural depression and appearance of the boll weevil destroyed the profitability of cotton and spurred a sizeable out-migration of blacks. The 25-percent decline in number of tenants during the New Deal needs to be viewed against a 16-percent decline during the 1920s and an 18-percent decline in the 1940s.[44] Moreover, as mentioned earlier in this chapter, comparatively little mechanization occurred before World War II.[45]

Crop diversification, except in soil-conserving crops, not only predated the New Deal but also received limited encouragement from it. Commercial truck cropping began in the 1910s, followed in the 1920s by wider crop diversification after the appearance of the boll weevil and the out-migration of blacks. Tobacco, the state's leading money crop in 1980, was already a major crop by 1921, when farmers planted 20 percent more acres than in 1932. Wheat farmers planted an annual average of 138,000 acres as early as the period from 1919 to 1923. After a decline in wheat production from the mid-1920s to the early 1930s, farmers planted an annual average of 151,000 acres during the New Deal (1934 to 1938), an increase in acreage over 1919 to 1923 of only 9 percent. Moreover, the average annual value of the wheat crop was $2.8 million in 1919–1923 and only $1.4 million in 1934–1938, a *decrease* in value of 50 percent. Clearly, the New Deal did not make wheat production either popular or profitable. By contrast, as nations began to stockpile food in anticipation of World War II, wheat production and profits soared. The 1939 crop of 210,000 acres was nearly 40 percent larger than the 1934–1938 average; the 1941 crop of 3.15 million bushels was twice as large as the average production of the previous 10 years.[46]

Other agricultural products popular after World War II tell the same story of limited encouragement by the New Deal. Soybeans, one of the two major field crops by 1980, was insignificant as late as 1940, when farmers harvested only 76,677 bushels, an increase in production over 1930 of only 29,351 bushels. By contrast, soybean production jumped more than 500 percent to 460,938 bushels between 1940 and 1950 and another 100 percent to 937,140 bushels by 1954. By 1978 the soybean crop of 29.3 million bushels was nearly five times more valuable than the cotton crop. Peach production in the upcountry did increase 32 percent during the New Deal, but this figure pales beside the 45-percent increase in the mid-1920s as part of the general trend toward diversification. During the New Deal the size of the state's swine herd increased 30 percent and the cattle herd 11 percent. But as late as 1939 the cattle herd was 17 percent smaller and 60 percent less valuable than in 1920; the swine herd, 31 percent smaller and 74 percent less valuable than in 1920.[47] The conclusion thus far seems to be threefold: the introduction of new commercial crops either predated or postdated the New Deal, depending on the crop; mechanization was a function of World War II and postwar prosperity; and land consolidation and tenant displacement, although they did occur, either predated the New Deal or would have resulted from postwar mechanization without the New Deal.

Even if the New Deal did not retrieve rural prosperity, destroy tenancy, mechanize agriculture, introduce new cash crops, or shape the configuration of agriculture for the remainder of the century, it was responsible for a minirevolution. Rural electrification eased the burden of life on the farm. Through a combination of higher prices, benefit payments, agricultural credit, and conservation measures, the New Deal stabilized land values and kept farmers from bankruptcy until they could reap the benefits of wartime and postwar prosperity. In the long run, of course, it forever altered the competitive market system through production controls and price fixing; its Agricultural Adjustment Act of 1938 created the framework for all agricultural programs for the remainder of the century; and its emphasis on conservation ridded the land of the curse of soil erosion. Finally, through land consolidation the New Deal increased average farm size by 32 percent to 82 acres, thus creating units that at last could be operated profitably. On these additional acres the farmer could pasture livestock or plant additional crops other than cotton that could either be sold for cash or consumed by the family in order to reduce monthly expenses.[48]

This problem of farms too small to yield adequate income had plagued South Carolina for decades before the New Deal. In 1933 the average size of a farm was sixty-two acres, although fully two-thirds were smaller than fifty acres. On farms such as these, operators cultivated no more than ten acres of corn, five acres of forage such as oats, and ten acres of cotton that produced about five bales. The Bankhead allotment for such a farm was four bales. After paying the Bankhead tax for the fifth bale, the farmer earned $275 for lint if cotton brought 12 cents a pound. Sale of two and one-half tons of cotton seed brought an additional $75, providing a total return of $350 for cotton. Since the average farmer was a tenant, the landlord not only claimed half of the cotton crop but also half of the corn and all of the forage to replace the feed consumed by the tenant's mule. The tenant was left with $175 (half of the $350 for cotton) plus $25 to $40 worth of corn for a gross income of $200 to $215. Although he received free rent, garden privileges, and wood, his living expenses for items such as clothing, doctor's bills, and taxes averaged $15 per month or $180 per year, which consumed the $175 from his cotton crop plus $5 of the $25 to $40 from his corn crop. At the end of the crop year, his disposable income was only $20 to $35 to cover everything else, including church support, education expenses for his children, recreation, travel to visit relatives, and routine medical expenses. Any unforeseen expense, such as an illness requiring costly medical attention or the need to replace a farm animal, put him in debt for years.[49]

The political effect of the New Deal was equally ambiguous. On the one hand, the New Deal did not alter existing political relationships. Not only did the same class of men who held office in 1932 do so in 1940, but no formally disfranchised class of South Carolinians had been empowered. In fact, those in power simply got control of New Deal agencies within the state and used them to their political advantage. For example, Byrnes, Smith, and the congressmen divided up the extensive patronage without regard for racial, gender, class, or even geographical equity. Maybank controlled thousands of jobs on the Santee-Cooper project. So great was the influence of Byrnes over major WPA appointments that the *Una News Review* opined that he could "still take care of [his] friends with supervisory positions," even if he succeeded in persuading Congress to reduce WPA expenditures.[50] In the counties, key politicians had a hand in appointments to relief agencies and indirectly decided who would receive relief.[51] Prominent farmers, who in many Black Belt counties ran the local Democratic Party, also dominated AAA and farm credit machinery. Cotton mill owners in textile counties had close ties to political leaders and thus controlled NRA compliance machinery.

On the other hand, the New Deal did make South Carolina Democrats a politically nervous breed. Not only were men such as Byrnes aware of the diminished voice of the South in Democratic councils, but men such as banker and former state legislator James A. Hoyt were conscious of the political realignment taking place in America. In 1939 Hoyt acknowledged privately that successful national Democratic candidates in the future would have to attract "the labor vote, the negro vote or the Jew vote . . . as well as the Catholic vote" because "those four elements control the elections in the big, doubtful States."[52] No doubt, Hoyt and Byrnes understood, to their dismay, this feat was something Southern white Protestant Democrats could not do.

Furthermore, opposition to the New Deal contributed to the demise of politicians such as Cole Blease and Thomas P. Stoney, while support for the New Deal enabled James F. Byrnes, Olin D. Johnston, and Burnet R. Maybank to achieve unusual prominence. After serving as unofficial administration floor leader in the 1930s, Byrnes was rewarded with a seat on the Supreme Court in 1941. He resigned in 1942 to become the "Assistant President" as director of war mobilization, barely missing the vice presidential nomination in 1944 before serving as secretary of state under Pres. Harry Truman. In 1950, as a result of his prestige, Byrnes was elected governor of South Carolina almost by acclamation. Soon afterward he lent his prestige to the Southern effort to elect Republicans to the presidency, which indirectly encouraged the ultimately successful movement to convert South Carolina from a one-party Democratic state into a two-party competitive, Republican leaning one. Thus, South Carolina politics at century's end bore the Byrnes stamp of pro-Republican.

Like Byrnes, Olin Johnston was already a political leader with a statewide following when the New Deal began. Born into a family of cotton mill workers in 1896, Johnston went to work at an Anderson County cotton mill at eleven years of age before eventually completing high school, Wofford College, and both graduate and law school at the University of South Carolina. In 1922, while still in law school, he was elected to the state legislature, where he quickly became a leader of the upcountry contingent. In 1930, by a margin of only 900 votes, he finished second to Ibra C. Blackwood in the race for governor. By supporting the New Deal, Johnston was able to win the governorship in 1934 and again in 1942 before defeating Senator Smith for reelection in 1944. Johnston remained in the Senate until his death in 1965.[53]

Unlike Byrnes and Johnston, Burnet R. Maybank lacked legislative experience when the New Deal began; but like them, he would use the New Deal to rise politically. Born into one of Charleston's patrician families in 1899, Maybank was graduated from the College of Charleston before engaging in his family's cotton export business and being elected to Charleston City Council in 1927. In 1930, at the age of thirty-two, he won election as mayor of Charleston, whose 65,000 citizens easily made it the largest city in South Carolina. He quickly broke with and neutralized his mentor, Thomas P. Stoney, and converted much of the Stoney following into a Maybank machine allied with Senator Byrnes. This organization controlled Charleston politics until 1947. Developing friendships with President Roosevelt and relief czar Harry Hopkins, Maybank was able to put Charleston on a sound financial footing before using more than $41 million in New Deal money to revitalize the local economy. New Deal projects saved the Navy Yard, beautified the city, built and renovated buildings at The Citadel and College of Charleston, preserved historic structures, provided low-cost housing, improved the airport, extended sewage and water systems, and also constructed a municipal incinerator, numerous recreational facilities, a fire station, and an orphanage.[54]

Not surprisingly, Maybank used his machine to advance New Deal candidates. His policemen not only served as poll workers, but they also allowed Maybank allies to vote repeatedly in the same precinct and at least once in several others. Maybank ensured that trusted followers gained seats on state and local relief councils and boards, where they could pass out jobs and favors to allies. He sat on three New Deal agencies: the State Board of Bank Control, Public Works Administration Advisory Board, and South Carolina Public Service Authority that oversaw the construction and operation of the Santee-Cooper project.[55] This machine helped elect Maybank governor in 1938 and United States senator in 1941, when he filled the vacancy created by the appointment of James F. Byrnes to the Supreme Court. Maybank remained there until his untimely death at fifty-four years of age in 1954.

Nevertheless, several intangible contributions more than compensated for New Deal failures and ambiguities. Through its literacy training program, the New Deal shored up individual self-esteem and increased a passion for learning. In the lower classes the New Deal reduced the feeling of alienation from government, recaptured the American spirit of community for all South Carolinians, and restored their faith in capitalism, democracy, and progress. When the New Deal began, South Carolina's illiteracy rate of nearly 15 percent was the highest in the nation. Illiteracy among blacks ranged from a low of 19 percent in Greenville County to a high of 46 percent in Allendale. Functional illiteracy—an inability to fill out a job application or read an instruction manual—was much higher in both races, approaching 51 percent of the total population.[56]

So successful were the SCERA, CWA, NYA, and WPA in reducing illiteracy that Hazel Iles Brochman, director of the Richland County Illiteracy Program, observed in 1940 that "with few exceptions only the aged, shiftless, and mentally incompetent are now actually illiterate."[57] WPA literacy instructors alone taught 62 percent of whites and 18 percent of blacks, who were listed as illiterate in the census of 1930, to read and write.[58]

Becoming literate invariably meant heightened self-esteem, passion for learning, and appreciation of education. In one family composed of two illiterate parents and four school-age daughters, the father insisted his daughters leave school and find a job after completing the seventh grade. Three daughters complied until their father's life-changing experience in an adult literacy program caused him to reverse his decision. Not only did he insist the youngest daughter remain in school, he also persuaded the three older girls to give up their jobs and finish high school. In another poor and illiterate family that lived in a tiny, dirty, dilapidated log cabin without ceilings, completion of an adult education program moved them beyond the embarrassment associated with illiteracy and helped them to grow in self-esteem. Proud of having become an educated citizen, the seventeen-year-old father tidied up the yard; his seventeen-year-old wife, the cabin. He scraped together enough lumber to fashion ceilings; she, enough cardboard from boxes to fashion a smooth surface on the log walls for wallpaper. Soon, she created a library of child-rearing guides for assistance in raising their three-month-old daughter. A third family lived in a small cabin with neither window screens nor sashes and with a water supply at a spring a quarter of a mile distant. Learning to read and write so expanded their horizons and so increased their self-esteem that they dug a well, modernized the windows, and even sacrificed necessities of life each month in order to subscribe to a newspaper and two magazines.[59] These three examples attest to the New Deal's renovation of the human spirit whose importance, though not measurable, was immeasurable.

No less important, for the first time in South Carolina history, the lower classes sensed some kinship with policies of the federal government and its leaders. One South Carolina mill hand wrote that Roosevelt was "the first man in the White House to understand that my boss is a son of a bitch." Another added that FDR was "the first President who made us feel that we really are part of the United States." A third praised the president's conviction that "the Constitution belonged to the poor man, too."[60] More illustrative and poignant was the case of a seventy-year-old widow named Sophie, who in 1935 lived in rural Charleston County in a tiny unpainted shack with two windows and two rooms, which to passersby resembled an outbuilding more than a dwelling. Her water supply was a well surrounded continuously with tubs and boilers that she used for laundry to earn the $10 a year she paid in rent. Although a victim of a stroke, which left her partially paralyzed, she still managed to raise a garden. She had never before encountered a government concerned with her plight and was grateful for the clothing and food provided by New Deal relief agencies to keep her warm and nourished. Most of all, she appreciated literacy training that enabled her to read her Bible. As she explained, before the SCERA began, "Many a times I be here by myself and yearn to read the Bible, but can't do a thing but look at pictures and make [up] stories about them." Sophies throughout South Carolina had nothing but praise for a national government that taught them to read and write and kept them from freezing and starving. "God bless the president" and "this blessed movement," they exclaimed.[61]

Most important of all the intangible contributions was restoration of faith in capitalism, democracy, and progress. The horror of the carnage of World War I, coupled with the misery of economic depression in the industrialized world of the 1920s and 1930s, discredited the three pillars of Western civilization: a belief in progress, a faith in the beneficent effects of capitalism, and a belief in the rectitude of liberal democracy. In the two decades following World War I, fascism and communism loomed as inevitable replacements for liberal democracy and capitalism; cynicism, as the antidote for a faith in progress. The editor of the *News Review* in Una, South Carolina, was certainly correct in observing, "Never has the Red god of revolution lurked nearer in the United States than in the early days of the Depression."[62]

South Carolinians from all stations in life realized that Roosevelt saved American capitalism and democracy with his New Deal. John W. Pollard, president of the South Carolina Federation of Textile Workers, called Roosevelt the savior who "rekindled the light of democracy."[63] Former banker and political leader James A. Hoyt affirmed that "Roosevelt has served best the very elements which hate him most, and perhaps that is why they hate him—the capitalist class. No one likes to be saved, especially after he is safe."[64] The editor of the *News Review* added that Roosevelt was "not only fighting to save the wage earners" but was also "seeking to save capital from itself."[65] James F. Miles, a poor twenty-four-year-old mill youth who was working to pay his way through the University of South Carolina, doubted that, without the New Deal, Americans "would even have a country today, hardly a democracy." He called it *"ironical"* that the aristocratic Roosevelt should be the savior of democracy. In fact, he was certain "no one but an aristocrat and one of the established order could have launched such a program for the good of the masses."[66]

Still, with eyes lovingly fixed on Roosevelt in 1939, these South Carolinians occasionally glanced backwards to the early 1930s. They recollected President Hoover's hollow promises of prosperity just around the corner, of tomorrow the dawn of a brighter day. They recalled the looks of fear and uncertainty on hundreds of faces. They remembered, too, that the New Deal brought hope in the future, which the *Columbia State* saw manifested in "different expressions" and "above all new smiles." In fact, Governor Blackwood was certain the New Deal's greatest achievement would be "the banishment of fear" and "the restoration of confidence."[67]

Repeatedly echoing this sentiment, and serving as a fitting epitaph for the New Deal in South Carolina, was "The Road Is Open Again" by Irving Kahal, the "Marching Song of the New Deal" sung in public schools across the state:

> There's a new day in view,
> There is gold in the blue,
> There is hope in the hearts of men.
> All the world's on the way, to a sunnier day,
> Cause the road is open again.
> There's a note of repair,
> There's a song in the air,
> It's the music of busy men.
> Every plow in the land, meets a happier hand
> Cause the road is open again.
> There's an Eagle blue
> In the White House, too.
> On the shoulders of our President there.
> With a lusty call, telling one and all,
> Brother, do your share!
> There's a new day in view,
> There is gold in the blue,
> There is hope in the hearts of men.
> From the plain to the hill,
> From the farm to the mill,
> All the road is open again.[68]

1934 LEGISLATION	BYRNES	SMITH	FULMER	GASQUE	MAHON	MCMILLAN	MCSWAIN	RICHARDS	TAYLOR
Civil Works Administration Bill(1)	Yea	Yea	Yea	Yea		Yea	Yea	Yes	N.V.
Bankhead Bill(1)	Yea	Yea	Yea	Yea		Yea	Yea	Yes	Yes
Conference Report on Bankhead(1)	Yea	Yea	Yea	Yea		Nay	Yea	Yea	Nay
Kerr-Smith Tobacco Act(1)			Yea	Yea		Nay	Yea	Yea	Nay
Gold Reserve Act(1)	Yea	Yea	Yea	Yea		Yea	Yea	Yea	Yea
Independent Offices Appropriation Bill over veto(2)	Nay	Yea	Yea	Yea		Yea	Yea	Yea	Yea
Silver Purchase Act(1)	Yea	Yea	Yea	N.V.		Yea	Yea	Yea	Yea
Reciprocal Trade Agreement Bill(1)	Yea	Yea	Yea	N.V.		Yea	Yea	N.V.	N.V.
Securities Exchange Bill(1)	Yea	Yea	N.V.	Yea		N.V.	N.V.	N.V.	Yea

1935 LEGISLATION	BYRNES	SMITH	FULMER	GASQUE	MAHON	MCMILLAN	MCSWAIN	RICHARDS	TAYLOR
Banking Bill(1)	N.V.	Yea	Yea	N.V.		Yea	N.V.	Yea	Yea
$4.8 billion Emergency Relief Bill(1)	N.V.	Yea	Yea	Yea		Yea	Yea	Yea	Yea
National Labor Relations Bill(1)	Yea	N.V.							
Tydings Amendment to the NLRB(2)	Nay	N.V.							
Public Utility-Holding Co. Bill(1)	Yea	Nay	Yea	Yea		Yea	Yea	Yea	Yea
Death Sentence of the Public Utility Holding Co. Bill(1)	Nay	Nay	Nay	Nay		Nay	Nay	Nay	Yea

	BYRNES	SMITH	FULMER	GASQUE	MAHON	MCMILLAN	MCSWAIN	RICHARDS	TAYLOR
1935 LEGISLATION continued									
Death Sentence after pressure from Roosevelt(1)	Yea		Yea	Nay		N.V.	N.V.	N.V.	Yea
Wealth Tax Bill(1)	Yea	Yea	Yea	Yea		N.V.	Yea	Yea	Yea
Social Security Bill(1)	Yea	N.V.	Yea	Yea		Yea	Yea	Yea	Yea
Amendment to strike out Title II of Social Security(2)	Nay	Yea							
1936 LEGISLATION	BYRNES	SMITH	FULMER	GASQUE	MAHON	MCMILLAN	MCSWAIN	RICHARDS	TAYLOR
Soil Conservation and Domestic Allotment Act(1)	Yea	Yea	Yea	Yea	Yea	Yea	N.V.	Yea	Yea
Revenue Bill of 1936(1)	Yea	Nay	Yea	Yea		Yea	Yea	Yea	Yea
1937 LEGISLATION	BYRNES	SMITH	FULMER	GASQUE	MAHON	MCMILLAN	MCSWAIN	RICHARDS	TAYLOR
Civilian Conservation Corps Bill(1)	Yea	Yea	N.V.	Yea	Yea	Yea		Yea	Yea
Byrd Amendment to the CCC Bill(2)	Yea	Nay							
Wagner-Steagall Housing Bill(1)	Nay	Nay	N.V.	N.V.	Nay	Nay		Nay	Nay
Sit-Down Strike Bill(2)	Yea	N.V.							
Bankhead-Jones Farm Tenancy Bill(1)			Yea	Yea	Yea	Nay		Yea	Yea
$1.5 billion Relief Bill			N.V.	Yea	Yea	N.V.		Yea	Yea
Reduce the Relief Bill appropriation to $1 billion(2)	Yea		N.V.	Yea	Yea	Yea		Yea	Yea
Court-Packing Bill(1)	Yea	Nay	(For)	(For)		(Against)			

1937 DECEMBER SPECIAL SESSION	BYRNES	SMITH	FULMER	GASQUE	MAHON	MCMILLAN	MCSWAIN	RICHARDS	TAYLOR
Agricultural Adjustment Bill(1)	Yea	Yea	Yea	N.V.	Yea	Nay		Yea	Yea
Recommit Fair Labor Standards Bill(2)			Yea	Yea	Yea	Yea		Nay	Yea

1938 LEGISLATION	BYRNES	SMITH	FULMER	GASQUE	MAHON	MCMILLAN	MCSWAIN	RICHARDS	TAYLOR
AAA Conference Report(1)	Yea	Yea	Yea	Yea	Yea	Nay		Yea	Nay
Fair Labor Standards Bill(1)	Nay	Nay	Nay	Nay	Yea	Nay		Yea	Nay
Conference Report on Fair Labor Standards Bill(1)			Yea	Nay	Yea	N.V.		Yea	Nay
$3.75 billion Relief Bill(1)	Yea	Yea	Yea	N.V.	Yea	Yea		Yea	N.V.

1939 LEGISLATION	BYRNES	SMITH	FULMER	J. MCMILLAN	BRYSON	T. MCMILLAN	RICHARDS	HARE
$725 million WPA Appropriation (instead of $875(2)	Yea	Yea	Yea	Yea	Yea	Yea	Yea	Yea
Government Reorganization Bill(1)	Yea	Yea	Yea	Yea	Yea	Yea	Yea	Yea
Amendments to weaken the Government Reorganization Bill(2)	Nay	Yea						
Vote to investigate the NLRB(2)			Yea	Yea	Nay	Yea	Nay	Nay
Public Housing Bill(1)			Yea	Yea	Yea	Nay	Yea	Nay
$2.4 billion Public Works Bill(1)	Yea	Nay	Yea	Yea	Yea	Nay	Nay	Yea

NOTES

PREFACE

1. Created in 1935 by executive order, the Works Progress Administration was renamed the Work Projects Administration in 1939, when it was merged into the larger Federal Works Agency. Because most Americans know the agency by its original name, and to avoid confusion, the name Works Progress Administration will be used throughout the book to describe the agency in the years 1935 to 1943.

2. Walter Edgar, *South Carolina: A History* (Columbia: University of South Carolina Press, 1998), 482.

CHAPTER 1—A SOUTH CAROLINA PRIMER

1. In 1941 the WPA *Guide to the Palmetto State* acknowledged the importance of heritage by remarking that the first question asked of any stranger attempted "to place him as to family, religion, and region of birth." Writers' Program of the Works Progress Administration, *South Carolina: A Guide to the Palmetto State* (New York: Oxford University Press, 1941; reprint, 1973), 107 (page citations are to the reprint edition) (hereafter cited as WPA, *Guide*).

2. Ibid., 3.

3. "Palmetto Stump—Thirties Style," in *Perspectives in South Carolina History: The First 300 Years,* ed. Ernest M. Lander, Jr., and Robert K. Ackerman (Columbia: University of South Carolina Press, 1973), 349; V. O. Key, Jr., *Southern Politics in State and Nation* (New York: Alfred A. Knopf, 1949), 130–31; Bernard L. Poole, "The Presidential Election of 1928 in South Carolina," in *Proceedings of the South Carolina Historical Association,* (1954): 10–16 (hereafter cited as Poole, "1928 Election").

4. David Duncan Wallace, *The History of South Carolina,* 4 vols. (New York: American Historical Society, 1934), iii, 422–23; John D. Stark, *Damned Upcountryman: William Watts Ball* (Durham, N.C.: Duke University Press, 1968), 163 (hereafter cited as Stark, *Ball*); James F. Byrnes to Franklin D. Roosevelt, 8 November 1933, James Francis Byrnes Papers, Robert M. Cooper Library, Clemson University, Clemson, S.C. Curiously, the issue of alcohol was even intertwined with the issue of race. In early 1932 one South Carolina congressman wrote: "With the legal sale of liquor at reasonable prices, there would be no safety on our highways with negroes [*sic*], automobiles, whiskey and gasoline mixed in one mass." Henry

C. Ferrell, Jr., "John Jackson McSwain: A Study in Political Technique" (master's thesis, Duke University, 1957), 78.

5. Francis Butler Simkins, *Pitchfork Ben Tillman,South Carolinian* (Baton Rouge: Louisiana State University Press, 1967 [1944]), 490; C. Vann Woodward, *Origins of the New South, 1877–1913* (Baton Rouge: Louisiana State University Press, 1967 [1951]), 394.

6. Daniel Walker Hollis, "Coleman Livingston Blease," in *Dictionary of American Biography: Supplement Three* (New York: Charles Scribner's Sons, 1973), 77–78; Simkins, *Tillman,* 485–504; Daniel Walker Hollis, "Cole L. Blease and the Senatorial Campaign of 1924," in *Proceedings of the South Carolina Historical Association* (1978): 53–68.

7. I. A. Newby, *Plain Folk in the New South* (Baton Rouge: Louisiana State University Press, 1989), 389–417; Robert G. Torbet, *A History of the Baptists* (Valley Forge: The Judson Press, 1969), 451–52.

8. WPA, *Guide,* xxiii–xxvii, 191.

9. Ibid., 100.

10. Richard Hofstadter, *The American Political Tradition and the Men Who Made It* (New York: A. A. Knopf, 1948; reprint, with a foreword by Christopher Lasch, Vintage Books, 1974), 92 (page citations are to the reprint edition).

11. WPA, *Guide,* 184–211.

12. Ibid., 5.

13. Ibid., 5, 35; Walter Edgar, *South Carolina: A History* (Columbia: University of South Carolina Press, 1998), 507.

14. WPA, *Guide,* 66.

15. Edgar, *South Carolina,* 468.

16. David L. Carlton, *Mill and Town in South Carolina, 1880–1920* (Baton Rouge: Louisiana State University Press, 1982), 129–70, 203, 228–31.

17. WPA, *Guide,* 3, 38, 58.

18. Ibid., 219–23.

19. Ibid., 7.

20. Edgar, *South Carolina,* xx.

21. Thomas D. Clark, *The Emerging South,* 2d ed. (New York: Oxford University Press, 1968), 11–13; Olin Pugh, *Difficult Decades of Banking: A Comparative Study of Banking Developments in South Carolina and the United States, 1920–1940* (Columbia: University of South Carolina School of Business Administration, 1964), 3; Department of Agriculture, Commerce and Industries of the State of South Carolina, *Yearbook of the Department of Agriculture, Commerce and Industries of the State of South Carolina, 1938–1939* (Columbia, 1939), 112 (hereafter cited as S.C. Dept. ACI, *Yearbook); Charleston News and Courier,* 22 June 1932, 4; William B. Hesseltine and David L. Smiley, *The South in American History,* 2d ed. (Englewood Cliffs, N.J.: Prentice-Hall, Inc., 1960), 531; U.S. Bureau of the Census, *Historical Statistics of the United States: Colonial Times to*

1970, Vol. 1 (Washington, D.C.: Government Printing Office, 1976), 517–18; George Brown Tindall, *The Emergence of the New South: 1913–1945* (Baton Rouge: Louisiana State University Press, 1967), 29, 33–37, 60, 111, 112, 121, 138; Mary Katherine Davis Cann, "The Morning After: South Carolina in the Jazz Age" (Ph.D. diss., University of South Carolina, 1984), 24–25; S.C. Dept. ACI, *Yearbook, 1935–1936*, 22.

22. In 1933 the state's 101,585 workers in manufacturing produced goods worth $235 million and earned wages of $54 million. The 80,154 workers in textiles produced goods worth $168 million and earned wages of $43 million. *South Carolina: Economic and Social Conditions in 1944* (Columbia: University of South Carolina Press, 1945), 50, 60 (hereafter cited as *S.C. Economic and Social*); S.C. Dept. ACI, *Yearbook, 1932–1933*, 103; WPA, "Unemployment in South Carolina," July 1939, WPA Records, RG 69, box 29, National Archives.

23. Edgar, *South Carolina*, 488; William Wilker Thompson, Jr., "A Managerial History of a Cotton Textile Firm: Spartan Mills, 1888–1958" (Ph.D. diss., University of Alabama, 1960), 104–16.

24. *Charleston News and Courier*, 19 May 1932, 4.

25. Marvin Leigh Cann, "Burnet Rhett Maybank and the New Deal in South Carolina, 1931–1941" (Ph.D. diss., University of North Carolina, 1967), 71 (hereafter cited as Cann, "Maybank"); *Chester News*, 2 Feb. 1932, 2; *Charleston News and Courier*, 28 Sept. 1932, 2; William P. Jacobs, *Facts about South Carolina and Her Textile Mills* (N.p.: Jacobs Press, 1937), 22.

26. *Charleston News and Courier*, 2 Jan. 1932, 1; 3 Jan. 1932, 1, 2; 5 Jan. 1932, 1; 8 Jan. 1932, 6; *Walterboro Press and Standard*, 18 May 1932, 2.

27. *Sixth Annual Report of the Department of Labor of the State of South Carolina* (Columbia: South Carolina Department of Labor, 1941), 75; Lawrence M. Pinckney, Business and Economic Report for South Carolina, February 1940, Works Progress Administration Collection, South Caroliniana Library, University of South Carolina.

28. *Columbia State*, 1 May 1932, 32; Cann, "Maybank," 72, 76; *Charleston News and Courier*, 28 Jan. 1932, 1; 19 Feb. 1932, 3.

29. Carl Gibbs, telephone interview by author, Wellford, S.C., 12 February 1999; Elizabeth M. Hayes, telephone interview by author, Latta, S.C., 10 February 1999; Ezra Dewitt, telephone interview by author, Rock Hill, S.C., 11 February 1999; Allison P. Simons, telephone interview by author, Columbia, S.C., 10 February 1999; Roy Altman, telephone interview by author, Okatie, S.C., 8 February 1999.

30. Julia Woodson, telephone interview by author, Liberty, S.C., 17 February 1999; Eunice H. Whitaker, telephone interview by author, Batesburg, S.C., 11 February 1999; Gibbs, interview.

31. Paul Wilkerson, telephone interview by author, Seneca, S.C., 11 February 1999; Ellison E. Jamison, telephone interview by author, Walhalla, S.C., 11 February

1999; Wilburn Hembree, telephone interview by author, Spartanburg, S.C., 8 February 1999, Gibbs, interview; Simons, interview.

32. Levi Tillman Fulmer, telephone interview by author, Graniteville, S.C., 8 February 1999; Mrs. Saluda D. Forest, telephone interview by author, Saluda, S.C., 10 February 1999; Hembree, interview; Gibbs, interview; Simons, interview; Wilkerson, interview; see also Ronald L. Heinemann, *Depression and New Deal in Virginia: The Enduring Dominion* (Charlottesville: University Press of Virginia, 1983), 23.

33. Forest, interview, Simons, interview, Hembree, interview; Fulmer, interview; Hayes, interview.

34. Fulmer, interview; Woodson, interview; Gibbs, interview.

35. Fulmer, interview; Hembree, interview; Wilkerson, interview; Simons, interview.

36. Gilbert C. Fite, *Cotton Fields No More: Southern Agriculture,1865–1980* (Lexington: University of Kentucky Press, 1984), 137.

37. Ibid., 137–38; see also Fulmer, interview; Gibbs, interview.

38. Frank E. Cain, Jr., telephone interview by author, Bennettsville, S.C., 12 February 1999; Fulmer, interview; Gibbs, interview; Edgar, *South Carolina*, 500.

39. Simons, interview; Woodson, interview; Wilkerson, interview; Whitaker, interview.

40. *Congressional Quarterly's Guide to U.S. Elections,* 3d ed. (Washington, D.C.: Congressional Quarterly, Inc., 1994), 361–94, 440–52, 658, 806.

41. Byrnes to Roosevelt, 12 November 1928, Byrnes Papers; James F. Byrnes, *All in One Lifetime* (New York: Harper and Brothers, 1958), 61.

42. F. B. Summers to Mendel L. Smith, 8 and 19 August 1932, Mendel L. Smith Papers, South Caroliniana Library, University of South Carolina, Columbia; Mary Dewson to Ibra C. Blackwood, 28 November 1931, Ibra C. Blackwood Papers, South Carolina Department of Archives and History, Columbia; Byrnes, *All in One Lifetime,* 62; see Rexford G. Tugwell, *How They Became President* (New York: Simon and Schuster, 1964), 415; Lionel V. Patenaude, "The New Deal and Texas" (Ph.D. diss., University of Texas, 1953), 28–29; Ewing Laporte, *Official Record of the Proceedings of the Democratic National Convention, 1932,* 601–2 (hereafter cited as *Proceeding*); *Charleston News and Courier,* 3 July 1932, 4; 5 July 1932, 9; *Spartanburg Herald,* 3 July 1932, 4; 4 July 1932, 4; *Chester Reporter,* 4 July 1932, 2; *Columbia State,* 4 July 1932, 4; 23 July 1932, 11; *Edgefield Advertiser,* 6 July 1932, 2; *Walterboro Press and Standard,* 27 July 1932, 2.

43. *Charleston News and Courier,* 17 Aug. 1932, 1.

44. *Spartanburg Herald,* 20 May 1932, 4; 23 Sept. 1932, 4; *Charleston News and Courier,* 4 Sept. 1932, 4; *Columbia State,* 22 Aug. 1932, 4.

45. *Barnwell People-Sentinel,* 28 Jan. 1832, 2; *Camden Wateree Messenger,* 22 Mar. 1932, 2; *Lexington Dispatch News,* 11 May 1932, 4; *Bamberg County Times,* 28 July 1932, 4; *Chester News,* 4 Nov. 1932, 2.

46. *Columbia State,* 17 Oct. 1932, 2; 25 Oct. 1932, 1; Clint T. Graydon, *In Memoriam: Claud N. Sapp, 1886–1947* (n.p., n.d.), 16; Charles H. Gerald to John S. Cohen, Western Union Telegram, 21 October 1932, Blackwood Papers. Not all Brains Trusters agree on Byrnes's role. Raymond Moley, who liked Byrnes, says Roosevelt invited Byrnes to advise. Rexford Tugwell, who did not like Byrnes, wrote that Byrnes and Pittman "asserted their right to be consulted." Raymond Moley, *27 Masters of Politics* (New York: Funk and Wagnalls Co., 1949), 252; Rexford Tugwell, *The Brains Trust* (New York: Viking Press, 1968), 481.

47. *Columbia State,* 14 Oct. 1932, 5; 27 Oct. 1932, 6; 29 Oct. 1932, 6.

48. Edgar Eugene Robinson, *They Voted for Roosevelt* (Stanford, Calif.: Stanford University Press, 1947), 42–46, 150–51.

49. See Tindall, 388.

50. Henry Lee Moon, *Balance of Power: The Negro Vote* (Garden City, N.Y.: Doubleday and Co., 1949), 65. The identification of the African American with the Republican Party was the decisive factor causing South Carolina to give Al Smith more than 90 percent of the state's popular vote in 1928, despite his Roman Catholicism and "wetness." Pool, "1928 Election," 10–16.

51. *Columbia State,* 15 Aug. 1932, 8; 25 Aug. 1932, 4; *Spartanburg Herald,* 21 Aug. 1932, 4; 19 Sept. 1932, 4; *Edgefield Advertiser,* 24 Aug. 1932, 2.

52. *Spartanburg Herald,* 5 Nov. 1932, 4; 10 Nov. 1932, 4; *Columbia State,* 7 Jan. 1932, 1; 16 Feb. 1932, 4; *Charleston News and Courier,* 7 Feb. 1932, 1; *Columbia State,* 4 July 1932, 4.

53. *Charleston News and Courier,* 13 Apr. 1932, 1; *Columbia State,* 19 May 1932, 1; 29 Oct. 1932, 6. As late as 1938 the *Columbia State* agreed that "Wade Hampton was of his day Franklin D. Roosevelt of today." *Columbia State,* 22 Aug. 1938, 9. See also W. J. Cash, *The Mind of the South* (New York: Alfred A. Knopf, 1941), 365.

54. *Spartanburg Herald,* 9 Nov. 1932, 4; *Barnwell People-Sentinel,* 10 Nov. 1932, 2.

55. *Columbia State,* 9 Sept. 1932, 9.

CHAPTER 2—THE CONGRESSIONAL DELEGATION AND THE NEW DEAL: 1933–1939

1. James A. Hoyt to Harry L. Watson, 12 July 1935, Harry L. Watson Papers, South Caroliniana Library, University of South Carolina, Columbia.

2. The eight bills included the Emergency Banking Act (1933), Economy Act (1933), compromise currency amendment to the Agricultural Adjustment Act (1933), Farm Credit Act (1933), Home Owners Loan Act (1934), Independent Offices Appropriation Act (1934), Emergency Relief Appropriation Act (1935), and Government Reorganization Act (1937–1938).

3. Clipping titled "The Political Traffic Cop," *Today,* 17 Jan. 1934; Byrnes Scrapbook, 1934, James Francis Byrnes Papers, Robert M. Cooper Library, Clemson University, Clemson, S.C.; Winfred Bobo Moore, "New South Statesman: The

Political Career of James Francis Byrnes" (Ph.D. diss., Duke University, 1975), 133–37 (hereafter cited as Moore, "Byrnes").

4. Moore, "Byrnes," 116.

5. Not only was Smith the "Dean of Democrats" in 1933, but he had also served more years in the Senate than all but 12 of the 1,356 members since 1789. Clipping, hand-dated "3/18/37," Ellison D. Smith Papers, South Caroliniana Library, University of South Carolina, Columbia. See also David Robertson, *Sly and Able: A Political Biography of James F. Byrnes* (New York: W. W. Norton and Company, 1994), 190.

6. Daniel W. Hollis, "Cotton Ed Smith—Showman or Statesman?" *South Carolina Historical Magazine* 71 (Oct. 1970), 240–45 (hereafter cited as Hollis, "Smith"); James T. Patterson, *Congressional Conservatism and the New Deal: The Growth of a Conservative Coalition in Congress, 1933–1939* (Lexington: University of Kentucky Press, 1967), 42.

7. Henry C. Ferrell, Jr., "John Jackson McSwain: A Study in Political Technique" (master's thesis, Duke University, 1957), 5.

8. *New York Times,* 7 Aug. 1936, 19; John C. Weaver, "Lawyers, Lodges, and Kinfolk: The Workings of a South Carolina Political Organization, 1920–1936," *South Carolina Historical Magazine* 78 (Oct. 1977), 272–85; James M. Richardson, *History of Greenville County, South Carolina: Narrative and Biographical, by James M. Richardson* (Atlanta: A. H. Cawston, 1930; reprint, with a new index by Margaret H. Cannon, Spartanburg, S.C.: The Reprint Company, 1980), 140–42 (page citations are to the reprint edition); McSwain was a member of Kiwanis, Masons, Odd Fellows, Knights of Pythias, Elks, Order of the Moose, Woodmen of the World, and Red Men.

9. *New York Times,* 30 Sept. 1939, 17; Doyle W. Boggs, "Charleston Politics, 1900–1930: An Overview," *Proceedings of the South Carolina Historical Association* (1979), 1–13.

10. *New York Times,* 18 June 1938, 15; *Biographical Directory of the United States Congress: 1744–1989* (Washington, D.C.: Government Printing Office, 1989), 1048, 1481.

11. *South Carolina Newsview,* 9 May 1936, 7; David Duncan Wallace, *The History of South Carolina,* vol. 4 (New York: American Historical Society, 1934), 299; J. C. Hemphill, ed., *Men of Mark in South Carolina: Ideals of American Life: A Collection of Biographies of Leading Men of the State,* vol. 3 (Washington, D.C.: Men of Mark Publishing Company, 1908), 299; *Who's Who in South Carolina, 1934–1935* (Columbia: Current Historical Association, 1935), 160, 170, 290, 345, 398, 471; *Biographical Directory,* 1713–14, 1916; folder marked "Richards, James Biographical Info," James P. Richards Papers, South Caroliniana Library, University of South Carolina, Columbia.

12. *New York Times,* 9 Sept. 1936, 2; Archie Vernon Huff, Jr,. *Greenville: The History of the City and County in the South Carolina Piedmont* (Columbia:

University of South Carolina Press, 1995), 342; *Who's Who in South Carolina: 1934–1935* (Columbia: Current Historical Association, 1935), 65, 290.

13. *Biographical Directory,* 692, 1133, 1480.

14. William E. Leuchtenburg, *Franklin D. Roosevelt and the New Deal* (New York: Harper and Row, 1963), 48–49 (hereafter cited as Leuchtenburg, *FDR*).

15. *Congressional Record,* 73d Cong., Special Sess., 675–76, 1139–43, 4712; *Columbia State,* 22 Mar. 1933, 1.

16. *Congressional Record,* 73d Cong., Special Sess., 1949.

17. *Congressional Record,* 73d Cong., Special Sess., 1447; *Columbia State,* 8 Apr. 1933, 1.

18. *Congressional Record,* 73d Cong., Special Sess., 1387; *Columbia State,* 1 Apr. 1933, 1; 2 Apr. 1933, 1.

19. *Congressional Record,* 73d Cong., Special Sess., 2551, 2562; Leuchtenburg, *FDR,* 50; James F. Byrnes, *All in One Lifetime* (New York: Harper and Brothers, 1958), 75–76. The Farm Credit Act to expand farm credit and to centralize federal farm lending agencies under the Farm Credit Administration was fathered by Byrnes, who guided it through the Banking and Currency Committee, the Senate floor, and the conference committee. Smith gave only grudging support, charging that the measure smacked too much of "commercial banking." Smith had wanted a system of agricultural banks lending directly to the farmer. Under the Farm Credit Act the farmer had to purchase stock in the Production Credit Association from which he then borrowed. *Congressional Record,* 73d Cong., Special Sess., 5521–29, 5614.

20. *Columbia State,* 13 June 1933, 1; 15 June 1933, 1; 21 June 1933, 1.

21. *Congressional Record,* 73d Cong., 2d Sess., 1441–42.

22. Ibid, 4196–97, 4436–40.

23. Ibid; see also Joseph Edward Lee, "'America Comes First with Me': The Political Career of James Richards, 1932–1957" (Ph.D. diss., University of South Carolina, 1987), 61–80.

24. In January, Smith had informed Roosevelt that he would support the Bankhead Bill only if a majority of cotton farmers favored it. Secretary Wallace sent out questionnaires, and 85 percent of the respondents favored the bill. *Congressional Record,* 73d Cong., 2d Sess., 5407–10; *Columbia State,* 27 Mar. 1934, 1.

25. *Congressional Record,* 73d Cong., 2d Sess., 5413–18.

26. Ibid., 5712; *Columbia State,* 25 Apr. 1934, 3.

27. *Congressional Record,* 73d Cong., 2d Sess., 9310, 10657–58, 10667; *Columbia State,* 18 May 1934, 1. Although supportive of acreage reduction in principle, Taylor and McMillan deserted their four colleagues and voted against the Kerr Bill because they claimed it discriminated against small farmers.

28. *Columbia State,* 11 June 1934, 1; *Congressional Record,* 73d Cong., 2d Sess., 10817–23.

29. *Columbia State,* 10 Jan. 1936, 7; 12 Jan. 1936, 10-A; 15 Jan. 1936, 8.

30. Ibid., 6 Jan. 1936, 1; *Congressional Record,* 74th Cong., 2d Sess., 1570, 1585, 2165, 2578.

31. *Columbia State,* 31 Jan. 1937, 14-B; *Congressional Record,* 75th Cong., 1st Sess., 8270–81.

32. *Columbia State,* 6 Aug. 1937, 7-A; 14 Aug. 1937, 5; 20 Aug. 1937, 1.

33. Ibid., 9 Sept. 1937, 1.

34. Ibid., 2 Oct. 1937, 8.

35. Ibid., 19 Oct. 1937, 2; 20 Oct. 1937, 1; *Congressional Record,* 75th Cong., 2d Sess., 439. This informal referendum in South Carolina stymied Smith, who had agreed earlier to abide by the wishes of cotton farmers when he formulated the new agricultural bill. Smith had no choice but to surrender. As he explained it: "A majority of the cotton growers said, 'We want it with teeth.' Some said, 'We want it with tusks. . . .' This is what they said they want, and . . . this is what they are going to get."

36. *Congressional Record,* 75th Cong., 2d Sess., 1042.

37. Ibid., 1280.

38. Ibid.

39. Ibid., 1290, 1768; Ibid., 75th Cong., 3d Sess., 1764–1770, 1881, Appendix, 811; *Columbia State,* 19 Feb. 1938, 7.

40. Half determined to leave industrial recovery for the regular session, the president was jarred into action on 16 April by Sen. Hugo Black's Thirty-hour Bill that would use the Interstate Commerce Clause to create a six-hour day, five-day workweek in order to create six million new jobs. The Senate passed Black's measure by a vote of fifty-three to thirty. Smith voted for and Byrnes against the measure. *Columbia State,* 7 Apr. 1933, 1; Leuchtenburg, *FDR,* 56. For Byrnes's efforts to amend the National Industrial Recovery Bill to outlaw the stretch-out in the textile industry, see *Congressional Record,* 73d Cong., Special Sess., 4737, 5224, 5290–91, 5424, 5861. *Columbia State,* 1 June 1933, 1; Moore, "Byrnes," 126; Ellis W. Hawley, *The New Deal and the Problem of Monopoly* (Princeton: Princeton University Press, 1966), 31; Bernard Bellush, *The Failure of the NRA* (New York: W. W. Norton and Co., 1975), 26.

41. *Columbia State,* 10 Oct. 1935, 8.

42. *Congressional Record,* 73d Cong., Special Sess., 2305, 2584.

43. Clipping, McSwain Scrapbook, 1932–1935, 136, John Jackson McSwain Papers, Duke University Library, Durham, N.C.

44. Ibid., 134, 139; G. H. Mahon to McSwain, 30 May 1934, McSwain Papers.

45. *Congressional Record,* 74th Cong., 1st Sess., 940, 942.

46. *Congressional Record,* 73th Cong., Special Sess., 2808, 2274–82, 2340, 3084, 3374, 3590–600; *New York Times,* 14 Mar. 1933, 4; *Columbia State,* 20 May 1933, 1. For McSwain's role in the Muscle Shoals controversy in the 1920s, see Preston J. Hubbard, *Origins of the TVA: The Muscle Shoals Controversy, 1920–1932*

(Nashville: Vanderbilt University Press, 1961), 119, 215; Erwin C. Hargrove and Paul K. Conkin, *TVA: Fifty Years of Grass-Roots Bureaucracy* (Urbana: University of Illinois Press, 1983), 27–29; Roy Talbert, Jr., *FDR's Utopian: Arthur Morgan of the TVA* (Jackson: University Press of Mississippi, 1987), 87; C. Herman Pritchett, *The Tennessee Valley Authority: A Study in Public Administration [by] C. Herman Pritchett . . .* (New York: Russell and Russell, 1971), 29.

47. *New York Times,* 4 May 1937, 13. See also *Congressional Record,* 75th Cong., 1st Sess., Appendix, 1075–77; *New York Times,* 24 Dec. 1936, 2.

48. Undated memorandum titled "Federal, State, and Local Funds Used for Relief and Work Programs in New York and South Carolina," Byrnes Papers; Moore, "Byrnes," 229–30.

49. Byrnes to W. H. Beattie, 17 July 1937, Byrnes Papers. Byrnes offered less resistance the following year to a $3.75 billion Work Relief Bill. A recession that began in September 1937 plunged many farmers and industries nearly to 1933 levels of production and profits. By April 1938 an additional four million workers were unemployed. Now, in the midst of a new emergency, Byrnes helped to write the bill in committee and guided it through the upper house before also serving on the conference committee. He acknowledged that by the spring of 1938, "each piece" of his constituent mail was "a prayer and plea from hungry people in South Carolina for help." Once again the "good order and the harmony of the whole community" was in jeopardy. *Congressional Record,* 75th Cong., 3d Sess., 7851; Leuchtenburg, *FDR,* 257; Moore, "Byrnes," 268.

50. *Congressional Record,* 75th Cong., 1st Sess., 4923, 5227, 5816; *Time,* 28 June 1937, 10; Moore, "Byrnes," 232–33.

51. *Congressional Record,* 75th Cong., 1st. Sess., 342–43, 887. Byrnes also worked closely with Senate Finance Committee chairman Pat Harrison to repeal the New Deal taxes on undistributed profits and capital gains. E. D. Easterby to Byrnes, 8 May 1937, Byrnes Papers; *New York Times,* 6 Nov. 1937, 4; *Congressional Record,* 75th Cong., 3d. Sess., 2578; *Time,* 2 May 1938, 8; Leuchtenburg, *FDR,* 260. And yet in 1939 most of the lawmakers from the Palmetto State avoided the anti–New Deal coalition on measures that either benefited South Carolina or were popular in particular congressional districts. A $2.4 million antirecession public works bill, which passed the Senate but failed in the House, found Senator Byrnes and representatives Bryson, Fulmer, Hare, and John McMillan voting for it, with Senator Smith and Representatives Richards and Thomas McMillan against it. *Congressional Record,* 76th Cong., 1st Sess., 2502–4, 3104–5, 9592–93, 10512, 10717, 10957–58; Patterson, *Congressional Conservatism,* 299–323.

52. Please see the appendix for a description of the voting by each lawmaker. Incidently, Congressman McSwain supported the New Deal on 91 percent of his votes.

53. Robertson, *Sly and Able,* 253; Leuchtenburg, *FDR,* 233; Byrnes, *All in One Lifetime,* 97; Moore, "Byrnes," 217.

54. Quoted in the *Columbia State,* 25 Mar. 1937, 3-A. See also Thomas S. McMillan to John Grace, 16 February 1937, John P. Grace Papers, Set 2, Duke University Library, Durham, N.C.

55. Byrnes, *All in One Lifetime,* 97.

56. Robertson, *Sly and Able,* 255.

57. Ibid.; Moore, "Byrnes," 218; *Congressional Record,* 75th Cong., 1st Sess., 276–78.

58. Moore, "Byrnes," 218; *Congressional Record,* 75th Cong., 1st Sess., 276–78, 2583; *Columbia State,* 22 Aug. 1937, 2.

59. Ku Klux Klan, Broadside, n.d., Byrnes Papers; Moore, "Byrnes," 219–20.

60. *Congressional Record,* 75th Cong., 1st Sess., 2186, 2191.

61. Robertson, *Sly and Able,* 260; Moore, "Byrnes," 221.

62. John H. Bankhead to Byrnes, 20 July 1937, Byrnes Papers.

63. Robertson, *Sly and Able,* 262.

64. *Time,* 26 July 1937, 13; Moore, "Byrnes," 235–36; Robertson, *Sly and Able,* 263.

65. Byrnes to Bankhead, 5 August 1937, Byrnes Papers; *Time,* 2 Aug. 1937, 10; Byrnes, *All in One Lifetime,* 99–100; Robertson, *Sly and Able,* 263–66; Moore, "Byrnes," 237–40.

66. Robertson, *Sly and Able,* 256–58; Moore, "Byrnes," 222.

67. *Congressional Record,* 74th Cong., 1st. Sess., 6534–45; see also Arthur M. Schlesinger, Jr., *The Politics of Upheaval* (Boston: Houghton Mifflin Company, 1960), 437, and Winfred B. Moore, Jr., "'Soul of the South': James F. Byrnes and the Racial Issue in American Politics, 1911–1941," *Proceedings of the South Carolina Historical Association* (1978): 48–49.

68. *Congressional Record,* 74th Cong., 1st Sess., 5749.

69. Ibid., 6616.

70. *Columbia State,* 17 Mar. 1935, 1.

71. *Time,* 24 Jan. 1938, 8–9; *Congressional Record,* 75th Cong., 3d. Sess., 228–31.

72. *Congressional Record,* 75th Cong., 3d Session, 306–10; *Time,* 24 Jan. 1938, 9.

73. Patterson, *Congressional Conservatism,* 184, 332–37.

74. *Congressional Record,* 75th Cong., 3d Sess., 1835, Appendix, 486–89.

75. *Congressional Record,* 75th Cong., 1st Sess., 7881–83. Nevertheless, the labor standards bill finally passed into law in 1938. In the lower house Fulmer, Taylor, Gasque, and McMillan opposed the measure; Mahon and Richards supported it. The previous year Richards had been the only South Carolinian to vote yea. Mahon probably joined him in 1938 with an eye to textile votes since he represented the textile counties of Greenville and Spartanburg. On the conference report Fulmer, whose district also contained a sizeable textile vote, changed his vote from nay to yea. *Congressional Record,* 75th Cong., 3d Sess., 7450, 9267; *Columbia State,* 15 June 1938, 8; Leuchtenburg, *FDR,* 262.

76. *Congressional Record,* 75th Cong., 1st Sess. 8373, 9293; Leuchtenburg, *FDR,* 135–36.

77. Leuchtenburg, *FDR,* 279.

78. *Congressional Record,* 73d Cong., Special Sess., 67, 401, 539l; Leuchtenburg, *FDR,* 42–43.

79. *Congressional Record,* 73d Cong., 2d Sess., 1945, 2423, 5808, 8116, 8503–6, 8714, 8766, 10395, and Index, 63; Moore, "Byrnes," 148–50.

80. *Congressional Record,* 74th Cong., 1st Sess., 8948.

81. Ibid., 3464–65, 6069, 8747–48, 9053, 9065, 9648, 9650; Moore, "Byrnes," 174–75; Leuchtenburg, *FDR,* 155; *New York Times,* 20 June 1935, 13.

82. John Hammond Moore, *Columbia and Richland County* (Columbia: University of South Carolina Press, 1993), 340.

83. *Columbia State,* 21 June 1933, 10.

CHAPTER 3—RELIEF AT LAST

1. *Columbia State,* Aug. 2, 1933, 1; William E. Leuchtenburg, *Franklin D. Roosevelt and the New Deal,* Harper Torchbooks (New York: Harper and Row, 1963), 120 (hereafter cited as Leuchtenburg, *FDR*); Ronald Lynton Heinemann, "Depression and New Deal in Virginia" (Ph.D. diss., University of Virginia, 1968), 89 (hereafter cited as Heinemann, "New Deal in Virginia").

2. *Columbia State,* 15 Aug., 1933, 1; 24 Sept., 12-A; 6 Oct., 5; 8 Oct., 9-B.

3. Federal Emergency Relief Administration, *Federal Emergency Relief Administration: Unemployment Relief Census, October 1933,* no. 1 (Washington, D.C.: Government Printing Office, 1934), 5, 13 (hereafter cited as FERA, *Unemployment Relief Census No. 1*).

4. Ibid., 5, 7, 13, 34, 50; Federal Emergency Relief Administration, *Federal Emergency Relief Administration: Unemployment Relief Census, October 1933,* no. 2 (Washington, D.C.: Government Printing Office, 1934), 4, 5, 13, 14, map 1 (hereafter cited as FERA, *Unemployment Relief Census No. 2*).

5. Arthur E. Burns and Edward A. Williams, *A Survey of Relief and Security Programs* (Washington, D.C.: Government Printing Office, 1938), 22–28 (hereafter cited as Burns and Williams, *Relief Program Survey*).

6. *Columbia State,* 22 Nov. 1933, 1; 23 Nov. 1933, 1; 28 Nov. 1933, 1; 10 Dec. 1933, 1.

7. Civil Works Administration, Final Report of South Carolina, November 15, 1933–April 30, 1934, CWA Records, RG 69, National Archives, Washington, D.C.; Burns and Williams, *Relief Program Survey,* 94. Not all South Carolinians shared this young adult's appreciation. David R. Coker of Hartsville decried "spending millions unnecessarily" and "getting many of the well-to-do people out of the habit of responding to local charities." D. R. Coker to Kirkman G. Finlay, 27 March 1934, David R. Coker Papers, South Caroliniana Library, University of South Carolina, Columbia.

8. FERA, *Statistical Summary of Emergency Relief Activities, January 1933 through December 1935* (Washington, D.C.: Government Printing Office, 1936), 19–22 (hereafter cited as FERA, *Statistical Summary*); Burns and Williams, *Relief Program Survey*, 29; *Columbia State*, 21 Apr. 1934, 12; 2 Dec. 1934, 8-B.

9. *Columbia State*, 23 Sept. 1935, 2.

10. *Time*, 6 Dec. 1937, 41; South Carolina Works Progress Administration, *Work News*, Feb. 1937, 1–2; William Henry Hanckel, "The Preservation Movement in Charleston, 1920–1962" (master's thesis, University of South Carolina, 1962), 10.

11. Hanckel, "Preservation Movement," 9–10; Sidney R. Bland, *Preserving Charleston's Past, Shaping Its Future: The Life and Times of Susan Pringle Frost* (Columbia: University of South Carolina Press, 1999), 64–77.

12. Bland, *Preserving Charleston*, 89–94.

13. "Charleston Opens Historic Playhouse with Historic Play," *Architectural Record* 83, no. 1 (Jan. 1938): 20–25.

14. Frederick Johnson, "History of the Dock Street Theater," typescript of radio address [1947], South Caroliniana Library, University of South Carolina, Columbia.

15. Ibid.

16. *Columbia State*, 14 Oct. 1934, 1-A; 20 May 1935, 12.

17. Ibid., 19 Nov. 1934, 5; 10 Feb. 1935, 2-A.

18. Ibid., 29 Nov. 1933, 2; 11 Feb. 1934, 7-A; 4 Dec. 1934, 2-B.

19. Ibid., 6 May 1935, 12.

20. Ibid., 22 Aug. 1933, 1; 31 Aug. 1933, 3; 17 Sept. 1933, 5-A; 3 Oct. 1933, 9; 19 Apr. 1934, 7; 12 Sept. 1934, 12; 7 Nov. 1934, 11; 9 July 1935, 2; Burns and Williams, *Relief Program Survey*, 31–32; WPA, *Final Statistical Report of the Federal Emergency Relief Administration* (Washington, D.C.: Government Printing Office, 1942), 112, 297.

21. From April 1934, when the CWA ceased, until December 1935, when the SCERA ended, the largest monthly work quota in South Carolina was 45,878, with monthly earnings of $302,359. By contrast, the largest number of monthly cases receiving direct relief was 85,239, representing 353,820 persons, and the largest monthly appropriation for direct relief was more than $1 million. FERA, *Statistical Summary*, 4–8, 14–28.

22. *Columbia State*, 12 Aug. 1934, 14-B; 18 Oct. 1934, 2; 24 Oct. 1934, 3; 22 May 1935, 2; FERA, *Monthly Report of the Federal Emergency Relief Administration: November 1 through November 30, 1935* (Washington, D.C.: Government Printing Office, 1936), 62–69.

23. Burns and Williams, *Relief Program Survey*, 81–82, 93–94.

24. Quoted in B. A. Botkin, *Sidewalks of America* (Indianapolis: The Bobbs-Merrill Company, 1954), 509–10.

25. L. E. Jaeckel to Hugh Johnson, 4 December 1933, Civil Works Administration Records, RG 69, box 42, National Archives, Washington, D.C. (hereafter cited as CWA Records).

26. Ibid., folder marked "South Carolina Complaints, A–F," n.d.

27. Ibid., Fulmer to Harry Hopkins, 10 February 1934.

28. Ibid., McMillan to Hopkins, 13 February 1934; *Columbia State,* 26 Feb. 1934, 1.

29. Lawrence M. Pinckney to Frank C. Walker, 24 April 1934, 8 May 1934, National Emergency Council Records, RG 44, box 437, National Archives Branch, Federal Record Center, Suitland, Md. (hereafter cited as NEC Records).

30. *Columbia State,* 16 June 1934, 1. See also *Columbia State,* 9 June 1934, 1; 14 June 1934, 1.

31. Unemployed Citizens of Allendale County to Ibra C. Blackwood, 18 June 1934, Blackwood Papers.

32. *Columbia State,* June 18, 1934, 4. On June 19 Assistant State NEC director John W. Califf reported to the NEC that the charges of favoritism in the county ERAs were true. When the CWA had ended, he wrote, relatives of county relief administrators were transferred to the SCERA's emergency work program, while CWA workers without connections were left to shift for themselves. John W. Califf to Frank C. Walker, NEC Records.

33. *Columbia State,* 21 June 1934, 2; 30 June 1934, 1; 18 July 1934, 12.

34. Frederick A. Gutheim, "A Survey of the South Carolina Emergency Relief Administration," Federal Emergency Relief Administration Records, RG 69, National Archives, Washington, D.C., 3 (hereafter cited as Gutheim, "SCERA Survey").

35. Ibid., 4, 20.

36. Ibid., 4, 5, 7.

37. Ibid., 5, 8.

38. Ibid., 28.

39. Ibid.; see also 4, 5, 23, 24, 30.

40. *Columbia State,* 8 Sept. 1934, 1; 19 Oct. 1934, 1; Lawrence M. Pinckney to Donald R. Richberg, 23 October 1934, NEC Records.

41. *Columbia State,* 22 January 1934, 2; 6 March 1934, 8.

42. Philip M. Hauser, *Workers on Relief in the United States in March 1935,* vol. 1 (Washington, D.C.: Government Printing Office, 1938), 68–69.

43. This writer computed the relief and population percentages in the table above from figures given in Hauser, *Workers on Relief,* I, 788–90, and *Fifteenth Census of the United States, 1930,* vol. 3, part 2 (Washington, D.C.: Government Printing Office, 1932), 805–12.

44. Hauser, *Workers on Relief,* I, 84–86; Gutheim, "SCERA Survey," 67; *Columbia State,* 9 Feb. 1936, 11-A.

45. Gutheim, "SCERA Survey," 59–62.

46. Pinckney to Donald R. Richberg, 28 January 1935, NEC Records.

47. *Columbia State,* 13 Feb. 1935, 1; 20 Feb. 1935, 1; unidentified newsclipping, dated 20 Feb. 1935, Olin D. Johnston Scrapbook, 1935, Olin D. Johnston Papers,

South Caroliniana Library, University of South Carolina, Columbia, 225 (hereafter cited as Johnston Scrapbook).

48. Pinckney to Donald R. Richberg, 18 March 1935, NEC Records; unidentified clipping, Johnston Scrapbook, 227.

49. *Columbia State,* 15 Mar. 1935, 1; 19 Mar. 1935, 1; 21 Mar. 1935, 13; 26 Mar. 1935, 1; 29 Mar. 1935, 1; 2 Apr. 1935, 12.

50. Quoted in the *Columbia State,* 29 Mar. 1935, 1.

51. Ibid.

52. *Columbia Carolina Free Press,* 29 Mar. 1935, 1.

53. *Columbia State,* 30 July 1935, 1.

54. Ibid., 14 Nov. 1935, 1; 21 May 1936, 7.

55. Broadus Mitchell, *Depression Decade: From New Era through New Deal, 1929–1941* (New York: Harper and Row, 1947), 329.

56. Roy Altman, telephone interview by the author, Okatie, S.C., 8 February 1999; Ezra Dewitt, telephone interview by the author, Rock Hill, S.C., 11 February 1999; Levi Tillman Fulmer, telephone interview by the author, Graniteville, S.C., 8 February 1999; Ellison E. Jamison, telephone interview by the author, Walhalla, S.C., 11 February 1999; Paul Wilkerson, telephone interview by the author, Seneca, S.C., 11 February 1999; *The Pinopolian,* 24 January 1935, Civilian Conservation Corps Camp Newsletters, South Carolina Historical Society, Charleston (hereafter cited as CCC Camp Newsletters).

57. *The Pinopolian,* 30 April 1935, CCC Camp Newsletters.

58. *Cheraw Cherokean,* 12 November 1935, CCC Camp Newsletters.

59. Folders for the York County CCC Camp, CCC Records, RG 35, boxes 1183, 1184, National Archives, Washington, D.C.; *Columbia State,* 7 Apr. 1933, 8; 17 May 1933, 12; 19 June 1933, 2; 20 June 1933, 2; 29 Oct. 1933, 5-A; 21 May 1934, 5; 8 Aug. 1935, 8.

60. *The Pinopolian,* 7 Feb. 1935, CCC Camp Newsletters. See also 7 Mar. 1935, and *Cheraw Cherokean,* 12 Nov. 1935, CCC Camp Newsletters.

61. Altman, interview; Dewitt, interview; Fulmer, interview; Jamison, interview; Wilkerson, interview.

62. Office of Government Records, South Carolina: Report No. 10, NEC Records, 2, 21–22, 40–50 (hereafter cited as South Carolina Report No. 10).

63. *Columbia State,* 25 Nov. 1935, 2; 16 Mar. 1936, 4; 28 Mar. 1937, 3; 9 Feb. 1938, 4.

64. Ibid., 8 Aug. 1935, 8.

CHAPTER 4—RELIEF THAT LASTS

1. *South Carolina Social Welfare* 1 (July 1936), 2; newsclipping, Olin D. Johnston Scrapbook, Olin D. Johnston Papers, South Caroliniana Library, University of South Carolina, Columbia, 1936, 78 (hereafter cited as Johnston Scrapbook); Lawrence M. Pinckney to Eugene S. Leggett, 1 March 1936, National Emergency

Council Records, RG 44, box 437, National Archives, Washington, D.C. (hereafter cited as NEC Records); *Columbia State*, 11 May 1936, 5; 15 May 1936, 8-B.

2. *South Carolina Social Welfare* 1 (July 1936), 4.

3. Office of Government Reports, Activities and Accomplishments of Assistance Agencies in South Carolina, December 1939, NEC Records, RG 44, box 1477, 33–34 (hereafter cited as O.G.R., AAAASC); O.G.R., South Carolina Report No. 10, 25; *Columbia State*, 7 June 1936; Johnston Scrapbook, 1936, 1; 13 June 1936, 2; newsclipping, Johnston Scrapbook, 1936, 81; William R. Curtis, "The Development of Unemployment Insurance in the South," *Southern Economic Journal* 15 (July 1948), 43–53.

4. Quoted in *Annual Report of the State Department of Public Welfare,* May 1937–June 1938, 6 (hereafter cited as State Welfare Dapartment Annual Report); *Columbia State,* 22 Nov. 1936, 6-A.

5. *Columbia State,* 19 Feb. 1937, 1; 7 May 1937, 5-A; 13 May 1937, 4; see also *State Welfare Department Annual Report, May 1937–June 1938,* 6.

6. The other four social security programs were services for crippled children and maternal and child health services (both administered by the Children's Bureau of the Department of Labor), vocational rehabilitation (administered by the Office of Education in the Federal Security Administration), and public health services (administered by the U.S. Public Health Service). O.G.R., South Carolina Report No. 10, 24–27.

7. O.G.R., South Carolina Report No. 10, 24–27; *State Welfare Department Annual Report, May 1937–June 1938,* 7–9. The remaining social security program administered by the State Department of Public Welfare was the Child Welfare Service Program.

8. *State Welfare Department Annual Report, May 1937–June 1938,* 11–13, 30–31; O.G.R., AAAASC, 31. Even with the reduction in old-age assistance, South Carolina was still providing a higher monthly payment and to a higher percentage of her population than North Carolina, Georgia, Mississippi, and Alabama. The national average was $19.23 a month to only 21.7 percent of the aged population. *State Welfare Department Annual Report, May 1937–June 1938,* 13, 38–39; Ibid., *July 1, 1938–June 30, 1939,* 8, 24–25, 32–33.

9. *Columbia State,* 21 Aug. 1933, 1.

10. *Columbia State,* 21 June 1935, 1; 24 June 1935, 1; 18 July 1935, 10; 13 Aug. 1935, 12; 13 Sept. 1935, 5; 26 Jan. 1933, 7; Burns and Williams, *Relief Program Survey,* 46–48; Edward A. Williams, *Work, Relief and Security* (Washington, D.C.: Government Printing Office, 1941), 23, 24, 26 (hereafter cited as Williams, *Relief*); O.G.R., South Carolina Report No. 10, 39; Ronald Lynton Heinemann, "Depression and New Deal in Virginia" (Ph.D. diss., University of Virginia, 1967), 121; Lawrence M. Pinckney, Chart titled "Expenditures, Type of Employment, and Accomplishments," 30 June 1939, Wil Lou Gray Papers, South Caroliniana Library, University of South Carolina, Columbia.

11. *Charleston News and Courier,* 6 June 1931, 2; 13 June 1931, 1.

12. Lawrence M. Pinckney, Final State Report on Administration and Operation of WPA Programs in South Carolina, 1935–1943, 5 March 1943, Works Progress Administration Records, RG 69, Final State Reports series, National Archives, Washington, D.C., 1–3 (hereafter cited as Pinckney, Final WPA Report for South Carolina); Pinckney to Eugene S. Leggett, NEC Records, RG 44, box 437.

13. Works Progress Administration, *Report on Progress of the WPA Program* (Washington, D.C.: Government Printing Office, 1939) 172, 176–77 (hereafter cited as WPA, *Progress Report*); Works Progress Administration, *Final Report on WPA Programs, 1935–1943* (Washington, D.C.: Government Printing Office, 1947), 126–27, 135–36 (hereafter cited as WPA, *Final Report*).

14. J. Rion McKissick et al., Report of the State [WPA] Appraisal Committee, 23 March 1938, WPA Records, RG 69, box 217, National Archives, Washington, D.C., 5–7 (hereafter cited as McKissick, State Appraisal Committee Report); Lawrence M. Pinckney to Alfred Edgar Smith, 17 December 1936, James Francis Byrnes Papers, Robert M. Cooper Library, Clemson University, Clemson, S.C. (hereafter cited as Byrnes Papers).

15. McKissick, State Appraisal Committee Report, 7; see also 5–8; WPA, *Progress Report,* 176–77; WPA, *Final Report,* 135–36.

16. McKissick, State Appraisal Committee Report, 2–3; *Columbia State,* 16 May 1936, 2; Works Project Administration of South Carolina, *A Short Synopsis of the Projects in the Community Service Section of the Professional and Service Division* (Columbia: N.p., 1940), 1 (hereafter cited as WPA of S.C., *Community Service Section Synopsis*). See also folder titled 10 Mss., c. 1936, Olin W. Bundrick Papers, South Caroliniana Library, University of South Carolina, Columbia.

17. O.G.R., AAAASC, 17, 20; McKissick, State Appraisal Committee Report, 8; O.G.R., South Carolina Report No. 10, 23; NYA, Final Report of South Carolina, National Youth Administration Records, RG 119, Final State Report series, National Archives, Washington, D.C. Of the $1.1 million paid to college and high school students by March 1938, $726,101 went to aid 10,972 white students and $269,331 to 8,331 black students.

18. McKissick, State Appraisal Committee Report, 10–11. In 1935 only four tax-supported county libraries existed in the counties served by the WPA library project. By 1940, through encouragement from the WPA, nine tax-supported libraries were operating. WPA of S.C., *Community Service Section Synopsis,* 3.

19. McKissick, State Appraisal Committee Report, 21–22; *Columbia State,* 26 Mar. 1938, 16; Lawrence M. Pinckney to Eugene S. Leggett, 27 January 1936; Pinckney to C. H. Cotter, 14 September 1936, NEC Records, RG 44, box 437; Pinckney to Harry L. Hopkins, 15 March 1937, Byrnes Papers.

20. Pamphlet titled "Publications: South Carolina Writers' Project," WPA Records, Final State Report series, RG 69, box 10; WPA of S.C., *Community Service Section Synopsis,* 9; WPA, introduction to *South Carolina Guide,* 1988 reprint, v.

21. WPA, introduction to *South Carolina Guide*, 1988 reprint, v–xiii.

22. Roberta V. Copp, "South Carolina's Historic Records Survey, 1935–1942" (master's thesis, University of South Carolina, 1988), vii, 25–48, 50, 52, 70, 72, 81; Works Progress Administration of South Carolina, *Research and Records Work in South Carolina* (Columbia: N.p., 1940), 7–8; McKissick, State Appraisal Committee Report, 12–13.

23. Lawrence M. Pinckney to Harry L. Hopkins, 15 March 1937, Byrnes Papers; WPA of S.C., *Community Service Section Synopsis*, 8; *Columbia State*, 15 Mar. 1936, 10-A.

24. Susan G. Hiott, "New Deal Art in South Carolina: The WPA Federal Art Project," http://people.clemson.edu/hiott/text/pwap.htm, 6 January 1998, 1–7 (hereafter cited as Hiott, WPA/FAP).

25. Lise C. Swensson and Nancy M. Higgins, ed., *New Deal Art in South Carolina* (Columbia: South Carolina State Museum, 1990), 30–32.

26. WPA, *Progress Report*, 172; WPA, *Final Report,* 135–36; McKissick, State Appraisal Committee Report, 15.

27. Lawrence M. Pinckney to Eugene S. Leggett, 5 February 1936, NEC Records, RG 44, box 437; *Columbia State*, 27 Nov. 1935, 1.

28. Pinckney, Final WPA Report for South Carolina, 7–8.

29. Lawrence M. Pinckney to Addison G. Foster, 13 November 1937, NEC Records, RG 44, box 437; F. C. Harrington to Pinckney, 19 April 1938, WPA Records, RG 69, box 2505; A. Willis Spells to Harry L. Hopkins, 15 August 1938; Pinckney to Aubrey Williams, 4 October 1938, WPA Records, RG 69, box 2505.

30. Irene Allen to Aubrey Williams, 13 August 1936, WPA Records, RG 69, box 2514; Lawrence M. Pinckney to Nels Anderson, 26 August 1936, WPA Records, RG 69, box 2514.

31. Folders marked WPA 1938, WPA 1939, WPA 1940, John L. McMillan Papers, South Caroliniana Library, University of South Carolina, Columbia (hereafter cited as McMillan Papers).

32. Lawrence M. Pinckney to Harry L. Hopkins, 5 March 1936, NEC Records, RG 44, box 1477; *Columbia State*, 6 May 1936, 1, 13.

33. Edgar B. Chase to James F. Byrnes, 6 May 1936, Byrnes Papers; Lawrence M. Pinckney to Harry L. Hopkins, 5 March 1936, NEC Records, RG 44, box 1477.

34. Lawrence M. Pinckney to Nels Anderson, 20 November 1936, WPA Records, RG 69, box 2514.

35. Lawrence M. Pinckney to James F. Byrnes, 1 October 1936, Byrnes Papers.

36. John A. Peel to James F. Byrnes, 30 June 1936, Byrnes Papers; Lawrence M. Pinckney to Nels Anderson, 20 November 1936, WPA Records, RG 69, box 2514; *South Carolina Newsview* 2 (4 July 1936), 23.

37. Nels Anderson to Lawrence M. Pinckney, 12 November 1936, WPA Records, RG 69, box 2514. Lewis Brookshire, past president of the South Carolina Federation of Labor, warned Pinckney that Labor commissioner Nates was trying

to get control of WPA appointments "in an effort to buy enough (labor) votes to secure reelection" as commissioner. Brookshire to Pinckney, 4 November 1936, Byrnes Papers.

38. James F. Byrnes to Harry L. Hopkins, 16 November 1936, WPA Records, RG 69, box 2514.

39. H. L. H. [Harry L. Hopkins] to Nels Anderson, 18 November 1936, WPA Records, RG 69, box 2514.

40. David R. Coker to James F. Byrnes, 2 June 1937, David R. Coker Papers, South Caroliniana Library, University of South Carolina, Columbia (hereafter cited as Coker Papers). Pinckney's policy was to discharge a worker from the WPA when a farmer agreed to pay him a "living wage." But, Pinckney added, "Investigation has disclosed that the farmers are unwilling to pay a living wage." Lawrence M. Pinckney to C. H. Cotter, 13 April 1937, NEC Records, RG 44, box 437; see also David R. Coker to William E. Dodd, 20 December 1933, and David R. Coker to Frank Graham, 4 June 1934, Coker Papers; J. H. Welch to John McMillan, 11 July 1938, McMillan Papers.

41. Marvin Cann, "Small Town Stuff: Robert Quillen's View of the New Deal," 12 April 1985, Robert Quillen Papers, South Caroliniana Library, University of South Carolina, Columbia.

42. *Congressional Record,* 75th Cong., 1st Sess., 473.

43. Lawrence M. Pinckney to Harry L. Hopkins, 25 February 1937, WPA Records, RG 69, box 2505.

44. *Bennettsville Pee Dee Advocate,* 11 Feb. 1937, 1; *Columbia State,* 26 July 1937, 4; 17 Sept. 1937, 4-B; 25 Sept. 1937, 16; W. J. Cash, *The Mind of the South* (New York: Alfred A. Knopf, 1941), 409.

45. WPA, *Final Report,* 115, 120, 135–36, 172.

46. Hiott, WPA/FAP, 1–7; Hiott, "New Deal Art in South Carolina: Conclusion," http://people.clemson.edu/hiott/text/pwap.htm, 6 January 1999, 1.

47. *Columbia State,* 30 Nov. 1936, 4; Lawrence M. Pinckney to C. H. Cotter, 14 Sept. 1936, NEC Records, RG 44, box 437; WPA, *Final Report,* 110–12; *Columbia State,* 8 Dec. 1938, 9.

48. National Appraisal Committee, *U.S. Community Improvement Appraisal: A Report on the Work Program of the Works Progress Administration* (Washington, D.C.: Works Progress Administration, 1939), 59.

49. O.G.R., South Carolina Report No. 10, 42; William E. Leuchtenburg, *Franklin D. Roosevelt and the New Deal* (New York: Harper and Row, 1963), 53 (hereafter cited as Leuchtenburg, *FDR*); In May 1934 Congress amended the Home Owners Loan Act to require monthly payments to begin in 1934 instead of 1936. *Columbia State,* 3 May 1934, 4.

50. *Columbia State,* 10 Sept. 1933, 1.

51. Lawrence M. Pinckney to Frank C. Walker, 27 March 1934, 24 April 1934, 23 October 1934, NEC Records, RG 44, box 437.

52. O.G.R., AAAASC, 13–14; *Columbia State,* 15 July 1934, 1; 11 Aug. 1936, 5; 16 Mar. 1938, 4.; O.G.R., AAASC, 8, 13; South Carolina Bankers Association, *Report of Proceedings of the Annual Convention of the South Carolina Bankers Association, 1935,* 41 (hereater cited as SCBA).

53. O.G.R., South Carolina Report No. 10, 43; O.G.R., AAAASC, 8; SCBA, *Bankers Convention Report, 1935,* 41.

CHAPTER 5—CHANGING THE FACE OF THE PALMETTO STATE

1. Don C. Reading, "A Statistical Analysis of New Deal Economic Programs in the Forty-Eight States, 1933–1939" (Ph.D. diss., Utah State University, 1972), 257.

2. Public Works Administration, *America Builds: The Record of the PWA* (Washington, D.C.: Government Printing Office, 1939), 1, 36, 43, 85, 86; Jack F. Isakoff, *The Public Works Administration* (Urbana: University of Illinois Press, 1938), 121; *Columbia State,* 27 July 1933, 1; 31 Aug. 1933, 2; 20 Aug. 1936, 14; Pinckney to C. H. Cotter, NEC Records, RG 44, box 437, FRC, Suitland.

3. O.G.R., South Carolina Report No. 10, 34; *Columbia State,* 27 Oct. 1933, 7; 13 Oct. 1934, 12.

4. Pinckney to Eugene S. Leggett, 1 Mar. 1936, 14 Mar. 1936, NEC Records, RG 44, box 437, FRC, Suitland; William Suttles, typescript history of the South Carolina Highway Department, in possession of William Suttles, Columbia, South Carolina, 145–46, 158, 193, 268.

5. O.G.R., South Carolina Report No. 10, 32, 34; Marvin Leigh Cann, "Burnet Rhett Maybank and the New Deal in South Carolina, 1931–1941" (Ph.D. diss., University of North Carolina, 1967), 115 (hereafter cited as Cann, "Maybank"); "Re-elect Thomas S. McMillan," 1938 Congressional Campaign Pamphlet, James A. Hoyt Papers, South Caroliniana Library, University of South Carolina, Columbia (hereafter cited as Hoyt Papers); Fritz P. Hamer, "A Southern City Enters the Twentieth Century: Charleston, Its Navy Yard, and World War II, 1940–1948" (Ph.D. diss., University of South Carolina, 1998), 15–20 (hereafter cited as Hamer, "Charleston Navy Yard").

6. Hamer, "Charleston Navy Yard," 45–47, 285, abstract.

7. A. R. Clas to G. M. McTeer, 4 March 1936, Public Housing Administration Records, RG 196, box 330, FRC, Suitland; Housing Survey of Charleston: H-8900, 21 December 1935, ibid., box 400, ibid.; Cann, "Maybank," 103.

8. *Columbia State,* 30 Aug. 1935, 1, 9; Memorandum: Paul M. Pearson to the Director of Housing, 19 February 1937, Public Housing Administration Records, RG 196, box 331, FRC, Suitland.

9. *Columbia State,* 27 Sept. 1935, 1; Cann, "Maybank," 104.

10. Pinckney to Eugene S. Leggett, 28 October 1935, NEC Records, RG 44, box 437, FRC, Suitland.

11. Pinckney to Eugene S. Leggett, 3 February 1936, NEC Records, RG 44, box 437.

12. Quoted in Cann, "Maybank," 105.

13. Pinckney to Eugene S. Leggett, 1 March 1936, NEC Records, RG 44, box 437, FRC, Suitland; *Columbia State,* 27 Apr. 1936, 1; Cann, "Maybank," 106.

14. O.G.R., South Carolina Report No. 10, 37–38; Cann, "Maybank," 107.

15. O.G.R., South Carolina Report No. 10, 37–38.

16. Ibid., 33–35; Public Works Administration, *America Builds,* 177, 284; Status of Completed Non-federal Allocated Projects, Report No. 5, July 26, 1939, Public Works Administration Records, RG 135, National Archives, Washington, D.C., 83–86.

17. Public Works Administration, *America Builds,* 277.

18. Harold Ickes, *Back to Work: The Story of the PWA* (New York: The Macmillan Co., 1935), 140; *Columbia State,* 20 July 1934, 1, 2; 30 July 1934, 5.

19. Quoted in Ickes, *Back to Work,* 141.

20. Quoted in Ickes, *Back to Work,* 142.

21. Ibid., 143.

22. Geer to Byrnes, 26 June 1934, Byrnes Papers.

23. Byrnes to Ickes, 26 June 1934, Postal Telegram, Byrnes Papers.

24. Byrnes to Geer, 29 June 1934, Byrnes Papers.

25. Geer to Byrnes, 30 June 1934, Byrnes Papers.

26. Nicholson to Byrnes, 14 July 1934, Byrnes Papers; Miss Cassie Connor to Nicholson, 16 July 1934, Byrnes Papers.

27. Ickes, *Back to Work,* 144; *Columbia State,* 4 July 1934, 1; 16 July 1934, 5; 17 July 1934, 1; 21 July 1934, 7.

28. Byrnes to Nicholson, 20 July 1934, Byrnes Papers.

29. *Columbia State,* 6 Oct. 1934, 1; 16 Oct. 1934, 3; 3 Nov. 1934, 13.

30. *Columbia State,* 13 Apr. 1935, 1; 6 Dec. 1935, 9; 13 Dec. 1935, 1; 24 Dec. 1935, 1; 9 June 1936, 12; 23 Feb. 1936, 1; 18 Apr. 1936, 1; 15 Dec. 1936, 1.

31. Daniel T. Duncan to Burnet Maybank, 17 May 1935, Duncan, Kinard, Sanders, and Tucker Family Papers, South Caroliniana Library, University of South Carolina, Columbia; Duncan to W. W. Burgiss, 21 December 1934, and E. L. Brooks to the Federal Trade Commission, 15 February 1935, Duncan et al. Family Papers.

32. *Columbia State,* 1 Dec. 1934, 1; 26 Apr. 1935, 2; 24 Aug., 1. Even Byrnes was publicly critical of Duke Power Company for charging exorbitant rates and then engaging in charities "of its own choosing" with other people's money. *Columbia State,* 11 May 1935, 1.

33. *Columbia State,* 3 June 1937, 1, 7; 7 Aug. 1937, 1; *Duke Power Company et al. v. Greenwood County et al.,* 82 Lawyers Edition, 381–82. A week after the Supreme Court decision, President Roosevelt wrote his congratulations to the citizens of Greenwood County in a letter to the *Greenwood Index Journal. Columbia State,* 18 Jan. 1938, 5.

34. *Greenwood Index Journal*, 6 Jan. 1938, 1.

35. F. A. Porcher, *The History of the Santee Canal: Dedicated to the South Carolina Historical Society, 1875* (Charleston: South Carolina Historical Society, 1903), 3–12; David Robertson, *Sly and Able: A Political Biography of James F. Byrnes* (New York: W. W. Norton and Company, 1994), 203; Walter B. Edgar, *History of Santee Cooper, 1934–1984* (Columbia: R. L. Bryan Co., 1984), 3 (hereafter cited as Edgar, *Santee Cooper*).

36. Cann, "Maybank," 141–45.

37. Jefferies to the Federal Emergency Administration of Public Works, 19 December 1933, Byrnes Papers.

38. James F. Byrnes, Typescript account of Byrnes's actions on behalf of Santee Cooper, Byrnes Papers, 1–2 (hereafter cited as Byrnes, Santee Cooper Typescript).

39. Jefferies to Byrnes, 5 January 1934, 15 January 1934, Byrnes Papers; Cann, "Maybank," 150.

40. Edgar, *Santee Cooper*, 6–7.

41. C. M. Clark to John B. Gadsden, 27 December 1933, Byrnes Papers.

42. R. A. Easterling to Byrnes, 30 January 1934, Byrnes Papers.

43. Cann, "Maybank," 15–53.

44. Quoted in ibid., 151.

45. Cann, "Maybank," 151–52, 154–56; Byrnes, Santee Cooper Typescript, 2–3.

46. Byrnes to Maybank, 4 December 1934, Byrnes Papers.

47. Byrnes to Ickes, 14 December 1934,Byrnes Papers. See also Robertson, *Sly and Able,* 202, and Harold L. Ickes, *The Secret Diary of Harold Ickes,* vol. 1 (New York: Simon and Schuster, 1953–1954), 443, 488–90, 498; Ickes, *Secret Diary of Harold Ickes,* vol. 2, 64, 92.

48. Byrnes, Santee Cooper Typescript, 4–5; Report on Santee Cooper, 11 July 1935, copy in Byrnes Papers.

49. Byrnes to Roosevelt, 11 September 1935, Byrnes Papers; Cann, "Maybank," 159; Byrnes, Santee Cooper Typescript, 5–8.

50. Byrnes, Santee Cooper Typescript, 9–11; Byrnes to Roosevelt, 19 September 1935, Byrnes Papers.

51. Byrnes to Marguerite LeHand, 14 August 1935, Byrnes Papers.

52. Byrnes to Maybank, 19 August 1935, Byrnes Papers.

53. Byrnes to Roosevelt, 11 September 1935, Byrnes Papers.

54. Byrnes to Hopkins, 18 September 1935, Byrnes Papers.

55. Byrnes, Santee Cooper Typescript, 10.

56. Cann, "Maybank," 162.

57. Byrnes to Roosevelt, 12 October 1935, Byrnes Papers.

58. Report of the [Santee Cooper] Board of Review, 4 November 1935, Byrnes Papers.

59. *Columbia State,* 20 Dec. 1935, 1.

60. Cann, "Maybank," 164–69; Robertson, *Sly and Able,* 230–33; Edgar, *Santee Cooper,* 7.

61. Cann, *Maybank,* 170; Robertson, *Sly and Able,* 233–35.

62. Cann, "Maybank," 173–74, 184–85; Public Works Administration, *America Builds,* 277; Robertson, *Sly and Able,* 203, 213, 238–40, 243–44; Edgar, *Santee Cooper,* 7–10.

63. Edgar, *Santee Cooper,* 11, 20, 95–96.

64. Ibid., 95–96.

CHAPTER 6—HOORAY FOR THE NRA

1. James A. Hodges, "The New Deal Labor Policy and the Southern Cotton Textile Industry, 1933–1941" (Ph.D. diss., Vanderbilt University, 1963), 164–66 (hereafter cited as Hodges, "The New Deal and Southern Textiles"); Jack M. Blicksilver, *Cotton Manufacturing in the Southeast: An Historical Analysis* (Atlanta: Georgia State College of Business Administration, 1959), 98–99; *Columbia State,* 11 Mar. 1933, 5; *New York Times,* 11 Mar. 1933, 22; James A. Hodges, *New Deal Labor Policy and the Southern Cotton Textile Industry, 1933–1941* (Knoxville: University of Tennessee Press, 1986), 48 (hereafter cited as Hodges, *New Deal Textiles*); William Wilker Thompson, Jr., "A Managerial History of a Cotton Textile Firm: Spartan Mills, 1888–1958," 119; Anthony J. Badger, *North Carolina and the New Deal* (Raleigh: North Carolina Department of Cultural Resources, 1981), 5.

2. Robert H. Zieger, *Organized Labor in the Twentieth Century South* (Knoxville: University of Tennessee Press, 1996), 7; David L. Carlton, *Mill and Town in South Carolina, 1880–1920* (Baton Rouge: Louisiana State University Press, 1982), 245–47.

3. William Hays Simpson, *Life in Mill Communities* (Clinton, S.C.: Presbyterian College Press, 1941), 21–27, 34–49, 55–67 (hereafter cited as Simpson, *Mill Communities*); Hodges, *New Deal Textiles,* 26–42.

4. Gavin Wright, *Old South, New South: Revolutions in the Southern Economy since the Civil War* (New York: Basic Books, 1986), 146.

5. Janet C. Irons, "Testing the New Deal: The General Textile Strike of 1934" (Ph.D. diss., Duke University, 1988), 545–46; I. A. Newby, *Plain Folk in the New South* (Baton Rouge: Louisiana State University Press, 1989), 235–36, 389–417; Zieger, *Organized Labor,* 35–45.

6. Irons, "Testing the New Deal," 32–39, 103–21, 149–50.

7. Hodges, *New Deal Textiles,* 32; Simpson, *Mill Communities,* 86.

8. Quoted in Hodges, *New Deal Textiles,* 65; *Columbia State,* 23 May 1971, 2-E; Hodges, "The New Deal and Southern Textiles," 162; *Columbia State,* 24 May 1933, 7; 30 May 1933, 1; 5 June 1933, 5.

9. Interview with Mr. E. T. Kirkland, Secretary of the South Carolina Labor Council, 5 August 1971 (hereafter cited as Kirkland, interview); *Columbia State,* 6

May 1933, 5; 9 May 1933, 1; 17 May 1933, 1; 24 May 1933, 7; 27 May 1933, 1; 30 May 1933, 1; 31 May 1933, 1; 1 June 1933, 15; 5 June 1933, 1; 8 June 1933, 1; 10 June 1933, 1; 14 June 1933, 7; 21 June 1933, 5, 10; 22 June 1933, 12; 27 June 1933, 9; Newby, *Plain Folk,* 260–86.

10. *Columbia State,* 22 July 1933, 1; 23 July 1933, 1; 28 July 1933, 1.

11. Ibid., 28 July 1933, 1, 5; 29 July 1933, 1; 30 July 1933, 8, 10-A; 1 Aug. 1933, 7; 2 Aug. 1933, 1; 5 Aug. 1933, 12; 7 Aug. 1933, 3; 3 Sept. 1933, 5-A; Archie Vernon Huff, Jr., *Greenville: The History of the City and County in the South Carolina Piedmont* (Columbia: University of South Carolina Press, 1995), 349.

12. Hodges, "The New Deal and Southern Textiles," 159–72; John Wesley Kennedy, "The General Strike in the Textile Industry, September 1934" (master's thesis, Duke University, 1947), 9 (hereafter cited as Kennedy, "Textile Strike"); *Proceedings: Annual Convention, American Cotton Manufacturers Association,* 37th convention (n.p., 1933), 1–9 (hereafter cited as *A.C.M.A. Convention*); *A.C.M.A. Convention,* 38th convention, 27.

13. Badger, *North Carolina,* 29–30; Hodges, "The New Deal and Southern Textiles," 174–86; *A.C.M.A. Convention,* 37th convention, 141–49; *Columbia State,* 1 July 1933, 1.

14. Photocopy of selected portions of the minutes of the annual meeting of the Cotton Manufacturers Association of South Carolina, 7 July 1933, in the possession of the Cotton Manufacturers Association of South Carolina, Columbia (hereafter cited as CMASC).

15. *Columbia State,* 8 July 1933, 1.

16. NRA, Official Hearing on the Stretchout System, copy in Byrnes Papers; CMASC, The Effect of the Stretch-out on Textile Employment, Byrnes Papers.; *Columbia State,* 30 June 1933, 5; 14 July 1933, 1, 12; 15 July 1933, 1.

17. Hodges, "The New Deal and Southern Textiles," 216.

18. Ibid., 214.

19. *Columbia State,* 26 July 1933, 1; Kennedy, "Textile Strike," 11.

20. Department of Agriculture, Commerce and Industries of the State of South Carolina, *Yearbook of the Department of Agriculture, Commerce and Industries of the State of South Carolina, 1932–1933,* 79, 94 (hereafter cited as S.C. Dept. ACI, *Yearbook*); S.C. Dept. ACI, *Yearbook, 1933–1934,* 20; *Columbia State,* 15 July 1933, 1; 16 July 1933, 10-A; 18 July 1933, 7; 20 July 1933, 10.

21. Elliott Springs, "Elliott Springs to George A. Sloan," 20 December 1933, reproduced in *Clothes Make the Man* (N.p., 1948; reprint as *Clothes Make the Man; or, How to Put the Broad in Broadcloth,* New York: Empyrean Press, 1954), 110 (page citations are to the reprint edition).

22. *Columbia State,* 13 Dec. 1933, 2; 31 Aug. 1933, 8; 4 Sept. 1933, 3; J. J. McSwain to Franklin D. Roosevelt, 12 August 1933, John Jackson McSwain Papers, Duke University Library, Durham, N.C.

23. *Columbia State,* 19 July 1933, 1.

24. Alvin W. Byars. *Olympia Pacific: The Way It Was, 1895–1970* (N.p., privately printed, 1981), 38.

25. *Columbia State*, 29 July 1933, 6.

26. Ibid., 27 July 1933, 1; 28 July 1933, 6; 29 July 1933, 10; 9 Aug. 1933, 1; 15 Aug. 1933, 10-B; 18 Aug. 1933, 9; 19 Aug. 1933, 5; 21 Aug. 1933, 1; 26 Aug. 1933, 2.

27. Ibid., 26 July 1933, 10.

28. Ibid., 14 Aug. 1933, 8.

29. Ibid., 30 July 1933, 1; 25 Aug. 1933, 7; 14 Dec. 1933, 2; Hodges, "The New Deal and Southern Textiles," 208; Kirkland, interview.

30. Springs, *Clothes Make the Man,* 68.

31. Ibid.

32. Peel to Byrnes, 14 November 1933, Byrnes Papers; Robert W. Bruere et al. to T. F. Cawthen, 1 June 1934, NRA Records, RG 9, box 562, National Archives, Washington, D.C.; *Columbia State,* 16 Nov. 1933, 10.

33. G. A. Franklin to Hugh Johnson, 13 July 1933, NRA Records, RG 9, box 558.

34. *Columbia State,* 21 Oct. 1933, 1; 22 Oct. 1933, 12-A; 25 Oct. 1933, 5: 27 Oct. 1933, 1; 28 Oct. 1933, 1, 9; 31 Oct. 1933, 1.

35. Ibid.

36. Decisions Issued by the Cotton Textile National Industrial Relations Board, 8 August 1933 to 8 August 1934, NRA Records, RG 9, Series 402, 1, 2, 6, 8, 141 (hereafter cited as CTNIRB Decisions); *Columbia State,* 4 Nov. 1933, 1; 5 Nov. 1933, 1; 5 Dec. 1933, 1.

37. H. H. Willis to Robert W. Bruere, 12 April 1934, NRA Records RG9, box 558; CTNIRB Decisions, 142–43; *Columbia State,* 15 Feb. 1934, 1.

38. H. H. Willis to E. Gillespie, 23 March 1934, NRA Records, RG 9, box 585; Notarized Affidavit of E. Gillespie et al., 6 January 1934, NRA Records, RG 9, box 585; Notarized Affidavit of W. E. Mathes, 30 December 1933, NRA Records, RG 9, box 585; L. T. Mills to Frances Perkins, 15 January 1934, NRA Records, RG 9, box 585; CTNIRB Decisions, 161–63.

39. Rogers to L. R. Gilbert, 29 June 1934, NRA Records, RG 9, box 585.

40. Ibid.

41. Typescript of a telephone conversation between Geer and Bruere, 23 July 1934, NRA Records, RG 9, box 585.

42. H. Landermilk to Bruere, 7 June 1934, NRA Records, RG 9, box 585; Notarized Affidavit of L. J. Mills et al., 4 June 1934, NRA Records, RG 9, box 585; H. H. Willis to L. R. Gilbert, 27 June 1934, NRA Records, RG 9, box 585; W. C. Hamrick to H. H. Willis, 10 July 1934, NRA Records, RG 9, box 585; L. J. Mills et al. to the South Carolina Industrial Relations Board, n.d., NRA Records, RG 9, box 585; Notarized Affidavit of J. E. Cabaness, 23 July 1934, NRA Records, RG 9, box 585; W. C. Hamrick to L. R. Gilbert, 25 July 1934, NRA Records, RG 9, box 585;

Columbia State, 22 July 1934, 14-B. For the disposition of other disputes in South Carolina by the Willis and Bruere boards, see CTNIRB Decisions, 140–77.

43. *Columbia State,* 7 Mar. 1934, 1.

44. *Congressional Record,* 73d Cong., 2d Sess., 7952, 7954.

45. *Columbia State,* 7 Mar. 1934, 1.

46. Ibid., 8 Mar. 1934, 13.

47. *Congressional Record,* 73d Cong. 2d Sess., 7950–57; *Columbia State,* 7 Mar. 1934, 1. The smaller lumber companies were not subject to the minimum price provision of the lumber code. Thus, when smaller companies disobeyed the wages and hours provisions and sold cheaply, the larger companies were squeezed economically. At least three large lumber companies in South Carolina—Florence Plywood Manufacturing Company, Hardwood Manufacturing Company of Florence, and O. T. Smith of Charleston—lost their Blue Eagles for selling below the minimum price provision in order to compete with the smaller operators. *Columbia State,* 19 Dec. 1934, 2.

48. Pinckney to Frank C. Walker, 15 February 1934, NEC Records, RG 44, box 437, FRC, Suitland; *Columbia State,* 18 Sept. 1935, 3.

49. Pinckney to Donald R. Richberg, 18 March 1935; 28 January 1935, 13 May 1935; and Pinckney to Frank C. Walker, 1 March 1934; 14 March 1934, NEC Records, RG 44, box 437, FRC, Suitland; *Columbia State,* 13 June 1934, 2.

50. T. R. Waring [Sr.] to Howard Davis, 5 January 1935, Thomas R. Waring Papers, South Carolina Historical Society, Charleston.

CHAPTER 7—THE GENERAL TEXTILE STRIKE OF 1934 AND ITS AFTERMATH

1. Peel to Byrnes, 13 February 1934, James Francis Byrnes Papers, Robert M. Cooper Library, Clemson University, Clemson, S.C. (hereafter cited as Byrnes Papers).

2. *Columbia State,* 22 Apr. 1934, 8-A; Archie Vernon Huff, Jr., *Greenville: The History of the City and County in the South Carolina Piedmont* (Columbia: University of South Carolina Press, 1995), 351.

3. *Columbia State,* 20 May 1934, 1.

4. T. M. Marchant, "Cotton Manufacturers' Problems," *Manufacturers Record* 103 (Jan. 1934): 19.

5. *Proceedings: Annual Convention, American Cotton Manufacturers Association,* 38th convention (n.p., 1933), 1–9, 41 (hereafter cited as *ACMA Convention*).

6. James A. Hodges, "The New Deal Labor Policy and the Southern Cotton Textile Industry, 1933–1941" (Ph.D. diss., Vanderbilt University, 1963), 124–25, 260–61 (hereafter cited as Hodges, "The New Deal and Southern Textiles").

7. *Columbia State,* 23 May 1934, 2; John Wesley Kennedy, "The General Strike in the Textile Industry, September 1934" (master's thesis, Duke University, 1947), 14–25 (hereafter cited as Kennedy, "Textile Strike"); *Time,* 3 Sept. 1934, 4; George

A. Sloan, "First Flight of the Blue Eagle: The Cotton Textile Code in Operation," *Atlantic Monthly* 153 (Mar. 1934): 324.

8. Bryant Simon, "A Fabric of Defeat: The Politics of South Carolina Textile Workers in State and Nation, 1920–1938" (Ph.D. diss., University of North Carolina, 1992), 188–95.

9. *Columbia State,* 2 June 1934, 1; 31 May 1934, 1; 1 June 1934, 1; Kennedy, "Textile Strike," 14–25; Hodges, "The New Deal and Southern Textiles," 258–60.

10. *Columbia State,* 5 June 1934, 9; 9 June 1934, 2; 21 June 1934, 1; 14 July 1934, 9; 15 July 1934, 1, 13-A; 16 July 1934, 1; 17 July 1934, 1; 20 July 1934, 1; F. B. Rogers to Bruere, 16 July 1934, NRA Records, RG 9, box 575, National Archives, Washington, D.C.

11. *Columbia State,* 22 July 1934, 14-B.

12. *New York Times,* 17 Aug. 1934, 7.

13. For a description of the 1934 strike, see Jacquelyn Dowd et al., *Like a Family: The Making of a Southern Cotton Mill World* (Chapel Hill: University of North Carolina Press, 1987), 289–357.

14. Janet C. Irons, "Testing the New Deal: The General Textile Strike of 1934" (Ph.D. diss., Duke University, 1988), abstract.

15. *Columbia State,* 17 Aug. 1934, 1; 19 Aug. 1934, 11-A; 20 Aug. 1934, 1; 24 Aug. 1934, 1; Anthony J. Badger, *North Carolina and the New Deal* (Raleigh: Department of Cultural Resources, 1981), 31.

16. Gorman to Blackwood, 1 September 1934, Postal Telegram, Ibra C. Blackwood Papers, South Carolina Department of Archives and History, Columbia (hereafter cited as Blackwood Papers).

17. *Columbia State,* 4 Sept. 1934, 1.

18. William R. Whitmire to Winder Gary, 4 September 1934, Blackwood Papers.

19. Blackwood to Sheriff W. A. Clamp, 8 September, 1934, Western Union Telegram, Blackwood Papers.

20. Blackwood to J. M. Cantey, Jr., 4 September 1934, Blackwood Papers; Charles H. Gerald to Superintendent Lonsdale Manufacturing Company, 11 September 1934, Blackwood Papers; Gerald to James C. Dozier, 7 January 1935, Blackwood Papers.

21. *Columbia State,* 5 Sept. 1934, 1, 6, 9; 6 Sept. 1934, 1. Usually, the presence of the flying squadron was sufficient to close the mill. On one occasion where it was not, members of the flying squadron entered the mill and shut off the machinery. *Columbia State,* 5 Sept. 1934, 9.

22. Byrnes to Roosevelt, 4 September 1934, Byrnes Papers; Newsclipping, dated "Sept. 5, 1934," Byrnes Scrapbook, 1933–1934, Byrnes Papers.

23. *Columbia State,* 6 Sept. 1934, 1, 11, 12, 13; Huff, *Greenville,* 353–54.

24. H. P. Burbage to A. L. Wirin, 29 September 1934, American Civil Liberties Union Papers, microfilm roll 113, vol. 756.

25. *New York Times,* 8 Sept. 1934, 1; *Columbia State,* 7 Sept. 1934, 1, 9; 21 Feb. 1934, 11; E. H. Shanklin et al. to Gov. I. C. Blackwood, 6 September 1934, Western Union telegram, Blackwood Papers.

26. *Columbia State,* 9 Sept. 1934, 1. Two weeks later the county solicitor charged eleven men in the shooting, among them the chief of police. In November a grand jury indicted only two of the eleven, who were acquitted in February 1935. *Time,* 17 Sept. 1934, 13; *New York Times,* 9 Sept. 1934, 3; Kennedy, "Textile Strike," 65; *Columbia State,* 26 Sept. 1934, 1; 24 Nov. 1934, 1; 21 Feb. 1935, 1.

27. *Columbia State,* 7 Sept. 1934, 1, 9, 11; *Time,* 24 Sept. 1934, 22.

28. Hodges, "The New Deal and Southern Textiles," 287–88; *Columbia State,* 8 Sept. 1934, 11.

29. *Columbia State,* 8 Sept. 1934, 1; 9 Sept. 1934, 1.

30. Ibid., 12 Sept. 1934, 1; 14 Sept. 1934, 1; 16 Sept. 1934, 1; Hodges, "The New Deal and Southern Textiles," 279; *Congressional Record,* 74th Cong., 2d Sess., 2079–81. Strike leaders even organized street dances in the evenings to maintain striker solidarity. One of these events was so festive that students at a nearby college were unable to sleep, causing them to miss their morning classes. Elizabeth Watson to Mother (Ella Watson), 19 September 1934, Watson Family Papers, South Caroliniana Library, University of South Carolina, Columbia.

31. *Columbia State,* 18 Sept. 1934, 1; 19 Sept. 1934, 7; 20 Sept. 1934, 1; 21 Sept. 1934, 1; 22 Sept. 1934, 1; 23 Sept. 1934, 1, 9; Hodges, "The New Deal and Southern Textiles," 291; Kennedy, "Textile Strike," 78–80; Glenn Gilman, *Human Relations in the Industrial Southeast* (Chapel Hill: University of North Carolina Press, 1956), 188.

32. *Columbia State,* 24 Sept. 1934, 1.

33. Ibid., 25 Sept. 1934, 1; 26 Sept. 1934, 1; 28 Sept. 1934, 11-A; 9 Dec. 1934, 5-A; 10 Dec. 1934, 3.

34. Quoted in Hodges, "The New Deal and Southern Textiles," 325; *Columbia State,* 20 Jan. 1935, 1; 13 May 1935, 1; *ACMA Convention,* 39th convention, 131. See also Francis J. Gorman to Byrnes, 28 May 1935, Byrnes Papers.

35. Quoted in James A. Hodges, *New Deal Labor Policy and the South Cotton Textile Industry: 1933–1941* (Knoxville: University of Tennessee Press, 1986), 130.

36. *Columbia State,* 28 Nov. 1934, 2.

37. Ibid., 27 Nov. 1934, 1; 8 Dec. 1934, 5; 19 Dec. 1934, 2; 10 Jan. 1935, 2.

38. Complaint, Pelzer Manufacturing Company, received 10 April 1935, NRA Records, RG 9, box 465; Report, J. L. Bernard to the Textile Labor Relations Board, 20 April 1935, NRA Records, RG 9, box 465, National Archives, Washington, D.C.; John Peel to Samuel R. McClurd, 3 July 1935, ibid.; W. B. Taliaferro to Samuel R. McClurd, 10 July 1935, ibid.; Typescript of a telephone conversation between Bernard and Samuel R. McClurd, 17 July 1935; ibid.; Bernard to Samuel R. McClurd, 1 April 1935, ibid.; ibid., 21 July 1935, ibid.; *Columbia State,* 16 July

1935, 1; 17 July 1935, 1; 20 July 1935, 1; 31 July 1935, 16; 3 Aug. 1935, 3; Bernard to the Textile Labor Relations Board, 27 August 1935, ibid.; *Columbia State,* 30 Aug. 1935, 1; 3 Aug. 1935, 1; 4 Aug. 1935, 1; 6 Aug. 1935, 1; 27 Aug. 1935, 9; W. Ney Evans to Alan McNab, 17 August 1935, NRA Records, RG 9, box 465; J. L. Bernard to the Textile Labor Relations Board, 29 August 1935, ibid.; Pelzer Strike Agreement, dated "September 6, 1935," NRA Records, RG 9, box 465; *Columbia State,* 3 Sept. 1935, 1, 6; 4 Sept. 1935, 1; 7 Sept. 1935, 1; Newsclipping, undated, Johnston Scrapbook, 1935, 370; see also JoAnn Deakin Carpenter, "Olin D. Johnston, the New Deal, and the Politics of Class in South Carolina, 1934–1938" (Ph.D. diss., Emory University, 1987), 235–43.

39. Ibid.

40. Bryant Simon, "Fabric," 333–34.

41. W. A. Taliaferro to Samuel R. McClurd, 11 December 1934, NRA Records, RG 9, box 507.

42. Bernard to Samuel R. McClurd, 2 March 1935, NRA Records, RG 9, box 383.

43. Henry Baker to McClurd, 11 May 1936, NRA Records, RG 9, box 507; George Kamenow and L. S. Harding to McClurd, 8 June 1936, NRA Records, box 507; Kamenow and Henry Baker to the Textile Labor Relations Board, 4 April 1936, NRA Records, box 383; Kamenow and Henry Baker to the Textile Labor Relations Board, 15 April 1936, NRA Records, box 383; Kamenow and Henry Baker to the Textile Labor Relations Board, 22 April 1936, NRA Records, box 383; Kamenow and Henry Baker to the Textile Labor Relations Board, 1 May 1936, NRA Records, box 383; *South Carolina Newsview,* 6 June 1936, 18–19.

44. L. S. Harding to Samuel R. McClurd, 23 June 1936, NRA Records, RG 9, box 383; George Kamenow to the Textile Labor Relations Board, 11 June 1936, NRA Records, box 383; Textile Labor Relations Board to the Gaffney Manufacturing Company, 5 September 1936, NRA Records, box 383; Kamenow to the Textile Labor Relations Board, 27 October 1936, NRA Records, box 383.

45. Harding, Preliminary Report, 20 June 1935, NRA Records, RG 9, box 301.

46. D. Yates Heafner to Walter C. Taylor, 25 August 1935, NRA Records, RG 9, box 301; Taylor to W. S. Montgomery, 21 August 1935, NRA Records, box 301; George Kamenow to Taylor, 23 August 1935, NRA Records, box 301; Montgomery to Taylor, 23 August 1935, NRA Records, box 301; S. O. Neal to the Textile Labor Relations Board, n.d., NRA Records, box 301; Samuel McClurd to J. L. Bernard, 24 May 1935, NRA Records, box 301.

47. Ibid. See also D. Yates Haefner, undated memorandum, NRA Records, RG 9, box 301; Haefner to the Textile Labor Relations Board, 15 September 1935, ibid; Walter C. Taylor to Haefner, 24 September 1935, ibid; S. O. Neal to Taylor, 11 November 1935, Western Union telegraph, ibid.

48. George Kamenow to the Textile Labor Relations Board, 18 November 1935, ibid.; ibid.; 25 November 1935, ibid.

49. Newsclipping, *Greenville News,* 10 Feb. 1936, ibid.

50. George Kamenow to the Textile Labor Relations Board, 10 February 1936, ibid.

51. Ibid., 22 February 1936; 4 March 1936; 7 March 1936; 31 March 1936, ibid.; Newsclipping, n.d., ibid.

52. Kamenow and Harding to the Textile Labor Relations Board, 25 June 1936; 31 March 1936, NRA Records, RG 9, box 301; Newsclipping, n.d., ibid., Harding and Kamenow to S. R. McClurd, 23 June 1936, ibid.; Newsclipping, 21 Apr. 1936, ibid.

53. *Columbia State,* 29 May, 1935, 1; 30 May 1935, 1; 8 June 1935, 2; 13 June 1935, 8; June 1935, 5; 14 Feb. 1937, 13-A; *Spartanburg Herald,* 8 July 1935, 12; Hodges, "The New Deal and Southern Textiles," 343.

54. Hodges, "The New Deal and Southern Textiles," 363.

55. *Columbia State,* 27 Aug. 1935, 2; *Decisions and Orders of the National Labor Relations Board* (Washington, D.C.: Government Printing Office, 1936), vol. 1, 97–122 (hereafter cited as *NLRB Decisions*); *First Annual Report of the National Labor Relations Board for the Fiscal Year Ended June 30, 1936* (Washington, D.C.: Government Printing Office, 1936), 147–49; *Labor Relations Reference Manual* (Washington, D.C.: Bureau of National Affairs, 1937), 345–60; *Columbia State,* 4 July 1937, 8-A; *NLRB Decisions,* vol. 2, 1081–93.

56. *South Carolina Newsview,* 9 Sept. 1936, 10–11; *Columbia State,* 15 July 1936, 10-A; Hodges, "The New Deal and Southern Textiles," 367; John Wesley Kennedy, "A History of the Textile Workers Union of America, C.I.O." (Ph.D. dissertation, University of North Carolina, 1950), 58–70 (hereafter cited as Kennedy, "TWUA"); *Annual Reports of the Department of Labor of the State of South Carolina,* 2d annual report (Columbia, 1937), 18–19 (hereafter cited as *SC Labor Report*); *Columbia State,* 18 Nov. 1936, 1; 19 Mar. 1937, 1; 20 Mar. 1936, 1; Henry Cooper Ellenberg, "The Congress of Industrial Organization in South Carolina, 1938–1945" (master's thesis, University of South Carolina, 1951), 25–26 (hereafter cited as Ellenberg, "CIO in SC").

57. The slowness and lack of success in collective bargaining forced the Textile Workers Organizing Committee to alter its policy and charter locals before contracts were secured.

58. Quoted in Ellenberg, "CIO in SC," 32, 21, 24.

59. Ibid., 29–32; *Columbia State,* 8 May 1937, 1; 17 May 1937, 1; *Textile World,* June 1937, 73.

60. *NLRB Decisions,* vol.5, 100–105, 398–402; *NLRB Decisions,* vol. 6, 92–93; *NLRB Decisions,* vol. 7, 960–63; *NLRB Decisions,* vol. 8, 619–20, 1224–27; *NLRB Decisions,* vol. 9, 13–18; *NLRB Decisions,* vol. 10, 345–46; *Columbia State,* 12 Aug. 1938, 5-B; Ellenberg; "CIO in SC," 46–60; WPA Writers Project, *South Carolina Guide,* 80; National Youth Administration in South Carolina, *The Textile Industry in South Carolina* (Columbia, S.C.: N.p., 1939), 100.

61. *Una News Review,* 24 September 1937, 6.

62. *Una News Review,* 12 Aug. 1938, 2; 18 Feb. 1938, 6.

63. Ibid., 19 May 1939, 1; 11 Aug. 1938, 1.

64. Carl Gibbs, telephone interview by author, Wellford, S.C., 12 February 1999.

65. Irons, "Testing the New Deal," 532.

66. George Brown Tindall, *The Emergence of the New South, 1913–1945* (Baton Rouge: Louisiana State University Press, 1967), 520.

67. *NLRB Decisions,* vol. 24, 1–70.

68. Ibid.

69. Quoted in Kennedy, "TWUA," 135–36. The *News Review,* a labor organ in Una, South Carolina, warned evangelists such as Preacher Paul, "If we understand the teachings of the Bible, the Christian religion is above all the religion of the downtrodden. Christ didn't align himself with the money changers. He drove them from the temple." 1 July 1938, 2.

70. *NLRB Decisions,* vol. 24, 10–60.

71. Quoted in Kennedy, "TWUA," 136.

72. James C. Self to Byrnes, 13 February 1935, Byrnes Papers; Sydney Bruce to Byrnes, 7 February 1935, Byrnes Papers.

73. Photocopy of selected portions of the minutes of the annual meeting of the Cotton Manufacturers Association of South Carolina, May 23, 1936, in possession of the Cotton Manufacturers Association of South Carolina, Columbia; *Columbia State,* 22 May 1936, 1; 1 June 1936, 15; Jack M. Blicksilver, *Cotton Manufacturing in the Southeast: An Historical Analysis* (Atlanta: Georgia State College of Business Administration, 1959), 113–16; Hodges, "The New Deal and Southern Textiles," 354–56.

74. Handwritten report titled "Textiles—Cotton Mill Profits," n.d., Byrnes Papers; *Columbia State,* 1 Dec. 1936, 7.

75. *Columbia State,* 18 Apr. 1938, 5; Hodges, "The New Deal and Southern Textiles," 354; Hodges, *New Deal Textiles,* 155.

76. Hodges, *New Deal Textiles,* 192; Thomas E. Terrill, "'No Union for Me': Southern Textile Workers and Organized Labor," in *The Meaning of South Carolina History: Essays in Honor of George C. Rogers, Jr.,* ed. David Chesnutt and Clyde N. Wilson (Columbia: University of South Carolina Press, 1991), 202–13. The New Deal aided South Carolina textile workers in one final way. Since the New Deal's wages and hours legislation rendered labor costs an invariable cost factor, textile manufacturers searched for ways to reduce expenses in other areas. This need, coupled with the increased purchasing power of the mill worker and the fact that factory ownership of the mill village became a "strategic liability" when the owner appeared before the National Labor Relations Board, induced mills to begin selling their villages to their workers. Mills such as the Springs chain, Pacific Mills, and the Whitney Manufacturing Company had their houses appraised on the bases of worth and the workers' ability to pay, and effected plans for selling the houses at low interest rates over a ten-year (or longer) period. The mill worker at last began

to enjoy the blessings and burdens of home ownership, which further helped to make him the greatest beneficiary of the New Deal's program for industrial recovery. Blicksilver, *Cotton Manufacturing,* 126; *Textile World,* Aug. 1937, 72; WPA Writers Project, *South Carolina Guide,* 79–80; E. T. Kirkland, interview by author, Columbia, S.C., 5 August 1971.

CHAPTER 8—AGRICULTURE

1. *Columbia State,* 12 Jan. 1936, 10-A.

2. Department of Agriculture, Commerce and Industries of the State of South Carolina, *Yearbook of the Department of Agriculture, Commerce and Industries of the State of South Carolina, 1932–1933,* 13, 79 (hereafter cited as S.C. Dept. ACI, *Yearbook*); S.C. Dept. ACI, *Yearbook, 1938–1939,* 112; Henry I. Richards, *Cotton and the AAA* (Washington, D.C.: The Brookings Institution, 1936), 14; Agricultural Adjustment, A report of administration of the *Agricultural Adjustment Act, May 1933 to February 1934* (Washington, D.C.: Government Printing Office, 1934), 21, 33 (hereafter cited as *Agricultural Adjustment*).

3. S.C. Dept. ACI, *Yearbook, 1934–1935,* 24–25; University of South Carolina, *South Carolina: Economic and Social Conditions in 1944* (Columbia: University of South Carolina Press, 1945), 106; David Duncan Wallace, *The History of South Carolina,* vol. 3 (New York: American Historical Society, 1934), 478.

4. *Fifteenth Census of the United States, 1930,* vol. 2, part 2: *Agriculture* (Washington, D.C.: Government Printing Office, 1932), 466, 480; University of South Carolina, *South Carolina: Economic and Social,* 107–8; S.C. Dept. ACI, *Yearbook, 1932–1933,* 8.

5. *Fifteenth Census,* vol. 2, part 2: *Agriculture,* 462; University of South Carolina, *South Carolina: Economic and Social,* 135; Cyril B. Busbee, "Farm Tenancy in South Carolina" (master's thesis, University of South Carolina, 1938), 9–12.

6. Tom E. Terrill and Jerrold Hirsch, *Such As Us: Southern Voices of the Thirties* (Chapel Hill: University of North Carolina Press, 1978), 85.

7. William E. Leuchtenburg, *Franklin D. Roosevelt and the New Deal* (New York: Harper and Row, 1963), 75–76, 130–38 (hereafter cited as Leuchtenburg, *FDR*); Gilbert C. Fite, *Cotton Fields No More: Southern Agriculture, 1865–1980* (Lexington: University of Kentucky Press, 1984), 130–38.

8. *Congressional Record,* 73d Cong., Spec. Sess., 4713; Richards, *Cotton and the AAA,* 44; *Columbia State,* 20 June 1933, 1, 9. Farmers could receive rental payments either in cash, as explained above, or in cash plus government-held (option) cotton. The AAA graduated the cash-plus-option payments from $6 per acre destroyed yielding 100 to 124 pounds to $12 per acre destroyed yielding more than 275 pounds in the base period. A farmer electing the cash-plus-option plan was allotted option cotton equal to the amount of cotton he had destroyed. The farmer could then direct the secretary of agriculture to sell the farmer's option cotton at anytime between 1 December 1933 and 1 May 1935, with the farmer receiving the difference between what the cotton sold for and 6 cents per pound.

Thus, a farmer who destroyed one acre of cotton usually yielding 276 pounds and who directed Wallace to sell his 276 pounds of option cotton when cotton was selling for 10 cents, received $12 plus 4 cents (10 cents minus 6 cents) multiplied by 276 equals $23.04. If the same farmer had chosen cash, he would have received only $20.

9. *Columbia State*, 21 June 1933, 5; 20 June 1933, 1; 23 June 1933, 3; 24 June 1933, 1; 25 June 1933, 12-A.

10. Ibid., 28 June 1933, 7.

11. Ibid., 27 June 1933, 1.

12. James E. Dickson, Monthly Reports, 21 June 1933, 26 July 1933, James E. Dickson Papers, South Caroliniana Library, University of South Carolina, Columbia. Privately, Coker was skeptical of the plow-up: "I sincerely hope that Mr. Wallace and his advisors are not going to make themselves the laughing stock of the country. . . by advising the plowing up of cotton," he wrote. David R. Coker to Dr. W. W. Long, 22 May 1933, David R. Coker Papers. Newspaperman Robert Quillen opined that the farm problem could not be solved "by plowing up cotton while millions need more sheets." Quoted in Marvin Cann, "Small Town Stuff: Robert Quillen's View of the New Deal," 12 April 1985, Robert Quillen Papers, South Caroliniana Library, University of South Carolina, Columbia; Unfortunately, not all farmers were as enthusiastic. Neil O'Donnell of Sumter refused to sign because of dissatisfaction with the estimate of his base-period production. In retaliation, a force of "night riders" descended on 25 July and destroyed two acres of his cotton. *Columbia State*, 21 June 1933, 1; 27 June 1933, 2; 28 June 1933, 1; 29 June 1933, 1; 2 July 1933, 5-A; 3 July 1933, 1; 26 July 1933, 2.

13. *Columbia State*, 27 June 1933, 1; 29 June 1933, 7; 9 July 1933, 1; 19 July 1933, 1; 26 July 1933, 9; S.C. Dept. ACI, *Yearbook, 1932–1933*, 14; Richards, *Cotton and the AAA*, 120; Department of Agriculture, *Yearbook of Agriculture, 1934* (Washington, D.C.: Government Printing Office, 1934); 722 (hereafter cited as USDA, *Yearbook of Agriculture*).

14. *Columbia State*, 13 Sept. 1933, 10.

15. Richards, *Cotton and the AAA*, 213–17; *Columbia State*, 13 Sept. 1933, 1, 10; 14 Sept. 1933, 2; 19 Sept. 1933, 1; 22 Sept. 1933, 1.

16. S.C. Dept. ACI, *Yearbook, 1932–1933*, 15; S.C. Dept. ACI, *Yearbook, 1937–1938*, 46; *Columbia State*, 11 Aug. 1933, 1; 25 Aug. 1933, 7; 27 Aug. 1933, 1; Harold B. Rowe, *Tobacco under the AAA* (Washington, D.C.: The Brookings Institution, 1935) 100–102; Gov. I. C. Blackwood, Proclamation, State of South Carolina, 1 September 1933, Ibra C. Blackwood Papers, South Carolina Department of Archives and History, Columbia (hereafter cited as Blackwood Papers).

17. *Columbia State*, 5 Sept. 1933, 1; 9 Sept. 1933, 1; 13 Sept. 1933, 1; 15 Sept. 1933, 1; Rowe, *Tobacco under the AAA*, 155.

18. Rowe, *Tobacco under the AAA*, 113–15; *Columbia State*, 27 Sept. 1933, 1; 13 Oct. 1933, 11; 15 Oct. 1933, 6-A; S.C. Dept. ACI, *Yearbook, 1937–1938*, 46.

19. *Columbia State*, 3 Feb. 1934, 1; S.C. Dept. ACI, *Yearbook, 1933–1934*, 14; S.C. Dept. ACI, *Yearbook, 1934–1935*, 13; S.C. Dept. ACI, *Yearbook, 1938–1939*, 118; *Agricultural Adjustment*, 296–97.

20. *Columbia State*, 5 Jan. 1934, 2; 12 Jan. 1934, 9; Edwin G. Nourse et al., *Three Years of the Agricultural Adjustment Administration* (Washington, D.C.: The Brookings Institution, 1937), 95–98 (hereafter cited as Nourse, *AAA*).

21. *Columbia State*, 15 Feb. 1934, 1; 16 Feb. 1934, 11; 13 Apr. 1934, 1; USDA, *Yearbook of Agriculture, 1935*, 696; Nourse, *AAA*, 96. South Carolina's average production from 1928 to 1932 was 805,470 bales, which the AAA reduced to approximately 600,000 bales under the Bankhead program.

22. Richards, *Cotton and the AAA*, 74–81; *Columbia State*, 4 Aug. 1934, 12; James M. Eleazer, interview by author, Clemson, S.C., 2 March 1971 (hereafter cited as Eleazer, interview). The decentralization of the AAA minimized complaints of federal regimentation. The AAA in Washington approved contracts; county and state farmers on the committees and boards secured the contracts, ordered adjustments, and checked compliance. With the Bankhead plan, the AAA did no more than make the state allotment. The state board set county and farm allotments under Bankhead.

23. Nourse, *AAA*, 343; Richards, *Cotton and the AAA*, 53.

24. Frederick A. Gutheim, "A Survey of the South Carolina Emergency Relief Administration," Federal Emergency Relief Administration Records, RG 69, National Archives, Washington, D.C., 78 (hereafter cited as Gutheim, "SCERA Survey").

25. *Columbia State*, 16 Oct. 1934, 6; 6 May 1934, 13-B; 19 May 1934, 8; 22 May 1934, 3; 18 July 1934, 1; 4 Aug. 1934, 12; 4 Oct. 1934, 8; 14 Nov. 1934, 10; Stoll Sweatmen to Gov. Ibra C. Blackwood, 28 September 1934, Blackwood Papers.

26. S.C. Dept. ACI, *Yearbook, 1934–1935*, 7, 13; S.C. Dept. ACI, *Yearbook, 1936–1937*, 22; Richards, *Cotton and the AAA*, 220; *Columbia State*, 29 Dec. 1934, 14; 12 Sept. 1935, 11; 14 Dec. 1935, 1; USDA, *Yearbook of Agriculture, 1936*, 1154.

27. Rowe, *Tobacco under the AAA*, 283–96; *Columbia State*, 3 May 1934, 3; 8 Aug. 1935, 7.

28. S.C. Dept. ACI, *Yearbook, 1934–1935*, 7; *Columbia State*, 10 Aug. 1934, 1; 16 Sept. 1934, 8-A; 14 Oct. 1934, 5-A; 18 Nov. 1934, 1; 22 Dec. 1934, 1.

29. *Columbia State*, 8 Aug. 1935, 7.

30. S.C. Dept. ACI, *Yearbook, 1934–1935*, 31; Clemson Agricultural College, *Extension Work in South Carolina, 1935* (Clemson, 1935), 2; USDA, *Yearbook of Agriculture, 1935*, 697; Rowe, *Tobacco under the AAA*, 283–96; *Columbia State*, 8 Aug. 1935, 7; 9 Aug. 1935, 1; 15 Nov. 1935, 1.

31. *Columbia State*, 9 Jan. 1936, 1.

32. *Columbia State*, 8 Jan. 1936, 1; 21 Mar. 1936, 1-B; 1 Apr. 1936, 2; 18 Nov. 1936, 3; Murray R. Benedict, *Farm Policies of the United States, 1790–1950* (New York: The Twentieth Century Fund, 1953), 350–51.

33. *Congressional Record,* 74th Cong., 1st Sess., 205–6, 3551–52.

34. *Columbia State,* 5 May 1935, 2-A; 18 Apr. 1935, 5; Press release, 13 June 1935, Civilian Conservation Corps Records, RG 35, box 1453, National Archives, Washington, D.C.; D. W. Ross, "Inspection of Projects of Soil Erosion Service . . . Spartanburg, South Carolina, August 1934," Public Works Administration Records, RG 135, Series 46; *Congressional Record,* 74th Cong., 1st Sess., 205–6, 3551–52.

35. Lawrence M. Pinckney to Eugene S. Leggett, 3 August 1936, National Emergency Council Records, RG 44, box 437, FRC, Suitland (hereafter cited as NEC Records); Pinckney to C. H. Cotter, October 10, 1936, NEC Records.

36. *Agricultural Adjustment, 1937–1938,* 258–62, 289–91; S.C. Dept. ACI, *Yearbook, 1938–1939,* 110.

37. *Columbia State,* 22 Apr. 1936, 1.

38. S.C. Dept. ACI, *Yearbook, 1936–1937,* 22; S.C. Dept. ACI, *Yearbook, 1936–1937, 1938–1939,* 110; *Columbia State,* 13 Mar. 1936, 8-B; 2 Apr. 1936, 1.

39. Katie Lou to James F. Miles, 17 September 1937, James F. Miles Papers, South Caroliniana Library, University of South Carolina, Columbia.

40. *Agricultural Adjustment, 1937–1938,* 264–70; S.C. Dept. ACI, *Yearbook, 1936–1937,* 57; S.C. Dept. ACI, *Yearbook, 1938–1939,* 110; *Columbia State,* 23 Jan. 1937, 3; 11 Aug. 1937, 1; 19 Oct. 1937, 1; 20 Oct. 1937, 1; 8 Nov. 1937, 1.

41. Benedict, *Farm Policies,* 375–78; Gilbert C. Fite, *American Agriculture and Farm Policy since 1900* (Washington, D.C.: The American Historical Association, Service for Teachers of History, 1964), 19; *Columbia State,* 15 Feb. 1938, 15; 18 Feb. 1938, 11-A; Ronald Lynton Heinemann, "Depression and New Deal in Virginia" (Ph.D. diss., University of Virginia, 1968), 171.

42. O.G.R., South Carolina, Report No. 10, 1940 Supplement, 17; S.C. Dept. ACI, *Yearbook, 1938–1939,* 10, 46, 112, 118.

43. *Columbia State,* 17 Nov. 1938, 6.

44. Ibid., 12 Dec. 1938, 1; O.G.R., South Carolina, Report No. 10, 1940 Supplement, 17; S.C. Dept. ACI, *Yearbook, 1938–1939,* 57; S.C. Dept. ACI, *Yearbook, 1939–1940,* 43–44.

45. Farm Credit Administration, *Annual Reports of the Farm Credit Administration* (Washington, D.C.: Government Printing Office, 1934), First Annual Report, 1933, vi; O.G.R., South Carolina Report No. 10, 1940 Supplement, 10–11; *Columbia State,* 14 May 1933, 1; 24 July 1933, 4; 22 Sept. 1933, 10; 21 Nov. 1933, 11; 5 Dec. 1933, 12; 3 Jan. 1934, 2; 2 May 1934, 5; 12 May 1934, 9; 17 June 1934, 16-A; 3 July 1934, 14; 21 Mar. 1936, 10-C.

46. *Columbia State,* 4 Nov. 1934, 2-A; 13 Jan. 1935, 3; 3 Feb. 1935, 14-A; 21 Feb. 1935, 2; Gutheim, "SCERA Survey," 76.

47. O.G.R., South Carolina Report No. 10, 1940 Supplement, 11, 15; Lawrence Pinckney to C. H. Cotter, 14 September and 10 October 1936, NEC Records, box 437; Resettlement Administration, *First Annual Report: Resettlement Administration* (Washington, D.C.: Government Printing Office, 1936), 159, 170.

48. William David Hiott, "New Deal Resettlement in South Carolina" (master's thesis, University of South Carolina, 1986), 1–2, 6–8, 100–101.

49. Ibid., 79, 100; Constance B. Schulz, *A South Carolina Album: 1936–1948* (Columbia: University of South Carolina Press, 1992), 10.

50. Eleazer, interview; *Columbia State,* 30 July 1934, 1; 19 Oct. 1934, 2; 30 Oct. 1934, 14, 24 May 1938, 6; 25 May 1938, 6.

51. Eleazer, interview; Frate Bull, Cooperative Activities Recommended for the Ashwood Project, August 8, 1936, Farmers Home Administration Records, RG 96, box 616, National Archives, Washington, D.C. (hereafter cited as FHA Records); Farm Security Administration, Audit Report: Ashwood Plantation Cooperative . . . 22 September 1936 to December 1940, FHA Records, box 612; Farm Security Administration, *Report of the Administration of the Farm Security Administration: 1941* (Washington, D.C.: Government Printing Office, 1941) 34, 35, 37 (hereafter cited as FSA, *Report*).

52. *Columbia State,* 16 July 1937, 9-A; 9 Aug. 1937, 14; 2 Dec. 1937, 1; 25 June 1938, 2; 13 July 1938, 3; Busbee, "Farm Tenancy in South Carolina," 67; FSA, *Report, 1941,* 32. Actually, the FSA negotiated only 718 tenant loans in South Carolina for the 1937–1940 period, instead of the 1,030 loans that were allotted to the state.

53. Rural Electrification Administration, *Report of the Rural Electrification Administration, 1937* (Washington, D.C.: Government Printing Office, 1938), 5 (hereafter cited as REA, *Report*); REA, *Report,* 1938, 174–75; *Columbia State,* 10 Sept. 1934, 8; 15 Mar. 1935, 1; 7 Nov. 1935, 1; Lawrence Pinckney to Addison G. Foster, 13 November 1937, NEC Records, box 437.

54. Eleazer, interview.

55. REA, *Report, 1938,* 174–75; Clemson Agricultural College, *Extension Work in South Carolina, 1937,* 29; Clemson Agricultural College, *Extension Work in South Carolina, 1938,* 28; Clemson Agricultural College, *Extension Work in South Carolina, 1939,* 31; Eleazer, interview; *Columbia State,* 14 July 1935, 2-A; 28 Jan. 1936, 14; 30 Apr. 1936, 3; 2 Oct. 1936, 3-B; 16 Oct. 1936, 8-B.

56. S.C. Dept. ACI, *Yearbook, 1932–1933,* 13;S.C. Dept. ACI, *Yearbook, 1938–1939,* 57, 112, 118; O.G.R., South Carolina Report No. 10, 1940 Supplement, 5, 9, 10.

57. O.G.R., South Carolina Report No. 10, 1940 Supplement, 4, 6, 9; S.C. Dept. ACI, *Yearbook,* 1938–1939, 112.

CHAPTER 9—THE NEW DEAL IN POLITICS AND PUBLIC OPINION IN SOUTH CAROLINA: 1933–1939

1. *Marion Star,* 8 Mar. 1933, 4; *Congressional Record,* 74th Cong., 1st Sess., 2282–83; *Columbia State,* 24 Feb. 1933, 4.

2. *Columbia State,* 7 Mar. 1933, 1; 25 Mar. 1934, 4; 19 May 1934, 7; 23 May 1934, 10; 16 June 1934, 1; 17 June 1934, 1; 28 June 1934, 2; 5 Aug. 1934, 12; 20

Aug. 1934, 1; 31 May 1935, 1; William F. Stevenson to John J. McSwain, 10 July 1933, John Jackson McSwain Papers, Duke University Library, Durham, N.C. (hereafter cited as McSwain Papers); Folder marked "Democratic Committee," James Francis Byrnes Papers, Robert M. Cooper Library, Clemson University, Clemson, S.C. (hereafter cited as Byrnes Papers); *Columbia State,* 18 June 1933, 12-A; 20 July 1933, 10.

3. W. R. Bradley to W. W. Ball, 9 June 1933, William Watts Ball Papers, Duke University Library, Durham, N.C. (hereafter cited as Ball Papers); Byrnes to Henry Morgenthau, Jr., 7 November 1933, Byrnes Papers; Walter Brown to Byrnes, 18 November 1933, Byrnes Papers; *Columbia State,* 10 June 1933, 1; 16 Nov. 1933, 7; 3 Dec. 1933, 10-A.

4. Harold Ickes, *The Secret Diary of Harold Ickes,* vol. 1 (New York: Simon and Schuster, 1953), 164.

5. Bernard Sternsher, *Rexford Tugwell and the New Deal* (New Brunswick, N.J.: Rutgers University Press, 1964), 253–55; *Time,* 25 June 1934, 10; *Columbia State,* 22 Mar. 1934, 1; 7 June 1934, 1.

6. W. D. Workman to Byrnes, 19 December 1934, Byrnes Papers.

7. Folder marked "McSwain, J. J., General, June, July, 1936," McSwain Papers; J. H. Price to McSwain, 17 April 1936, McSwain Papers; McSwain to George K. Langley, 11 April 1936, McSwain Papers; *Columbia State,* 4 July 1934, 1; 24 Aug. 1935, 14; 30 Aug. 1935, 1, 8; 9 Jan. 1937, 7; 19 Jan. 1937, 1.

8. *Columbia State,* 14 Mar. 1933, 4.

9. *Marion Star,* 29 Mar. 1933, 2; *Columbia State,* 25 Mar. 1933, 4; 27 Mar. 1933, 4; 17 May 1933, 4; *Manning Times,* 16 Aug. 1933, 4; *Clinton Chronicle,* 29 June 1933, 4; 3 Aug. 1933, 4; *Hartsville Messenger,* 22 June 1933, 4; *Chester News,* 21 Mar. 1933, 2; *Spartanburg Herald,* 9 Apr. 1933, 4; 17 Apr. 1933, 4; 10 May 1933, 4; 2 June 1933, 4; 17 June 1933, 4; 23 June 1933, 4; Levi Tillman Fulmer, telephone interview by author, Graniteville, S.C., 8 February 1999; B. W. Gettys, telephone interview by author, West Columbia, S.C., 10 February 1999.

10. *Horry Herald,* 23 Mar. 1933, 4; 18 May 1933, 8; 20 July 1933, 4; 7 Sept. 1933, 1; 19 Oct. 1933, 8; 16 Nov. 1933, 1, 8.

11. Henry Herbert Lesesne, "Opposition to the New Deal in South Carolina, 1933–1936" (master's thesis, University of South Carolina, 1995), 19–25.

12. Ball to Burnet Maybank, May 6, 1933, Ball Papers.

13. Ball to James A. Hoyt, May 14, 1933, Ball Papers.

14. John D. Stark, *Damned Upcountryman: William Watts Ball* (Durham, N.C.: Duke University Press, 1968), 160; *News and Courier,* 3 Apr. 1933, 4; 11 May 1933, 4; 8 June 1933, 4; 15 June 1933, 4; 16 June 1933, 4.

15. *Columbia State,* 1 Jan. 1934, 4.

16. David R. Coker to D. S. Freeman, 22 March 1934, David R. Coker Papers, South Caroliniana Library, University of South Carolina, Columbia (hereafter cited as Coker Papers).

17. *Horry Herald,* 1 Feb. 1934, 4; 15 Mar. 1934, 4; 20 Dec. 1934, 4; Stark, *Damned Upcountryman,* 162; *Manning Times,* 21 Nov. 1934, 1; *Columbia State,* 7 July 1934, 11; 13 Aug. 1934, 4.

18. Quoted in Bryant Simon, "A Fabric of Defeat: The Politics of South Carolina Textile Workers in State and Nation, 1920–1938" (Ph.D. diss., University of North Carolina, 1992), 161.

19. *Columbia State,* 7 Jan. 1934, 8-A; 17 May 1934, 1; *Spartanburg Herald,* 17 May 1934, 1, 2; *Manning Times,* 30 May 1934, 1; *Marion Star,* 18 July 1934, 1, 5. Although a prohibitionist, Johnston stated during the campaign that he would sign any "reasonable" legislation legalizing the sale of intoxicating beverages.

20. *Columbia State,* 5 July 1934, 2; 27 July 1934, 10; 3 Aug. 1934, 13; *Walhalla Keowee Courier,* 15 Aug. 1934, 1, 5; 22 Aug. 1934, 4; *Marion Star,* 25 July 1934, 1; J. J. McSwain to C. L. Gipson, 21 June 1934, McSwain Papers; Frank E. Jordan, Jr., *The Primary State* (N.p., n.d.), 106, 111, 116, 120 (hereafter cited as Jordan, *Primary State*).

21. Byrnes to Edward Keating, 14 September 1935, Byrnes Papers.

22. Claiming that "nothing would remain of state rights," Senator Smith opposed Byrnes's efforts to amend the Constitution. Clipping, hand-dated "June 13, 1935," Ellison D. Smith Papers, South Caroliniana Library, University of South Carolina, Columbia (hereafter cited as Ellison D. Smith Papers).

23. Chart titled "The Old Art of Smearing a Farm Program," folder 267, Stanley F. Morse Papers, South Caroliniana Library, University of South Carolina, Columbia (hereafter cited as Morse Papers). See also press release, Farmers' Independence Council of America, 25 September 1936, Morse Papers.

24. D. R. Coker to Olin D. Johnston, 12 October 1936, Coker Papers.

25. *Columbia State,* 12 Mar. 1935, 4; Rodger E. Stroup, "The Kingfish Solicits the Youth," Seminar Paper for History 858, University of South Carolina, 13 August 1971, typescript in possession of its author, 6–9; *Columbia State,* 19 Mar. 1935, 9; 21 Mar. 1935, 13.

26. *Columbia State,* 23 Mar. 1935, 1; 24 Mar. 1935, 1, 3; 25 Mar. 1935, 9; *New York Times,* 24 Mar. 1935, 32; *Winnsboro News and Herald,* 28 Mar. 1935, 4; James Johnson to Byrnes, 2 April 1935, Byrnes Papers; Stroup, "The Kingfish Solicits the Youth," 10–12.

27. *New York Times,* 25 Feb. 1936, 6.

28. Gen. Johnson Hagood to Congressman John J. McSwain and Sen. James F. Byrnes, Western Union telegram, 12 February 1936, Johnson Hagood Papers, South Carolina Historical Society, Charleston, S.C. (hereafter cited as Hagood Papers).

29. *New York Times,* 25 Feb. 1936, 6; 29 Feb. 1936, 13; Byrnes to William E. Gonzales, 5 March 1936, Byrnes Papers; Memorandum, Malin Craig to George H. Dern, [15 February 1936], Hagood Papers.

30. *New York Times,* 25 Feb. 1936, 6.

31. Cole L. Blease to McSwain, 25 February 1936, McSwain Papers.

32. *Congressional Record,* 74th Cong., 2d Sess., 3029–30.

33. *Columbia State,* 26 Feb. 1936, 4; 3 Mar. 1936, 4; American Liberty League, "The Story of an Honest Man," Doc. no. 107, March 1936 (Washington, D.C.: American Liberty League, 1936); Folders marked "General Hagood," Byrnes Papers.

34. Byrnes to Gonzales, 5 March 1936, Byrnes Papers.

35. *Spartanburg Herald,* 8 Apr. 1933, 4.

36. Byrnes to Gonzales, 5 March 1936, Byrnes Papers; *Columbia State,* 14 Apr. 1936, 1; 15 Apr. 1936, 4; 5 May 1936, 1.

37. Byrnes to Robert G. Elbert, 25 March 1936, Byrnes Papers.

38. Byrnes to Hugh O. Hanna, 23 December 1935, Byrnes Papers; *Congressional Record,* 74th Cong., 2d Sess., 7659, 7838–41; *Columbia State,* 21 May 1936, 1. Born in 1889, Stoney had received his education at the University of the South and the law school of the University of South Carolina. He was mayor of Charleston from 1923 to 1931. Harllee was born in 1877 and was educated at The Citadel, the University of North Carolina, West Point, and the Army and Navy War Colleges. He had been a career officer and a Marine since 1900. Harllee was also a member of the prestigious New York Yacht Club.

39. *Manning Times,* 10 June 1936, 1. See also working papers and notes for speeches and press releases in the 1936 election, Thomas P. Stoney Papers, South Carolina Historical Society, Charleston, S.C.

40. *Columbia State,* 10 June 1936, 1; 11 June 1936, 11; 13 June 1936, 1; 16 June 1936, 1; 19 June 1936, 8-B; James F. Byrnes, *All in One Lifetime* (New York: Harper and Brothers, 1958), 93–94; *Time,* 24 Aug. 1936, 18.

41. Clippings, June 1936, Ellison D. Smith Papers.

42. *Columbia State,* 25 June 1936, 2; 26 June 1936, 1; 28 June 1936, 1; John E. Huss, *Senator for the South: A Biography of Olin D. Johnston* (Garden City: Doubleday and Co., 1961), 84 (hereafter cited as Huss, *Johnston*); Byrnes, *All in One Lifetime,* 94.

43. Newsclippings, Johnston Scrapbook, Olin D. Johnston Papers, South Caroliniana Library, University of South Carolina, Columbia, 1936, 171 (hereafter cited as Johnston Scrapbook).

44. *Clinton Chronicle,* 2 July 1936, 4; *Horry Herald,* 2 July 1936, 1; *Walterboro Press and Standard,* 1 July 1936, 4; *Columbia State,* 2 July 1936, 4-A; *Marion Star,* 1 July 1936, 4.

45. *New York Times,* 3 July 1936, 5.

46. *South Carolina Newsview* (25 July 1936): 7.

47. O. F. Armfield, an opponent of the New Deal and editor of the *Newberry Herald and News,* had offered for the legislature from Newberry County. He anticipated making his campaign an anti—New Deal one, stressing race, wasted money, and the abuses of the AAA. The Johnston forces in Newberry County agreed to support Armfield only if the editor would agree to follow Johnston's example and support the New Deal. *Horry Herald,* 2 July 1936, 4.

48. A. Frank Lever to Cassie Connor, 22 July 1936, Asbury F. Lever Papers, Robert M. Cooper Library, Clemson University, Clemson, S.C. (hereafter cited as Lever Papers); Lever to Byrnes, 27 July 1936, Lever Papers; *Hartsville Messenger,* 16 July 1936, 4; *Columbia State,* 30 June 1936, 2; 5 July 1936, 10-A; 22 Aug. 1936, 9; *Horry Herald,* 6 Aug. 1936, 5; 20 Aug. 1936, 10.

49. *Columbia State,* 26 Aug. 1936, 1; 13 Sept. 1936, 1, 2; 3 Nov. 1936, 1; 10 Nov. 1936, 1; 28 Nov. 1936, 1; *New York Times,* 27 Aug. 1936, 10; 29 Sept. 1936, 19; Huss, *Johnston,* 86; Byrnes, *All in One Lifetime,* 94.

50. *Columbia State,* 26 Aug. 1936, 1; 8 Nov. 1936, 1; 20 Feb. 1937, 4; 4 Mar. 1937, 2; *Walterboro Press and Standard,* 11 Feb. 1937, 4; *Clinton Chronicle,* 11 Feb. 1937, 4; *Horry Herald,* 25 Feb. 1937, 4; *Spartanburg Herald,* 7 Feb. 1937, 4; *Marion Star,* 10 Feb. 1937, 4; *Winnsboro News and Herald,* 18 Feb. 1937, 4; *Hartsville Messenger,* 18 Feb. 1937, 4.

51. *Columbia State,* 7 Feb. 1937, 14-A.

52. *Manning Times,* 21 July 1937, 6.

53. W. H. Ambrose to Byrnes, 19 February 1937, Byrnes Papers.

54. H. D. Burgiss to Byrnes, 20 February 1937, Byrnes Papers.

55. Cormack to Byrnes, 22 February 1937, Byrnes Papers; Lever to Byrnes, 27 March 1937, Byrnes Papers; George Brown Tindall, *The Emergence of the New South, 1913–1945* (Baton Rouge: Louisiana State University Press, 1967), 622. Support among mill workers for court reform was almost unanimous. Their spokesman, the *News Review* of Una, opined that in the absence of a reformed court, "no power under heaven" could protect American workers from "the ruthless greed of the sweatshop boss." John W. Pollard, president of the South Carolina Federation of Textile Workers, was certain that the coalition against court reform consisted of no one except "economic royalists" and "agents of entrenched greed." *Una News Review,* 12 June 1936, 3; 5 Mar. 1937, 2. See also 19 Feb. 1937, 2; 26 Feb. 1937, 2; 19 Mar. 1937, 2; 16 Apr. 1937, 2.

56. *Columbia State,* 4 Mar. 1937, 13; newsclipping, dated "March 4, 1937," Byrnes Papers; *Columbia State,* 10 Feb. 1937, 9; 18 Feb. 1937, 16; 19 Feb. 1937, 6-A; 26 Feb. 1937, 1.

57. *Congressional Record,* 75th Cong., 1st Sess., 2186, 2191.

58. Ibid.; *Columbia State,* 5 Mar. 1937, 1, 5-A; 11 Mar. 1937, 8; *Walterboro Press and Standard,* 11 Mar. 1937, 4; Donald Russell to Byrnes, Saturday (n.d.), Byrnes Papers; C. C. Wyche to Byrnes, 20 February 1937, C. C. Wyche Papers, Duke University Library, Durham, N.C. In late March the annual convention of the South Carolina Bar Association entertained a resolution to disapprove of court reform. Convinced that the resolution would carry, James H. Hammond and Clint Graydon forced through a proposal requiring voting members to sign their names to their ballots. Of the 250 lawyers in attendance, 86 voted for the resolution, 37 voted against it, and 127 fled rather than vote against Byrnes and Roosevelt. A. Frank Lever to Byrnes, 27 March 1937, Byrnes Papers.

59. Newsclipping, *Anderson Daily Mail,* undated, Johnston Scrapbook, 1937.

60. Harry M. Arthur to Byrnes, 26 June 1937, Johnston Scrapbook; T. M. Marchant to Byrnes, 2 April 1937, Johnston Scrapbook; Christie Benet to Byrnes, 8 April 1937, Johnston Scrapbook; M. E. Brockman to Byrnes, 4 May 1937, Johnston Scrapbook; Arthur [J. Stoney] to Wyndham Manning, 12 June 1937, Wyndham Manning Papers, South Caroliniana Library, University of South Carolina, Columbia (hereafter cited as Manning Papers).

61. *Marion Star,* 18 Sept. 1935, 4; *Columbia State,* 8 Aug. 1936, 4; 7 Oct. 1936, 4; *Horry Herald,* 20 Aug. 1936, 10; undated newsclipping, *Greenville Observer,* Byrnes Papers; *Walterboro Press and Standard,* 25 Feb. 1937, 4.

62. A. G. Kennedy to Byrnes, 5 June 1937, Byrnes Papers.

63. Cole L. Blease, speech delivered at Greenville, S.C., 11 September 1937, Ball Papers; *Manning Times,* 21 July 1937, 6; 8 Sept. 1937, 6; 15 Sept. 1937, 6; *Walhalla Keowee Courier,* 9 Dec. 1937, 2.

64. Roosevelt's support of the Fair Labor Standards Bill symbolized his alliance with Northern Democrats. For South Carolina's reaction, see *Marion Star,* 16 June 1937, 4; *Manning Times,* 23 June 1937, 4; *Walhalla Keowee Courier,* 24 June 1937, 4; *Horry Herald,* 1 July 1937, 1; *Columbia State,* 22 July 1937, 2; *Clinton Chronicle,* 5 Aug. 1937, 4.

65. *Congressional Record,* 75th Cong., 3d Sess., 493.

66. *Clinton Chronicle,* 27 Jan. 1938, 4; *Lee County Messenger,* quoted in the *Walhalla Keowee Courier,* 17 Feb. 1938, 2; *Walhalla Keowee Courier,* 20 Jan. 1938, 2; 24 Feb. 1938, 2.

67. *Walhalla Keowee Courier,* 12 May 1938, 2; See also *Manning Times,* 4 May 1938, 6; 11 May 1938, 4.

68. *Columbia State,* 19 May 1938, 1, 5. With public opinion so uncertain, candidates in the gubernatorial primary treated the New Deal gingerly. The large field included Burnet Maybank and Wyndham Manning as front-runners, the perennial Cole Blease, Chairman Neville Bennett of the House Ways and Means Committee, WPA critic Ben Adams, and three also-rans. Maybank campaigned on his record as mayor of Charleston, success in obtaining public funds from the Roosevelt administration, and successful efforts to secure the Santee Cooper project. The other candidates campaigned against Maybank on the issue of law and order, which meant Charleston's traditional disregard of laws regulating alcoholic beverages and prostitution. Although Blease and occasionally Manning took swipes at Santee Cooper as a Maybank campaign fund, Manning was careful not to oppose the New Deal too strenuously. Maybank led in the first primary, followed by Manning, Blease, Bennett, and Adams. In the runoff between Maybank and Manning, Maybank won with 52 percent of the vote. The congressional primaries were similar. In congressional districts 1, 2, 5, and 6 the New Deal was less an issue than incumbency or constituent services. Congressional districts 3 and 4 were different.

Textile workers, who lived there in large numbers, constituted the New Deal's most loyal following. Votes by Congressmen Taylor and Mahon against the New Deal, and especially against the Fair Labor Standards Act, helped defeat both men. Marvin L. Cann, "The End of a Political Myth: The South Carolina Gubernatorial Campaign of 1938." *South Carolina Historical Magazine* 82 (July 1971): 142–46. Sectionalism blotted out pro– and anti–New Deal distinctions. The nearly "100 percent" New Deal *News and Herald* of Winnsboro supported Manning over Maybank, and the upcountry counties where the New Deal remained popular went to Manning. Maybank's victory stemmed from his huge vote in Charleston, the promises his lieutenants made in every county of jobs with Santee Cooper, and his help from Byrnes. V. O. Key, Jr., *Southern Politics in State and Nation* (New York: Alfred A. Knopf, 1949), 137–38; Jordan, *Primary State,* 42–43; *Winnsboro News and Herald,* 4 Aug. 1938, 4; *Walterboro Press and Standard,* 30 June 1938, 8; J. M. Nickles to Wyndham Manning, 24 September 1938, Manning Papers; *Columbia State,* 27 Aug. 1938, 2; 1 Sept. 1938, 7; *Walterboro Press and Standard,* 14 July 1938, 1; Campaign Broadside [1945], Butler B. Hare Papers, South Caroliniana Library, University of South Carolina, Columbia; *Walhalla Keowee Courier,* 28 July 1938, 8; 4 Aug. 1938, 1; James M. Baker to Byrnes, 5 September 1938, Byrnes Papers; *Spartanburg Herald,* 31 Aug. 1938, 2; *Clinton Chronicle,* 18 Aug. 1939, 8; 15 Sept. 1939, 1; *Una News Review,* 4 Sept. 1936, 4.

69. James T. Patterson, *Congressional Conservatism and the New Deal: The Growth of a Conservative Coalition in Congress, 1933–1939* (Lexington: University of Kentucky Press, 1967), 202–7.

70. Huss, *Johnston,* 88; W. D. Workman, Jr., *The Bishop from Barnwell* (Columbia, S.C.: R. L. Bryan Co., 1963), 219–22; *Columbia State,* 9 May 1938, 1; 17 May 1938, 1; newsclipping, Johnston Scrapbook, 1938, 341–42.

71. *Columbia State,* 15 June 1938, 1, 9; Huss, *Johnston,* 92–93; Workman, *Bishop,* 222–23.

72. *Columbia State,* 16 June 1938, 15; 18 June 1938, 1; 12 July 1938, 3; 16 July 1938, 7; 30 July 1938, 7; Workman, *Bishop,* 225–30.

73. *Columbia State,* 16 June 1938, 15; 17 June 1938, 12; 18 June 1938, 1; 22 June 1938, 8; 23 June 1938, 3; 12 July 1938, 3; 30 July 1938, 7.

74. Quoted in Daniel Walker Hollis, "Cotton Ed Smith—Showman or Statesman?" *South Carolina Historical Magazine* 71 (Oct. 1970): 251 (hereafter cited as Hollis, "Smith"); and in Anthony Barry Miller, "Palmetto Politician: The Early Political Career of Olin D. Johnston, 1896–1945" (Ph.D. diss., University of North Carolina, 1976), 303; *Columbia State,* 30 July 1938, 7.

75. *New York Times,* 23 Aug. 1938, 5.

76. Quoted in Hollis, "Smith," 251.

77. Byrnes, *All in One Lifetime,* 101–2; Byrnes to B. M. Baruch, 16 August 1938, Byrnes Papers; Byrnes to Miss M. A. Boyle, 17 August 1938, Byrnes Papers.

78. W. W. Ball to H. L. Watson, 9 October, 1938, Harry L. Watson Papers, South Caroliniana Library, University of South Carolina, Columbia (hereafter cited as Harrry L. Watson Papers).

79. Workman, *Bishop*, 231–32.

80. *Columbia State*, 12 Aug. 1938, 1; Hollis, "Smith," 253; Byrnes, *All in One Lifetime*, 103; Huss, *Johnston*, 95; Workman, *Bishop*, 232; Archie Vernon Huff, Jr., *Greenville: The History of the City and County in the South Carolina Piedmont* (Columbia: University of South Carolina Press, 1995), 358–59.

81. Byrnes to Baruch, 16 August 1938, Byrnes Papers. See also Byrnes to James A. Farley, 23 August 1938, Byrnes Papers, for the same conclusion by Byrnes. The junior senator advised Farley that there would be a runoff between Smith and Johnston. Brown's mill vote would go to Johnston, and his support from the highway department would go to Smith.

82. Byrnes to Miss M. A. Boyle, 17 August 1938, Byrnes Papers.

83. Byrnes to B. M. Baruch, 16 August 1938, Byrnes Papers.

84. Byrnes to Farley, 23 August 1938, Byrnes Papers; *Spartanburg Herald,* 12 Aug. 1938, 1; *Clinton Chronicle,* 1Aug. 8 1938, 6; *Walhalla Keowee Courier,* 18 Aug. 1938, 1; *Winnsboro News and Herald,* 18 Aug. 1938, 4; *Columbia State,* 13 Aug. 1938, 1; 14 Aug. 1938, 4-A; 19 Aug. 1938, 1; 27 Aug. 1938, 1, 5; 28 Aug. 1938, 1. For Brown's reasons for withdrawing, see Workman, *Bishop,* 233–34. The press, with the exception of the Anderson and Spartanburg papers, denounced Roosevelt's intervention.

85. Quoted in Workman, *Bishop*, 236.

86. Olin D. Johnston to Edgar A. Brown, 29 August 1938, Western Union telegram, Edgar A. Brown Papers, Robert M. Cooper Library, Clemson University, Clemson, S.C. (hereafter cited as Brown Papers); Edgar A. Brown to Olin D. Johnston, 29 August 1938, Brown Papers.

87. Workman, *Bishop,* 236–38; Hollis, "Smith," 254. For a more complete discussion of the 1938 election, see David Robertson, *Sly and Able,* 269–80; JoAnn Deakin Carpenter, "Olin D. Johnston, the New Deal, and the Politics of Class in South Carolina, 1934–1938" (Ph.D.diss., Emory University, 1987), 361–97; Miller, "Palmetto Politician," 296–318; Roger P. Leemhuis, "Olin Johnston Runs for the Senate: 1938 to 1962," *Proceedings of the South Carolina Historical Association* (1986): 57–69.

88. *Walterboro Press and Standard,* 25 Aug. 1938, 7. For examples of support given Smith by the South Carolina Federation of Labor (AFL), see *Una News Review,* 1 July 1938, 1.

89. *Spartanburg Herald,* 1 Sept. 1938, 2.

90. McMaster to Jim [A. Hoyt], 5 July 1938, James A. Hoyt Papers, South Caroliniana Library, University of South Carolina.

91. Walter Edgar, *South Carolina: A History* (Columbia: University of South Carolina Press, 1998), 510.

92. W. W. Ball to H. L. Watson, 5 March 1938, Harry L. Watson Papers; W. W. Ball to Fitz Hugh McMaster, 2 July 1938, Fitz Hugh McMaster Papers, South Caroliniana Library, University of South Carolina.

CHAPTER 10—A NEW DEAL FOR AFRICAN AMERICANS

1. Theodore Hemingway, "Beneath the Yoke of Bondage: A History of Black Folks in South Carolina, 1900–1940" (Ph.D. disseration, University of South Carolina, 1976), 254–338 (hereafter cited as Hemingway, "Yoke").

2. Edwin D. Hoffman, "The Genesis of the Modern Movement for Equal Rights in South Carolina, 1930–1939," *Journal of Negro History* 44 (July 1959): 346.

3. Hemingway, "Yoke," 4–49.

4. Benjamin E. Mays, *Born to Rebel* (New York: Charles Scribner's Sons, 1971), 7–8 (hereafter cited as Mays, *Rebel*).

5. Hemingway, "Yoke," 53–64; Mays, *Rebel*, 24, 33.

6. I. A. Newby, *Black Carolinians: A History in South Carolina from 1895 to 1968* (Columbia: University of South Carolina Press, 1973), 207.

7. Mays, *Rebel*, 6.

8. Mr. and Mrs. Dock Belton, interview conducted by the author, Ridgeway, S.C., 28 January 2000.

9. Hemingway, "Yoke," 397; Newby, *Black Carolinians*, 248.

10. Hoffman, "Genesis," 347–48; Hemingway, "Yoke," 243–45, 397.

11. Mays, *Rebel*, 22.

12. Hemingway, "Yoke," 84, 85, 100–106, 114, 149–56, 245, 248, 315, 324; Newby, *Black Carolinians*, 240–41; Hoffman, "Genesis," 349.

13. Hemingway, "Yoke," 140–45, 149–57.

14. Quoted in Newby, *Black Carolinians*, 232–33.

15. "I Am a Negro," South Carolina WPA Federal Writers' Project Life Histories, Works Progress Administration Collection, South Caroliniana Library, University of South Carolina, Columbia.

16. Ibid.

17. Quoted in Newby, *Black Carolinians*, 233. See also Mays, *Rebel*, 25.

18. Quoted in Newby, *Black Carolinians*, 232.

19. John A. Salmond, "The Civilian Conservation Corps and the Negro," *Journal of American History* 52 (June 1965): 79; Newby, *Black Carolinians*, 245–46, 265; Hoffman, "Genesis," 361.

20. Quoted in Ralph J. Bunche, *The Political Status of the Negro in the Age of FDR* (Chicago: University of Chicago Press, 1973), 514.

21. Ibid., 514; James E. Dickson, Monthly Reports, June and July 1933, James E. Dickson Papers, South Caroliniana Library, University of South Carolina, Columbia.

22. Newby, *Black Carolinians*, 214, 218, 219, 224; Hemingway, "Yoke," 335.

23. Hemingway, "Yoke," 399–404.

24. Belton, interview.

25. Robert Earl Martin, "Negro-White Participation in the AAA Cotton and Tobacco Referenda in North and South Carolina: A Study in Differential Voting and Attitudes in Selected Areas" (Ph.D. diss., University of Chicago, 1947), 288–89.

26. Newby, *Black Carolinians*, 193, 221, 265–66; Roger Biles, *The South and the New Deal* (Lexington: University Press of Kentucky, 1994), 116.

27. 1 June 1935, 4. See also David R. Coker to D. S. Freeman, 22 March 1934, David R. Coker Papers, South Caroliniana Library, University of South Carolina, Columbia. Coker wrote: "The labor provisions of the NRA will, in the long run, affect the negro workers unfavorably, as it will result in some shift from negro to white labor." See also Biles, *The South and the New Deal*, 111–12.

28. *Sixteenth Census of the United States: 1940, Agriculture*, vol. 1, part 3 (Washington, D.C.: Government Printing Office, 1942), 434, 442. While there were 17,168 fewer black tenants in 1940 than in 1930 (a 28 percent decline), there were also 8,416 fewer white tenants (a 20 percent decline). In addition, the effects of the AAA on blacks in agriculture were only slightly more severe than those of the boll weevil in the 1920–1925 period, when the number of black farm operators declined 17 percent from 109,005 to 90,581. *1950 United States Census of Agriculture: North Carolina and South Carolina* (Washington, D.C.: Government Printing Office, 1952), 358–59.

29. 11 January 1936, 4.

30. "WPA Road," South Carolina WPA Federal Writers' Project Life Histories, Works Progress Administration Collection, South Caroliniana Library, University of South Carolina, Columbia.

31. Quoted in Bunche, *Political Status*, 514.

32. Harvard Sitkoff, "The Impact of the New Deal on Black Southerners," in James C. Cobb and Michael V. Namorato, *The New Deal and the South* (Jackson: University Press of Mississippi, 1984), 130 (hereafter cited as Sitkoff, "Impact").

33. Quoted in ibid.

34. Newby, *Black Carolinians*, 185; Hemingway, "Yoke," 392; Biles, *The South and the New Deal*, 123.

35. Biles, *The South and the New Deal*, 123.

36. Bunche, *Political Status*, 426. See also 153–58.

37. Hoffman, "Genesis," 363. See also 346–70, and Cobb and Namorato, *The New Deal and the South*, 125–34.

38. Typescript folder marked "Simkins, Biographical Papers, 1913–1992," Modjeska Monteith Simkins Papers, South Caroliniana Library, University of South Carolina, Columbia (hereafter cited as Simkins Papers).

39. Hoffman, "Genesis," 361

40. Hoffman, "Genesis," 361–62; Paul Lofton, "The Columbia Black Community in the 1930s," *Proceedings of the South Carolina Historical Association* (1984): 233–34.

41. Quoted in Hoffman, "Genesis," 364.

42. Quoted in Bunche, *Political Status*, 360.

43. Patricia Sullivan, *Days of Hope: Race and Democracy in the New Deal Era* (Chapel Hill: University of North Carolina Press, 1996), 144 (hereafter cited as Sullivan, *Hope*).

44. Quoted in Bunche, *Political Status*, 322.

45. Ibid.

46. Bunche, *Political Status,* 322–23, 359–63, 419.

47. Sullivan, *Hope,* 144.

48. Quoted in Bunche, *Political Status,* 419.

49. Ibid., 420.

50. Ibid., 322.

51. Ibid., 431.

52. Bunche, *Political Status,* 416.

53. Quoted in ibid., 419.

54. Bunche, *Political Status,* 419.

55. Hemingway, "Yoke," 387; Sullivan, *Hope,* 144; Bunche, *Political Status,* 421–22.

56. Quoted in Bunche, *Political Status,* 204.

57. Ibid.

58. Ibid., 320.

59. Hemingway, "Yoke," 388.

60. Quoted in Bunche, *Political Status,* 423.

61. Hoffman, "Genesis," 366–67; Hemingway, "Yoke," 388; Sullivan, *Hope,* 145; Bunche, *Political Status,* 423.

62. *Columbia Palmetto Leader,* 26 Jan. 1935, 4; 2 Mar. 1935, 4; 16 Mar. 1935, 4; 6 Apr. 1935, 4; 13 Apr. 1935, 4; Archie Vernon Huff, Jr., *Greenville: The History of the City and County in the South Carolina Piedmont* (Columbia: University of South Carolina Press, 1995), 358.

63. *Columbia Palmetto Leader,* 3 Apr. 1937, 4; Telegram, Interdenominational Ministers Union to Franklin D. Roosevelt, 26 December 1938, Simkins Papers.

64. 6 July 1935, 4; 10 August 1935, 4; 3 April 1937, 4; 9 October 1937, 4.

65. Folder titled "Simkins, Topical Files: Republican Party, 1938–1951," Simkins Papers.

66. 12 November 1932, 1; 29 October 1938, 2.

67. Newby, *Black Carolinians,* 251.

68. Quoted in Bunche, *Political Status,* 427–28.

69. Ibid., 428.

70. Ibid.

71. Ibid., 429.

72. Hoffman, "Genesis," 365–68; A. J. Collins et al. to Franklin D. Roosevelt, telegram, n.d., Simkins Papers.

73. Newby, *Black Carolinians,* 235.

74. Quoted in Hoffman, "Genesis," 368–69. See also Newby, *Black Carolinians,* 234–35; Hemingway, "Yoke," 390–91; Miles S. Richards, "Osceola E. McKaine and the Struggle for Black Civil Rights: 1917–1946" (Ph.D. diss., University of South Carolina, 1994), 108–9 (hereafter cited as Richards, "McKaine").

75. Hoffman, "Genesis," 346; Sullivan, *Hope,* 142; Mrs. Andrew (Modjeska M.) Simkins, telephone interview by the author, 25 January 1972; Lofton, "Columbia Black Community," 86–95; Barbara Woods Aba-Mecha, "Black Woman Activist in Twentieth Century South Carolina: Modjeska Monteith Simkins" (Ph.D. diss., Emory University, 1978), 153–228; Barbara W. Aba-Mecha, "South Carolina Conference of NAACP: Origin and Major Accomplishments, 1939–1954," *Proceedings of the South Carolina Historical Association,* 1981, 3, 7–9.

76. Richards, "McKaine," 97–124; Newby, *Black Carolinians,* 303–4.

77. Richards, "McKaine," 132–41.

78. Quoted in ibid., 145–46.

79. Richards, "McKaine," 143–48.

80. Newby, *Black Carolinians,* 280–81; Sullivan, *Hope,* 145–47.

81. Newby, *Black Carolinians,* 281; Sullivan, *Hope,* 147.

82. Quoted in Sullivan, *Hope,* 147.

83. Ibid., 169.

84. Newby, *Black Carolinians,* 281–82; Sullivan, *Hope,* 148; James O. Farmer, Jr., "The End of the White Primary in South Carolina: A Southern State's Fight to Keep Its Politics White" (master's thesis, University of South Carolina, 1969), 25–42 (hereafter cited as Farmer, "White Primary").

85. John Egerton, *Speak Now against the Day* (New York: Alfred A. Knopf, 1994), 549.

86. Quoted in Richards, "McKaine," 171–73.

87. Richards, "McKaine," 171–73.

88. Quoted in Sullivan, *Hope,* 170–71.

89. Richards, "McKaine," 177–84; Sullivan, *Hope,* 171.

90. Richards, "McKaine," 188.

91. Ibid., 193.

92. Quoted in ibid., 198.

93. Richards, "McKaine," 183–98.

94. Ibid., 202–4.

95. Quoted in Newby, *Black Carolinians,* 285. See also "Judge Waring on the Civil Rights Issue," *Nation* 174 (1 June 1952): 540.

96. Egerton, *Speak,* 407–9; Newby, *Black Carolinians,* 284–85; Cassandra Maxwell Birnie, "Race and Politics in Georgia and South Carolina," *Phylon* 13 (Sept. 1952): 242.

97. Quoted in Newby, *Black Carolinians,* 285; Farmer, "White Primary," 54–74.

98. Newby, *Black Carolinians,* 286–87; clipping dated 29 May 1948, Scrapbook 1948–1952, John H. McCray Papers, South Caroliniana Library, University of South Carolina.

99. Minutes of the meetings of the Board of Trustees of the University of South Carolina, 8 July 1938, 26–28; 26 October 1938, 51; 7 December 1938, 49; 28 July 1939, 45; Charles Bruce Bailey, telephone interview by the author, Columbia, S.C., 25 January 1972.

100. Newby, *Black Carolinians,* 350–51; Egerton, *Speak,* 409.

101. Egerton, *Speak,* 589–90; Richards, "McKaine," 117; Newby, *Black Carolinians,* 305.

102. Quoted in Egerton, *Speak,* 590.

103. Ibid., 590–91; Newby, *Black Carolinians,* 306.

104. Robert F. Cushman, ed., *Cases in Constitutional Law,* 4th ed. (Englewood Cliffs, N.J.: Prentice-Hall, Inc., 1975), 628.

105. Quoted in Egerton, *Speak,* 595.

106. Ibid., 597. See also 591–602 and Cushman, *Cases in Constitutional Law,* 627.

107. Quoted in Cushman, *Cases in Constitutional Law,* 631.

108. Egerton, *Speak,* 611.

109. Sitkoff, "Impact," 133.

110. Ibid., 134.

111. Ibid., 133.

112. Hemingway, "Yoke," 411.

CHAPTER 11—THE IMPACT OF THE NEW DEAL IN SOUTH CAROLINA

1. Paul S. Lofton, "A Social and Economic History of Columbia, South Carolina, during the Great Depression, 1929–1940" (Ph.D. diss., University of Texas, Austin, 1977), 245–49.

2. Don C. Reading, "A Statistical Analysis of New Deal Economic Programs in the Forty-Eight States, 1933–1939" (Ph.D. diss., Utah State University, 1972), 257. The $533 million in 1933–1938 dollars would equal approximately $7.12 billion in October 2000 dollars.

3. O.G.R., South Carolina Report No. 10, 2–3; O.G.R., South Carolina Report No. 10, 1940 Supplement, 3–4; Congress, Senate, *Federal, State, and Local Government Fiscal Relations,* Sen. Doc. 69, 78th Cong., 1st sess., 1943, 192–93; *Columbia State,* 31 Dec. 1933, 5-A, 7-A, 8-A, 8-B, 11-B; 30 Dec. 1934, 1, 8-A, 14-A; 21 Dec. 1935, 1; Lawrence M. Pinckney, "Business and Economic Report: South Carolina, February 1940 and April 1940" (Works Progress Administration Collection, South Caroliniana Library, Columbia).

4. Clinch Heyward Belser, "Banking in South Carolina, 1910–1940" (master's thesis, University of South Carolina, 1940), 45; Olin Pugh, *Difficult Decades of*

Banking: A Comparative Study of Banking Developments in South Carolina and the United States,1920–1940 (Columbia: University of South Carolina School of Business Administration, 1964), 58; *Columbia State,* 29 Oct. 1938, 6; O.G.R., South Carolina: Report No. 10, 5; O.G.R., South Carolina: Report No. 10, 1940 Supplement, 4; W. H. Steiner, "South Carolina Cash Depositories," *Southern Economic Journal* 4 (July 1937): 28–32.

5. John G. Sproat and Larry Schweikart, *Making Change: South Carolina Banking in the Twentieth Century* (Columbia: South Carolina Bankers Association, 1990), 79; John Dean Minton, "The New Deal in Tennessee, 1932–1938" (Ph.D. diss., Vanderbilt University, 1959), 40; William E. Leuchtenburg, *Franklin D. Roosevelt and the New Deal* (New York: Harper and Row, 1963), 38–39.

6. *Columbia State,* 6 Mar. 1933, 4.

7. Ibid., 1, 5.

8. Thomas H. Daniel, *Twenty-eighth Annual Report of the State Banking Department of South Carolina, 1934* (Columbia, 1934), 10–11 (hereafter cited as Daniel, *Banking Department Report*); Daniel, *Banking Department Report, 1935,* 9; Daniel, *Banking Department Report, 1936,* 10; Daniel, *Banking Department Report, 1937,* 16–17; *Columbia State,* 29 Apr. 1933, 12; 9 Jan. 1934, 10. The liquidated banks included the Bank of Camden, Commerce Bank in Clinton, Carolina Bank and Trust Company in Denmark, Commercial Bank in Easley, Bank of Eutawville, Lucas Bank in Laurens, Lockhart Bank at Lockhart, Lyman Savings Bank, and Spartan Savings Bank of Spartanburg. O.G.R., South Carolina Report No. 10, 4–5. Personal income increased from $290 million to $490 million, while bank deposits increased from $48.7 million to $134.9 million. Also attesting to the healthier banking environment was the increase in bank assets from an average of $813,000 per bank in 1934 to $1.2 million per bank by 1940. Pugh, *Difficult Decades,* 95. Also important was the provision in the Glass-Steagall Banking Act of 1933 that forced national banks to divorce themselves from their state bank affiliates. During the speculative mania of the 1920s, the Federal Reserve System had imposed stiff investment guidelines on national banks. National banks circumvented these guidelines by using funds to capitalize state banks (affiliates) with unlimited investment potential. This system made the safety of the national banks indirectly dependent upon the stock market investments of their affiliates. How extensive the system of affiliates was in South Carolina is unknown, although the Glass-Steagall Act forced at least two affiliates to merge with their parent national banks. The two were the Conway Savings Bank, which merged with the Conway National Bank, and the Piedmont Savings Bank and Trust Company, which merged with the First National Bank of Greenville. *Columbia State,* 19 Apr. 1934, 1; Daniel, *Banking Department Report, 1934,* 13; Frederick Lewis Allen, *The Lords of Creation* (New York: Harper and Brothers, 1935), 174–75, 440.

9. Federal Deposit Insurance Corporation, *Annual Report of the Federal Deposit Insurance Corporation for the Year Ending December 31, 1934* (n.p., n.d.),

180–83 (hereafter cited as FDIC, *Annual Report*); FDIC, *Annual Report, 1938*, 131, 152.

10. *Columbia State*, 11 Aug. 1934, 12; 29 Oct. 1938, 6; O.G.R., South Carolina Report No. 10, 45; Leo T. Crawley to Byrnes, 18 March 1935, James Francis Byrnes Papers, Robert M. Cooper Library, Clemson University, Clemson, S.C.

11. FDIC, *Annual Report, 1938*, 131.

12. Simon, "Fabric," 313–30; Carpenter, "Johnston," 226–51, 278–90; Miller, "Palmetto Politician," 115–46, 225–27, 249–62.

13. Olin D. Johnston, governor of South Carolina, *Annual Messages of Olin D. Johnston, Governor* (Columbia, 1935), 5–17 (hereafter cited as Johnston, *Governor's Annual Messages*); Johnston, *Governor's Annual Messages, 1936*, 7–20; Johnston, *Governor's Annual Messages, 1937*, 4–11; Johnston, *Governor's Annual Messages, 1938*, 6–26; *Charleston News and Courier*, 19 May 1935, 1, 2-A; 22 May 1937, 1; 8 May 1938, 1; *Columbia State*, 4 Apr. 1935, 14; 11 Apr. 1935, 2; 17 May 1945, 1; 18 May 1935, 1; 25 May 1935, 3; 26 Mar. 1936, 16; 27 Mar. 1936, 1-B; 1 Apr. 1936, 11; 11 Apr. 1936, 2; 16 Apr. 1936, 15; 10 May 1936, 1; 14 May 1936, 14; 31 May 1936, 1; 11 June 1936, 4; 29 Oct. 1936, 5; 16 Apr. 1937, 8-B; 1 May 1937, 14; 18 Feb. 1938, 5-B.

14. *Labor Information Bulletin* 2 (Sept. 1935): 3; *Labor Information Bulletin* 4 (Aug. 1937): 5; *Monthly Labor Review* 43 (Dec. 1936): 1444, 1446, 1451; *Monthly Labor Review* 46 (Jan. 1938), 132, 137, 143, 150, 154, 156; *Monthly Labor Review* 47 (Oct. 1938), 808, 810; *Textile World* (June 1938), 91; Clippings, Johnston Scrapbook (1935), Olin D. Johnston Papers, South Caroliniana Library, University of South Carolina, Columbia, 65; (1937); John E. Huss, *Senator for the South: A Biography of Olin D. Johnston* (Garden City, N.Y.: Doubleday and Co., 1961), 56–59.

15. Ibid.

16. *Columbia State*, 15 Apr. 1933, 1; 17 Apr. 1933, 2.

17. Ibid., 3 Oct. 1933, 5; 4 Nov. 1933, 1; 23 Nov. 1933, 5.

18. South Carolina General Assembly, *Acts and Joint Resolutions of the General Assembly of the State of South Carolina* (Columbia, 1935), 325–40; *Charleston News and Courier*, 30 Aug. 1934, 1; Solomon Blatt, interview by the author, Columbia, S.C., 19 January 1972.

19. *Report of the Comptroller General of South Carolina for the Fiscal Year 1930* (Columbia: 1931), 4, 13, 18 (hereafter cited as *Comptroller General Report*); *Comptroller General Report, 1931*, 14–16; *Comptroller General Report, 1932*, 11–13; *Comptroller General Report, 1933*, 23–25; *Comptroller General Report, 1934*, 15–17; *Comptroller General Report, 1935*, 22–24; *Comptroller General Report, 1936*, 25–27; *Comptroller General Report, 1937*, 24–26; *Comptroller General Report, 1938*, 14; House of Representatives, *Journal of the House of Representatives of the State of South Carolina* (Columbia, 1934), 2212–16. Until 1934 the fiscal year in South Carolina ran from 1 January to 31 December. Appropriations for a fiscal year were not made until four months after the fiscal year had begun,

forcing the state to borrow. Voters in 1932 accepted a constitutional amendment to change the fiscal year to 1 July to 30 June, and the 1933 legislature passed legislation to make it effective. South Carolina General Assembly, *Acts and Joint Resolutions, 1933,* 218, 591.

20. Blackwood, *Governor's Annual Messages, 1933,* 3–17; James T. Patterson, *The New Deal and the States* (Princeton, N.J.: Princeton University Press, 1969), 47; *Charleston News and Courier,* 6 May 1933, 1.

21. Blackwood, *Governor's Annual Messages, 1934,* 3–12; *Charleston News and Courier,* 15 Apr. 1934, 2-A; *Columbia State,* 3 Mar. 1934, 12; 17 Apr. 1934, 9; 14 Nov. 1934, 4.

22. *Charleston News and Courier,* 2 July 1939, 7; Marvin Leigh Cann, "Burnet Rhett Maybank and the New Deal in South Carolina, 1931–1941" (Ph.D. diss., University of North Carolina, 1967), 200–222, 242–54 (hereafter cited as Cann, "Maybank").

23. Addison T. Cutler, "Labor Legislation in the Thirteen Southern States," *Southern Economic Journal* 7 (Jan. 1941): 297–314.

24. State Planning Board, *Progress Report on State Planning in South Carolina* (Columbia, 1938); Patterson, *New Deal and the States,* 118–20.

25. David L. Carlton, "Unbalanced Growth and Industrialization: The Case of South Carolina," in *Developing Dixie: Modernization in a Traditional Society,* ed. Winfred B. Moore, Jr., Joseph F. Tripp, and Lyon G. Tyler, Jr. (New York: Greenwood Press, 1988), 111–30; Miller, "Palmetto Politician," 17, 29; Jay Bender, "Olin D. Johnston and the Highway Department Controversy," *Proceedings of the South Carolina Historical Association* (1972), 51.

26. D. R. Coker to Neville Bennett, 20 March 1937, David R. Coker Papers, South Caroliniana Library, University of South Carolina (hereafter cited as Coker Papers).

27. Mrs. M. B. Hall to Wil Lou Gray, 5 February 1935, Wil Lou Gray Papers, South Caroliniana Library, University of South Carolina (hereafter cited as Gray Papers).

28. James Miles to Wil Lou Gray, 11 January 1935, Gray Papers.

29. Helen Atkins to Wil Lou Gray, 22 November 1944, Gray Papers.

30. W. W. Ball to H. L. Watson, 25 December 1939, Harry L. Watson Papers, South Caroliniana Library, University of South Carolina (hereafter cited as Harry L. Watson Papers).

31. I. (T.) to Gertrude Maginnis, 29 January 1929, Gray Papers.

32. Charlotte Stevenson to Dear Girls, 1 December 1941, Elizabeth Belser Fuller Papers, South Caroliniana Library, University of South Carolina, Columbia.

33. Department of Labor, *Sixth Annual Report of the Department of Labor of the State of South Carolina, July 1, 1939–June 30, 1940,* 73; William Hays Simpson, *Life in Mill Communities* (Clinton, S.C.: Presbyterian College Press, 1941), 20.

34. William P. Jacobs, *Facts about South Carolina and Her Textile Mills* (N.p.: Jacobs Press, 1937), 13; Department of Labor, *Fifth State Labor Department Report,* in *Annual Reports of the Department of Labor of the State of South Carolina* (Columbia, 1935–1945, 1936–1946), 73. For the year 1935 the state's 235 mills operated 230 days, employed 83,592 workers, paid total wages of $52,126,622 and an average wage of $623.58. Therefore, average daily wages were $2.71; the average number of workers per mill was 356. Computations using 0.88 percent as the profit figure and 25.57 percent as the wage cost yield total profits of approximately $1.79 million and per mill profits of $7,634.

35. Jas. C. Self to Harry Riemer, 29 February 1939, Harry L. Watson Papers.

36. *Sixth State Labor Department Report,* 38–41; *Seventh State Labor Department Report,* 44–51, 62–66; *Eighth State Labor Department Report,* 31–34; *Ninth State Labor Department Report,* 40–43; *Eleventh State Labor Department Report,* 34; Department of Agriculture, Commerce and Industries of the State of South Carolina, *Yearbook of the Department of Agriculture, Commerce and Industries of the State of South Carolina, 1938–1939* (Columbia, 1939), 122–25 (hereafter cited as S.C. Dept. ACI, *Yearbook*). Incidentally, inflation for the four years of 1941 to 1945 totaled only 22 percent. Federal Reserve Bank of Minneapolis, "What Is a Dollar Worth?" http://woodrow.mpls.frb.fed.us/economy/calc/cphihome.html (25 May 1998) (hereafter cited as Minneapolis, "Dollar").

37. *1950 United States Census of Agriculture: North Carolina and South Carolina* (Washington, D.C.: Government Printing Office, 1952), 364–68 (hereafter cited as *1950 Census*); S.C. Dept. ACI, *Yearbook, 1938–1939,* 112, 130; S.C. Dept. ACI, *Yearbook,, 1941,* 19, 20, 25; S.C. Dept. ACI, *Yearbook, 1941–42,* 48, 50, 51, 93; S.C. Dept. ACI, *Yearbook, 1943–1944,* 45–46; S.C. Dept. ACI, *Yearbook, 1945,* 44; S.C. Dept. ACI, *Yearbook, 1946,* 48. On the other hand, tobacco farmers did fare better under the New Deal. The average price in the 1920s was 18.2 cents per pound; the average price during the New Deal, 19.3 cents. At the same time, tobacco prices shot up during the war from 25 cents to 43.9 cents. The average wartime price of 40.8 cents was more than double the average New Deal price of 19.3 cents.

38. *Sixteenth Census of the United States: 1940, Agriculture,* vol. 1, part 3 (Washington, D.C.: Government Printing Office, 1942), 423–25; *1950 Census,* 357.

39. *1950 Census,* 357, 360, 368.

40. Ibid., 358. The average AAA payment of approximately $77 per farmer per year included administrative expenses, which, of course, the farmer would not have received. Nevertheless, agriculturalist David R. Coker of Hartsville was certain that AAA payments were critical to the farmers' well-being. His Coker's Pedigreed Seed Company, a farming, seed breeding, and seed merchandising operation that depended on farmers with disposable income, was so unprofitable from 1928 to 1933 that it had to raise $300,000 through the sale of $150,000 in stock and

$150,000 in notes in order to avoid bankruptcy. By contrast, the combination of better prices and AAA payments made the years 1934 to 1937 so profitable that the company was able to retire its $150,000 debt and to show a half-year profit of $50,000 in June 1937. David R. Coker to James F. Byrnes, 2 June 1937, Coker Papers.

41. Cotton production began to decline long before the New Deal. Farmers planted 2.63 million acres in 1920, 2 million acres in 1925, and 1.97 million acres in 1930. *United States Census of Agriculture: 1954, Volume 1, Part 16, North Carolina and South Carolina* (Washington, D.C.: Government Printing Office, 1956), 326 (hereafter cited as *Census of Agriculture: 1954*).

42. Charles F. Kovacik and John J. Winberry, *South Carolina: The Making of a Landscape* (Columbia: University of South Carolina Press, 1987), 160–64.

43. Roger Biles, *The South and the New Deal* (Lexington: University of Kentucky Press, 1994), 36; Pete Daniel, "The New Deal, Southern Agriculture, and Economic Change," in *The New Deal and the South,* ed. James C. Cobb and Michael Namorato (Jackson: University Press of Mississippi, 1984), 37–61.

44. In terms of proportion, tenancy did begin to decline in the 1930s, particularly after 1936 when changes in the administration of New Deal programs encouraged a shift from tenancy to wage labor. Nevertheless, this decline was greater after World War II when South Carolina agriculture mechanized. For example, the proportion of farms operated by tenants declined 14 percent during the 1930s but more than 27 percent in the period 1945 to 1954. *Census of Agriculture: 1954,* 326.

45. *Census of Agriculture: 1954,* 319.

46. S.C. Dept. ACI, *Yearbook, 1932,* 12; S.C. Dept. ACI, *Yearbook, 1934–1935,* 16–17; S.C. Dept. ACI, *Yearbook, 1935–1936,* 13, 15, 19–20, 46; S.C. Dept. ACI, *Yearbook, 1938–1939,* 9, 65, 110, 132, 134, 137–39, 142, 148; S.C. Dept. ACI, *Yearbook, 1940–1941,* 91.

47. Ibid.; *Census of Agriculture: 1954,* 364; *United States Census of Agriculture: 1978, Part 40, South Carolina* (Washington, D.C.: Government Printing Office, 1980), 17.

48. Kovacik and Winberry, *South Carolina Landscape,* 126; *1950 Census,* 357.

49. D. R. Coker to D. S. Freeman, 20 September 1935, Coker Papers.

50. *Una News Review,* 14 Apr. 1939, 2.

51. See John W. Califf to Frank C. Walker, 19 June 1934, National Emergency Council Records, National Archives Branch, Federal Record Center, Suitland, Md., RG 44, Box 437.

52. James A. Hoyt to Harry L. Watson, 28 July 1939, Harry L. Watson papers.

53. Miller, "Palmetto Politician," 2–20.

54. Walter J. Fraser, Jr., *Charleston! Charleston! The History of a Southern City* (Columbia: University of South Carolina Press, 1989), 381–83; Cann, "Maybank," 85–95.

55. Fraser, *Charleston,* 382; Cann, "Maybank," 88, 127.

56. Hazel Iles Brochman, Report of Richland County Illiteracy Program, 15 January to 15 April 1940, Gray Papers.

57. Ibid.

58. Pinckney, "Business and Economic Report," 30 June 1939.

59. Handwritten report titled "FERA Adult Education Evaluation for Saluda, 1935," Gray Papers; Handwritten report titled "FERA Adult Education Evaluation for Clarendon, Colleton, and Darlington, 1935," Gray Papers; Typescript titled "Evaluation of Adult Education in Florence, 1937," Gray Papers.

60. Simon, "Fabric," 163.

61. Anabelle T. Harris, "An Incident [in] the Recruiting Campaign," 1935, Gray Papers; Florence Gainey, "Something That Happened While on My Trip of Recruiting Work," 1935, Gray Papers.

62. *Una News Review,* 4 Nov. 1938, 2.

63. Ibid., 5 Mar. 1937, 5.

64. James A. Hoyt to W. W. Ball, 14 December 1938, Fitz Hugh McMaster Papers, South Caroliniana Library, University of South Carolina, Columbia.

65. 7 October 1938, 2.

66. James F. Miles to Eleanor Roosevelt, circa 1937, James F. Miles Papers, South Caroliniana Library, University of South Carolina, Columbia.

67. *Columbia State,* 31 Dec. 1933, 1, 7-A; James M. Eleazer, interview by the author, Clemson, S.C., 2 March 1971.

68. Edward Kohn, *South Carolina on Parade,* 7 April 1935, Gray Papers; The Road Is Open Again. By: Sammy Fain and Irving Kahal © 1933 (renewed) Warner Bros. Inc. All rights reserved. Used by permission. Warner Bros. Publications U.S. Inc., Miami, FL 33014.

BIBLIOGRAPHY

MANUSCRIPT COLLECTIONS

Duke University Library, Durham, N.C.

William Watts Ball Papers
John P. Grace Papers
John Jackson McSwain Papers
C. C. Wyche Papers

National Archives, Washington, D.C.

National Recovery Administration Records (RG 9)
Civilian Conservation Corps Records (RG 35)
Social Security Records (RG 47)
Civil Works Administration Records (RG 69)
Federal Emergency Relief Administration Records (RG 69)
Works Progress Administration Records (RG 69)
Farmers Home Administration Records (RG 96)
National Youth Administration Records (RG 119)
Public Works Administration Records (RG 135)
Agricultural Adjustment Administration Records (RG 145)

National Archives Branch, Federal Record Center, Suitland, Md.

National Emergency Council Records (RG 44)
Public Housing Administration Records (RG 196)

Robert M. Cooper Library, Clemson University, Clemson, S.C.

Edgar A. Brown Papers
James Francis Byrnes Papers
Asbury F. Lever Papers

South Carolina Historical Society, Charleston, S.C.

Civilian Conservation Corps Newsletters
Johnson Hagood Papers
Thomas P. Stoney Papers
Thomas R. Waring Papers

South Carolina Department of Archives and History, Columbia

Ibra C. Blackwood Papers

South Caroliniana Library, University of South Carolina, Columbia

American Civil Liberties Union Papers (1932–1940)
Solomon Blatt Papers
Olin W. Bundrick Papers
Clifton Manufacturing Company Papers
David R. Coker Papers
James E. Dickson Papers
Duncan, Kinard, Sanders, and Tucker Family Papers
Elizabeth Belser Fuller Papers
Allard H. Gasque Papers
Wil Lou Gray Papers
Butler B. Hare Papers
W. H. Hare Papers
James A. Hoyt Papers
Olin D. Johnston Papers
Wyndham Manning Papers
John H. McCray Papers
Fitz Hugh McMaster Papers
John L. McMillan Papers
James F. Miles Papers
Stanley F. Morse Papers
Robert Quillen Papers
James P. Richards Papers
Modjeska Monteith Simkins Papers
Ellison D. Smith Papers
Mendel L. Smith Papers
Leah Townshend Papers
Watson Family Papers
Harry L. Watson Papers
Works Progress Administration Collection

Wilson Library, University of North Carolina at Chapel Hill

Bass, Jack. Transcript of interview with J. Drake Edens, 13 February 1974. Southern Oral History Program, Southern Historical Collection

NEWSPAPERS

Bamberg County Times
Barnwell People-Sentinel

Bennettsville Pee Dee Advocate
Bishopville Lee County Messenger
Camden Wateree Messenger
Charleston News and Courier
Chester News
Chester Reporter
Clinton Chronicle
Columbia Carolina Free Press
Columbia Palmetto Leader
Columbia State
Conway Horry Herald
Edgefield Advertiser
Greenville Piedmont
Greenwood Index Journal
Hartsville Messenger
Lexington Dispatch News
Manning Times
Marion Star
New York Times
Saluda Standard
Spartanburg Herald
Spartanburg Herald-Journal
Una News Review
Walhalla Keowee Courier
Walterboro Press and Standard
Washington Herald
Winnsboro News and Herald

PUBLIC DOCUMENTS: SOUTH CAROLINA

Blackwood, I. C. *Annual Messages of I. C. Blackwood, Governor.* Columbia, 1933–1934.

Clemson Agricultural College. *Extension Work in South Carolina.* Clemson, 1935–1939.

Daniel, Thomas H. *Annual Reports of the State Banking Department of South Carolina.* Columbia, 1934–1939.

Department of Agriculture, Commerce and Industries. *Yearbook of the Department of Agriculture, Commerce and Industries of the State of South Carolina.* Columbia, 1933–1939.

Department of Labor. *Annual Reports of the Department of Labor of the State of South Carolina.* Columbia, 1936–1946.

House of Representatives. *Journal of the House of Representatives of the State of South Carolina.* Columbia, 1934, 1935, 1937.

Johnston, Olin D., Governor of South Carolina. *Annual Messages of Olin D. Johnston, Governor.* Columbia, 1935–1939.

Reports of the Comptroller General of South Carolina. Columbia, 1929–1940.

South Carolina General Assembly. *Acts and Joint Resolutions of the General Assembly of the State of South Carolina.* Columbia, 1933–1938.

South Carolina Public Welfare Statistics. Columbia, 1938.

State Department of Public Welfare. *Annual Reports of the State Department of Public Welfare.* Columbia, 1937–1940.

State Highway Department. *Annual Reports of the South Carolina State Highway Department.* Columbia, 1929–1939.

State Planning Board. *Progress Report on State Planning in South Carolina.* Columbia, 1938.

Works Progress Administration of South Carolina. *Research and Records Work in South Carolina.* Columbia, 1940.

———. *A Short Synopsis of the Projects in the Community Service Section of the Professional and Service Division.* Columbia, 1940.

PUBLIC DOCUMENTS: UNITED STATES

Agricultural Adjustment. A report of administration of the *Agricultural Adjustment Act, May 1933 to February 1934.* Washington, D.C.: Government Printing Office, 1934.

———. A report of administration of the *Agricultural Adjustment Act, 1934.* Washington, D.C.: Government Printing Office, 1934.

———. A report of administration of the *Agricultural Adjustment Act, 1933 through 1935.* Washington, D.C.: Government Printing Office, 1935.

———. A report of administration of the *Agricultural Adjustment Act, 1935.* Washington, D.C.: Government Printing Office, 1935.

———. A report of administration of the *Agricultural Adjustment Act, 1936.* Washington, D.C.: Government Printing Office, 1936.

———. A report of administration of the *Agricultural Adjustment Act, 1937–1938.* Washington, D.C.: Government Printing Office, 1938.

———. A report of administration of the *Agricultural Adjustment Act, 1938–1939.* Washington, D.C.: Government Printing Office, 1939.

———. A report of administration of the *Agricultural Adjustment Act, 1939.* Washington, D.C.: Government Printing Office, 1939.

———. A report of administration of the *Agricultural Conservation Act, 1936.* Washington, D.C.: Government Printing Office, 1936.

———. A report of administration of the *Agricultural Conservation Act, 1937.* Washington, D.C.: Government Printing Office, 1937.

Biographical Directory of the United States Congress: 1744–1989. Washington, D.C.: Government Printing Office, 1989.

Biographical Dictionary of the American Congress: 1774–1971. Washington, D.C.: Government Printing Office, 1971.

Burns, Arthur E., and Edward A. Williams. *A Survey of Relief and Security Programs.* Washington: Government Printing Office, 1938.

Comptroller of the Currency. *Annual Report of the Comptroller of the Currency, 1933.* Washington, D.C.: Government Printing Office, 1933.

————. *Annual Report of the Comptroller of the Currency, 1934.* Washington, D.C.: Government Printing Office, 1934.

Congress. Senate. *Federal, State, and Local Government Fiscal Relations.* Senate Doc. 69. 78th Cong., 1st sess., 1943.

Congressional Record. Washington, D.C., 1933–1939.

Duke Power Company et al. v. Greenwood County et al. 82 Lawyers Edition 381–82.

Farm Credit Administration. *Annual Reports of the Farm Credit Administration.* Washington, D.C.: Government Printing Office, 1933–1938.

————. *Annual Reports of the Farm Credit Administration.* Washington, D.C.: Government Printing Office, 1934–1939.

Farm Security Administration. *Report of the Administration of the Farm Security Administration: 1941.* Washington, D.C.: Government Printing Office, 1941.

Federal Deposit Insurance Corporation. *Annual Reports of the Federal Deposit Insurance Corporation.* 1934–1938. N.p., n.d.

Federal Emergency Relief Administration. *Federal Emergency Relief Administration: Unemployment Relief Census, October 1933,* no. 1, 2. Washington, D.C.: Government Printing Office, 1934.

————. *Monthly Report of the Federal Emergency Relief Administration: November 1 through November 30, 1935.* Washington, D.C.: Government Printing Office, 1936.

————. *Monthly Reports of the Federal Emergency Relief Administration* (1933–1936). Washington, D.C.: Government Printing Office, 1934–1936.

————. *Final Statistical Report of the Federal Emergency Relief Administration.* 1942.

Fifteenth Census of the United States, 1930. Washington, D.C., Government Printing Office, 1932.

Gibbes v. Zimmerman. 54 Sup. Ct. 140–42.

————. *Statistical Summary of Emergency Relief Activities, January 1933 through December 1935.* Washington, D.C.: Government Printing Office, 1936.

Hauser, Philip M. *Workers on Relief in the United States in March 1935.* 2 vols. Washington, D.C.: Government Printing Office, 1938.

Historical Statistics of the United States: Colonial Times to 1970. Washington, D.C., Government Printing Office, 1976.

Labor Relations Reference Manual. Washington, D.C.: Bureau of National Affairs, 1937.

National Labor Relations Board. *Decisions and Orders of the National Labor Relations Board.* Washington, D.C.: Government Printing Office, 1936–1943.

——. *First Annual Report of the National Labor Relations Board for the Fiscal Year Ended June 30, 1936.* Washington, D.C.: Government Printing Office, 1936.

Resettlement Administration. *First Annual Report: Resettlement Administration,* Washington, D.C.: Government Printing Office, 1936.

National Appraisal Committee. *U.S. Community Improvement Appraisal. A Report on the Work Program of the Works Progress Administration.* Washington, D.C.: Works Progress Administration, 1939.

1950 United States Census of Agriculture: North Carolina and South Carolina. Washington, D.C.: Government Printing Office, 1952.

Public Works Administration. *America Builds: The Record of the PWA.* Washington, D.C.: Government Printing Office, 1939.

Public Works Administration Housing Division. *Urban Housing: The Story of the PWA Housing Division, 1933–1936.* Washington, D.C.: Government Printing Office, 1936.

Works Progress Administration. *Report on Progress of the WPA Program.* Washington, D.C.: Government Printing Office 1939.

Rural Electrification Administration. *Reports of the Rural Electrification Administration.* Washington, D.C.: Government Printing Office, 1937–1938.

Sixteenth Census of the United States: 1940, Agriculture, vol. 1, part 3. Washington, D.C.: Government Printing Office, 1942.

United States Census of Agriculture: 1954, Volume 1, Part 16, North Carolina and South Carolina. Washington, D.C.: Government Printing Office, 1956.

United States Census of Agriculture: 1978. Washington, D.C.: Government Printing Office, 1980.

Williams, Edward A. *Work, Relief and Security.* Washington, D.C.: Government Printing Office, 1941.

Work Projects Administration. *Final Report on WPA Programs, 1935–1943.* Washington, D.C.: Government Printing Office, 1947.

Department of Agriculture. *Yearbook of Agriculture.* Washington, D.C.: Government Printing Office, 1934–1939.

MINUTES AND PROCEEDINGS

Laporte, Ewing. *Official Record of the Proceedings of the Democratic National Convention, 1932.* N.p., n.d.

Photocopy of selected portions of the minutes of the annual meetings of the Cotton Manufacturers Association of South Carolina (1933, 1936, 1937). In possession of the Cotton Manufacturers Association of South Carolina, Columbia, South Carolina.

Proceedings: Annual Conventions, American Cotton Manufacturers Association. N.p., 1933–1938.

Report of Proceedings of the Annual Conventions of the South Carolina Bankers Association. Columbia: R. L. Bryan Company, 1933–1939.

University of South Carolina. Minutes of the meetings of the Board of Trustees of the University of South Carolina (1938–1940). In possession of the University of South Carolina, Columbia.

INTERVIEWS

All interviews were conducted by the author.

Altman, Roy. Telephone interview. Okatie, S.C., 8 February 1999.

Bailey, Charles Bruce. Telephone interview. Columbia, S.C., 25 January 1972.

Belton, Mr. and Mrs. Dock. Ridgeway, S.C., 28 January 2000.

Blatt, Solomon. Columbia, S.C. 19 January 1972.

Bloodworth, Louise. Telephone interview. Batesburg, S.C., 7 May 1999.

Bowie, George, Jr. Telephone interview. Pickens County, S.C., 7 May 1999.

Boylston, William. Telephone interview. West Columbia, S.C., 7 May 1999.

Browne, Wilton M. Telephone interview. McCormick, S.C., 7 May 1999.

Cain, Frank E., Jr. Telephone interview. Bennettsville, S.C., 12 February 1999.

Dewitt, Ezra. Telephone interview. Rock Hill, S.C., 11 February 1999.

Eleazer, James M. Clemson, S.C., 2 March 1971.

Forest, Mrs. Saluda D. Telephone interview. Saluda, S.C., 10 February 1999.

Fulmer, Levi Tillman. Telephone interview. Graniteville, S.C., 8 February 1999.

Gettys, B. W. Telephone interview. West Columbia, S.C., 10 February 1999.

Gibbs, Carl. Telephone interview. Wellford, S.C., 12 February 1999.

Hayes, Elizabeth M. Telephone interview. Latta, S.C., 10 February 1999.

Hembree, Wilburn. Telephone interview. Spartanburg, S.C., 8 February 1999.

Jamison, Ellison E. Telephone interview. Walhalla, S.C., 11 February 1999.

Kirkland, E. T. Columbia, S.C., 5 August 1971.

Mahon, Elizabeth. Telephone interview. Greenville, S.C., 25 August 1997.

Sapp, Joseph. Columbia, S.C., 7 August 1970.

Simkins, Modjeska Monteith. Telephone interview. Columbia, S.C., 25 January 1972.

Simons, Allison P. Telephone interview. Columbia, S.C., 10 February 1999.

Whitaker, Eunice H. Telephone interview. Batesburg, S.C., 11 February 1999.

Wilkerson, Paul. Telephone interview. Seneca, S.C., 11 February 1999.

Woodson, Julia. Telephone interview. Liberty, S.C., 17 February 1999.

UNPUBLISHED MANUSCRIPTS

Aba-Mecha, Barbara Woods. "Black Woman Activist in Twentieth Century South Carolina: Modjeska Monteith Simkins." Ph.D. diss., Emory University, 1978.

Belser, Clinch Heyward. "Banking in South Carolina, 1910–1940." Master's thesis, University of South Carolina, 1940.

Busbee, Cyril B. "Farm Tenancy in South Carolina." Master's thesis, University of South Carolina, 1938.

Cann, Marvin Leigh. "Burnet Rhett Maybank and the New Deal in South Carolina, 1931–1941." Ph.D. diss., University of North Carolina, 1967.

Cann, Mary Katherine Davis. "The Morning After: South Carolina in the Jazz Age." Ph.D. diss., University of South Carolina, 1984.

Carpenter, JoAnn Deakin. "Olin D. Johnston, the New Deal, and the Politics of Class in South Carolina, 1934–1938." Ph.D.diss., Emory University, 1987.

Copp, Roberta V. "South Carolina's Historic Records Survey, 1935–1942," Master's thesis, University of South Carolina, 1988.

Ellenberg, Henry Cooper. "The Congress of Industrial Organization in South Carolina, 1938–1945." Master's thesis, University of South Carolina, 1951.

Farmer, James O., Jr. "The End of the White Primary in South Carolina: A Southern State's Fight to Keep Its Politics White." Master's thesis, University of South Carolina, 1969.

Ferrell, Henry C., Jr. "John Jackson McSwain: A Study in Political Technique." Master's thesis, Duke University, 1957.

Garrison, Joseph Yates. "Paul Revere Christopher: Southern Labor Leader, 1910–1974." Ph.D. diss., Georgia State University, 1976.

Gutheim, Frederick A. "A Survey of the South Carolina Emergency Relief Administration." Federal Emergency Relief Administration Records. RG 69. National Archives, Washington, D.C.

Hanckel, William Henry. "The Preservation Movement in Charleston, 1920–1962." Master's thesis, University of South Carolina, 1962.

Hamer, Fritz P. "A Southern City Enters the Twentieth Century: Charleston, Its Navy Yard, and World War II, 1940–1948." Ph.D. diss., University of South Carolina, 1998.

Heinemann, Ronald Lynton. "Depression and New Deal in Virginia." Ph.D. diss., University of Virginia, 1968.

Hemingway, Theodore. "Beneath the Yoke of Bondage: A History of Black Folks in South Carolina, 1900–1940." Ph.D. diss., University of South Carolina, 1976.

Hiott, William David. "New Deal Resettlement in South Carolina." Master's thesis, University of South Carolina, 1986.

Hodges, James A. "The New Deal Labor Policy and the Southern Cotton Textile Industry, 1933–1941" Ph.D. diss., Vanderbilt University, 1963.

Irons, Janet C. "Testing the New Deal: The General Textile Strike of 1934." Ph.D. diss., Duke University, 1988.

Kennedy, John Wesley. "The General Strike in the Textile Industry, September 1934." Master's thesis, Duke University, 1947.

———. "A History of the Textile Workers Union of America, C.I.O." Ph.D. diss., University of North Carolina, 1950.

Lee, Joseph Edward. "'America Comes First with Me': The Political Career of James P. Richards, 1932–1957." Ph.D. diss., University of South Carolina, 1987.

Lesesne, Henry Herbert. "Opposition to the New Deal in South Carolina, 1933–1936." Master's thesis, University of South Carolina, 1995.

Lofton, Paul S. "A Social and Economic History of Columbia, South Carolina, during the Great Depression, 1929–1940." Ph.D. diss., University of Texas, Austin, 1977.

Martin, Robert Earl. "Negro-White Participation in the AAA Cotton and Tobacco Referenda in North and South Carolina: A Study of Differential Voting and Attitudes in Selected Areas." Ph.D. diss., University of Chicago, 1947.

McKissick, J. Rion et al. Report of the State [WPA] Appraisal Committee. Works Progress Administration Records. RG 69. National Archives, Washington, D.C.

Miller, Anthony Barry. "Palmetto Politician: The Early Political Career of Olin D. Johnston, 1896–1945." Ph.D. diss., University of North Carolina, 1976.

Minton, John Dean. "The New Deal in Tennessee, 1932–1938." Ph.D. diss., Vanderbilt University, 1959.

Moore, Winfred Bobo. "New South Statesman: The Political Career of James Francis Byrnes." Ph.D. diss., Duke University, 1975.

Office of Government Records. "Activities and Accomplishments of Assistance Agencies in South Carolina." National Emergency Council Records. RG 44. Federal Record Center, Suitland, Maryland.

———. "South Carolina: Report Number 10." National Emergency Council Records. RG 44. Federal Record Center, Suitland, Maryland.

———. "South Carolina: Report Number 10, 1940 Supplement." National Emergency Council Records. RG 44. Federal Record Center, Suitland, Maryland.

Patenaude, Lionel V. "The New Deal and Texas." Ph.D. diss., University of Texas, 1953.

Pinckney, Lawrence M. "Business and Economic Report: South Carolina, February 1940." Columbia, S.C.: Works Progress Administration, 1940.

———. "Federal Departments and Agencies in South Carolina." Columbia, S.C.: National Emergency Council, 20 Dec. 1935.

Reading, Don C. "A Statistical Analysis of New Deal Economic Programs in the Forty-Eight States." Ph.D. diss., Utah State University, 1972.

Richards, Miles S. "Osceola E. McKaine and the Struggle for Black Civil Rights: 1917–1946." Ph. D. diss., University of South Carolina, 1994.

Simon, Bryant. "A Fabric of Defeat: The Politics of South Carolina Textile Workers in State and Nation, 1920–1938." Ph.D. diss., University of North Carolina, 1992.

Stroup, Rodger E. "The Kingfish Solicits the Youth." Seminar paper for History 858, University of South Carolina, 13 Aug. 1971. In possession of its author, Columbia, S.C.

Suttles, William. "The History of the South Carolina State Highway Department." Typescript in possession of its author, Columbia, S.C.

Thompson, William Wilker, Jr. "A Managerial History of a Cotton Textile Firm: Spartan Mills, 1888–1958." Ph.D. diss., University of Alabama, 1960.

ESSAYS, ARTICLES, AND PAMPHLETS

Aba-Mecha, Barbara W. "South Carolina Conference of NAACP: Origin and Major Accomplishments, 1939–1954." *Proceedings of the South Carolina Historical Association* (1981): 1–21.

Alsop, Joseph. "Sly and Able." *Saturday Evening Post,* 20 July 1940, 16, 19, 21, 41–42, 44–45.

American Liberty League. "The Story of an Honest Man." Doc. no. 107, March 1936, Washington, D.C. American Liberty League, 1936.

Bender, Jay. "Olin D. Johnston and the Highway Department Controversy." *Proceedings of the South Carolina Historical Association, 1972.* Anderson: South Carolina Historical Association, 1972. 39–54.

Birnie, Cassandra Maxwell. "Race and Politics in Georgia and South Carolina." *Phylon* 13 (Sept. 1952): 236–44.

Boggs, Doyle W. "Charleston Politics, 1900–1930: An Overview." *Proceedings of the South Carolina Historical Association, 1979.* Aiken: South Carolina Historical Association, 1979. 1–13.

Cann, Marvin L. "Burnet Maybank and Charleston Politics in the New Deal Era." *Proceedings of the South Carolina Historical Association, 1970.* Columbia: South Carolina Historical Association, 1970. 39–48.

———. "The End of a Political Myth: The South Carolina Gubernatorial Campaign of 1938." *South Carolina Historical Magazine* 82 (July 1971): 139–49.

Carlton, David L. "Unbalanced Growth and Industrialization: The Case of South Carolina." In *Developing Dixie: Modernization in a Traditional Society.* Ed. by Winfred B. Moore, Jr., Joseph F. Tripp, and Lyon G. Tyler, Jr., 111–30. New York: Greenwood Press, 1988.

"Charleston Opens Historic Playhouse with Historic Play." *Architectural Record* 83, no. 1 (Jan. 1938): 20–25.

Curtis, William R. "The Development of Unemployment Insurance in the South." *Southern Economic Journal* 15 (July 1948): 43–53.

Cutler, Addison T. "Labor Legislation in the Thirteen Southern States." *Southern Economic Journal* 7 (Jan. 1941): 297–314.

DeVyver, Frank T. "The Present Status of Labor Unions in the South." *Southern Economic Journal* 5 (April 1939): 485–98.

———. "The President Status of Labor Unions in the South—1948." *Southern Economic Journal* 16 (July 1949): 1–22.

Graham, Grace. "Negro Education Progresses in South Carolina." *Social Forces* 30 (May 1954): 429–438.

Hoffman, Edwin D. "The Genesis of the Modern Movement for Equal Rights in South Carolina, 1930–1939." *Journal of Negro History* 44 (July 1959): 346–70.

Hollis, Daniel Walker. "Cole L. Blease and the Senatorial Campaign of 1924." In *Proceedings of the South Carolina Historical Association, 1978*. Lancaster: South Carolina Historical Association, 1978. 53–68.

———. "Coleman Livingston Blease." In *Dictionary of American Biography: Supplement Three,*77–78. New York: Charles Scribner's Sons, 1973.

———. "Cotton Ed Smith—Showman or Statesman?" *South Carolina Historical Magazine* 71 (Oct. 1970): 235–56.

Janeway, Eliot. "Jimmy Brynes." *Life* 14 (4 Jan. 1943): 63–71.

"Judge Waring on the Civil Rights Issue." *Nation* 174 (1 June 1952): 540–41.

Leemhuis, Roger P. "Olin Johnston Runs for the Senate: 1938–1962." *Proceedings of the South Carolina Historical Association, 1986*. Aiken: South Carolina Historical Association, 1986. 57–69.

Lofton, Paul. "The Columbia Black Community in the 1930s." *Proceedings of the South Carolina Historical Association, 1984*. Aiken: South Carolina Historical Association, 1984. 86–95.

Marchant, T. M. "Cotton Manufacturers' Problems." *Manufacturers Record* 103 (Jan. 1934), 19.

Martin, Harold H., and Gault, Harper. "The Gay Banker of Rock Hill." *Saturday Evening Post,* 219 (23 November 1946), pp. 9–11, 151–52.

Moloney, John F. "Some Effects of the Federal Fair Labor Standards Act upon Southern Industry." *Southern Economic Journal* 9 (July 1942): 15–23.

Moore, Winfred B., Jr. "' Soul of the South': James F. Byrnes and the Racial Issue in American Politics, 1911–1941." *Proceedings of the South Carolina Historical Association, 1978*. Lancaster: South Carolina Historical Association, 1978. 42–52.

Patterson, James T. "A Conservative Coalition Forms in Congress, 1933–1939." *Journal of American History* 52 (Mar. 1966): 757–72.

———. "The New Deal and the States." *American Historical Review* 73 (October 1967): 70–84.

Poole, Bernard L. "The Presidential Election of 1928 in South Carolina." *Proceedings of the South Carolina Historical Association, 1954*. Columbia: South Carolina Historical Association, 1954. 5–16.

Salmond, John A. "The Civilian Conservation Corps and the Negro." *Journal of American History* 52 (June 1965): 75–88.

Simkins, Francis Butler. "New Viewpoints of Southern Reconstruction." *Journal of Southern History* 5 (Feb. 1939): 49–61.

Sloan, George A. "First Flight of the Blue Eagle: The Cotton Textile Code in Operation." *Atlantic Monthly* 153 (Mar. 1934): 321–25.

Smith, Selden K. "'Cotton Ed' Smith's Response to Economic Adversity." *Proceedings of the South Carolina Historical Association, 1971*. Clinton: South Carolina Historical Association, 1971. 16–23.

Spencer, Thomas T. "Daniel C. Roper and the 1932 Presidential Campaign." *South Carolina Historical Magazine* 85 (Jan. 1984): 22–32.

Steiner, W. H. "South Carolina Cash Depositories." *Southern Economic Journal* 4 (July 1937): 28–37.

Terrill, Thomas E. "'No Union for Me': Southern Textile Workers and Organized Labor." In *The Meaning of South Carolina History: Essays in Honor of George C. Rogers, Jr.,* edited by David R. Chesnutt and Clyde N. Wilson, 202–13. Columbia: University of South Carolina Press, 1991.

Weaver, John C. "Lawyers, Lodges, and Kinfolk: The Workings of a South Carolina Political Organization, 1920–1936." *South Carolina Historical Magazine* 78 (Oct. 1977): 272–85.

PERIODICAL PUBLICATIONS

Labor Information Bulletin (1935–1939)
Manufacturers Record (1933–1939)
Monthly Labor Review (1933–1939)
South Carolina Newsview (1939)
South Carolina Social Welfare (1936)
Textile World (1933–1939)
Time (1933–1939)
Works Progress Administration of South Carolina, *Work News,* February 1937

BOOKS

Allen, Frederick Lewis. *The Lords of Creation.* New York: Harper and Brothers, 1935.

Badger, Anthony J. *North Carolina and the New Deal.* Raleigh: Department of Cultural Resources, 1981.

Bellush, Bernard. *The Failure of the NRA.* New York: W. W. Norton and Co., 1975.

Benedict, Murray R. *Farm Policies of the United States, 1790–1950.* New York: The Twentieth Century Fund, 1953.

Biles, Roger. *The South and the New Deal.* Lexington: University of Kentucky Press, 1994.

Bland, Sidney R. *Preserving Charleston's Past, Shaping Its Future: The Life and Times of Susan Pringle Frost.* Columbia: University of South Carolina Press, 1999.

Blicksilver, Jack M. *Cotton Manufacturing in the Southeast: An Historical Analysis.* Atlanta: Georgia State College of Business Administration, 1959.

Botkin, B. A. *Sidewalks of America.* Indianapolis: Bobbs-Merrill Company, 1954.

Bunche, Ralph J. *The Political Status of the Negro in the Age of FDR.* Chicago: University of Chicago Press, 1973.

Byars, Alvin W. *Olympia Pacific: The Way It Was, 1895–1970.* N.p.: Privately printed, 1981.

Byrnes, James F. *All in One Lifetime.* New York: Harper and Brothers, 1958.

Carlton, David L. *Mill and Town in South Carolina, 1880–1920.* Baton Rouge: Louisiana State University Press, 1982.

Cash, W. J. *The Mind of the South.* New York: Alfred A. Knopf, 1941.

Cauthen, John K. *Speaker Blatt: His Challenges Were Greater.* Columbia, S.C.: R. L. Bryan Co., 1965.

Clark, Thomas D. *The Emerging South,* 2d. ed. New York: Oxford University Press, 1968.

Cobb, James C., and Namorato, Michael V. *The New Deal and the South.* Jackson: University Press of Mississippi, 1984.

Congressional Quarterly's Guide to U.S. Elections, 3d. ed. Washington, D.C.: Congressional Quarterly, Inc., 1994.

Cushman, Robert F., ed. *Cases in Constitutional Law,* 4th ed. Englewood Cliffs: Prentice-Hall, Inc., 1975.

Hall, Jacquelyn Dowd et al. *Like a Family: The Making of a Southern Cotton Mill World.* Chapel Hill: University of North Carolina Press, 1987.

Edgar, Walter. *History of Santee Cooper: 1934–1984.* Columbia, S.C.: R. L. Bryan Co., 1984.

———. *South Carolina: A History.* Columbia: University of South Carolina Press, 1998.

Egerton, John. *Speak Now against the Day.* New York: Alfred A. Knopf, 1994.

Ezell, John Samuel. *The South since 1865.* New York: The Macmillan Co., 1963.

Farley, James A. *Behind the Ballots.* New York: Harcourt Brace and Co., 1938.

———. *Jim Farley's Story: The Roosevelt Years.* New York: McGraw, Hill Book Co., 1948.

Fite, Gilbert C. *American Agriculture and Farm Policy since 1900.* Washington, D.C.: The American Historical Association, Service Center for Teachers of History, 1964.

———. *Cotton Fields No More: Southern Agriculture, 1865–1890.* Lexington: University of Kentucky Press, 1984.

Fraser, Walter J., Jr. *Charleston! Charleston! The History of a Southern City.* Columbia: University of South Carolina Press, 1989.

Freidel, Frank. *F.D.R. and the South.* Baton Rouge: Louisiana State University Press, 1965.

———. *Franklin D. Roosevelt: The Triumph.* Boston: Little, Brown, and Co., 1956.

Galenson, Walter. *The CIO Challenge to the AFL.* Cambridge: Harvard University Press, 1960.

Gilman, Glenn. *Human Relations in the Industrial Southeast.* Chapel Hill: University of North Carolina Press, 1956.

Graydon, Clint T. *In Memoriam: Claud N. Sapp, 1886–1947.* N.p., n.d.

Hargrove, Erwin C., and Paul K. Conkin. *TVA: Fifty Years of Grass-Roots Bureaucracy.* Urbana: University of Illinois Press, 1983.

Hawley, Ellis W. *The New Deal and the Problem of Monopoly.* Princeton: Princeton University Press, 1966.

Heinemann, Ronald L. *Depression and New Deal in Virginia: The Enduring Dominion.* Charlottesville: University Press of Virginia, 1983.

Hemphill, J. C., ed. *Men of Mark in South Carolina: Ideals of American Life: A Collection of Biographies of Leading Men of the State.* 4 vols. Washington, D.C.: Men of Mark Publishing Company, 1907–9.

Hesseltine, William B., and David L. Smiley. *The South in American History,* 2d ed. Englewood Cliffs, N.J.: Prentice-Hall, Inc., 1960.

Hicks, John D. *Republican Ascendancy, 1921–1933.* Harper Torchbooks. New York: Harper and Row, 1960.

Hodges, James A. *New Deal Labor Policy and the South Cotton Textile Industry: 1933–1941.* Knoxville: University of Tennessee Press, 1986.

Hofstadter, Richard. *The American Political Tradition and the Men Who Made It.* New York: A. A. Knopf, 1948. Reprint, with a foreword by Christopher Lasch, New York: Vintage Books, 1974.

Hubbard, Preston J. *Origins of the TVA: The Muscle Shoals Controversy, 1920–1932.* Nashville: Vanderbilt University Press, 1961.

Huff, Archie Vernon, Jr. *Greenville: The History of the City and County in the South Carolina Piedmont.* Columbia: University of South Carolina Press, 1995.

Hull, Cordell. *The Memoirs of Cordell Hull.* 2 vols. New York: The Macmillan Co., 1948.

Huss, John E. *Senator for the South: A Biography of Olin D. Johnston.* Garden City, N.Y.: Doubleday and Co., 1961.

Ickes, Harold. *Back to Work: The Story of the PWA.* New York: The Macmillan Co., 1935.

———. *The Secret Diary of Harold Ickes.* 3 vols. New York: Simon and Schuster, 1953.

Isakoff, Jack F. *The Public Works Administration.* Urbana: University of Illinois Press, 1938.

Jacobs, William P. *Facts about South Carolina and Her Textile Mills.* N.p.: Jacobs Press, 1937.

Jordan, Frank E., Jr. *The Primary State.* N.p., n.d.

Key, V. O., Jr. *Southern Politics in State and Nation.* New York: Alfred A. Knopf, 1949.

Kovacik, Charles F., and John J. Winberry. *South Carolina: The Making of a Landscape.* Columbia: University of South Carolina Press, 1987.

Lahne, Herbert J. *The Cotton Mill Worker.* New York: Farrar and Rinehart, 1944.

Lander, Ernest M., Jr. *A History of South Carolina.* Chapel Hill: University of North Carolina Press, 1960.

Lander, Ernest M., Jr., and Ackerman, Robert K. *Perspectives in South Carolina History: The First 300 Years.* Columbia: University of South Carolina Press, 1973.

Leuchtenburg, William E. *Franklin D. Roosevelt and the New Deal.* Harper Torchbooks. New York: Harper and Row, 1963.

Lewinson, Paul. *Race, Class and Party: A History of Negro Suffrage and White Politics in the South.* London, New York: 1932. Reprint, New York: Russell and Russell, 1963.

Lorwin, Lewis L., and Arthur Wubnig. *Labor Relations Boards.* Washington, D.C.: The Brookings Institution, 1935.

Mays, Benjamin E. *Born to Rebel.* New York: Charles Scribner's Sons, 1971.

Mencken, H. L. *Making a President: A Footnote to the Saga of Democracy, by H. L. Mencken.* New York: A. A. Knopf, 1932.

Michie, Allan A., and Ryhlick, Frank. *Dixie Demagogues.* New York: The Vanguard Press, 1939.

Mitchell, Broadus. *Depression Decade: From New Era through New Deal, 1929–1941.* New York: Harper and Row, 1947.

Moley, Raymond. *27 Masters of Politics.* New York: Funk and Wagnalls, Co., 1949.

Moon, Henry Lee. *Balance of Power: The Negro Vote.* Garden City, N.Y.: Doubleday and Co., 1949.

Moore, John Hammond. *Columbia and Richland County.* Columbia: University of South Carolina Press, 1993.

National Youth Administration in South Carolina. *The Textile Industry in South Carolina.* Columbia, S.C.: N.p., 1939.

Newby, I. A. *Black Carolinians: A History of Blacks in South Carolina from 1895 to 1968.* Columbia: University of South Carolina Press, 1973.

———. *Plain Folk in the New South.* Baton Rouge: Louisiana State University Press, 1989.

Nourse, Edwin G. et al. *Three Years of the Agricultural Adjustment Administration.* Washington, D.C.: The Brookings Institution, 1937.

Patterson, James T. *Congressional Conservatism and the New Deal: The Growth of a Conservative Coalition in Congress, 1933–1939.* Lexington: University of Kentucky Press, 1967.

———. *The New Deal and the States.* Princeton, N.J.: Princeton University Press, 1969.

Peel, Roy V., and Thomas C. Donnelly. *The 1932 Campaign: An Analysis.* New York: Farrar and Rinehart, 1935.

Porcher, F. A. *The History of the Santee Canal.* Charleston: The South Carolina Historical Society, 1903 [1875].

Pritchett, C. Herman. *The Tennessee Valley Authority: A Study in Public Administration [by] C. Herman Pritchett . . . .* New York: Russell and Russell, 1971.

Pugh, Olin. *Difficult Decades of Banking: A Comparative Study of Banking Developments in South Carolina and the United States,1920–1940.* Columbia: University of South Carolina School of Business Administration, 1964.

Reynolds, Emily Bellinger, and Joan Reynolds Faunt. *Biographical Dictionary of the Senate of the State of South Carolina, 1776–1964.* Columbia: South Carolina Department of Archives and History, 1964.

Richards, Henry I. *Cotton and the AAA.* Washington, D.C.: The Brookings Institution, 1936.

Richardson, James M. *History of Greenville County, South Carolina: Narrative and Biographical, by James M. Richardson.* Atlanta: A. H. Cawston, 1930. Reprint, with a new index by Margaret H. Cannon. Spartanburg, S.C.: The Reprint Company, 1980.

Robertson, David. *Sly and Able: A Political Biography of James F. Byrnes.* New York: W. W. Norton and Company, 1994.

Robinson, Edgar Eugene. *They Voted for Roosevelt.* Stanford, Calif.: Stanford University Press, 1947.

Rollins, Alfred B., Jr. *Roosevelt and Howe.* New York: Alfred A. Knopf, 1962.

Roosevelt, Franklin D. *The Public Papers and Addresses of Franklin D. Roosevelt.* 13 vols. New York: Random House, 1938–1950.

Rowe, Harold B. *Tobacco under the AAA.* Washington, D.C.: The Brookings Institution, 1935.

Saloutos, Theodore. *The American Farmer and the New Deal.* Ames: Iowa State University Press, 1982.

Sass, Herbert Ravenel. *Outspoken: 150 Years of "The News and Courier."* Columbia: University of South Carolina Press, 1953.

Schlesinger, Arthur M., Jr. *The Coming of the New Deal.* Boston: Houghton Mifflin Company, 1959.

———. *The Politics of Upheaval.* Boston: Houghton Mifflin Company, 1960.

Schulz, Constance B. *A South Carolina Album: 1936–1948.* Columbia: University of South Carolina Press, 1992.

Simkins, Frances Butler. *A History of the South.* New York: Alfred A. Knopf, 1956.

———. *Pitchfork Ben Tillman, South Carolinian.* Baton Rouge: Louisiana State University Press, 1967 [1944].

Simpson, George Lee, Jr. *The Cokers of Carolina.* Chapel Hill: University of North Carolina Press, 1956.

Simpson, William Hays. *Life in Mill Communities.* Clinton, S.C.: Presbyterian College Press, 1941.

South Carolina. Chicago: Lewis Publishing Co., 1920.

Springs, Elliott. *Clothes Make the Man.* New York: J. J. Little and Ives Co., 1948, and New York: The Empyrean Press, 1953.

Sproat John G., and Larry Schweikart. *Making Change: South Carolina Banking in the Twentieth Century.* Columbia: South Carolina Bankers Association, 1990.

Stark, John D. *Damned Upcountryman: William Watts Ball.* Durham, N.C.: Duke University Press, 1968.

Sternsher, Bernard. *Rexford Tugwell and the New Deal.* New Brunswick, N.J.: Rutgers University Press, 1964.

Sullivan, Patricia. *Days of Hope: Race and Democracy in the New Deal Era.* Chapel Hill: University of North Carolina Press, 1996.

Swensson, Lise C., and Nancy M. Higgins, ed., *New Deal Art in South Carolina.* Columbia: South Carolina State Museum, 1990.

Talbert, Roy, Jr. *FDR's Utopian: Arthur Morgan of the TVA.* Jackson: University Press of Mississippi, 1987.

Tindall, George Brown. *The Emergence of the New South, 1913–1945.* Baton Rouge: Louisiana State University Press, 1967.

Terrill, Tom E., and Jerrold Hirsch. *Such As Us: Southern Voices of the Thirties.* Chapel Hill: University of North Carolina Press, 1998.

Torbet, Robert G. *A History of the Baptists.* Valley Forge: The Judson Press, 1969.

Tugwell, Rexford G. *The Brains Trust.* New York: Viking Press, 1968.

———. *How They Became President.* New York: Simon and Schuster, 1964.

University of South Carolina. *South Carolina: Economic and Social Conditions in 1944.* Columbia: University of South Carolina Press, 1945.

Wallace, David Duncan. *The History of South Carolina.* 4 vols. New York: American Historical Society, 1934.

Wecter, Dixon. *The Age of the Great Depression, 1929–1941.* New York: The Macmillan Co., 1948.

Who's Who in South Carolina, 1934–1935. Columbia: Current Historical Association, 1935.

Wolfskill, George. *The Revolt of the Conservatives: A History of the American Liberty League.* Boston: Houghton Mifflin Co., 1962.

Woodward, C. Vann. *Origins of the New South, 1877–1913.* Baton Rouge: Louisiana State University Press, 1967 [1951].

Workman, W. D., Jr. *The Bishop from Barnwell.* Columbia, S.C.: R. L. Bryan Co., 1963.

Writers' Program of the Work Projects Administration. *South Carolina: A Guide to the Palmetto State.* New York: Oxford University Press, 1941.

Wright, Gavin. *Old South, New South: Revolutions in the Southern Economy since the Civil War.* New York: Basic Books, 1986.

Zieger, Robert H. *Organized Labor in the Twentieth Century South.* Knoxville: University of Tennessee Press, 1996.

INTERNET SOURCES

Federal Reserve Bank of Minneapolis, "What Is a Dollar Worth?" http://woodrow.mp/s.frb.us/economy/calc/cphihome.html, 25 May 1998.

Hiott, Susan G. "New Deal Art in South Carolina: Conclusion." http://people.-clemson.edu/hiott/text/pwap.htm, 6 January 1998.

―――. "New Deal Art in South Carolina: The WPA Federal Art Project." http://people.clemson.edu/hiott/text/pwap.htm, 6 January 1998.

http://people.clemson.edu/hiott/text/wpafap.htm, 6 January 1998.

MISCELLANEOUS

Johnson, Frederick. "History of the Dock Street Theater." Typescript of radio address [1947], South Caroliniana Library, University of South Carolina, Columbia.

The Road Is Open Again. By: Sammy Fain and Irving Kahal © 1933 (renewed) Warner Bros. Inc. All rights reserved. Used by permission. Warner Bros. Publications U.S. Inc., Miami, FL 33014.

INDEX